COLOSSIANS AND PHILEMON
FOR THE PRACTICAL MESSIANIC

COLOSSIANS
AND
PHILEMON
FOR THE PRACTICAL MESSIANIC

J.K. MCKEE

MESSIANIC APOLOGETICS
messianicapologetics.net

COLOSSIANS AND PHILEMON
FOR THE PRACTICAL MESSIANIC

Published by Messianic Apologetics, a division of Outreach Israel Ministries
P.O. Box 850845
Richardson, Texas 75085
(407) 933-2002

www.outreachisrael.net
www.messianicapologetics.net

originally produced by TNN Press 2009 in Kissimmee, Florida

Front cover image is of the mountain range of Denizli, Turkey, adjacent to Ancient Colossae
Back cover image is of the Ephesus Road
©Istockphoto.com

Unless otherwise noted, Scripture quotations are from the *New American Standard, Updated Edition* (NASU), © 1995, The Lockman Foundation.

Unless otherwise noted, quotations from the Apocrypha are from the *Revised Standard Version* (RSV), © 1952, Division of Education of the National Council of the Churches of Christ in the United States of America.

TABLE OF CONTENTS

ABBREVIATION CHART AND SPECIAL TERMS

The following is a chart of abbreviations for reference works and special terms that are used in publications by Outreach Israel Ministries and Messianic Apologetics. Please familiarize yourself with them as the text may reference a Bible version, i.e., RSV for the Revised Standard Version, or a source such as *TWOT* for the *Theological Wordbook of the Old Testament*, solely by its abbreviation. Detailed listings of these sources are provided in the Bibliography.

Special terms that may be used have been provided in this chart:

ABD: *Anchor Bible Dictionary*

AMG: *Complete Word Study Dictionary: Old Testament, New Testament*

ANE: Ancient Near East(ern)

Apostolic Scriptures/Writings: the New Testament

Ara: Aramaic

ASV: American Standard Version (1901)

ATS: ArtScroll Tanach (1996)

b. Babylonian Talmud (*Talmud Bavli*)

B.C.E.: Before Common Era or B.C.

BDAG: *A Greek-English Lexicon of the New Testament and Other Early Christian Literature* (Bauer, Danker, Arndt, Gingrich)

BDB: *Brown-Driver-Briggs Hebrew and English Lexicon*

BKCNT: *Bible Knowledge Commentary: New Testament*

C.E.: Common Era or A.D.

CEV: Contemporary English Version (1995)

CGEDNT: *Concise Greek-English Dictionary of New Testament Words* (Barclay M. Newman)

CHALOT: *Concise Hebrew and Aramaic Lexicon of the Old Testament*

CJB: Complete Jewish Bible (1998)

DRA: Douay-Rheims American Edition

DSS: Dead Sea Scrolls

ECB: *Eerdmans Commentary on the Bible*

EDB: *Eerdmans Dictionary of the Bible*

EJ: *Encyclopaedia Judaica*

ESV: English Standard Version (2001)

EXP: *Expositor's Bible Commentary*

Ger: German

GNT: Greek New Testament

Grk: Greek

halachah: lit. "the way to walk," how the Torah is lived out in an individual's life or faith community

HALOT: *Hebrew & Aramaic Lexicon of the Old Testament* (Koehler and Baumgartner)

HCSB: Holman Christian Standard Bible (2004)

Heb: Hebrew

HNV: Hebrew Names Version of the World English Bible

IDB: *Interpreter's Dictionary of the Bible*

IDBSup: *Interpreter's Dictionary of the Bible Supplement*

ISBE: *International Standard Bible Encyclopedia*

IVPBBC: *IVP Bible Background Commentary (Old & New Testament)*

Jastrow: *Dictionary of the Targumim, Talmud Bavli, Talmud Yerushalmi, and Midrashic Literature* (Marcus Jastrow)

JBK: New Jerusalem Bible-Koren (2000)

JETS: *Journal of the Evangelical Theological Society*

KJV: King James Version

Lattimore: The New Testament by Richmond Lattimore (1996)

LITV: *Literal Translation of the Holy Bible* by Jay P. Green (1986)

LS: *A Greek-English Lexicon* (Liddell & Scott)

LXE: *Septuagint with Apocrypha* by Sir L.C.L. Brenton (1851)

LXX: Septuagint

m. Mishnah

MT: Masoretic Text

NASB: New American Standard Bible (1977)

NASU: New American Standard Update (1995)

NBCR: *New Bible Commentary: Revised*

NEB: New English Bible (1970)

Nelson: *Nelson's Expository Dictionary of Old Testament Words*

NIB: *New Interpreter's Bible*

NIGTC: *New International Greek Testament Commentary*

NICNT: *New International Commentary on the New Testament*

NIDB: *New International Dictionary of the Bible*

NIV: New International Version (1984)

NJB: New Jerusalem Bible-Catholic (1985)

NJPS: Tanakh, A New Translation of the Holy Scriptures (1999)

NKJV: New King James Version (1982)

NRSV: New Revised Standard Version (1989)

NLT: New Living Translation (1996)

NT: New Testament

orthopraxy: lit. "the right action," how the Bible or one's theology is lived out in the world

OT: Old Testament

PreachC: *The Preacher's Commentary*

REB: Revised English Bible (1989)

RSV: Revised Standard Version (1952)

t. Tosefta

Tanach (Tanakh): the Old Testament

Thayer: *Thayer's Greek-English Lexicon of the New Testament*

TDNT: *Theological Dictionary of the New Testament*

TEV: Today's English Version (1976)
TNIV: Today's New International Version (2005)
TNTC: *Tyndale New Testament Commentaries*
TWOT: *Theological Wordbook of the Old Testament*
UBSHNT: United Bible Societies' 1991 Hebrew New Testament revised edition
v(s). verse(s)

Vine: *Vine's Complete Expository Dictionary of Old and New Testament Words*
Vul: Latin Vulgate
WBC: *Word Biblical Commentary*
Yid: Yiddish
YLT: Young's Literal Translation (1862/1898)

PROLOGUE

How many times have you heard a Messianic Bible teacher quote from Colossians at a *Shabbat* service? If you can count the number of times on a single hand, then you are not alone. How many times have you heard a Messianic Bible teacher even quote from Philemon? I hate to say this, but the only Messianic teacher I have ever heard refer to Philemon has actually been *myself*. Colossians and Philemon are two letters of the Pauline corpus that do not get a great deal of attention within Messianic circles (that is, when Paul's epistles are even addressed). Often we just do not know what to do with these two letters, even though Colossians may get a quote here or there to make a teaching sound exciting. At best, we might find a tertiary level of engagement, but we do not know that much about the content, message, and purpose of Colossians-Philemon.

In 2008 we just finished a Bible study of the Epistle of Ephesians, a six-chapter letter which undoubtedly has connections to Colossians. It would be inappropriate of me to continue our Wednesday Night Bible Study program and skip over Colossians-Philemon, especially given all of the connections that we see between Ephesians and Colossians. In all likelihood, Colossians was written immediately prior to Ephesians, and so we will be examining the first letter written before the more general letter was composed.

Having been in the Messianic movement since 1995, I have always wondered why short books of the Bible like Colossians and Philemon often do not merit a great deal of our attention. Is it because they are so short that we already think we know what they mean, and we really do not think that we need to expel the time or effort to understand them? Is it because these texts make us go back to an historical period in the First Century that causes us to feel uncomfortable? Is it because when Paul asserts that *something* has been nailed to the cross (Colossians 2:14), today's Torah observant Messianics would like to just act as though this statement were not present in our Bibles? Furthermore, might some of the refutations that Paul makes against ancient proto-Gnosticism (Colossians 2:18, 20) have some contemporary applications that would disturb some populist teachings floating around today's Messianic world? And Philemon, it obviously forces us to deal with the question of slavery. *We just don't want to "go there."*

I suppose there are more questions that I could list from examining Colossians-Philemon that relate to our present Messianic non-engagement with these two letters. As we prepare to embark upon a study of these two letters—which in case you are wondering were written at the same time, as the same people who greet the Colossians (Colossians 4:9-15) are the same who greet Philemon (Philemon 22-24)—I write this during a season when Messianic Biblical Studies themselves are in a severe state of flux. Regardless of whether we deal with the Apostolic Scriptures or the Tanach (or preferably *both*), there is a shift that is beginning to take place as individuals start to realize that only addressing the weekly Torah portion is not enough for their spiritual diet. Entire sectors of the Bible have been overlooked by us for far too long. Colossians is a text frequently referred to by Christians who think that we are in error for committing ourselves to a life of Torah obedience. So obviously, it is high time we examine Colossians and Philemon—not only for what *they* say about it—but also for what it might teach *us* and how we may need to improve.

Many of you do know that in recent years old theological debates over Christology—the identity of the Messiah—have arisen in the Messianic movement. Is Yeshua the Messiah Divine, or was He just a human being empowered by God? Colossians has some things to teach us about this (Colossians 1:15-20; 2:9). A much lesser debate, but one that is obviously significant to anyone who follows the Scriptures, is what we are to do with Philemon. Is this just a one-page letter that Paul wrote to a First Century colleague that made it into our Bibles by happenstance? What does it have to tell us about the First Century social setting and composition of who many of the early Believers were? How many of us have found ourselves *assuming things* about the First Century that we should not be assuming?

Because there has been so little attention given to Colossians-Philemon in the Messianic world, I am actually very excited about what we are all going to learn. I have been convinced over the past few years that many of the answers that our faith community needs are found in these kinds of short books of the Bible, which unfortunately, very few people read *much less discuss.* As we mature as a movement—and actually read texts like Colossians-Philemon—I believe God will mold us to be more effective for His service. We may be shown some things that make us feel uncomfortable at first, revealing some things among us that need to be improved and/or changed, **but it will make us stronger and more able to accomplish His tasks in the long term.** Are there any "Colossian" congregations to be found today's Messianic movement? What would be their strengths and weaknesses?

What do you think you are going to learn as a Messianic Believer preparing to examine Colossians-Philemon? Have you even sat down and read the entire text of these two letters before? Have you really contemplated what it means to "Set your mind on the things above, not on the things that are on earth," because "When Messiah, who is our life, is revealed, then you also will be revealed with Him in glory" (Colossians 3:2, 4)? Likewise, what is Paul's intention of saying, "Let the word of Messiah richly dwell within you, with all wisdom teaching and admonishing one another with psalms *and* hymns *and* spiritual songs, singing with thankfulness in your hearts to God" (Colossians 3:16)? As much as we may think we have to sort through negative admonitions and rebukes, and then encounter Paul's opinion of slavery, we actually do have some significantly positive things to contemplate.

Just like you, I am looking forward to this being yet another opportunity to learn more about the masterpiece of God's Word!

J.K. McKee
Editor, Messianic Apologetics

COLOSSIANS

INTRODUCTION TO COLOSSIANS

When was the last time you really studied Colossians, for more than just a snippet of information, or a sound byte here or there? Colossians can be a very easy-to-overlook text in one's Bible study, largely because the only reference we have to the Colossian Believers is seen in this letter. There is no reference to who the Colossians were outside of the epistle that bears their name, with no direct information given to us in the Book of Acts. N.T. Wright mentions how "it is easy to lose track of the overall thread of the letter and merely...pick out a few details."[1] Most examinations of Colossians only focus on the high points of what its author is countering, so much so that not enough attention is often given to the positive features of what he says. This can only exemplify the need for people to read Colossians as a whole, hopefully motivating them to examine it verse-by-verse. Just as the Apostle Paul desires Yeshua the Messiah to be "all, and in all" (3:11), so must our faith experience—and engagement with Colossians—be.

The Epistle to the Colossians[2] (Grk. *Pros Kolossaeis*, ΠΡΟΣ ΚΟΛΟΣΣΑΕΙΣ) invites us into a very complex, ancient religious world, where Believers in Yeshua the Messiah (Jesus Christ) can be affected by any one, *or many*, diverse religious streams of error. We know from history that errant religious streams affected many of the Christians of the Second and Third Centuries, but not enough are aware of how negative religious influences crept into parts of the Jewish Synagogue several centuries earlier. While it contains important doctrine that cannot be excluded from one's understanding of God and the Bible, Colossians is not a major theological treatise as much as it is a letter of admonition to a group of Believers that Paul is concerned about, having been informed about them from Epaphras (1:7). Commentators who approach Colossians have the task to piece together what *they think* might have been the original circumstances necessitating this letter, and thus to correctly interpret what was actually being communicated.

It is difficult for one to avoid the fact that Colossians does address some kind of false teaching (2:8-13). But what were the specifics of this false teaching? Who were the false teachers bringing in error? Many are agreed today that Colossians likely addresses some kind of Gnosticism and/or mysticism affecting the Colossian Believers. But was it a proto-Gnosticism, something relatively undefined and unorganized, or the kind of full-blown Gnosticism that we see in the Second-Third Centuries C.E.?[3] Theologically, Colossians is known for presenting an advanced Christology (1:15-20), and for refuting some kind of dangerous syncretism that affected a group of Believers (2:6-23). Yet the details which required these things and others to be addressed, are largely left to informed speculation and recognizing that confused people have to be put back on the proper course of faith.

Both conservatives and liberals recognize the unique connections—both theological and linguistic—that exist between Colossians and Ephesians,[4] but beyond this there are many disagreements. It is difficult to fully reconstruct the events that required Colossians to be written. There are different proposals made about what the religious errors countered in Colossians actually are. And, even the authorship of the letter itself is disputed, with many denying that the Apostle Paul had a direct hand in its composition.

---

[1] N.T. Wright, *Tyndale New Testament Commentaries: Colossians and Philemon* (Grand Rapids: Eerdmans, 1986), 19.

[2] Please note that in spite of the common reference to Colossians as "the Book of Colossians," I am going to purposefully refer to the text as either the Epistle to the Colossians or Paul's letter to the Colossians, and not use this reference. By failing to forget that this text is a letter written to a specific audience in a specific setting, we can make the common error of thinking that this was a text written *directly to us*. Our goal as responsible interpreters is to try to reconstruct what this letter meant *to its original audience first*, before applying its message in a modern-day setting.

[3] That is, the kind vehemently protested against by Church Fathers like Irenaeus in his *Against Heresies*, and best epitomized by the Nag Hammadi literature.

[4] Previously addressed in the author's commentary *Ephesians for the Practical Messianic*.

WHO WAS THE AUTHOR OF THIS LETTER?

The Epistle to the Colossians is part of a collection commonly known as the Deutero-Pauline letters (also including: Ephesians, 2 Thessalonians, 1&2 Timothy, Titus), meaning that not all theologians agree that it was written by the Apostle Paul. The text of Colossians itself claims some degree of Pauline authorship, with the Apostle Paul extending opening greetings to his audience (1:1, 23). It is very hard to dismiss the closing claim, "I, Paul, write this greeting with my own hand" (4:18), a practice that he employed to apparently authenticate all of his letters (cf. 2 Thessalonians 3:17). Douglas J. Moo points out, "The letter's claim to be written by Paul is no casual matter. It is a claim built into the warp and woof of the letter, elaborated with detail after detail."[5] No one from ancient times denied genuine Pauline authorship of Colossians, and many find it difficult to assume that its author is completely pseudonymous. Indeed, unlike its companion Ephesians which does not list any major personal references, it is quite difficult to assume pseudonymity when real, genuine people are listed as extending greetings to the Colossians (4:7-17; cf. Philemon 2, 23, 24), with the courier Tychicus carrying the epistle to them (4:7).

The composition of Colossians is closely connected to the composition of Philemon, precisely because of the personal references seen in both letters. Most of the same people who extend greetings to the Colossians also extend greetings to Philemon:

PERSONAL REFERENCES AND GREETINGS	
COLOSSIANS	PHILEMON
...Timothy our brother... (1:1)	...Timothy our brother... (1)
Aristarchus, my fellow prisoner, sends you his greetings; and *also* Barnabas's cousin Mark (about whom you received instructions; if he comes to you, welcome him)...Epaphras, who is one of your number, a bondslave of Yeshua the Messiah, sends you his greetings...Luke, the beloved physician, sends you his greetings, and *also* Demas (4:10-12, 14)	Epaphras, my fellow prisoner in Messiah Yeshua, greets you, *as do* Mark, Aristarchus, Demas, Luke, my fellow workers (23-24)
Say to Archippus, "Take heed to the ministry which you have received in the Lord, that you may fulfill it" (4:17)	...and to Archippus our fellow soldier... (2)
...and with him Onesimus, *our* faithful and beloved brother, who is one of your *number*... (4:9)	I appeal to you for my child Onesimus... (10)

One feature of Colossians that should be noted is how it opens up with both Paul *and* Timothy extending greetings (1:1), and so some kind of Timothean involvement with the letter is not at all impossible. The only part of Colossians that is actually attested to have been written by Paul's own hand is the closing

---

[5] Douglas J. Moo, *Pillar New Testament Commentary: The Letters to the Colossians and to Philemon* (Grand Rapids: Eerdmans, 2008), pp 28-29.

salutation (4:18). Supposed stylistic differences appearing in Colossians, which may not appear in some of Paul's other letters, could easily be the result of Paul employing an amanuensis or secretary in writing down the letter or assisting him in its composition. Timothy, because of his being mentioned by name, has often been proposed as a possible co-author of Colossians. F.F. Bruce does observe, though, "if Paul and Timothy were in any degree joint-authors of a letter, the probability is that, while the literary style might be Timothy's, the ultimate authorship would be Paul's."[6]

The early Christian Church of the Second-Third Centuries C.E. recognized genuine Pauline authorship of Colossians,[7] and there was no dispute over Colossians' authorship in the further ancient centuries. While it is true that the Epistle to the Colossians may not have been appealed to in early Christian teaching as much as its companion, Ephesians, the authorship of Colossians was never an issue.

It was not until the Nineteenth Century with the emergence of liberal German scholarship when Colossians' stated authorship via the Apostle Paul was questioned, with it then being classified among the so-called Deutero-Pauline Epistles. A fair number of today's New Testament scholars, similar to Ephesians, consider Colossians to be pseudonymous, perhaps as many as sixty percent. Yet many who consider Ephesians to have been written by a successor of the Apostle Paul, in a kind of "Pauline school," do in fact consider Colossians to be authentically Pauline in its theological scope, with Ephesians to perhaps be further from Paul, a reworked epistle based on Colossians.

Is it so impossible for the Epistle to the Colossians to be authentically written by Paul, with problems so abounding for it to be a direct product of the eminent Apostle? Many of the claims that liberals make against genuine Pauline authorship regard some stylistic differences with other letters that all scholars are agreed[8] are direct products of Paul (Romans, 1&2 Corinthians, Galatians, Philippians, 1 Thessalonians, Philemon). Those who advocate pseudonymity for Colossians have a much more difficult task, when compared to Ephesians, because unlike Ephesians the letter to the Colossians is fairly personal. Liberal resources like *IDB* are forced to indicate, "Whereas Ephesians is dull and impersonal, Col. 2:6-4:6 is lively with personal feeling; definite people and places appear (1:2, 5-8, 27; 2:1; 4:7 ff, 13). We have to do with a real letter."[9] Its entry further concludes, surprisingly, "The links between Colossians and PHILEMON support authenticity" (*IDB*),[10] at least recognizing that the authorship an interpreter accepts for one letter must be accepted for the other. And few liberals today actually deny genuine Pauline authorship of Philemon.

Even though many liberals assume that the authorship of Colossians is pseudonymous, it is still recognized that "The overall structure of Colossians conforms to that of the typical Pauline letter" (*ABD*), and "Most of the lexical differences between Colossians and the letters that are certainly Paul's do not weigh very heavily against Pauline authorship" (*ABD*).[11] D.A. Carson and Douglas J. Moo, holding to genuine Pauline authorship, conclude in their New Testament introduction that "Differences in vocabulary may be accounted for in part by his use of words needed to oppose a new heresy."[12] So in this case, the circumstances that Colossians originally addressed required a variance of vocabulary, not seen in the other Pauline letters. In fact, Ben Witherington III goes a step further, indicating how,

"[T]he expansive and redundant nature of the style of Colossians is...characteristic of Asiatic rhetoric, which was characterized by long lugubrious sentences, piling up synonyms for rhetorical effect, and the absence of conjunctions so that the sentences keep flowing in the torrent of eloquence."[13]

---

[6] F.F. Bruce, *New International Commentary on the New Testament: The Epistles to the Colossians, to Philemon, and to the Ephesians* (Grand Rapids: Eerdmans, 1984), 30.

[7] Curtis Vaughan, "Colossians," in Frank E. Gaebelein, ed. et. al., *Expositor's Bible Commentary* (Grand Rapids: Zondervan, 1978), 11:64.

[8] Obviously excluding those scholars who deny Pauline authorship of *all* his attributed letters.

[9] G. Johnston, "Colossians, Letter to the," in George Buttrick, ed. et. al., *The Interpreter's Dictionary of the Bible*, 4 vols. (Nashville: Abingdon, 1962), 1:659.

[10] Ibid.

[11] Victor Paul Furnish, "Colossians, Epistle to the," in David Noel Freedman, ed., *Anchor Bible Dictionary*, 6 vols. (New York: Doubleday, 1992), 1:1090, 1093.

[12] D.A. Carson and Douglas J. Moo, *An Introduction to the New Testament*, second edition (Grand Rapids: Zondervan, 2005), 518.

[13] Ben Witherington III, *The Letters to Philemon, the Colossians, and the Ephesians: A Socio-Rhetorical Commentary on the Captivity Epistles* (Grand Rapids: Eerdmans, 2007), 18.

Other claims against genuine Pauline authorship for Colossians regard what are considered to be theological differences seen between Colossians and the agreed-upon genuine Pauline letters.[14] It is thought that there is a stress upon the life of the resurrection to be experienced now (2:12-13), as opposed to it being something exclusively of the future (Romans 6:5; Philippians 3:11-12). There is no language of "justification" seen in Colossians, as is seen elsewhere in Paul. Some themes first appearing in Galatians are developed further in Colossians 2:8-23, thought to be the hand of a Pauline successor. Paul's apostleship appears to be presented as universal to those who have never seen him (2:1-2), a reflection of those who came after him. And, those who deny Pauline authorship often argue that Colossians is combating a much later, full-fledged Gnosticism seen in the late First or early Second Century C.E., rather than an incipient proto-Gnosticism in the mid First Century C.E.

But is the authorship of the Apostle Paul for Colossians completely in doubt? There are many good reasons for us, in fact, to believe that Colossians **was simply written late in Paul's ministry.** It is a unique letter addressing some specific circumstances conveyed to him by the Colossian Epaphras, and the letter was carefully crafted for a series of complex needs—tailored for what the audience needed to hear. It need not be thought that the theological themes seen in Colossians are in conflict with other letters, agreed upon by all, to have been written by Paul.

Yet if Paul is not the author of the Epistle to the Colossians, than who was it? Was it simply an anonymous Believer in Asia Minor who wanted to honor Paul? Or could it have been Timothy, the other name mentioned in the opening greeting?

It is interesting that those who interpret the text of Colossians, denying Pauline authorship, still cannot deny some kind of Pauline connection. Morna D. Hooker thus refers to the author of Colossians as "Paul" in quotation marks in *ECB*.[15] James D.G. Dunn considers that if Colossians really is Deutero-Pauline, then it must be one of the very early Deutero-Pauline texts, and similarly that it should be considered "Pauline" in quotation marks.[16] And lest we think that many who deny genuine Pauline authorship of Colossians have a low opinion of the role that it plays in theology, this is simply not true when we evaluate many of their thoughts. Many commentators who hold to Colossians being Deutero-Pauline very much consider it to have a significant role in our spiritual and theological experiences today. Andrew T. Lincoln summarizes,

"If…it was intended for a specific group of readers in Asia Minor after Paul's death and came from one of Paul's close followers, it is reasonable to believe that its readers would have known of such a significant event as the death of the apostle and, therefore, would have taken the letter as a product of a trusted Pauline teacher who was presenting his teaching not simply as his own but as in the Pauline apostolic tradition."[17]

Dunn is notable among those who deny Pauline authorship of Colossians, taking a somewhat different approach. He describes his view of how "it is difficult to envisage a scenario where 4:7-17 can be easily explained on a full-blown post-Pauline (say, fifteen years after his death) hypothesis,"[18] namely all of the personal interactions that are depicted between "Paul," his associates, the Colossian audience, and the overlap

[14] Summarized by Morna D. Hooker, "Colossians," in James D.G. Dunn and John W. Rogerson, eds., *Eerdmans Commentary on the Bible* (Grand Rapids: Eerdmans, 2003), 1404.

[15] Ibid.

[16] James D.G. Dunn, *New International Greek Testament Commentary: The Epistles to the Colossians and to Philemon* (Grand Rapids: Eerdmans, 1996), 19.

[17] Andrew T. Lincoln, "The Letter to the Colossians," in Leander E. Keck, ed., et. al., *New Interpreter's Bible*, Vol. 11 (Nashville: Abingdon, 2000), 582.

If you are Messianic Believer, currently struggling with various assertions made in Colossians (i.e., 2:14), and you find liberal commentators denying Pauline authorship to be an appealing reason to dismiss the text as valid Scripture—*think again!* Lincoln describes how those denying genuine Pauline authorship of Colossians is similar to how "In the Jewish Scriptures writings are attributed to great personages like Moses, David, Solomon, and Isaiah…[being] written in [their] name" (Ibid.), but not actually being written by any of them. So, *if* you are going to deny genuine Pauline authorship of Colossians, you are *also* required to hold the Torah to the same standard, and you must consider the many proposals made regarding non-Mosaic authorship of Genesis, Exodus, Leviticus, Numbers, and Deuteronomy. Few Messianics today (including this author) are willing to accept the JEDP documentary hypothesis, though. (Much less consider the Torah to be Ancient Israel's "mythology"!)

For a further discussion, consult the author's entries on the Pentateuchal books in *A Survey of the Tanach for the Practical Messianic*.

[18] Dunn, 37.

with Philemon. He concludes that the most likely author of Colossians was, in fact, Paul's disciple Timothy. He describes, "We may…envisage Paul outlining his main concerns to a secretary (Timothy) who was familiar with the broad pattern of Paul's letter-writing," also commenting, "we should perhaps more accurately describe the theology of Colossians as the theology of Timothy, or…the theology of Paul as understood by Timothy."[19]

As already mentioned, a Timothean composition and/or authorship of Colossians, via the Apostle Paul's direct guidance, does not seem impossible—at least among all of the alternatives available. (From this angle, at least, Timothy writing Colossians would not be that different from the possibility of Baruch being the author of Lamentations, and not Jeremiah.)[20] Carson and Moo indicate, "Certainly this theory is preferable to the one that judges the present 'shell' to be non-Pauline."[21] Witherington likewise considers Timothy "perhaps as a coauthor…but at least as a co-authority addressing these audiences [Colossians-Philemon, Ephesians]."[22]

This commentary accepts genuine Pauline authorship of Colossians, but we will be engaging with some commentators who deny it in varying degrees (Hooker, Lincoln, Dunn). I do not think it is at all a stretch to say that Timothy did have some role in its composition, though, either as an amanuensis or one who counseled Paul on what he needed to say to the Colossians.[23]

PAUL AND HIS RELATIONSHIP TO THE COLOSSIANS

The only reference to the Asian (Minor) city of Colossae that appears in the Bible is in the letter that bears the title "Colossians." But this does not mean that the good Apostle Paul had no relationship, even an indirect one (cf. 2:1), with the Colossians. The Colossian who receives the most amount of attention in Paul's letter is Epaphras, who Paul says "is one of your number" (4:12). Archippus was also a leader among the Colossian Believers (4:17).

While there is no record in the Book of Acts that Paul ever visited Colossae, we do know that Paul had spent about three years proclaiming the gospel and teaching in the adjacent city of Ephesus during his Third Missionary Journey (52-55 C.E.; Acts 18:23-21:16). It was during this time that Paul was able to lecture in the hall of Tyrannus for two years, and "all who lived in Asia heard the word of the Lord, both Jews and Greeks" (Acts 19:10), meaning that the message spread throughout the region. Epaphras had likely been converted to faith in Yeshua during this time, and he took the gospel that Paul preached back to Colossae (1:7-9), presumably his hometown. Many Colossians had received it with eagerness.

The Believers who had sprung up in Colossae, forming some kind of community or *ekklēsia*, would have fallen under Paul's ministerial influence—and he would have been responsible for them in some way. They were almost all non-Jewish Believers (1:21; cf. Ephesians 2:12), especially given the list of pagan vices that Paul speaks against (3:5-7). Just as Epaphras would have met Paul during his time in Ephesus, it is possible that some from Colossae had also met him and recognized him as an elder leader of the Body of Messiah.

Given the Apostle Paul's indirect relationship with the Colossian Believers, it is surmised that the letter written to them was composed at Epaphras' request. The Epistle to the Colossians could be taken as Paul representing himself as some kind of "grandfather" over the Colossian assembly.[24] Donald Guthrie remarks, "Probably Epaphras could not cope with the specious arguments and assumed humility of the leader of the

---

[19] Ibid., 38.

[20] Consult the author's entry for the Book of Lamentations in *A Survey of the Tanach for the Practical Messianic*.

[21] Carson and Moo, 520.

[22] Witherington, pp 24-25.

[23] For those wishing to investigate the authorship of Colossians in more detail, consult Donald Guthrie, *New Testament Introduction* (Downers Grove, IL: InterVarsity, 1990), pp 527-577; Peter. T. O'Brien, *Word Biblical Commentary: Colossians, Philemon*, Vol. 44 (Nashville: Thomas Nelson, 1982), xlii-xlix; and especially Moo, 28-41 for a thorough explanation and defense of Pauline authorship. Also consider O'Brien, "Colossians, Letter to the," in Gerald F. Hawthorne, Ralph P. Martin, and Daniel G. Reid, eds., *Dictionary of Paul and His Letters* (Downers Grove, IL: InterVarsity, 1993), pp 150-152.

[24] Moo, 27.

false teachers and needed the greater wisdom of the apostle."[25] From this vantage point, then, Colossians was put together to meet the specific needs of a confused group of individuals.

WHERE WAS PAUL WHEN HE WROTE THIS LETTER?

Colossians is considered to be one of the Prison Epistles, along with Ephesians, Philippians, and of course its companion Philemon. Paul does ask the Colossians, "pray for us…so that we may proclaim the mystery of Christ, for which I am in chains" (4:3, NIV). It is most probable that the imprisonment referred to by Paul in Colossians is his detainment in Rome (Acts 28:16-31), as there is no record given of the outcome of Paul's trial. In support of the traditional view of a Roman composition for Colossians, Luke, who is present among the "we" with Paul in Rome (Acts 28:14, 16), is also listed among those who extend greetings to the Colossians (4:14), and to Philemon (24).

Rome as the place of Colossians' composition requires Epaphras to somehow have made his way to Rome to visit him, even sharing some kind of detainment with him as seen in Philemon 23, where Paul calls him "my fellow prisoner." Epaphras actually having to transverse a distance of 1,200 miles from Colossae to Rome—to consult Paul in person—makes one realize how significantly bad the circumstances were for the Colossians.

Likewise to be considered, given Colossians' connection to Philemon, is how the slave Onesimus would have escaped to Rome. This would have been one of the farthest places he could have traveled as a runaway, and being a large city he would have had many places to hide.

While many Colossians' commentators today have little difficulty with Rome as the place of the letter's composition, a lesser number of scholars propose Caesarea. The ancient Marcionite Prologue actually listed Ephesus as the place of origin. This is something followed by Wright, as he considers the letter to address a relatively new congregation of Believers being errantly persuaded, also considering it much more likely that Onesimus only escaped to Ephesus and not to Rome.[26] But this has a problem because just as Tychicus is listed as the courier who carried Colossians (3:7), so is he also the carrier for the letter that was later entitled "Ephesians" (Ephesians 6:21; cf. 1:1, Grk.) (The only way around this would be to suggest that Paul actually wrote the circular epistle "Ephesians" from Ephesus.)

Considering the fact that Colossians does represent a relatively advanced stage in Paul's theological thought, Rome seems like the most likely place of composition.[27] **Our analysis of Colossians will stand by the traditional view that the letter was written by Paul when he was in Rome.**

WHEN DID PAUL WRITE THIS LETTER?

If Rome was indeed the location where Colossians was composed by Paul, then this places Colossians being written between 60-62 C.E., at around the same time of Ephesians. Conservatives such as Bruce, who accept genuine Pauline authorship, consider Colossians and Ephesians to appear later in the scope of Paul's writings, because "his presentation of the Church [or, the *ekklēsia*] as the body of Christ in Colossians and Ephesians marks a later and more advanced stage of his thought on this subject than the stage represented by 1 Corinthians (*ca.* A.D. 55) and Romans (*ca.* A.D. 57)" (*ISBE*).[28] Dunn, who believes in a Timothean authorship of Colossians, similarly thinks that the letter was written during 60-62 C.E., in his words being "the last Pauline letter to be written with the great apostle's explicit approval."[29]

Those advocating an Ephesian authorship for Colossians propose a much earlier period, such as 52-55 C.E. And those who deny genuine Pauline authorship of Colossians propose the broad period of 65-90 C.E.

---

[25] Guthrie, *New Testament Introduction*, 565.

[26] Wright, pp 35-36.

[27] O'Brien, *Colossians-Philemon*, l-li.

[28] F.F. Bruce, "Colossians, Epistle to the," in Geoffrey Bromiley, ed., *International Standard Bible Encyclopedia*, 4 vols. (Grand Rapids: Eerdmans, 1988), 1:733.

[29] Dunn, 41.

There is discussion among those who accept genuine Pauline authorship of Colossians, though, as to whether Colossians-Philemon or Ephesians was written first. It is very difficult to deny a literary connection between these epistles (compare Colossians 4:7-9 and Ephesians 6:21-22). Many lean toward Colossians being the specific letter written first, with Ephesians being the more general version following. It is easy to just say that Colossians-Philemon and Ephesians were both written at about the same time.[30]

WHO WAS THE TARGET AUDIENCE OF THIS LETTER?

The ancient city of *Kolossai* (Κολοσσαί) was located in southeastern Asia Minor, with the Colossians living along the east-west trade route between the Aegean coast and Asian interior. The road from Ephesus and Sardis made its way all to the Euphrates River and onto Mesopotamia. It is not difficult to see how the Epistles of Ephesians and Colossians are related, especially since Colossae was located only about 100 miles east of Ephesus. Colossae was located on the Lycus River along with Hierapolis and Laodicea, which is important because Paul's letter to the Colossians was intended to be read by the Laodiceans as well, and mention is made of Believers in both Hierapolis and Laodicea within Colossians (4:13). This is evidence of how the Believers in this general area were closely connected (2:1).

Paul actually instructed the Colossians' letter to be read to the Believers in Laodicea, and also that a letter he wrote to the Laodiceans would be coming to them (4:16). While some think that this is a lost letter of Paul's, this second letter could very well be what became entitled as "Ephesians," as "in Ephesus" is missing from the oldest manuscripts (cf. Ephesians 1:1, RSV), originally composed as a circular epistle for those in Asia Minor.

Much of what we know about the city of Colossae has to be pieced together from ancient witnesses, as there has yet to be any significant archaeological activity conducted at its location. The city was substantially demolished by an earthquake in the early 60s C.E., and was probably not rebuilt.

The general region of Asia Minor had once been a part of the ancient Phrygian Kingdom (Twelfth-Seventh Centuries B.C.E.), and by Paul's day had been consecutively conquered by a variety of ancient empires, including (but not limited to) the Persians, Greeks, Seleucids, and the Romans. The Greek writer Xenophon commented how during the Persian Wars, Cyrus marched through Phrygia and was brought "to the large and prosperous inhabited city of Colossae" (*Anabasis* I.2.6).[31] The Greek historian Herodotus similarly recorded how "Xerxes...arrived at the large city of Colossae" (*Histories* 7.30).[32] At one point in the past, the city of Colossae was considered to be large and prosperous, the main population being a mix of Phrygian locals, and later Greeks.

The religion in the region was syncretistic, with a great number of diverse cults. In the First Century C.E., mainline Greco-Roman religion was present, along with Roman emperor worship, as well as local mystery religions. Religious practices from the many travelers that came through Colossae were also present. "Numismatic evidence points most frequently to the worship of the Ephesian Artemis and the Laodicean Zeus, but also to Artemis (the huntress), Men, Selene, Demeter, Hygieia, Helios, Athena, Tyche, Boule, as well as the Egyptian deities Isis and Sarapis" (*ABD*).[33] Guthrie further specifies,

"A combination of ideas would have found ready acceptance in Asia with its flourishing cults and its considerable Jewish population. In Colossae in particular the worship of the heathen goddess Cybele was deeply rooted and showed a tendency towards love of extravagances among the people. Oriental speculation would easily spread along the trade routes of the Lycus valley and be hungrily absorbed by the populace."[34]

Five centuries prior to Paul writing his letter, Colossae the city had been quite important and prosperous, but by the First Century C.E. had diminished in importance for the adjacent cities of Laodicea and/or Hierapolis (the former of which is admonished by Yeshua in Revelation 3:14). Still, even with its

---

[30] Witherington, pp 103-104.
[31] Xenophon: *The Persian Expedition*, trans. George Cawkwell (London: Penguin Books, 1949), 59.
[32] Herodotus: *The Histories*, trans. Aubrey de Sélincourt (London: Penguin Books, 1954), 456.
[33] Clinton E. Arnold, "Colossae," in *ABD*, 1:1089.
[34] Guthrie, *New Testament Introduction*, 569.

decline the city of Colossae did exhibit some importance within the Lycus Valley, as "The economic success of the cities of this valley was derived primarily from their textile industries. Colossae was famous for the distinctive purple color of its wool, which was commonly called *colossinius*" (ABD).[35]

image reproduced from *NIB*, 11:581

---

[35] Arnold, "Colossae," in *ABD*, 1:1089.
Cf. Bruce, *Colossians-Philemon-Ephesians*, pp 3-8 for a more detailed historical overview of the cities of the Lycus Valley.

The main audience of Colossians, as already stated, were likely non-Jewish Believers who had received the gospel as a result of Epaphras' and his colleagues' work (1:7; 4:12-13), themselves having heard the gospel via Paul's preaching in Ephesus (Acts 19:10). Yet it is notable that Colossae was not a city without a Jewish population, as there had been a Jewish presence in Phrygia going back to the Sixth Century B.C.E., with considerable numbers of Jews living in the region by the 200s B.C.E. This is attested by both Philo and Josephus:

> ...[T]here are vast numbers of Jews scattered over every city of Asia and Syria... (Philo *Embassy to Gaius* 245).[36]

> King Antiochus to Zeuxis his father, sends greetings. "If you are in health, it is well. I also am in health. Having been informed that a sedition has arisen in Lydia and Phrygia, I thought that matter required great care; and upon advising with my friends what was fit to be done, it has been thought proper to remove two thousand families of Jews, with their effects, out of Mesopotamia and Babylon, to the citadels and places that lie most convenient; for I am persuaded that they will be well disposed guardians of our possessions, because of their piety toward God, and because I know that my predecessors have borne witness to them, that they are faithful, and with alacrity do what they are desired to do. I will, therefore, though it be a laborious work, that you remove these Jews; under a promise that they shall be permitted to use their own laws; and when you shall have brought them to the places before mentioned, you shall give everyone of their families a place for building their houses, and a portion of the land for their husbandry, and for the plantation of their vines; and you shall discharge them from paying taxes of the fruits of the earth for ten years; and let them have a proper quantity of wheat for the maintenance of their servants, until they receive grain out of the earth; also let a sufficient share be given to such as minister to them in the necessities of life, that by enjoying the effects of our humanity, they may show themselves the more willing and ready about our affairs. Take care likewise of that nation, as far as you are able, that they may not have any disturbance given them by anyone." Now these testimonials which I have produced are sufficient to declare the friendship that Antiochus the Great bore to the Jews (Josephus *Antiquities of the Jews* 12.148-153).[37]

It is estimated that in the First Century C.E. that as many as 7,500 Jewish freemen were present in a region of around 50,000,[38] with a possible Jewish population in Colossae itself of around two to three thousand.[39] Recognize how there were Jews from the region of Asia and Phrygia present at Jerusalem on the day of *Shavuot*/Pentecost (Acts 2:9-10).

No scholar, conservative or liberal, has ever proposed a Hebrew or Aramaic origin of Colossians, as "During the Hellenistic and Roman periods the use of the Greek language naturally spread in this region" (*IDB*).[40] The claim by some Messianics that Paul would have written to the Colossians in Hebrew or Aramaic is without historical merit, especially when the Jews of Colossae, widely lax in their observance of the Torah (as evidenced by some of the religious problems confronted in the epistle), would not have been using it for daily conversation. A written Greek origin for Colossians is well-assured. And if Greek were not the composition language of the letter, then some kind of local Phrygian dialect would be the only other major option available for the author.

In the early 60s C.E., following the earthquake that rocked Colossae, many of its residents were forced to relocate to the surrounding towns and villages, likely including Laodicea. It is notable that Colossae was a place for cold springs of water,[41] which would make their way to Laodicea, possibly a reference to Yeshua's

---

[36] Philo Judaeus: *The Works of Philo: Complete and Unabridged*, trans. C.D. Yonge (Peabody, MA: Hendrickson, 1993), 780.

[37] Flavius Josephus: *The Works of Josephus: Complete and Unabridged*, trans. William Whiston (Peabody, MA: Hendrickson, 1987), pp 317-318.

Do note that this Antiochus the Great (reigned 222-187 B.C.E.) is different from the Antiochus Epiphanes (reigned 175-164 B.C.E.) who defamed the Second Temple during the time of the Maccabees.

[38] Arnold, "Colossae," in *ABD*, 1:1089.

[39] Dunn, 22.

[40] F.V. Filson, "Phrygia," in *IDB*, 3:806.

[41] Bruce, *Colossians-Philemon-Ephesians*, 15.

word in Revelation 3:15, "I wish that you were cold..." It may also be that concurrent with the problems Paul addresses in Colossians, his word to Timothy, "You are aware of the fact that all who are in Asia turned away from me" (2 Timothy 1:15), regards how this audience could have left his teachings and did not heed his warnings.

WHAT IS THE THEOLOGICAL MESSAGE OF COLOSSIANS?

All interpreters who approach Colossians are agreed that some kind of false teaching had affected the Colossian Believers, enacted by some kind of false teachers and/or philosophers. Determining who these people were is difficult, as they are only known to us in the letter as "no one" (2:4, 8, 16, 18). There are a variety of threads to consider as a person reads Colossians, giving us clues as to what the false teachings confronted involved. Most significant to our understanding of the problem(s) in Colossae regard Paul's emphasis on a proper and high Christology (1:15-20; 2:9), as Yeshua the Messiah is represented as the Deity (2:9), Lord (1:10; 2:6), and Head (1:18).[42] The false teaching in Colossae undoubtedly subtracted who Yeshua should have been for the Colossian Believers. Conservative interpreters can often agree that Colossians addressed the beginning of a problem later witnessed in the Second Century in a much more serious form.

An interpreter, even while knowing that there are false teachings combated in Colossians, has to infer a great deal from the text regarding what they actually are. *Was there a coherent false teaching in Colossae?*[43] Moo points out how "Paul and the false teachers are indirectly engaged in a sort of debate the Colossians are listening in to...Paul naturally presupposes that the Colossians know what the false teachers were saying, and so he only alludes to their teaching in making his own points."[44] This does not aid the modern interpreter who has to attempt to reconstruct the original events which necessitated composition of the epistle. The only thing almost all can agree upon is how the author labels the problem as *philosophia* (φιλοσοφία) in Colossians 2:8. This does not help that much, as such "philosophy" could range across the spectrum from being normative, Synagogue-based Judaism all the way to outright paganism—with much left to consider in between. It is safe to assert that whatever this philosophy was, it was taking the Colossians away from a focus on Yeshua and His work for them (2:8-9, 15, 19). But that is about all one can say for sure.

There are a variety of proposals made for what the "Colossian heresy" or false teaching might have been—ranging from ceremonialism to asceticism to angel worship (2:18) to secret knowledge (2:4, 8). In all likelihood, these were more than just bad tendencies or influences that the Colossians were to be aware of.[45] Guthrie indicates how "the apostle is dealing with a specific situation and it will be convenient to refer to this situation as a heresy."[46] But while the description "Colossian heresy" has been traditionally attributed to the problems, Moo urges some caution and only suggests that "the time-honored phrase 'false teaching' is...the best option,"[47] for referring to the problems addressed in Colossians, likely because not all commentators are agreed on what the concern actually was.

Regardless of what the false teaching specifically was, it depreciated Yeshua the Messiah in the view of those influenced. Was this false teaching manifested in a singular, united error—or an amalgamation of errors? Rather than the problems being theological, were they at all astrological? If the latter is the case, it is not surprising why Yeshua needs to be portrayed as exalted over the cosmos (1:16; 2:15), and why the Colossians need not appeal to angelic forces for their deliverance (2:10).

Could there have been a grafting of local Phrygian religious customs onto Jewish Synagogue observance, resulting in a fused mess that Paul wanted the Colossians to stay away from? Some commentators conclude that the problem was first Jewish, then pagan;[48] and others conclude that the problem was first

---

[42] Cf. Moo, pp 52, 61-63.

[43] Consult Ibid., pp 50-51 for a list that most Colossians' interpreters are agreed upon.

[44] Ibid., 49.

[45] For a summary of the various options proposed in recent scholarship, consult O'Brien, *Colossians-Philemon*, xxxiii-xxxviii.

[46] Guthrie, *New Testament Introduction*, 565.

[47] Ibid., 48.

[48] Norman Geisler, "Colossians," in John F. Walvoord and Roy B. Zuck, eds., *The Bible Knowledge Commentary: Old Testament* (Wheaton, IL: Victor Books, 1985), 668.

pagan, then Jewish.[49] Some argue for Colossians addressing an exclusively Jewish problem,[50] with commentators like Witherington thinking that it may have had "some ascetic practices,"[51] but on the whole is similar to what is addressed in Galatians and Philippians 3.[52] Against the Colossian errors being exclusively Jewish, Moo notes "the silence of Colossians on three key elements of Judaism...the Old Testament, circumcision, and the law."[53]

On the whole, most evangelical commentators on Colossians consider the error addressed to be something of, as Robert H. Gundry summarizes, a blend "together [of] Jewish mysticism, Greek philosophic speculation, and Oriental mysticism."[54] This mess of errors would easily account for Paul speaking against a kind of self-abasement (2:18, 23), which Peter T. O'Brien concludes "was a term used by opponents to denote ascetic practices that were effective for receiving visions of heavenly mysteries and participating in mystical experiences."[55]

A definite possibility is that the problems facing the Colossians originated from a kind of Jewish Gnosticism, or at least a "Gnosticizing" Judaism. A cursory examination of Jewish history will show how errant influences had infected parts of the Synagogue prior to the First Century C.E. "Tradition" (2:9) can be understood in either a Jewish or a pagan context, but it does seem that the ascetic practices confronted (2:16) are of some kind of Jewish origin. The Epistle to the Colossians could be a testimony to the diversity of Diaspora Judaism, and here a form of Judaism that the Apostle Paul wanted his audience to stay away from (as opposed to *all* of Judaism representing something that today's Christians should not appreciate). There may be some (limited) parallels between the Judaism represented in Colossians and that witnessed in the Qumran materials, particularly in angelology.

Guthrie explains that "although" things like angel worship "would have been strongly resisted by orthodox Jews with their tenacious monotheism," it is nevertheless true that there was a "Jewish transcendental theology"[56] present in ancient times. Local paganism did occasionally—or in some cases, frequently—affect the Jewish people in their religious beliefs and practices. In Colossians, it is best for us to *first* argue that pagan beliefs had influenced the Judaism present in Colossae, manifesting itself in various strange and abnormal practices observed in the Synagogue, in turn being errors advocated by the false teachers confronted by Paul. Lincoln comments, "the evidence for a syncretistic mixing of Jewish angelic and pagan divine names in magical practice is clear. Elements of Jewish belief about angels could be combined with pagan deity cults."[57] Moo has an excellent approach to this, concluding,

"People in Colossae, a cosmopolitan city exposed to a wide variety of religions and philosophies, were likely quite susceptible to these kinds of mixtures. It is this possibility that bedevils any attempt to come up with a 'neat' identification of the false teaching."[58]

What is witnessed in Paul's letter to the Colossians by no means would have been a normative Judaism for the First Century. With astral forces in view, *tapeinophrosunē* (ταπεινοφροσύνη) or self-abasement manifested itself in superstitions regarding food, drink (2:16), not touching certain things (2:20-21), and some kind of severe treatment of the body. Lincoln references how *tapeinophrosunē* is used in the early Second Century

---

[49] O'Brien, *Colossians-Philemon*, xxxii-xxxiii.

[50] Wright, 27; Dunn, pp 29-35.

[51] Witherington, 110.

[52] Wright does indicate, thought, that "this is a controversial claim" (p 23).

Please also note that even though Wright considers the problem in Colossians to be non-Jews being lured into the Synagogue, he believes that Paul's problems with Judaism in the letter are concurrent with the larger problems of fallen humanity (p 29), rightfully speaking against any Christian who would "deny [Jews] their rights, including the right to practise their ancestral religion" (p 30).

[53] Moo, 56.

[54] Robert H. Gundry, *A Survey of the New Testament*, third edition (Grand Rapids: Zondervan, 1994), 395.

[55] O'Brien, "Colossians, Letter to the," in *Dictionary of Paul and His Letters*, 149.

Dunn, in contrast, feels "the peculiar beliefs and practices of the Jews are explained or expressed in categories and language more conductive to winning the respect of cultured Hellenists" (p 32), arguing for a level of commonality between Colossians and the argumentation style seen in Philo.

[56] Guthrie, *New Testament Introduction*, 568.

[57] Lincoln, in *NIB*, 11:563.

[58] Moo, 58.

Christian works *Shepherd of Hermas* and *Similitudes*,[59] noting "Sometimes" these things were "the preparation specifically for entrance into the heavenly realm. All this is highly relevant to Col 2:18, where the two elements associated with fasting are 'the worship of angels' and visionary experience."[60]

Many theologians have no difficulty recognizing that the Colossian error included a mix of both pagan/proto-Gnostic and Jewish errors, concurrent with the Phrygian spiritual environment of folk religion and/or mystery cults. This is perhaps not too much different than how people today might consult horoscopes,[61] even though they attend Church and study the Bible. The majority of evangelical interpreters today appear to agree that the problem in Colossae was a mishmash of errors,[62] but "The exact origin of the false teaching is unknown. Some find it in Essenism; others in incipient Gnosticism or in contemporary Judaism with a syncretistic addition of local Phrygian ideas" (*NIDB*).[63] The problem(s) countered by Paul in Colossians *cannot* be seen as entirely Jewish, even though some lay readers of Colossians—often with little or no knowledge of First Century religious complexities—may immediately assume this, when a closer reading of the text actually shows that more is at work.

Some have thought that various sentiments seen in the Dead Sea Scrolls (1QH 3.20-22; 11.10-12; 1QSb 4.25-26) can inform us as to what some of the Jewish errors may have been, as a hymn that would be prayed by the Qumran community indeed said, "You have opened within me knowledge in the mystery of Your insight" (1QH 20.13).[64] But how far we press the possible parallels and influences between Colossae and Qumran needs to be tempered. Bruce expresses how "It is unlikely that the Qumran community had members, even associate members, among the Jews of Phrygia...But the Qumran community, and the wider Essene order, represented a far-flung tendency sometimes called Jewish nonconformity."[65]

Further to be noted is that although many New Testament commentators have no difficulty recognizing that Jewish mystical errors are combated in Colossians, with the Colossians having died to "the elementary principles of the world" (2:10), many of the same have strong difficulty believing that the Influencers/Judaizers confronted in Galatians may have similarly had Jewish mystics among them (cf. Galatians 4:3; 6:16).[66]

When Paul writes to the Colossians, he makes a serious point to uplift Yeshua the Messiah to them (1:15-20; 2:9), and must assert that what they have been influenced by is deceptive human philosophy (2:8). Terms such as *gnōsis* (γνῶσις), *plērōma* (πλήρωμα), and *sophia* (σοφία) appear to be used to counter error (1:9-10, 26-28; 2:2-3; 3:10).[67] Paul uses these targeted terms in order to subvert false teachings among the Colossians, and "It is possible, but by no means certain, that the false philosophy required some kind of rite akin to that of the Hellenistic mystery cults" (*ABD*).[68] Rather than looking for knowledge, fullness, and wisdom in whatever sordid influences had come in—Paul appeals to the Colossians to find these things **in what Yeshua is for them.** Curtis Vaughan suggests that one of the massive errors countered in Colossians was that "In their view,

---

[59] "Now I was exceeding sad in regard to these appearances, for I longed much to know what the visions meant. Then I see the old woman in a vision of the night saying unto me: 'Every prayer should be accompanied with humility [*tapeinophrosunē*]: fast, therefore, and you will obtain from the Lord what you beg'" (*Shepherd of Hermas* 3.10.6).

"And you will do also as follows. Having fulfilled what is written, in the day on which you fast you will taste nothing but bread and water; and having reckoned up the price of the dishes of that day which you intended to have eaten, you will give it to a widow, or an orphan, or to some person in want, and thus you will exhibit humility [*tapeinophrosunē*] of mind, so that he who has received benefit from your humility [*tapeinophrosunē*] may fill his own soul, and pray for you to the Lord" (*Similitude* 5.3.7).

[60] Lincoln, in *NIB*, 11:563.

[61] Carson and Moo, pp 524-525.

[62] Moo, pp 57-60.

[63] Steven Barabas, "Colossians, the Letter to," in Merrill C. Tenney, ed., *The New International Dictionary of the Bible* (Grand Rapids: Zondervan, 1987), 227.

[64] Michael Wise, Martin Abegg, Jr., and Edward Cook, trans., *The Dead Sea Scrolls: A New Translation* (San Francisco: HarperCollins, 1996), 109.

[65] Bruce, *Colossians-Philemon-Ephesians*, 23.

[66] Important to note is the geographical proximity between Colossae, and the province of Galatia visited by Paul in Acts 13:13-14:28.

[67] Cf. Bruce, *Colossians-Philemon-Ephesians*, pp 20-22.

[68] Furnish, "Colossians, Epistle to the," in *ABD*, 1:1092.

Christ was only one of many intermediaries between God and the world…,"[69] with some kind of worship of Michael continuing in the region into the Fourth Century, condemned by the Council of Laodicea in the Fifth Century.[70] It should not at all surprise us that Paul admonishes the Colossians to hold firmly to the Lord Yeshua the Messiah *alone*, as He is over all things (3:11).

Aside from the admonitions issued in Colossians about ungodly philosophies, and their negative impact on the Colossians, a large part of the letter (ch. 3) is focused on getting the readers to consider the necessities of daily living and practical holiness—something that probably does not get enough attention as it should. Contemporary Christian theologians recognize how Colossians has a universal message, warning Believers against the errors of vain human philosophy (2:8), blending together their own eclectic mix of religions, with contemporary applications often warning against things like transcendental meditation or the occult. Instead, any Believer needs to be focused on what it means to *"put on* love, which is the perfect bond of unity. Let the peace of Messiah rule in your hearts, to which indeed you were called in one body; and be thankful" (3:14-15).

HOW DOES COLOSSIANS RELATE TO MESSIANIC BELIEVERS TODAY?

Colossians is not at all a text frequently read by today's Messianic Believers, and very little engagement is present in the current Messianic community. As of this writing (2009), there are presently no other Messianic commentaries on Paul's letter to the Colossians, save David H. Stern's twelve pages of selective notes in his *Jewish New Testament Commentary.*[71] Is this because we do not know what to do with Colossians? Is it because there are almost no direct quotes from the Tanach in Colossians? Were the Colossians not to be concerned with the Tanach Scriptures, or is Paul's letter simply targeted to address their situation?

Most of the attention given by Messianics to Colossians, which I have witnessed, almost only concerns Christological statements made by Paul (1:15-20; 2:9). While I **surely commend** those Messianic teachers who stand up against those who believe that Yeshua was just a human being empowered by God, and rightly affirm that Yeshua is indeed the LORD God made manifest in the flesh, there are *other issues* in Colossians that we cannot avoid—notably as it concerns the continued validity of the Torah (2:14, 16-17). What are we to make of Paul's references to circumcision (2:11; 3:11), food, feast days, New Moons, and Sabbaths (2:16, 20-21)? Are these widescale rejections of the Torah, or are they related to ascetic practices specific to Colossae and the local area, designed to curry angelic favors? Is Paul subverting the views of a Jewish mystery cult (cf. 1:26-27; 2:2), that to some degree may have had teachings similar to those witnessed at Qumran? Were the false teachers in Colossae some Hellenistic Jews who had been influenced by pagan religion, and significantly misused various Torah practices?

Among the various possibilities, Lincoln indicates, "It is quite possible that a Hellenistic Jew who had left the synagogue to join a Pauline congregation or a Gentile convert who had had some previous contact with the synagogue would advocate such a philosophy, and the writer evidently was concerned that it might appeal to others," actually considering this "an eminently plausible and fitting description of its [the philosophy's] components."[72] While it is true that not enough Christians approach Colossians, understanding the complexities of its locality, current Messianic understanding of Colossians may not be that much better. Few are aware that there are a considerable number of theologians who really do recognize the principal problem in Colossians as being primarily pagan, not Jewish—with paganism having affected the local Judaism, which was in turn affecting the Believers.

Today's Messianics often avoid Colossians because they do not want to engage with what appear to be disparaging remarks made against Ancient Judaism. Many people simply do not know what to do when someone like Bruce asserts, "Basically the heresy was Jewish. This seems obvious from the part played it in by legal ordinances, circumcision, food regulations, the Sabbath, new moon, and other prescriptions from the Jewish calendar." Yet he is clear to **further state**, "But it was not the same as the straightforward form of

---

[69] Vaughan, in *EXP*, 11:167.
[70] Barabas, "Colossians, the Letter to," in *NIDB*, 227.
[71] David H. Stern, *Jewish New Testament Commentary* (Clarksville, MD: Jewish New Testament Publications, 1995), pp 603-615.
[72] Lincoln, in *NIB*, 11:567.

Judaism...[but] was rather a development of Phrygian Judaism" (*ISBE*).[73] These are not entirely negative words, but nuanced warnings against Jewish errors seen in Colossae.

Still, Messianics today can often be accused of the kind of thing summarized by Carson and Moo: "they thought that Christ was no more than a beginning; to go on to spiritual maturity, it was necessary to follow their rules and practices,"[74] perhaps given the tenor of how Torah observance *can* be promoted in parts of the Messianic community as a lifestyle for Believers. (Yet how Torah observance is *actually* promoted needs to be considered on a case-by-case basis, given the youngness of the current Messianic movement.) O'Brien's conclusion is that Yeshua "had not only canceled the debt, or signed IOU, but also destroyed the document on which it was recorded,"[75] that document being God's Torah, even though Yeshua Himself said "Do not think that I came to destroy the Law" (Matthew 5:17, NKJV). Yeshua took away the penalty for sins via His sacrifice (2:14), not the righteous standard of God that condemns sinners! Wright actually goes even further, though, incorrectly concluding,

"The master-stroke in Paul's argument is thus that he warns ex-pagans by portraying Judaism itself as if it were just another pagan religion. It is a 'philosophy' (2:8), developed by human tradition (2:8, 22): and to follow it is to return to the same type of religion that the new converts had recently abandoned."[76]

Encountering these kinds of remarks, it is not difficult to see why many of today's Messianic teachers would just prefer to avoid Colossians altogether. But we are *not allowed* to do this as responsible Bible readers, and we are required to consider the fact that Paul is directly warning against a very odd, sectarian, and eclectic form of Judaism in his letter. Bruce correctly concludes that this was "a form of mysticism which tempted its adepts to look on themselves as a spiritual elite."[77] It was something to be considered "based on the elemental forces of the world" (2:8, HCSB; cf. 2:20), and we certainly see that many theologians (and indeed most evangelical commentators) have no difficulty recognizing that *anything but* mainline First Century Judaism is what is being refuted.[78] (But again, while we see that theologians have no difficulty recognizing the Colossians to be influenced by errant Jewish practices [2:8, 20], the same possibility is often not recognized for what affected the Galatians [Galatians 4:3, 9; cf. 6:13].)

Paul wants the Colossians' spiritual focus to be firmly placed on Yeshua, and in doing this he asserts that the Messiah is the substance (or, "the body"; Grk. σῶμα, *sōma*) of various aspects of the Torah (2:17), notably the appointed times. How should today's Messianics properly search for this substance in our wider Biblical Studies? O'Brien warns how "references to 'fullness,' specific ascetic injunctions (Col 2:21), regulations about food and holy days...[are] unusual phrases which seem to be catchwords of Paul's opponents and the strong emphasis on what Christ has *already achieved* by his death and resurrection, [so] it seems appropriate to speak of a 'heresy' which had just begun to make inroads into the congregation."[79] Sometimes, today's Messianics can be accused of promoting the same kinds of errors as confronted by Paul in Colossians, meaning that we need to take careful note of contemporary sentiments so as to not fall into the *actual errors* being refuted by Paul.

Most evangelical theologians would **not conclude** that Messianic congregations keeping the Sabbath or honoring the Passover are "heretical," per se. But a common accusation against us will be that we are looking *backward* in our salvation to Old Testament practices, rather than *forward* to the cross and Yeshua's resurrection. This is what Carson and Moo describe as, "distracting religious practices, the observance of religious festivals that subtract from what is central."[80] It is thought by many that by remembering the

---

[73] Bruce, "Colossians, Epistle to the," in *ISBE*, 1:733-734.

Here, Bruce considers the straightforward Judaism to be that "against which the churches of Galatia had to be put on their guard at an earlier date" (Ibid.). The author engages with thoughts from Bruce's Galatians commentary in his commentary *Galatians for the Practical Messianic*.

[74] Carson and Moo, 523.

[75] O'Brien, *Colossians-Philemon*, xxix.

[76] Wright, pp 24-25.

[77] Bruce, *Colossians-Philemon-Ephesians*, 22.

[78] Cf. O'Brien, "Colossians, Letter to the," in *Dictionary of Paul and His Letters*, pp 148-149.

[79] Ibid., 148.

[80] Carson and Moo, 529.

appointed times or eating kosher, we have lost sight of Yeshua the Messiah. And for some Messianics, sadly, this is in fact true. **We have the awesome responsibility of making sure that this is *never the case!*** If we have ever lost sight of Yeshua in our Torah observance or examination of the Tanach Scriptures, then it is necessary to rectify this and demonstrate lives where our Torah observance is evidence of our emulation of the Lord (Matthew 5:16-19).

Moo's thoughts are well taken, where he asserts how "Rules must never take the place of Christ as the source of spiritual nourishment and growth; and any rules that we propose to follow must be clearly rooted in and lead back to Christ." He further notes, "does Colossians 2:16 imply that Sabbath observance is optional for Christians? or does it teach that Sabbath observance not rooted in Christ is wrong?"[81], at least indicating how this verse can be interpreted as not being anti-Sabbath. So in any Messianic teachings about the Sabbath or appointed times, do we need to be careful about how far we push the motif of "fulfilled"? There are still *future* things for the Lord to accomplish represented by these Divine ordinances, and we need to be consciously aware of whether our observance of the *moedim* really does subtract from the substance of Yeshua. The ongoing debate Messianics face about the calendar, for example—and whether to follow the mainline Jewish calendar followed in today's Synagogue and Messianic Judaism, or one of the many alternatives available— *can* sometimes reduce the remembrance of the appointed times to a distracting religious practice, where we can totally forget what we are remembering.[82] *This need not be the case.*

At the very least, given the warnings issued against false religion and superstition in Colossians, there is an admonition seen for today's Messianics *not* to take a "Step on a crack and break your mother's back" view to the Sabbath, calendar, kosher laws, and appointed times. **We can often forget that the mercy of God *is there* to cover us when we slip up in our obedience to Him.**

Examining the Epistle to the Colossians will force today's Messianics to take more seriously their engagement with First Century B.C.E.-C.E. Judaism, and see that it is more realistically to be considered *Judaisms*.[83] The Apostle Paul encounters a socio-religious "soup" of beliefs in Colossians, including the possibility of some kind of *Merkavah* (מֶרְכָּבָה) mysticism, loosely based on the Prophet Ezekiel's visions (Ezekiel 1, 10).[84] In this errant strand of Judaism, one would try to enter into some kind of a trance to be brought to a higher spiritual plain. Bruce indicates, "For the gaining of such a vision punctilious observance of the *minutiae* of the law, not least the law of purification, was essential…[W]hen the heavenly ascent was attempted, the mediatorial role of angels was indispensable,"[85] making a reference to Rabbi Aqiba entering into Paradise as an example to be considered (t.*Haggigah* 2:3-4; b.*Haggigah* 14b). But Bruce also notes how it cannot be conclusively proven that the Colossian error was an early form of *Merkavah* mysticism, even though there are some parallels that cannot be ignored.[86]

Letters like Colossians demonstrate how knowledgeable Paul was not only of ancient Jewish thought, but also Greek thought as well, as he had to counter errors introduced *by both* into the assembly of Believers. Given the likelihood of the Colossian error being a mix of both local Greek/Phrygian and Jewish errors, today's Messianics **need to be quite assertive** in stating to others how the problems Paul addressed were *not* as clear cut as being exclusively "Jewish"—and thus the Messianic movement may be in error for even existing. Too often, lay readers of Colossians will not consider its historical backdrop, behooving us as

---

[81] Moo, 70.

[82] Do note that I am a firm advocate of following the mainline Rabbinical calendar, for *all* the dates of the appointed times. Consult the FAQ on the Messianic Apologetics website, "Biblical Calendar."

[83] Dunn, who considers Colossians to basically address a Jewish problem, does validly indicate, though, that "We cannot…assume… that the Judaism of the Colossian synagogues was wholly uniform" (p 30).

[84] Walter C. Kaiser, *The Promise-Plan of God: A Biblical Theology of the Old and New Testaments* (Grand Rapids: Zondervan, 2008), 289.

Cf. Marcus Jastrow, *Dictionary of the Targumim, Talmud Bavli, Talmud Yerushalmi, and Midrashic Literature* (New York: Judaica Treasury, 2004), 844.

[85] Bruce, *Colossians-Philemon-Ephesians*, pp 23, 24.

[86] Further summarized in Ibid., pp 24-26. Moo also remarks how "Jewish mysticism" is probably not "the best single option for describing the false teaching," yet "Jewish mysticism may…have played some role in the false teaching" (Moo, 55).

Messianic Believers to be more informed as to what the letter actually addressed given the complexities of circumstances available.

The challenge in understanding the diverse mix of pagan and Jewish errors countered in Colossians, is that a *contemporary* reflection on Colossians may force us to consider whether today's Messianic movement has been similarly affected by a fuse of human philosophical and Jewish errors. Would the promotion of the Jewish Kabbalah by some Messianics, for example, be something that Colossians speaks against? What about today's Jewish synagogues that promote Middle Eastern meditation, versus those who might only promote a social justice reading of Tanach books like Amos or Micah? Colossians 2:18 depicts an ecstatic kind of Judaism, outside the mainstream, that we need to make sure we not only avoid, but oppose should it crop up in our midst.

Eventually, like many other Pauline letters, Colossians asks today's Messianic Believers who or what is really at the center of their faith. **Is it Yeshua the Messiah?** Do we understand that regardless of who we are as individuals, that each person is equal in the eyes of the Lord (3:11). Do we make sure that we emphasize "Messiah in you, the hope of glory" (1:27)? Wright is entirely correct to observe, "The way to maturity for the people of God" lies in "the meaning of the death and resurrection of Jesus Christ."[87] Even though Wright is one commentator (an exception among evangelicals) who argues that Colossians is a polemic against the philosophy of Judaism, he is not incorrect in asserting how *our identity* is to be found in Yeshua the Messiah. His words also give today's Messianics a warning: "The emphasis of Paul's attack is against the adopting of a 'national' or racial religion in preference to faith in the one who is Lord of all."[88]

How often, for example, is the Torah given preferential treatment over the Messiah? Even while Yeshua may be considered important by today's Messianics, I have discovered *more than a few times* that the order that is emphasized is: Torah, Yeshua, and one's family/community. While Paul considered the Law to be spiritual (Romans 7:14) and important for instruction (2 Timothy 3:16), he would disagree with anyone placing the Torah before the Messiah (Philippians 3:9). Paul would most certainly disagree with one placing circumcision of the flesh over that of the heart (2:11), and circumcision being used as something to divide people in the Lord (3:11). Do today's Messianics rejoice more when the Torah is what is being proclaimed, or rather when one has "received Messiah Yeshua the Lord" and is able to "walk in Him" (2:6), as the Torah is to lead people to the Messiah (Galatians 3:24)?

Colossians need not be an impossible letter for us to understand or contemplate, but it is most certainly one that will ask today's Messianic Believers some rather targeted questions—just as it originally asked the Colossians some targeted questions. By living a life of Torah observance, we may be accused of missing the Torah's substance, Yeshua the Messiah, when in the case of many Messianics this is falsely placed. Some Messianics, though, may be legitimately accused of following the Torah in a very superstitious way, one which downplays God's grace when someone falls. There might be some contemporary application that warns us against Jewish error that we have allowed into the camp, evidencing itself in various populist teachings and trends. And perhaps most importantly, Colossians reminds us that we need to be a little more cognizant of the complexities of ancient religion when we read the Scriptures—something that needs to come through more frequently in *Shabbat* teaching and study.

How do we avoid the errors confronted in Colossians, and how do we hold to a very high view of who Yeshua is in our lives? Only by examining Colossians in detail can we actually find out how to do this.

On the technical side as you prepare to read this commentary on Colossians-Philemon, note that I have purposefully refrained from overly using Hebraic terminology, other than the name "Yeshua the Messiah" for Jesus Christ, and on occasion "Torah" instead of Law, for the familiarity of most readers, and those who can be easily confused by unfamiliar words. The 1995 New American Standard, Updated Edition is the base English translation used in these studies, because of its literalness and widespread usage among many conservative evangelical Christians. Other major English versions I consult include the Revised Standard Version and New International Version.

---

[87] Wright, 27.
[88] Ibid., pp 42-43.

References to the Greek Apostolic Scriptures are from United Bible Societies' 1998 Greek New Testament, Fourth Revised Edition, the same basic text as the Nestle-Aland Novum Testamentum Gracae, 27th Edition. If you have any competency in Greek, an excellent resource to employ in examining our text is the Nestle-Aland Greek-English New Testament, which includes the 27th Edition GNT and a parallel RSV.

ABBREVIATED OUTLINE OF COLOSSIANS

I. Greeting (1:1-2)
II. Thanksgiving (1:3-8)
III. Prayer (1:9-12)
IV. Doctrinal Section: An Exposition on the Doctrine of Messiah (1:13-2:23)
    a. A positive statement (1:13-2:7)
        i. Through Yeshua comes deliverance and redemption (1:13-14)
        ii. Yeshua is the "image of the invisible God" (1:15)
        iii. Yeshua is the Source and Upholder of Creation (1:16-17)
        iv. Yeshua is the Head of the *ekklēsia*, the Reconciler of all things to Himself (1:18-20)
        v. What Yeshua has done for the universe, He has done for the Colossians (1:21-28)
        vi. The readers are exhorted to be firmly established in faith (2:1-7)
    b. A polemical statements (2:8-23)
        i. Speculative philosophy is to be avoided (2:8-10)
            1. The Colossians need to focus on the true character found in the Messiah (2:11-15)
        ii. The Colossians are to remember the Messiah as the substance (*sōma*) of various aspects of Torah observance (2:16-17)
        iii. Worship of angels derides the supreme Lordship of Yeshua (2:18-19)
        iv. Rigid asceticism is to be shunned as superstitious (2:20-23)
V. Practical Section (3:1-4:6)
    a. The doctrinal basis of a Believer's life (3:1-4)
    b. The old life and the new (3:5-17)
    c. A Believer's homelife (3:18-4:1)
        i. Wives and husbands (3:18-19)
        ii. Children and parents (3:20-21)
        iii. Slaves and masters (3:22-4:1)
        iv. General behavior (4:2-6)
VI. Conclusion (4:7-18)
    a. Commendation of Tychicus and Onesimus (4:7-9)
    b. Greetings from Paul's companions (4:10-14)
    c. Messages to Laodicea and Archippus (4:15-17)
    d. Paul's own greeting (4:18)[89]

BIBLIOGRAPHY FOR INTRODUCTION TO COLOSSIANS

Arnold, Clinton E. "Colossae," in *ABD*, 1:1089-1090.
Banks, E.J. "Colossae," in *ISBE*, 1:732.
Barabas, Steven. "Colossae," in *NIDB*, 227.
_____. "Colossians, the Letter to," in *NIDB*, 227.
Bruce, F.F. "Colossians, Epistle to the," in *ISBE*, 1:733-735.

---

[89] Adapted from Guthrie, *New Testament Introduction*, pp 581-584.

_____. "Introduction to Colossians," in *NICNT: Colossians, Philemon, Ephesians*, pp 3-33.

Bullard, Roger. "The Letter of Paul to the Colossians," in *New Interpreter's Study Bible*, pp 2107-2113.

Carson, D.A., and Douglas J. Moo. "Colossians," in *An Introduction to the New Testament*, pp 516-531.

Dunn, James D.G. "Introduction," in *NIGTC: The Epistles to the Colossians and to Philemon*, pp 19-42.

Dunnam, Maxie D. "Introduction to Colossians," in *PreachC: Galatians, Ephesians, Philippians, Colossians, Philemon*, 31:319-323.

Francis, F.O. "Colossians, Letter to the," in *IDBSup*, pp 169-170.

Furnish, Victor Paul. "The Letter of Paul to the Colossians," in *The Interpreter's One-Volume Commentary on the Bible*, pp 856-864.

_____. "Colossians, Epistle to the," in *ABD*, 1:1090-1096.

Geisler, Norman. "Colossians," in *BKCNT*, pp 667-686.

Gundry, Robert H. "Colossians: Christ as the Head of the Church," in *A Survey of the New Testament*, pp 392-397.

Guthrie, Donald. "Colossians," in *NBCR*, pp 1139-1153.

_____. "The Epistle to the Colossians," in *New Testament Introduction*, pp 564-584.

Hay, David M. "Colossians, Letter to the," in *EDB*, pp 270-271.

Hooker, Morna D. "Colossians," in *ECB*, pp 1404-1412.

Johnston, G. "Colossians, Letter to the," in *IDB*, 1:658-662.

Kaiser, Jr., Walter C. "Colossians: The Primacy of Jesus and New Life in Christ," in *The Promise-Plan of God*, pp 285-290.

Lincoln, Andrew T. "The Letter to the Colossians," in *NIB*, 11:553-669.

Mellink, M.J. "Colossae," in *IDB*, 1:658

Moo, Douglas J. "Introduction to Colossians," in *Pillar New Testament Commentary*, pp 25-71.

Nash, Scott. "Colossae," in *EDB*, pp 269-270.

O'Brien, Peter T. "Introduction to Colossians," in *WBC: Colossians-Philemon*, 44:xxv-iiv.

_____. "Colossians, Letter to the," in *Dictionary of Paul and His Letters*, pp 147-153.

Stern, David H. *Jewish New Testament Commentary*, pp 603-615.

Vaughan, Curtis. "Colossians," in *EXP*, 11:163-226.

Witherington III, Ben. "Introduction," in *The Letters to Philemon, the Colossians, and the Ephesians: A Socio-Rhetorical Commentary on the Captivity Epistles*, pp 1-40.

_____. "The Letter to the Colossians," in Ibid., pp 99-113.

Wright, N.T. "Colossians: Introduction," in *TNTC: Colossians and Philemon*, pp 19-45.

COLOSSIANS 1
COMMENTARY

1 Paul, an apostle of Yeshua the Messiah by the will of God, and Timothy our brother, 2 to the saints and faithful brethren in Messiah *who are* **at Colossae: Grace to you and peace from God our Father.**

1:1 The Epistle to the Colossians opens with both Paul and Timothy extending greetings to the target audience (cf. Ephesians 1:1).[1] As this letter begins, Paul confidently asserts his apostolic authority "by the will of God," indicating that it has Divine origins (cf. Galatians 1:1). This is something important for him to emphasize to an audience he had never encountered (or, at least most of them) in person, in their native environment. Paul's authority as an apostle chosen by God—the Apostle to the nations—extended to congregations that he had not founded, such as the assembly he is writing to at Colossae, or previously the one at Rome (Romans 1:11-12). But Paul does not spend that much time asserting that he is an apostle called by God that they must respect and follow; he is more concerned about the Colossians' spiritual well being, and desires that they turn back to a proper course of faith.

Some commentators, as discussed in the Introduction, see the mention of Timothy to be a possible inference of co-authorship, or of Timothy serving as Paul's amanuensis. Strongly leaning toward Timothean authorship, James D.G. Dunn states, "the authority of the apostle [Paul] lay behind the letter, and that would be sufficient to ensure that the letter was treasured by the Colossians...subsequently to be included in the earliest collection(s) of Paul's letters."[2] Even though I am convinced that Paul is the primary author, we need not disregard any involvement of Timothy in helping Paul counsel Epaphras (vs. 7-8), or him playing a role in suggesting what needed to be written to the Colossians. To suggest that Timothy played a role in composing Colossians is acceptable, given that his name is mentioned in the text.

1:2 Paul's opening word to the Colossians is one not only of great respect, but is also rhetorically important for setting the tone of what he will be communicating. Paul issues a prayer to God on behalf of the Colossians. Ben Witherington III indicates, "Since Paul does not have a personal relationship with his audience it is all the more critical that he establish something positive with them so that they will be open to the discourse that follows."[3] Unlike the opening words of Galatians, for example, the Apostle Paul does not just go into a tirade against what is wrong with the Colossians. Instead, in spite of some of the problems that may be going on in Colossae, Paul recognizes the Colossians as both his fellow "saints" and as "faithful brothers and sisters" (NRSV).

The call to be *hagioi* (ἅγιοι) or saints/holy ones is something deeply rooted in the Tanach Scriptures. Israel was God's holy people (Exodus 19:6; Daniel 7:18, 22, 25, 27), called to be holy just as the Lord is holy (Leviticus 11:44; 19:2).[4] While rendered as "faithful" in the NASU, some argue that the best rendering for the adjective *pistos* (πιστός) is "believing."[5] Even if some of the Colossians were not entirely faithful to Yeshua when Paul wrote to them, they still no doubt believed in Him to some degree, and a status of faithfulness demonstrated to the Lord was certainly something that could be entirely restored in their lives. The Colossians

---

[1] Timothy also extends opening greetings in: 2 Corinthians 1:1; Philippians 1:1; 1 Thessalonians 1:1; 2 Thessalonians 1:1.

[2] Dunn, 44.

[3] Witherington, 118.

[4] Cf. O'Brien, *Colossians-Philemon*, 3.

[5] Lincoln, in *NIB*, 11:588.

are Paul's brothers and sisters "in Messiah," as their true identity is to be found in Him, something that he intends to see fully reestablished via his instructions to them (2:6).

The opening section of the epistle, which probably extends through 2:5, expresses that in the gospel and the salvation provided by God's Son, that the Colossians have everything that they need. The false teachers they have been listening to will not at all aid them. At the same time, as this is to be considered as one reads through Colossians, Witherington notes how there is only "one major problem [Paul] knows about in ch. 2," and "overall it is a mistake to see this whole letter as a broadside against this problem."[6] Any good communicator, either ancient or modern, knows that it is inappropriate, and perhaps even damaging, to only focus on negative aspects of a situation—as bad circumstances can surely be turned around as a chance for people to learn and see good prevail.

Paul tells the Colossians, "Grace to you and peace from God our Father," employing a combination of standard Greek and Jewish greetings: *charis humin kai eirēnē* (χάρις ὑμῖν καὶ εἰρήνη). *Chairein* (χαίρειν) was the normal Greek term employed for "greeting," but has been replaced with the similar sounding *charis*, meaning "grace." *Eirēnē* or "peace," should be understood via its Septuagint usage where it translates the Hebrew *shalom* (שָׁלוֹם)—which often regards the total peace, harmony, and tranquility that God desires between Himself, humanity, and Creation—as opposed to just its classical meaning of absence of war. Paul really does want the best for the Colossians.

Not to be overlooked is the author's usage of "God our Father," *patros hēmōn* (πατρὸς ἡμῶν). Dunn is correct for readers to consider that he has taken an Israel-specific claim and "appropriated it...[for] Gentile believers: '*our* God.' Paul's implicit claim is that by accepting the gospel of Christ and his Spirit Gentiles were incorporated into Israel/the family of God, now redefined as 'the household of faith'."[7] This is a theme that receives greater attention in Colossians' companion letter (Ephesians 2:11-12; 3:6)—not as a means of non-Jewish Believers replacing the Jewish people, but being incorporated into the community of Israel via their Messiah faith.

3 We give thanks to God, the Father of our Lord Yeshua the Messiah, praying always for you, 4 since we heard of your faith in Messiah Yeshua and the love which you have for all the saints; 5 because of the hope laid up for you in heaven, of which you previously heard in the word of truth, the gospel 6 which has come to you, just as in all the world also it is constantly bearing fruit and increasing, even as *it has been doing* in you also since the day you heard *of it* and understood the grace of God in truth;

1:3 This is the first of multiple times seen in Colossians where thanks are issued by the author (1:12; 2:7; 3:15-17; 4:2). The expression "We give thanks," rather than "I give thanks," is likely not the usage of an epistolary plural, but is intended to include Timothy and/or any other associates of Paul that have helped counsel Epaphras. Notably absent in these opening words, much unlike Galatians, is an urgency in which Paul's words were directed and targeted. While some direct statements surely do have to be made to the Colossians, there is no tone of significant urgency because of great upheaval.[8] On the contrary, in wanting to express such thanks, Paul and company say that they are "praying always" (Grk. *pantote...proseuchomenoi*, πάντοτε...προσευχόμενοι) for the Colossians. Paul could very well be referring to the common Jewish practice of praying three times a day (Daniel 6:11; Acts 3:1; 10:3), or that he simply prayed whenever he had the chance, now remembering the Colossians in his petitions to God.

The Epistle to the Colossians follows a standard, classical letter writing convention, where an expression of hope for the well being of the recipient begins the composition. This is a pattern consistent with all of the Pauline Epistles, the notable exception being Galatians.[9] As important as the statements of thanksgiving for the Colossians may be, they include significant reminders to them of the spiritual life they should be

---

[6] Witherington, 119.
[7] Dunn, 52.
[8] Ibid., 53.
[9] Bruce, *Colossians-Philemon-Ephesians*, 40.

experiencing in the Lord. This is a spiritual life they had lost sight of, and now needed to be refocused in a very careful and tactful way.

The Apostle Paul has a balanced view of the Godhead, as he speaks of "God, the Father of our Lord Yeshua the Messiah." Paul recognizes God as "Father," and Yeshua as "Lord" (cf. 1 Corinthians 8:6; Deuteronomy 6:4). By no means does Paul simply consider Yeshua to be a human master by calling Him *Kurios* (κύριος),[10] as will be demonstrated by the themes and concepts witnessed in vs. 15-20. The title *Kurios* was used in the Greek Septuagint to render the Divine Name YHWH (יהוה), and Paul absolutely considers Yeshua the Messiah to be the LORD manifested to the world in human flesh (2:9).[11] Yeshua the Messiah is very much recognized as a part of the Godhead, using available terms familiar to and employed within First Century Jewish monotheism.

1:4 Neither Paul nor his company have met their Colossian audience personally, as "we have heard of your faith in Christ Jesus and of the love which you have for all the saints" (RSV). They have only been told of the Colossians' spirituality—something that is marked by love toward God's people—via Epaphras (v. 7). Three major virtues of Believers in Messiah are listed by Paul: faith, love, and hope (v. 5), indicating a connection between Paul's other letters (Romans 5:2-5; 1 Corinthians 13:13; 1 Thessalonians 1:3; 5:8), and other Apostolic epistles (Hebrews 10:22-24; 1 Peter 1:21-22). *These are things present in the Colossians' lives, that thanks to God are issued for.* Paul and Timothy have heard a relatively positive report about the Colossians' life of faith, with the Colossians largely knowing Paul by reputation. Any of the Colossians who had actually known Paul, would have had to have been associates of Epaphras who had encountered him while he preached in Ephesus (Acts 19:10).

Peter T. O'Brien, reflecting one view, specifies how the faith of the Colossians is "'in Christ Jesus'…an expression which does not denote the object to which their faith is directed but rather indicates the sphere in which 'faith' lives and acts," further indicating how "Some of the implications of living under [Christ's] lordship will be spelled out in the later sections of the letter."[12] From this perspective, the faith in Messiah Yeshua (*tēn pistin humōn en Christō Iēsou*, τὴν πίστιν ὑμῶν ἐν Χριστῷ Ἰησοῦ) would be more how Believers are to be marked by His presence among them, demonstrated by an expression of love (Grk. *agapē*, ἀγάπη) toward others. Still, there are certainly commentators who take "faith in Messiah Yeshua" as simply meaning belief and trust in the Lord.

1:5 Confidence is expressed in the Colossians, because Paul issues thanks not only for their faith (v. 4), but also "because of the hope laid up for you in heaven. Of this you have heard before in the word of the truth, the gospel" (RSV). The Colossians' hope is not one that concerns this life only; it concerns another dimension where Yeshua the Messiah presently intercedes for Believers (Hebrews 7:21; 1 John 2:1), something to be further elaborated on (3:1-4). This ultimate hope that originates from Heaven is one of being crowned by the Lord at His Second Coming, where rewards are issued to the saints (2 Timothy 4:8).

While there are certainly future expectations of treasures in Heaven (Matthew 6:20), or an inheritance in Heaven (1 Peter 1:4) promised for the saints in the eschaton—Paul's letters express his view that these things are *not* entirely of the future. In order to receive such future treasures, *one must know* the Messiah today! F.F. Bruce comments how "The emphasis on hope reminds us that the salvation which believers enjoy in Christ has a future aspect. The hope is theirs here and now; its fulfillment lies ahead, in the resurrection age."[13] Douglas J. Moo similarly remarks, "Paul's eschatology, rooted in Jewish apocalyptic conceptions, combines the spatial and the temporal: that which will be 'revealed' even now exists in the transcendent realm of God's person and purposes."[14] The ultimate salvation occurs at the resurrection, when the complete being of a

---

[10] Cf. Romans 10:9, 13; Philippians 2:10.

[11] Cf. L.W. Hurtado, "Lord: Appellation Formulas (3.3)," in *Dictionary of Paul and His Letters*, 566.
As noted in this article: "[T]he single most frequently found use of *kyrios* [or 'Lord'] in Paul (about 100 times in the letters we are considering here) is as the designation of Jesus without any other title, simply 'the Lord.'"

[12] O'Brien, *Colossians-Philemon*, 11.

[13] Bruce, *Colossians-Philemon-Ephesians*, 41.

[14] Moo, 86.

person will be redeemed (Romans 13:11; Hebrews 9:28). Reaching toward this as salvation history progresses forward is to motivate Believers to capture that resurrection life in the present time.[15]

The hope of being rewarded for their faithfulness by the Lord is something that the Colossians had previously heard, with the gospel specifically labeled as *tō logō tēs alētheias* (τῷ λόγῳ τῆς ἀληθείας) or "the word of truth." Paul has directly appropriated a description reserved in the Tanach for the Torah as *devar-emet* (אֱמֶת־דְּבַר; Psalm 119:43, 142, 160), applying it to the good news of salvation in Yeshua. This should not be surprising, as he had previously written the Romans that "the gospel of God" was something "He promised beforehand through His prophets in the holy Scriptures" (Romans 1:1-2). God's Torah is not at all to be disregarded because of the good news of salvation in Yeshua, but just as the Torah was considered to be a reliable revelation of His truth, so was the gospel to be as well.

Paul's assertion that the Colossians had previously accepted the word of truth, in the good news, is definitely used to contrast the empty deceit of the false teachers in Colossae (2:8). Can they offer the Colossians the same things that the gospel has brought to their lives—*things that Paul has been told they have certainly experienced?*

1:6 In wanting to encourage the Colossians, Paul makes an important, yet bold claim about the expanse of the gospel. He recognizes that while the good news has come to them, "All over the world this gospel is bearing fruit and growing" (NIV). While saying that positive fruit has come forth from the good news, he does say that this has taken place "in all the world."

How are we to interpret Paul's claim that the gospel has spread *en panti tō kosmō* (ἐν παντὶ τῷ κόσμῳ)? Does "the world" pertain to only the Roman Empire, is it hyperbole, or is it an observation on Paul's behalf that the gospel has far-reaching results? Some take this as being exaggerated rhetoric. In Romans 1:8, Paul says "your faith is being proclaimed throughout the whole world," and in Romans 10:18 he quotes Psalm 19:4 (LXX), which expresses how "THEIR VOICE HAS GONE OUT INTO ALL THE EARTH, AND THEIR WORDS TO THE ENDS OF THE WORLD." Regardless of which option you may choose in how "all the world" is to be viewed, Paul's primary intent is to focus the Colossians' attention on the gospel, and how it is to affect—or will significantly affect—the Created order.

The most immediate affect that the good news provides is that it is "constantly bearing fruit and increasing," something that "*it has been doing* in you since the day you heard *of it* and understood the grace of God in truth." **Something that is to affect all the world has affected the Colossians personally.** The concept of bearing fruit is certainly language seen in the Tanach, including: the commandment given to people to multiply (Genesis 1:28; 8:17; 9:1, 7), God's promise that He would multiply the Patriarchs' seed (Genesis 17:20; 28:3; 35:11), or the fact that Israel would multiply while in Egypt (Genesis 48:4; Exodus 1:7). Even the post-exilic promise of multiplicity may be considered (Jeremiah 3:16; 23:3).

The connections of the spread of the gospel to bearing fruit likely regard God's original choosing of Israel, through which His Divine tasks would be accomplished (Hosea 10:1; 14:7-8). When we make the appropriate comparisons with the companion letter of Ephesians, the Apostle Paul does not at all seem to be promoting a separate entity with a separate purpose called "the Church" here. N.T. Wright sees connections between "bearing fruit and increasing" and Genesis 1:22 and 1:28, concluding that Paul is "highlighting the Jewish belief that in the call of Israel God was fulfilling his purposes for the whole world, undoing the sin of Adam by creating for himself a holy people."[16] Now with the arrival of Israel's promised Messiah, this original call would be greatly amplified, as the reliable and trustworthy message of His salvation would go forth, be sown, and great fruit would be borne. Moo further suggests,

"Paul may...be deliberately echoing a biblical-theological motif according to which God's original mandate to humans finds preliminary fulfillment in the nation Israel but ultimate fulfillment in the worldwide

---

[15] In the author's article "To Be Absent From the Body," he expresses the reality that while Believers are promised an intermediate afterlife in the presence of the Lord in Heaven prior to the resurrection (i.e., 2 Corinthians 5:8; Philippians 1:23), the Bible is more concerned with God's people capturing the life of the future age of resurrection in the present mission of the Body of Messiah—what may be termed "the life *after* the afterlife."

[16] Wright, 53.

transformation of people into the image of God by their incorporation into Christ, *the* image of God"[17] (cf. 3:10).

7 just as you learned *it* from Epaphras, our beloved fellow bond-servant, who is a faithful servant of Messiah on our behalf, 8 and he also informed us of your love in the Spirit.

1:7-8 The Colossians to whom Paul is writing originally learned of the gospel from Epaphras, who himself likely learned it from Paul while he was preaching in Ephesus (Acts 19:10), as a distance of only about 100 miles separated Colossae from Ephesus. Epaphras, who was a native of Colossae (4:12), has relayed a report to Paul on the Colossians' spiritual condition, while Paul was imprisoned in Rome, and how the Colossians' faith had been proceeding. Paul is clear to tell them, "[he] has made known to us your love in the Spirit" (RSV)—which is notably different from something like "He told us all about your problems..."

Because Epaphras will be returning to Colossae at some point, Paul finds it necessary to offer a word of commendation regarding him, as Epaphras will need to see that the Colossian Believers return to the proper course of faith. The Apostle Paul labels Epaphras as "our beloved fellow servant. He is a faithful minister of Christ," and denoting his approval, he adds that Epaphras serves "on our behalf" (RSV). Epaphras' faithfulness has been demonstrated by ministry service in nearby Laodicea and Hierapolis (4:13), and upon visiting Paul he had—in some degree—to be considered his fellow prisoner (Philemon 23). Perhaps in order to have access to Paul, Epaphras had to share a prison cell with him.

Just like Paul,[18] Epaphras is considered to be a *doulos* (δοῦλος)[19] or a servant of the Most High, accomplishing important work for the Lord. Similarly, he is also a *diakonos* (διάκονος) or a minister. Occupying these important offices, and with confidence expressed by the Apostle Paul, when Epaphras finally does return home the Colossians are to take him seriously.

9 For this reason also, since the day we heard *of it*, we have not ceased to pray for you and to ask that you may be filled with the knowledge of His will in all spiritual wisdom and understanding, 10 so that you will walk in a manner worthy of the Lord, to please *Him* in all respects, bearing fruit in every good work and increasing in the knowledge of God; 11 strengthened with all power, according to His glorious might, for the attaining of all steadfastness and patience; joyously 12 giving thanks to the Father, who has qualified us to share in the inheritance of the saints in Light.

1:9 The prayer that Paul and his colleagues have been issuing to the Lord on the Colossians' behalf is certainly one that is very encouraging for any of us to read, yet embedded within its words is definite instruction on what mature Believers should be doing and seeking. From the moment Paul and his associates heard of the Colossians' spiritual condition, they have not ceased in appealing to God for their well being. Parallels with how "Aaron shall carry the judgment of the sons of Israel over his heart before the LORD continually" (Exodus 28:30), or the Prophet Samuel's words, "far be it from me that I should sin against the LORD by ceasing to pray for you" (1 Samuel 12:23), have been suggested.

Paul appeals to God that the Colossians "may be filled with the knowledge of His will in all spiritual wisdom and understanding." Some of the terms that Paul uses here may be deliberate, in an effort to combat the claims made by the false teachers in Colossae: *hina* **plērōthēte** *tēn* **epignōsin** *tou thelēmatos* (ἵνα πληρωθῆτε τὴν ἐπίγνωσιν τοῦ θελήματος). The two terms to take note of are *plērōma* (πλήρωμα)[20] and *epignōsis* (ἐπίγνωσις), "fullness" and "knowledge," respectively. O'Brien comments, "Paul's use of 'knowledge'...here might be by way of contrast with the much-canvassed *gnosis* of the false teachers. Heretical *gnosis* was speculative and

---

[17] Moo, 88.

[18] Cf. Romans 1:1; 2 Corinthians 4:5; Galatians 1:10; Philippians 1:1; Titus 1:1.

[19] V. 7 actually employs the more specific *sundoulos* (σύνδουλος), meaning "fellow servant" (RSV). This would mean that Epaphras shares the same spiritual company as the Apostle Paul and his associates, and all of those previous servants of God in the Tanach who had preceded them.

[20] V. 9 actually employs the verb *plēroō* (πληρόω).

theoretical while the knowledge for which the apostle prayed concerned the 'will of God'."[21] This is a specific knowledge that is not to come from human flesh (cf. 1 Corinthians 8:1), but from the Holy Spirit inside of a person (1 Corinthians 2:5-6, 13). It manifests itself in a godly wisdom that can demonstrate useful, practical actions (James 1:5; 3:15). In contrast to this, Paul will say that the false teachers only possess "the appearance of wisdom" (2:23).

Wisdom and understanding are traits that are to originate from God's Spirit. Bezalel possessed it as he fashioned the various instruments to be used in the Tabernacle (Exodus 31:1; 35:31). Isaiah, prophesying of the Messiah to come, said, "The Spirit of the LORD will rest on Him, the spirit of wisdom and understanding" (Isaiah 11:2a). The Apocrypha also alludes to how wisdom and understanding are to be imbued on people from God's Spirit (Wisdom 9:17-18; Sirach 39:6; 4 Ezra 14:22). While certainly important to the Jewish community of the First Century, we should not dismiss the fact that wisdom and understanding are also seen as two of the most striking qualities in Aristotelian philosophy. Aristotle lists these as principal among virtues: "Some virtues are called intellectual and others moral; Wisdom and Understanding and Prudence are intellectual" (*Nicomachean Ethics* 1.13).[22] Many of the non-Jewish Colossians could very easily have sought for wisdom and understanding in the classical philosophy of their day, and so Paul would certainly want to communicate to them that these ever-important virtues **are to be found in the Holy Spirit**, and not in things of human origin (2:8). Witherington reminds us,

"In the pluralistic world in which the Colossians lived, the notion that one could achieve the highest level of generally recognized civic virtue by means of aid of the Holy Spirit would be welcome news and an impetus to continue to cultivate one's...faith."[23]

The false teachers in Colossae were coming from that same pluralistic world, a diverse cultural, philosophical, and religious environment with a great deal of perspectives to consider. And why did they advocate their false teachings? What might have made them so appealing to the Colossians? Were they things that were thought to help the Colossians give back to society, perhaps? There are certainly a great number of parallels to be found between classical philosophy and the Biblical message. But classical philosophy, or even the mystery religions and cults, could by no means **offer the personal presence of the Creator God** inside of a man or woman to positively impact others. In the Colossians' case, it got them very confused.

Proverbs 1:7a (LXX) says, "The fear of the Lord is the beginning of wisdom" (LXE). Paul wrote the Romans that because of humanity's widescale rejection of the Creator God, He "gave them over to a depraved mind, to do those things which are not proper" (Romans 1:28b). When one can manifest "all spiritual wisdom and understanding," improper and immoral actions will not be present, and born again Believers can accomplish the will of God. Curtis Vaughan remarks how "The will of God in its broadest and most inclusive sense is the whole purpose of God as revealed in Christ....To be 'filled' with the knowledge of the divine will suggests that such knowledge is to pervade all of one's being—thoughts, affections, purposes, and plans."[24] It is not insignificant that the verb *plērōthēte* (πληρωθῆτε), is a passive aorist, properly considered to be a Divine passive.[25] So, rather than going to fill themselves from what the false teachers are offering, Paul's prayer is that instead the Colossians will know how *God has filled* them with what they need.

In praying for the Colossians, what Paul has in mind relating to wisdom and understanding are practical concepts rooted in the Tanach. Obedience to God is a visible demonstration in the world of His greatness (Deuteronomy 4:6; Psalm 111:10), and it is something that only He can provide His people with (1 Chronicles 22:12), meaning that just like King Solomon men and women must diligently request it of Him (2 Chronicles 1:10-12). A leader like Joshua had wisdom imparted to him, as Moses commissioned him to lead Israel (Deuteronomy 34:9). The wisdom of God that can empower His people is not too difficult for them to

---

[21] O'Brien, *Colossians-Philemon*, 21.

[22] Aristotle: *Ethics*, trans. J.A.K. Thomson (Harmondsworth, UK: Penguin Books, 1979), 90.

[23] Witherington, 124.

[24] Vaughan, in *EXP*, 11:177.

[25] Moo, 93.

possess (1:27-28; 2:2-3), but they have got to want it. And in wanting it, they have got to be willing to fulfill what it mandates to righteous people:

"To know wisdom and instruction, to discern the sayings of understanding, to receive instruction in wise behavior, righteousness, justice and equity; to give prudence to the naive, to the youth knowledge and discretion, a wise man will hear and increase in learning, and a man of understanding will acquire wise counsel, to understand a proverb and a figure, the words of the wise and their riddles. The fear of the LORD is the beginning of knowledge; fools despise wisdom and instruction" (Proverbs 1:2-7).

1:10 Paul's prayer regarding the Colossians expresses a hope, because if they are empowered by wisdom and understanding, they will "walk in a manner worthy of the Lord, fully pleasing to him, bearing fruit in every good work and increasing in the knowledge of God" (ESV). Wright correctly indicates, "Understanding will fuel holiness; holiness will deepen understanding."[26] While some versions use a rendering like "live a life" (NIV), the Jewish character of Colossians' author comes through as he speaks of how to "walk" (i.e., Proverbs 2:12-20; 4:25-27), something that Dunn notes is "untypical of Greek thought,"[27] and is also something seen throughout the Pauline Epistles.[28] While the verb *peripateo* (περιπατέω) may be what is used for "walk," O'Brien notes how "The word is equivalent to the Hebrew *hālak/hithhallēk*,"[29] further indicating how it is used in the DSS to describe how the sons of light walk in an upright manner (1QS 1.8; 3.21).

Living in a manner worthy of the Lord, as important as this theme is to the Biblical tradition, may be some targeted words on Paul's behalf to confront some of the religious sentiments local to the Lycus Valley. Bruce remarks, "If pagans appreciated the importance of rendering worship which was worthy of the deities whose votaries they were, much more should Christians render the spiritual service of obedient lives to the living and true God and to his Son Jesus Christ."[30] Another angle to this walking properly in the Lord could be how Paul desired both Jewish and non-Jewish Believers to be one in Him. Dunn describes how "Paul and Timothy thought it desirable to emphasize just this fundamental feature of their common faith. The most obvious reason is that the Colossians were confronted by local Jews who were confident of the superiority of their own religious practice and who denigrated the claims of these Gentiles to share in their own Jewish heritage."[31] In living a life worthy of the Messiah, the Colossians would have to take a hold of a great heritage and mission presented to them in Israel's Scriptures.

The key to walking in a manner glorifying of God is for the Colossians to possess *panti ergō agathō* (παντὶ ἔργῳ ἀγαθῷ), which the NEB extrapolates as "active goodness of every kind." In his paralleling letter of Ephesians, Paul writes how salvation comes by God's grace (Ephesians 2:8-9), but He created us to accomplish good works (Ephesians 2:10). Even though Paul would very much oppose a doctrine of salvation by works or human effort, he nevertheless also promoted that those demonstrating proper faith were to have good works (Romans 13:3; 2 Corinthians 5:10; Galatians 6:10; 1 Thessalonians 5:15; 2 Thessalonians 2:17). The qualities that Believers are to manifest to the world at large are summarized by the Prophet Micah: "He has told you, O man, what is good; and what does the LORD require of you but to do justice, to love kindness, and to walk humbly with your God?" (Micah 6:8).

Paul employs the present participles *karpophorountes kai auxanomenoi* (καρποφοροῦντες καὶ αὐξανόμενοι) for "bearing fruit...and increasing," indicating the spiritual progress of the Colossians. Some have seen connections to Yeshua's parable of the sower (Mark 4:1-9, 13-20). Those who are bearing the required fruit of Believers will increase in their spiritual maturity, enabling them to have *tē epignōsei tou Theou* (τῇ ἐπιγνώσει τοῦ θεοῦ), "the knowledge of God." There could be echoes of Wisdom here, as "Having been disciplined a little, they will receive great good, because God tested them and found them worthy of himself" (Wisdom 3:5).

---

[26] Wright, 58.

[27] Dunn, 71.

[28] Romans 6:4; 8:4; 14:15; 2 Corinthians 4:2; Galatians 5:16; Ephesians 2:10; 4:1; 5:2, 15; Philippians 3:17.

[29] O'Brien, *Colossians-Philemon*, 22.

[30] Bruce, *Colossians-Philemon-Ephesians*, 47.

[31] Dunn, pp 68-69.

1:11 In order to possess the true knowledge of God—as opposed to whatever miniscule knowledge the false teachers might offer them—the Colossians are to "be made strong with all the strength which comes from his glorious power, so that you may be able to endure everything with patience" (Good News Bible). Tough times, or at least some kind of testing via life circumstances, may confront them. They would have to remember the word of Ezra and Nehemiah: "Do not be grieved, for the joy of the LORD is your strength" (Nehemiah 8:10). O'Brien properly notes, "This kind of endurance...does not derive from personal bravery or stoical fortitude. Rather, as in the OT and later Judaism...it is seen to spring from God who is its source."[32] And perhaps also to be wondered is whether or not the false teachers in Colossae could really provide a word of advice to those who may encounter hardship, that is, if their philosophy would even consider the possibility of people facing difficulties.

1:12 Paul gives thanks for the Colossians, because "the Father...has qualified us to share in the inheritance of the saints in Light." While versions like the NASU and RSV follow the reading *humas* (ὑμᾶς) or "us," which would include *both* Paul and the Colossians partaking of such an inheritance, other versions like the NIV, NRSV, and CJB follow the reading *hēmas* (ἡμᾶς) or "you." This does not significantly change the overall meaning, as Paul surely does desire the Colossians to be delivered into the realm of God's light. But have the Colossians merely strayed from the light, or are they yet to even reach it? Bruce M. Metzger notes that for the United Bible Societies GNT, "A majority of the Committee preferred ὑμᾶς....regarding ἡμᾶς...as an assimilation to ver. 13."[33] When "you" is considered as the reading, it could seem that Paul believes he and his associates to be the only ones brought into the sphere of God's light (v. 13), and the Colossians have yet to arrive in it. A reader would have to ask if his previous assertion that the gospel has borne fruit among them (v. 6) is only speaking of the general affects of the good news, or their actual salvation.

In the Tanach, the principal inheritance of God's people was considered to be the Promised Land (Numbers 26:52-56; 34:2, 13; Deuteronomy 10:9; 32:9; Joshua 19:9; Psalm 105:11; cf. Genesis 13:14-17). Paul's usage of *klēros* (κλῆρος) is significant, as in the Septuagint it speaks of God's apportionment of the Promised Land to Ancient Israel.[34] Building on this theme, it is asserted that Believers get to share *eis tēn merida tou klērou tōn hagiōn* (εἰς τὴν μερίδα τοῦ κλήρου τῶν ἁγίων), "in the inheritance of the saints," as Paul emphasizes how God's principal inheritance is actually found among His people. This is something he will refer to in Ephesians 1:18 as "the riches of the glory of His inheritance in the saints."

Certainly while this should motivate audiences such as the Colossians to consider the value that God places on their fellow brothers and sisters in the faith, it should also get them to consider the fact that they are different. Just like Ancient Israel, born again Believers have been called out by the Lord—but this is something much more profound than being called into the Land of milk and honey—as blessed as that would have been. O'Brien describes how "the inheritance to which Paul refers belongs to a higher plane and a more lasting order than any earthly Canaan."[35] Morna D. Hooker goes a step further, actually concluding, "Writing to Gentiles, Paul assures them that God has enabled them...to share in the lot of 'the saints'—that is, God's people Israel."[36] Far be it for the non-Jewish Colossians being a part of a separate "Church," Paul believes them to be a part of Israel as specified in his paralleling letter (Ephesians 2:11-12). This is a people who have been delivered into God's purposes via the salvific actions of His Son Yeshua.

Wisdom 5:5 in the Apocrypha notes that one who "has been numbered among the sons of God," whose "lot [is] among the saints," is he who has not fallen into unrighteousness and lawlessness. In the DSS, it is said "The source of righteousness, gathering of power, and abode of glory are from fleshly counsel hidden. To them He has chosen all these has He given—an eternal possession. He has made them heirs in the legacy of

---

[32] O'Brien, *Colossians-Philemon*, 24.

[33] Bruce M. Metzger, *A Textual Commentary on the Greek New Testament* (London and New York: United Bible Societies, 1975), 620; cf. Erwin Nestle and Kurt Aland, eds., *Novum Testamentum Graece, Nestle-Aland 27th Edition* (New York: American Bible Society, 1993), 524; Kurt Aland, et. al., *The Greek New Testament, Fourth Revised Edition* (Stuttgart: Deutche Bibelgesellschaft/United Bible Societies, 1998), 686.

[34] Cf. W. Foerster, "*klēros*," in Geoffrey W. Bromiley, ed., *Theological Dictionary of the New Testament*, abridged (Grand Rapids: Eerdmans, 1985), 442.

[35] O'Brien, *Colossians-Philemon*, 26.

[36] Hooker, in *ECB*, pp 1405-1406; cf. Moo, 101.

the Holy Ones" (1QS 11.6-8), further noting "if I stumble, God's loving-kindness forever shall save me. If through sin of the flesh I fall, my justification will be by the righteousness of God which endures for all time" (1QS 11.12).[37] Concurrent with these sentiments, even though Paul says that the Colossians have been rescued by the power of God, he surely desires them to live appropriate lives, rejecting sin and letting the Messiah reign in their hearts (3:5-10, 15, 17).

13 For He rescued us from the domain of darkness, and transferred us to the kingdom of His beloved Son, 14 in whom we have redemption, the forgiveness of sins.

1:13 Paul's word that "He has delivered us from the dominion of darkness and transferred us to the kingdom of his beloved Son" (RSV) seems pretty straightforward to understand. God's power has rescued Believers from the hold of Satan, and brought them into the reign of Yeshua! It is not difficult to see a connection with Ephesians 6:12, where he says "For our struggle is not against flesh and blood, but against the rulers, against the powers, against the world forces of this darkness, against the spiritual *forces* of wickedness in the heavenly *places.*" Similarly, the Apostle John's assertion that "In Him was life, and the life was the Light of men. The Light shines in the darkness, and the darkness did not comprehend it" (John 1:4-5), may also be considered.

As important as these themes are, in describing the salvation of Believers—and their removal from the realm of Satan to the realm of the Messiah—the Apostle Paul is directly applying themes from the Torah regarding the Exodus. The verb *rhuomai* (ῥύομαι) is used in the LXX where God says "I will deliver [*rhuomai*] you from bondage" (Exodus 6:6, LXE), and where "the Lord delivered [*rhuomai*] Israel in that day from the hand of the Egyptians" (Exodus 14:30, LXE). The salvation of Believers may be compared to God's power rescuing Ancient Israel from the clutches of Egypt—the same power that has now been unleashed via the gospel (Romans 1:16-17; 1 Corinthians 1:24)!

The themes of light and darkness are quite common to the Tanach, used to contrast good and evil (Isaiah 9:2; 58:8-10; 59:9; 60:1; cf. Luke 22:53). The Psalmist says after all, "The LORD is my light and my salvation" (Psalm 27:1). The Prophet Isaiah sees the Exile as being darkness, but deliverance from it being light (Isaiah 42:7, 16; 49:9). And as important as this prophesied restoration may be, what Paul specifically wants to highlight to the Colossians is what Messiah Yeshua has brought to them. Moo properly concludes, "The true and ultimate rescue from exile comes not in (physical) return to the land but in (spiritual) redemption from sin through Christ."[38] This is something that Paul was specifically commissioned by Yeshua to do in Acts 26:18: "to open their eyes so that they may turn from darkness to light and from the dominion of Satan to God, that they may receive forgiveness of sins and an inheritance among those who have been sanctified by faith in Me."

The themes of light and darkness also appear in the DSS, particularly as the dominion of Belial wages war against the faithful. A sinner is one whom "God shall separate out for a fate befitting his wickedness. He shall be cut off from all the Sons of Light because of his apostasy from God, brought about by unrepentance and the stumbling block of sin" (1QS 1.18).[39] God's faithful people are considered to be "created...for Yourself as an eternal people, and into the lot of light You cast us" (1QM 13.9).[40] Overseers in the community were to be those who were to guide others, "and assign him his standing according to his share in the allotment of Light" (CD 13.12).[41]

Believers in Messiah Yeshua have been delivered into His Kingdom, a Kingdom of Light. Yet it is not enough to simply reside in the light. As Daniel 12:3 should remind us, "Those who have insight will shine

---

[37] Michael Wise, Martin Abegg, Jr., and Edward Cook, trans., *The Dead Sea Scrolls: A New Translation* (San Francisco: HarperCollins, 1996), pp 142, 143.

[38] Moo, pp 103-104.

[39] Wise, Abegg, and Cook, 128.

[40] Ibid., 162.

[41] Ibid., 71.

brightly like the brightness of the expanse of heaven, and those who lead the many to righteousness, like the stars forever and ever." Redeemed people who live in God's light are to testify of His goodness, leading others to Him.

Also to be considered are Paul's teachings of the two ages: the present evil age (Galatians 1:4; Romans 5:21), and the future righteous age (1 Corinthians 15:23-28). The aorist verb *metestēsen* (μετέστησεν) is used for "transferred," depicts a past action that has already taken place. Vaughan indicates how *methistēmi* (μεθίστημι) "was used in secular literature in reference to removing persons from one country and settling them as colonists and citizens in another country."[42] If Believers have been brought out of the dominion of darkness into the dominion of light, then they are people of the righteous age to come, even with it yet to be fully manifest. Wright summarizes, "Paul conceived of the establishment of this kingdom as a two-stage process. First there is 'the kingdom of Christ', which begins with Christ's resurrection and exaltation and continues until all enemies are subdued. Then there comes the final kingdom of God, the restoration of all things."[43] Even with the Kingdom a future reality ahead, we must live out that future Kingdom now in the ministry and mission of the *ekklēsia!*

Romans 8:1 expresses the significant truth of how "Therefore there is now no condemnation for those who are in Messiah Yeshua," and Paul will later detail a list of sins from which the Colossians have been rescued (3:5-8). Having been removed from the realm of darkness, they seem to have found their way back into its influence via the false teachers. The Apostle Paul wants the Colossians back on the proper course of faith, exhibiting the practical wisdom and proper good works of citizens in Yeshua's Kingdom of Light.

The Jewish character of Colossians is seen in the designation of "the kingdom of His beloved Son," *tou huiou tēs agapēs autou* (τοῦ υἱοῦ τῆς ἀγάπης αὐτοῦ), which is literally "the Son of His love." Vaughan considers this to be "a Hebraic way of saying 'God's dear Son.'"[44] One can think of how at Yeshua's immersion by John, the Father declared from Heaven, "You are My beloved Son, in You I am well-pleased" (Mark 1:11). Yeshua portrayed as God's Son is an important indication in the Gospels that He accomplishes important work on the Father's behalf in the world of mortals (cf. Matthew 2:15 and Hosea 1:11), designated as their Deliverer. Moo rightly considers "the kingdom of the Son he loves" (NIV) to be an "indication of Paul's high Christology,"[45] seeing a likely allusion to the Messianic promise of 2 Samuel 7:12-16, and God's eternal love for the Messianic Kingdom (cf. Psalm 2:2).

1:14 Having used the terminology "kingdom of His beloved Son," Paul purposefully wants the Colossians to consider *more* than just their standing in God's light, but what it actually took to get them into that light—*and focus their attention back on the Messiah Yeshua.* In Yeshua "we have redemption, the forgiveness of sins." Not surprisingly, cognates of *apolutrōsis* (ἀπολύτρωσις) or "redemption," are used in the Septuagint to describe the deliverance from Egypt (Deuteronomy 7:8; 9:26; 13:5; 15:15; 24:18).[46] In considering the redemption provided by the Messiah, Wright believes there are not only allusions to the Exodus made, but also to the promised New Covenant of Jeremiah 31:31-34 and Ezekiel 36:16-36,[47] where God's Torah is written on the hearts of His people. Of significance to this would be what it took to inaugurate such redemption in the lives of human beings—the elimination of the Law of Moses *or* the nailing of the condemnation of sin to the cross (2:14)?

---

[42] Vaughan, in *EXP*, 11:180.

[43] Wright, 62.

[44] Vaughan, in *EXP*, 11:180.

[45] Moo, 105.

[46] Lincoln, in *NIB*, 11:596.

[47] Wright, 63.

15 He is the image of the invisible God, the firstborn of all creation. 16 For by Him all things were created, *both* in the heavens and on earth, visible and invisible, whether thrones or dominions or rulers or authorities—all things have been created through Him and for Him. 17 He is before all things, and in Him all things hold together.

1:15-20 This section of Colossians likely forms an early hymn or poem present in the ancient Messianic community,[48] used to exclaim the supremacy of Yeshua the Messiah over the cosmos. (Even if this is not a hymn, Paul is still expressing some significant thoughts about Yeshua.) This is probably the most important part of the entire epistle, due to its Christological claims, which would be specifically important for understanding the angle of the philosophy later referred to (2:8), something that errantly influenced the Colossians. Parallels can be seen between 1:15-20 and additional statements that will be made in ch. 2:

PAUL'S PARALLEL ARGUMENTS[49]	
COLOSSIANS 1:15-20	COLOSSIANS 2
For by Him all things were created, *both* in the heavens and on earth, visible and invisible, whether thrones or dominions or rulers or authorities—all things have been created through Him and for Him (v. 16)	He is the head over all rule and authority (v. 10b)
He is also head of the body, the [assembly] (v. 18a)	...and not holding fast to the head... (v. 19)
For it was the *Father's* good pleasure for all the fullness to dwell in Him (v. 19)	For in Him all the fullness of [the] Deity dwells in bodily form (v. 9)
and through Him to reconcile all things to Himself, having made peace through the blood of His cross; through Him, *I say*, whether things on earth or things in heaven (v. 20)	When He had disarmed the rulers and authorities, He made a public display of them, having triumphed over them through Him (v. 15)

When reviewing the hymn of Colossians 1:15-20, it is possible that its claims are derived from theological sentiments seen in First Century Judaism, as well as Diaspora Hellenistic Judaism,[50] where Proverbs 8, Genesis 1, and Wisdom of God beliefs are in some kind of view. The language of 1:15-20 is notably dissimilar from Paul, which indicates that he is quoting something—in this case to most likely refute how the false teachers of Colossae had been devaluing Yeshua the Messiah. Moo concludes, "Paul has quoted and redacted an earlier hymn,"[51] adapting it for his purposes in the letter. For Larry W. Hurtado, author of *Lord Jesus Christ: Devotion to Jesus in Earliest Christianity*, "it is likely that [the hymn] either originated within the context of early Christian praise and worship, as a hymn celebrating Jesus, or was composed by the author of Colossians himself as...an expression of Christ's supremacy."[52]

---

[48] For possible poetic, rhymnic divisions, consult Ibid., 65; Lincoln, in *NIB*, 11:602-604.
Also consult the discussions in R.P. Martin, "Hymns, Hymn Fragments, Songs, Spiritual Songs," in *Dictionary of Paul and His Letters*, pp 419-423.
[49] Cf Moo, 109.
[50] O'Brien, *Colossians-Philemon*, pp 38-39.
[51] Moo, 110.
[52] Larry W. Hurtado, *Lord Jesus Christ: Devotion to Jesus in Earliest Christianity* (Grand Rapids: Eerdmans, 2003), 506.

Why would 1:15-20 serve to be the most important part of the Epistle to the Colossians? It is not that difficult to see, because in these verses we see Yeshua the Messiah uplifted as the

1. Image of God (v. 15)
2. Firstborn (v. 15)
3. Creator (v. 16)
4. Head of the *ekklēsia* (v. 18)
5. Firstborn from the dead (v. 18)
6. Fullness of God (v. 19)
7. Reconciler of all Things (v. 20)[53]

How one interprets the claims that are made in 1:15-20 will significantly affect one's Christology. Most of today's evangelical Christians and Messianic Believers concur that this hymn reflects a high view of a Divine Messiah who would be incarnated as a human. The hymn was specifically employed by Paul to refute whatever false teaching(s) had circulated in Colossae, something which undoubtedly subtracted from the supremacy of Yeshua and His work. It is not unlikely that the various terms, used by the false teachers to denigrate Yeshua, were subverted by Paul to highlight and exalt Yeshua, being overturned. The hymn contains unique words and a unique message that are targeted to *both* non-Jewish pagans and Jewish non-Believers—philosophies that could errantly influence the Colossians. This does require modern readers, who often approach the text with no historical framework for the statements made, to expel some effort to follow what is said a bit more carefully.

Wright indicates how 1:15-20 "is a typical statement of Jewish-style monotheism, and would be a telling rejoinder to any dualistic theology which saw creation as inherently bad." But where a statement would be expected to be made of the LORD, the God of Israel, it "is now said in reference to Jesus Christ. He has not displaced the God of Abraham, the God of the exodus. He has made him known. If the hymn stands with mainline Judaism, over against paganism, it also stands over against Judaism itself."[54] From this vantage point, then, what is seen in 1:15-20 would be similar to what Paul does to the *Shema* in 1 Corinthians 8:1-6. There, he takes the confession "The LORD is our God, the LORD is one!" (Deuteronomy 6:4), and fills it in with content that speaks about Yeshua: "for us there is *but* one God, the Father, from whom are all things and we *exist* for Him; and one Lord, Yeshua the Messiah, by whom are all things, and we *exist* through Him" (1 Corinthians 8:6).[55]

The Apostle Paul is found here working within First Century Jewish monotheism, but is redefining it in light of the identity of Yeshua. Most significant to consider for the message of the hymn is the role of the Jewish Wisdom tradition, because Paul has previously labeled Yeshua as "the wisdom of God" (1 Corinthians 1:24).[56] Some of the titles and descriptions given to Yeshua in 1:15-20 are also given to the figure of Wisdom, evidenced in the Tanach, Apocrypha, and Philo. They include

1. Image of God (Wisdom 7:26; Philo *Allegorical Interpretation* 1.43)
2. Firstborn (Philo *Questions and Answers on Genesis* 4.97)
3. Agent of Creation (Proverbs 8:22-36; 3:19; Philo *On Flight and Finding* 109)
4. Beginning (Proverbs 8:23; Wisdom 6:22)

The most significant comparison that we will have to consider is how Wisdom is referred to as both "image" and "beginning," claims that are made of Yeshua the Messiah as well (vs. 15, 18). As is seen in the works of Philo:

---

[53] Geisler, in *BKCNT*, 672.
[54] Wright, 66.
[55] For a further evaluation, consult the author's article "What Does the Shema Really Mean?"
[56] Grk. *Theou sophian* (θεοῦ σοφίαν).

"And God planted a paradise in Eden, in the east: and there he placed the man whom he had formed [Genesis 2:8]:" for he called that divine and heavenly wisdom by many names; and he made it manifest that it had many appellations; for he called it the beginning, and the image, and the sight of God (*Allegorical Interpretation* 1.43).[57]

Now the image of God is the Word, by which all the world was made (*Special Laws* 1.81).[58]

When we consider how Yeshua the Messiah is specifically called the "image" and "beginning," what is being asserted here by the hymn? Generally speaking in theological studies today, those who hold to a low Christology will conclude that the author of Colossians widely associates the Messiah as being God's Wisdom—a quasi-personal emanation of God's mind or His thoughts. From this angle, Yeshua would be the most important mediator between the Father and humanity, but not that much more than a mediator. Perhaps the Messiah might be semi-Divine, but is not to be considered fully Divine as a part of the Godhead, and in all probability is a created being in some way. As personified Wisdom says in Sirach 24:9, "From eternity, in the beginning, [God] created me." For a theologian like Dunn, Wisdom was a way "of speaking of God's own outreach to and interaction with his world and his people," a manner "of speaking of God's immanence while safeguarding his transcendence—in a word, 'personifications' of God's wisdom rather than 'intermediaries.'"[59]

It is difficult to avoid the fact that the hymn of 1:15-20 does parallel some of the descriptions seen of Wisdom. Proverbs 8:22-23 notably says, "The LORD possessed me at the beginning of His way, before His works of old. From everlasting I was established, from the beginning, from the earliest times of the earth." This depicts a force from God existing before the world of humanity. Yet to what degree is Yeshua the Messiah to be associated with Wisdom? How far one pushes the Wisdom motif is an ongoing debate between theological conservatives and liberals, with conservatives arguing that *echoes* of Wisdom are in view, and that Yeshua is One who is far superior. Wisdom possesses some of the same qualities as Yeshua, but when the descriptions of Wisdom are fully tallied together, **Yeshua is testified to do things that Wisdom has not done and cannot do.** Lincoln observes, "At this early stage of christological reflection…no problem would have been contemplated in holding that, like Wisdom as God immanent in creation, Christ was both sovereign and first within creation as the divine agent of creation."[60] It is not what Yeshua and Wisdom have in common that is important to notice in 1:15-20; it is what classifies Yeshua as *different* that is important to notice.

While Yeshua might be thought of as God's "Wisdom," He is much, much more.[61] The major and significant difference between Wisdom and Yeshua the Messiah, as we will see, is that Wisdom was just an intangible, created force of God that emerges in history. Wisdom *was not* a personal being that is supreme over the cosmos, has created the cosmos, has brought final redemption to humanity, and actually desires a personal relationship with men and women. Witherington remarks how "the element of personal preexistence in this hymn goes beyond the personification of Wisdom in the Jewish sapiental material. The first stanza is about a person, not merely the power God exhibited in creation, for that power was exercised in person by the Son…Whereas Wisdom is seen as bringing God's people together in Sirach, Christ is given this role in the christology of Colossians and Ephesians."[62] Considering whether or not Yeshua is *just God's "Wisdom"*—or whether He goes *beyond Wisdom*—will determine whether or not the hymn of 1:15-20 reflects a high Christological view of the Messiah or not.

1:15a The opening of the hymn says that Yeshua the Messiah "is the image of the invisible God." Yeshua as the image of God is a concept seen elsewhere in the Apostolic Scriptures, specifically as He reflects the

---

[57] *The Works of Philo: Complete and Unabridged*, 29.

[58] Ibid., 541.

[59] Dunn, pp 88-89.

[60] Lincoln, in *NIB*, 11:598.

[61] Cf. Ibid., 11:607-608.

[62] Witherington, 132.

He further indicates, "This and the other christological hymns in the NT demonstrate what a high christology existed in the church, even before and during the time of Paul" (Ibid., pp 132-133).

Father's glory (2 Corinthians 4:4; Hebrews 1:3). It is also difficult to avoid that some kind of connection is made between Yeshua as God's "image," and the creation of humans in God's image (Genesis 1:26-27). How far can we push some of this, and could a low Christology of Yeshua being an exalted human really be in view?

This would be a very difficult conclusion to draw, because a very specific description is used: *eikōn tou Theou tou aoratou* (εἰκὼν τοῦ θεοῦ τοῦ ἀοράτου), *not* "the image of God," but instead "the image of the **invisible** God." In the Septuagint rendering of Genesis 1:27, human beings were only made in the *eikona Theou* (εἰκόνα θεοῦ).[63] Similarly, Wisdom is only said to be "an image of his goodness" (Wisdom 7:26) or *eikōn tēs agathotētos autou* (εἰκὼν τῆς ἀγαθότητος αὐτοῦ), and "the image, and the sight of God" (Philo *Allegorical Interpretation* 1.43)[64] or *eikona kai horasin Theou* (εἰκόνα καὶ ὅρασιν θεοῦ). Yeshua the Messiah, in stark contrast, represents something that cannot be seen or is invisible. The adjective *aoratos* (ἀόρατος) means "*unseen, not to be seen, invisible*" (LS).[65] Paul details how such invisibility is a quality that only God Himself possesses:

"Now to the King eternal, immortal, invisible [*aoratos*], the only God, *be* honor and glory forever and ever. Amen" (1 Timothy 1:17).[66]

The "invisible attributes" are considered by Paul to be "His eternal power and divine nature" (Romans 1:20). If Yeshua is the "image of the invisible God"—not just "the image of God"—what specific things would such invisibility relate to? Having taken on human flesh, what would the Messiah be able to reflect of His Father to the world of mortals? Ezekiel 1:26 gives us some important clues: "Now above the expanse that was over their heads there was something resembling a throne, like lapis lazuli in appearance; and on that which resembled a throne, high up, *was* a figure with the appearance of a man." Bruce remarks, "To say that Christ is the image of God is to say that in him the nature and being of God have been perfectly revealed—that in him the invisible has become visible."[67] So in asserting that Yeshua is "the image of the invisible God," the hymn makes a claim about Yeshua *that goes beyond* human beings made in only God's image, and likewise Wisdom being a force made in God's image.

It can certainly be suggested that several of the Tanach's most significant theophanies involved pre-incarnate manifestations of Messiah Yeshua, as such an "image of the invisible God." The author of Hebrews speaks of how Moses "persevered because he saw him who is invisible" (Hebrews 11:27, NIV), a reference to the burning bush, which is notably preceded by a statement about his service for the Messiah (Hebrews 11:26).[68] Yeshua being the "image of the invisible God," should be taken as proof of His pre-existence. Yeshua being the "image of the invisible God" highlights His unique identity, not only with the Father, but also in redemptive history. One should be able to see that with Yeshua asserted to be the "image of the invisible God," contrary to any other, how the claims of the hymn will continue to build, clarifying any misunderstandings that the ancient Colossians would have had.

Yet why refer to Yeshua as God's image at all, even if it is an invisible image that only He possesses? Consider our Lord's words in John 14:9, "Have I been so long with you, and *yet* you have not come to know Me, Philip? He who has seen Me has seen the Father." Yeshua has just been called "His beloved Son" (v. 13). When we see Yeshua as "the image of the invisible God," while it is absolutely true that we see His great power and authority present—as God Incarnate in human flesh—we also see "the exact representation of His nature" (Hebrews 1:3), something that extends to God's great love and compassion. Yeshua as "the image of the invisible God" does represent all of the fullness of God, but He also represents a fullness that Believers

---

[63] Heb. *tzelem Elohim* (צֶלֶם אֱלֹהִים).

[64] *The Works of Philo: Complete and Unabridged*, 29.

[65] H.G. Liddell and R. Scott, *An Intermediate Greek-English Lexicon* (Oxford: Clarendon Press, 1994), 86.

[66] Given the preceding verses in 1 Timothy 1:14-16 which describe Yeshua the Messiah, we are right to conclude that the designation of both *aoratos* and "the only God" applies to the Son, and not just the Father.

[67] Bruce, *Colossians-Philemon-Ephesians*, pp 57-58.

[68] "[C]onsidering the reproach of Messiah greater riches than the treasures of Egypt; for he was looking to the reward" (Hebrews 11:26).

To this can be added 1 Corinthians 10:4, "and all drank the same spiritual drink, for they were drinking from a spiritual rock which followed them; and the rock was Messiah."

should be trying to reach as they mature in faith (Ephesians 3:19; 4:13). Human beings, while only being the image of God and *not* "the image of the invisible God," should reflect enough of their Creator's basic character. For humans, being God's *eikōn* (εἰκών) still regards **"that which represents someth. else in terms of basic form and features"** (*BDAG*).[69]

Yeshua's association as God's image is something far closer than we can comprehend, even closer than Wisdom. John 1:18 explains how "No one has seen God at any time; the only begotten God who is in the bosom of the Father, He has explained *Him*." Yeshua is to reflect in the world of mortals what the Father is. If Paul had been confronting any kind of errant philosophical or Gnostic-style errors present in Colossae, where anything physical was considered to be evil, then the Messiah portrayed as *eikōn* would easily refute this. Yeshua the Messiah is a physical representation of His Father, incarnated in the flesh (v. 22). The Messiah only being God can reduce the importance of His redeeming work for fallen humanity, and the Messiah only being human can likewise reduce the gravity of His redeeming work, and what it has taken to reconcile us to the Father (cf. Psalm 49:7, 15). In Yeshua being God's *eikōn*, we can see who the Father truly is, but we can also see what someone can be without the presence of human sin.

Those who hold to a low Christology, of Yeshua the Messiah *only* being God's "Wisdom," would not make close observations about Him actually being "the image of the invisible God." There is a noticeable trend in such liberal theology to be over conciliatory to the Jewish theological tradition, which views the Messiah as only being a human and/or some (supernatural) agent empowered by God. Sadly enough, this view can be very tempting to some of today's Messianic Believers as well, even at the expense of key Biblical doctrines. Against such a tide, though, Wright would remind us,

"[I]t is only in Jesus Christ that we understand what 'divinity' and 'humanity' really mean: without him, we lapse into sub-Christian, or even pagan, categories of thought, and then wonder why the doctrine of incarnation causes us so much difficulty. Paul's way of expressing the doctrine is to say, poetically, that the man Jesus fulfills the purposes which God had marked out *both* for himself and for humanity."[70]

Far be it from Yeshua the Messiah just being another version of the force Wisdom, the Apostle Paul is clear to specify how "you are in Messiah Yeshua, who became to us wisdom from God, and righteousness and sanctification, and redemption" (1 Corinthians 1:30). Bruce concludes, "Christ was the personal (not personified) and incarnate Wisdom of God."[71] O'Brien summarizes how in Diaspora Jewish theology, the figure of Wisdom was "a quasi-personal way" to speak of a power of God, whereas in contrast, "the one spoken of in our paragraph of Colossians is the living person, Jesus Christ, whom Paul had met face to face on the Damascus road."[72] Yeshua the Messiah certainly does represent God's Wisdom, but He is more than just an intangible force witnessed throughout history. Yeshua the Messiah goes beyond Wisdom, and provides redemption for the human race—something which the Hellenistic Jewish idea of Wisdom did not do—demonstrating a *personal interest* in people, just as Paul had first encountered the Lord.

1:15b In the same opening line of the hymn, Yeshua the Messiah is exclaimed as "the firstborn of all creation." Some Bible readers, not knowing where this description originates, may immediately draw an assumption that Yeshua being "firstborn" means that He is a created being. But this is not at all what is being communicated. The designation of Yeshua as *prōtotokos pasēs ktiseōs* (πρωτότοκος πάσης κτίσεως) does not relate to a status of possession—as though the Earth were to own Him as only being human—but instead relates to a status of preeminence. Norman Geisler points out how *prōtotokos* is notably different from *prōtoktisis* (πρωτόκτίσις), which would mean "first-created."[73] The designation *prōtotokos pasēs ktiseōs* is best understood to mean "firstborn before all creation" (*NICNT*)[74] or "firstborn over all creation" (NIV), as Bruce describes how

---

[69] Frederick William Danker, ed., et. al., *A Greek-English Lexicon of the New Testament and Other Early Christian Literature*, third edition (Chicago: University of Chicago Press, 2000), 282.

[70] Wright, pp 70-71.

[71] Bruce, *Colossians-Philemon-Ephesians*, 60.

[72] O'Brien, *Colossians-Philemon*, 40.

[73] Geisler, in *BKCNT*, 673.

[74] Bruce, *Colossians-Philemon-Ephesians*, 59.

renderings like these are "designed to clarify the force of the genitive phrase,"[75] further consistent with "before all things" (v. 17). In the estimation of Daniel B. Wallace, the clause *prōtotokos pasēs ktiseōs* is a genitive of subordination, which would regard Yeshua's status as "the firstborn **over** all **creation**."[76]

Anyone familiar with the Tanach should immediately note how the title "firstborn" (Heb. *bekor*, בְּכוֹר) is one of high, preeminent status. It is applied to people regardless of where or when they were "born," sometimes even if they were actually not the first born in their family line. Firstborn describes Reuben the son of Jacob (Genesis 49:3-4), the people of Israel as God's "son" (Exodus 4:22), King David (Psalm 89:27), and the Northern Kingdom of Israel/Ephraim (Jeremiah 31:9). The title "firstborn," possessing royal distinction, is appropriate for the King of Kings and His ultimate authority (Revelation 1:17-18). As it was said of King David, "I will make him the first-born, the highest of the kings of the earth[77]" (Psalm 89:27, RSV). Similarly, Yeshua being firstborn of creation—and Him actually being the Creator of it all (vs. 16b)—by necessity draws *prōtotokos pasēs ktiseōs* to be "firstborn over all creation" (NIV), the One who is the preeminent over everything, Yeshua being the "heir of all things" (Hebrews 1:2).

The NEB paraphrases *prōtotokos pasēs ktiseōs* as "his is the primacy over all created things." Its translators are not at all trying to imply that Yeshua the Messiah is a created being, but are trying to convey, in more contemporary language, the dynamics of His Kingship. This rendering, however, can very much confuse people, who will often not take the time to read the text of the hymn a little closer, and consider the claims that it makes. The assertion that Yeshua is a created being, and not God Incarnate, can only be made if "firstborn" is divorced from its wider Biblical context (cf. Romans 8:29; Hebrews 1:6; Revelation 1:5). When we see Yeshua as the Agent of Creation, firstborn meaning "supreme" is best understood, as "When all things began, the Word already was" (John 1:1, NEB). Furthermore, we see that Yeshua being firstborn merits Him being worshipped, something that would be idolatrous if He were not God (Hebrews 1:6; cf. Psalm 97:7).

Even though ancient Jewish literature from the First Century period did portray various pre-existent figures or forces used by God, they did not possess *all of the qualities* that the Apostolic Scriptures portray Yeshua the Messiah as exercising. Bruce indicates how, "to none of them are such cosmic activity and significance ascribed as are here ascribed to the preexistent Christ."[78] While connections can be seen between Yeshua the Messiah and the figure of Wisdom, there should be no question that in comparison, Yeshua is the One who is unique. In his refutation of the Arians, who believed that Yeshua was just a created being, vs. 15-16 were pointed out by the Fourth Century theologian Athanasius as being of considerable importance:

"[T]he word 'First-born' has again the creation as a reason in connection with it, which Paul proceeds to say, 'for in Him all things were created.' But if all the creatures were created in Him, He is other than the creatures, and is not a creature, but the Creator of the creatures" (*Orations Against the Arians* II.62).[79]

Robert M. Bowman, Jr. and J. Ed Komoszewski properly add how, "The logic of Paul's reasoning from verse 15 to verse 16 (the son is the firstborn of all creation *because* everything was created in, through, and for him) really requires...that in this context the Son be distinguished from 'all creation.' In any case, then, Colossians 1:15 does not teach that the Son was the first creature whom God made."[80] The title "firstborn" is one of great status and rulership, and if a reader can understand that **firstborn=anointed king** in Colossians 1:15, it becomes obvious that Yeshua is not a created being, and it is perfectly legitimate to treat *prōtotokos pasēs ktiseōs* as a genitive of subordination: **"the firstborn over all creation"** (NIV/HCSB/TNIV).

1:16 After designating Yeshua as both "image" and "firstborn," the hymn makes the claim "for in him all things were created, in heaven and on earth, visible and invisible, whether thrones or dominions or

---

[75] Ibid.

[76] Daniel B. Wallace *Greek Grammar Beyond the Basics* (Grand Rapids: Zondervan, 1996), 104.

Other examples of a genitive of subordination provided by Wallace (Ibid., pp 103-104), include: Matthew 9:34; Mark 15:32; 2 Corinthians 4:4; 1 Timothy 1:17; Ephesians 2:2.

[77] Heb. *af-ani bekor et'neihu el'yon l'malkei-eretz* (אַף־אָנִי בְּכוֹר אֶתְּנֵהוּ עֶלְיוֹן לְמַלְכֵי־אָרֶץ).

[78] Bruce, *Colossians-Philemon-Ephesians*, 61.

[79] Cf. Lincoln, in *NIB*, 11:598.

[80] Robert M. Bowman, Jr. and J. Ed Komoszewski, *Putting Jesus in His Place: The Case for the Deity of Christ* (Grand Rapids: Kregel, 2007), 77.

principalities or authorities—all things were created through him and for him" (RSV). These are very broad sweeping categories, encompassing the whole of Creation, that to some degree are affected *en autō* (ἐν αὐτῷ) or "in Him." The role that Wisdom played in God creating the universe needs to be considered here, as Proverbs 3:19 says "The LORD by wisdom [*b'chokmah*, בְּחָכְמָה] founded the earth, by understanding He established the heavens." Proverbs 8:22-36 depicts Wisdom as a pre-existent force of God, able to carry out His bidding:

> "The LORD possessed me at the beginning of His way, before His works of old. From everlasting I was established, from the beginning, from the earliest times of the earth. When there were no depths I was brought forth, when there were no springs abounding with water. Before the mountains were settled, before the hills I was brought forth; while He had not yet made the earth and the fields, nor the first dust of the world. When He established the heavens, I was there, when He inscribed a circle on the face of the deep, when He made firm the skies above, when the springs of the deep became fixed, when He set for the sea its boundary so that the water would not transgress His command, when He marked out the foundations of the earth; then I was beside Him, *as* a master workman; and I was daily *His* delight, rejoicing always before Him, rejoicing in the world, His earth, and *having* my delight in the sons of men. Now therefore, O sons, listen to me, for blessed are they who keep my ways. Heed instruction and be wise, and do not neglect *it*. Blessed is the man who listens to me, watching daily at my gates, waiting at my doorposts. For he who finds me finds life and obtains favor from the LORD. But he who sins against me injures himself; all those who hate me love death."

Philo actually depicted God as the father of humanity, and Wisdom as the mother, further claiming that it was Wisdom "by means of whom [*di' hēs*, δι' ἧς] the universe arrived at creation" (*On Flight and Finding* 109).[81]

It is difficult to argue against echoes of Wisdom being present in Colossians 1:15-16, and those who hold to a low Christology often simply assume that Yeshua the Messiah was a created being or force of God, not at all dissimilar from Wisdom. Yet again, while there are similarities to be seen between Yeshua the Messiah and Wisdom, are there any significant dissimilarities? Lincoln is keen to note, "Col 1:16 goes further in its christological reflection so that here Christ can be said to be the goal of creation also. This addition of 'to him' or 'for him' also goes beyond what is said of Wisdom...[as] it adds to the conceptuality of the wisdom tradition."[82]

The activity of God the Father, working through the Son, is evidenced *hoti en autō* (ὅτι ἐν αὐτῷ), "for in Him..." Yeshua is to be considered "the firstborn of all creation" (v. 15) because of the specific reason "because in him were...all things created" (YLT). The reason Yeshua is to be considered the firstborn is because He made the universe! Dunn, who perhaps relies more heavily on the Wisdom tradition than he ought, is still forced to conclude, "That 'firstborn' must denote primacy over creation, and not just within creation, is indicated by the conjunction linking the two verses,"[83] making note of the construction between vs. 15-16: *prōtotokos pasēs ktiseōs, hoti en autō ektisthē* (πρωτότοκος πάσης κτίσεως, ὅτι ἐν αὐτῷ ἐκτίσθη).

The hymn claims that "all things have been created through Him," *di' autou* (δι' αὐτοῦ), similar to God's use of Wisdom in Philo. But Wisdom in Philo is only a force that assists God in creating the universe. Contrary to this, Yeshua's creation extends *ta panta en tois ouranois kai epi tēs gēs, ta horata kai ta aorata* (τὰ πάντα ἐν τοῖς οὐρανοῖς καὶ ἐπὶ τῆς γῆς, τὰ ὁρατὰ καὶ τὰ ἀόρατα), meaning that it is multi-dimensional. This includes "all things created, those in the heavens, and those upon the earth, those visible, and those invisible" (YLT). We may need to each be reminded of how God, and not only the Father but also the Son, being involved in the creation of the universe, is something clearly implied by Proverbs 30:4: "Who has ascended into heaven and descended? Who has gathered the wind in His fists? Who has wrapped the waters in His garment? Who has established all the ends of the earth? What is His name or His son's name? Surely you know!"

---

[81] *The Works of Philo: Complete and Unabridged*, 331.
[82] Lincoln, in *NIB*, 11:598.
[83] Dunn, 90.

Even more specifically than this, Yeshua is stated to be Creator of thrones, dominions, rulers, and authorities. Yeshua is supreme, especially over angels, a concept which will be important for Paul to stress as many of the Colossians had succumbed to angel worship (2:18). A reference to these various authorities can certainly be found in the literature of the Pseudepigrapha. *Testament of Levi* 3:8 refers to how in Heaven, "There with [God] are thrones and authorities."[84] Similarly in *1 Enoch* 61:10 are depicted "all the forces of the heavens...the cherubim, seraphim, ophanim, all the angels of governance...and the other forces on earth (and) over the water."[85] Just as Yeshua exercises creative power over these authorities, some of them could probably also be associated with the elemental forces of 2:8.

The Apostle Paul certainly believed that these kinds of angelic forces existed, but perhaps in contrast to some of the Colossians who believed that Yeshua was just another one of them—not unlike Wisdom—the hymn makes the claim that they are all subordinate to the Messiah. In his paralleling letter, Paul teaches that Yeshua is "far above all rule and authority and power and dominion, and every name that is named, not only in this age but also in the one to come" (Ephesians 1:21; cf. Revelation 4:4). This would be a significant contrast between Yeshua the Messiah and the Jewish Wisdom tradition. While Wisdom may be an important feature of comparison in the 1:15-20 hymn, what is seen in the Epistle to the Colossians, in Moo's words, "does not depend [exclusively] on that tradition," and here "Christ's relations to creation that *all things have been created...for him*, goes beyond any Jewish tradition about wisdom."[86]

Wisdom is only an impersonal force designated by God to do important tasks, and was used by Him in creating the universe. In stark contrast to Wisdom, not only in Yeshua were all things created, but also *di' autou kai eis auton* (δι' αὐτοῦ καὶ εἰς αὐτὸν), "through Him and for Him." Wisdom was used to create the universe on God's behalf; **Yeshua created the universe in Himself and for Himself** as a member of the Godhead, and is supreme over all authority. Yeshua the Messiah is the Creator, He exercises authority over the created forces of good and evil that He has made, and He is the One who will determine the final fate of those forces to which various Colossians had been making an appeal. There is no anticipation that Wisdom will be responsible for the final judgment of all beings, as such judgment is given to Yeshua alone (cf. Revelation 20:11). Paul's usage of the hymn would admonish the Colossians to turn to Yeshua for their deliverance, being the physical representation of everything the Father in Heaven is, demonstrated by His ministry on Earth.

1:17 Yeshua's ultimate supremacy is seen in the hymn's declaration "He is before all things, and in Him all things hold together." This is where those holding to a low Christology believe that their case is sealed, because as Sirach 1:4 says of Wisdom, "Wisdom was created before all things." Yeshua is before all things, and with the associations seen in vs. 15-16 previously, it is thought Yeshua must be a created being no different than Wisdom. Wisdom 7:24 would add, "For wisdom is more mobile than any motion; because of her pureness she pervades and penetrates all things." Could this not be a power granted to God's Messiah?

If the Colossians had been influenced by any errors that denigrated who Yeshua the Messiah was to be for them, and Paul had never encountered them in person before, we can expect the Apostle to subvert the terms and descriptions used by the false teachers to lead them astray—overturning them. So, if the false teachers were claiming that Yeshua had just been a created intermediary force of God, a force like Wisdom that scurries around the universe, Paul is going to use descriptions of Wisdom and describe how Yeshua possesses those same qualities, **but is also substantially different.** In this case, the hymn says *autos estin pro pantōn* (αὐτός ἐστιν πρὸ πάντων), "He is before all things" or "existed before all things" (Good News Bible), with the verb *estin* appearing in the present active indicative tense. Contrary to this, in Sirach 1:4, Wisdom *protera pantōn ektistai* (προτέρα πάντων ἔκτισται), or it "was created before all things," with the verb *ektistai* appearing in the perfect passive indicative tense. Yeshua just *is*, but Wisdom *was made* by an external force. Moo indicates, "while these texts assert that wisdom was the first thing created, the claim in our verse is bolder: Christ existed

---

[84] H.C. Kee, trans., "Testaments of the Twelve Patriarchs," in James H. Charlesworth, ed., *The Old Testament Pseudepigrapha*, Vol 1 (New York: Doubleday, 1983), 789.

[85] E. Isaac, "1 (Ethiopic Apocalypse of) Enoch," in Ibid., 42.

[86] Moo, 124.

before creation itself."[87] This is far more than just some statement of high status: "He was there before any of it came into existence" (The Message); **"is before all things"** is a statement which affirms Yeshua's pre-existence.

When the hymn claims that Yeshua the Messiah existed before all things, this "before all" (*pro pantōn*, πρὸ πάντων) relates to time. Yeshua said in John 8:58, "Truly, truly, I say to you, before Abraham was born, I am," and shortly after saying this, "they picked up stones to throw at Him" (John 8:59).[88] But not only does the hymn claim that Yeshua is "before all things," it also says that "in Him all things hold together," *ta panta en autō sunestēken* (τὰ πάντα ἐν αὐτῷ συνέστηκεν). A definite connection with Hebrews 1:3 can be seen, where Yeshua "upholds all things by the word of His power." O'Brien describes how "Not only was the universe created in the Son as the sphere, by him as the divine agent, and for him as the goal; it was also established permanently 'in him' alone." Notable to be considered is how this must be a continuous action, as seen by the perfect tense participle *sunistēmi* (συνίστημι). Without such action, as O'Brien indicates, "all would disintegrate."[89] Such were never the claims made of Wisdom. Wisdom works within the universe, whereas Yeshua *actually runs* and upholds the universe! As Moo is right to conclude,

"What holds the universe together is not an idea or a virtue, but a person: the resurrected Christ. Without him electrons with not continue to circle nuclei, gravity would cease to work, the planets would not stay in their orbits."[90]

Yeshua the Messiah is indeed, the supreme Creator! He is not just some agent within Creation.

18 He is also head of the body, the [assembly]; and He is the beginning, the firstborn from the dead, so that He Himself will come to have first place in everything.

1:18a In the previous verses of the hymn, Yeshua's role in creating and sustaining the universe has been described (vs. 16-17), and as such He is to be the most important One in the minds of those within the community of faith. Now the theme of the hymn shifts, as such significance will undoubtedly impact those who make up the congregation of the faithful: "He is the head of the body, the church; he is the beginning, the first-born from the dead, that in everything he might be pre-eminent" (RSV).

The first title Yeshua is given is as "head of the body," here a reference to the Body of Messiah, the *ekklēsia*. But while Yeshua has authority over both Earthly and cosmic powers (v. 16), is Yeshua as *hē kephalē tou sōmatos* (ἡ κεφαλὴ τοῦ σώματος) an exclusive claim of authority, or is it one of Yeshua being the origin of His Body? Speaking of the sphere of those affected by Yeshua, it might be best for us to consider how Paul writes in Romans 12:4-5, "For just as we have many members in one body and all the members do not have the same function, so we, who are many, are one body in Messiah, and individually members one of another." Yeshua as Head, would thus be the "brain" that directs the various parts in His Body (2:19). The Colossians were to be integrated into the supreme Yeshua, and not the cosmic powers (2:15, 18).

This is an issue more affected by what is seen in the paralleling letter of Ephesians, as Yeshua is exalted as "head over all things" (Ephesians 1:22), but then later as head is depicted as the One "from whom the whole body...[is] being fitted and held together" (Ephesians 4:15), as He is its origin. Likewise, per the debate over what Paul means by "the husband is the head of the wife" (Ephesians 5:23), this is best understood in light of the controlling statement "be subject to one another in the fear of Messiah" (Ephesians 5:21), and most significantly "husbands ought also to love their own wives as their own bodies" (Ephesians 5:28). These are

---

[87] Ibid., 125.

[88] About as close as the Messiah ever got to verbalizing the Divine Name of the Father, YHWH, appears at Yeshua's trial when He claimed to be the "I AM," and was considered blaspheming by the high priest (Mark 14:61-64; Luke 22:70-71). *Egō eimi* (ἐγώ εἰμι), appearing in the Gospels for many of His "I AM" statements, was used in the Septuagint to translate the Hebrew *ehyeh asher ehyeh* (אֶהְיֶה אֲשֶׁר אֶהְיֶה) where God reveals Himself to Moses as "I AM WHO I AM" (Exodus 3:13-14).

Consult G.M. Burge, "'I am' sayings," in Joel B. Green, Scot McKnight, and I. Howard Marshall, eds., *Dictionary of Jesus and the Gospels* (Downers Grove, IL: InterVarsity, 1992), pp 354-356.

[89] O'Brien, *Colossians-Philemon*, 47.

[90] Moo, pp 125-126.

statements that were radical for the First Century—in either a Hellenistic or a Jewish context—as they afforded considerable value to the woman, as the husband was to understand himself as *her origin*.

The hymn of Colossians 1:15-20, and the head-body issue, concerns more how the *ekklēsia* functions by the power of its Lord, and "head" in v. 18 is joined together with the titular rank of "firstborn." So in the words of Witherington, "Ideas of both authority and origin come together in this use of the word [*kephalē*] because the origin of something was thought to be determinative for what came forth or followed from it."[91] With this in mind—Yeshua as the Head of the assembly—Believers are to look to Him to be their preeminent example of how to live, with His thoughts flowing down to the diverse parts of His Body.

When one understands Yeshua as the Head of His Body, while some important claims are made about the Lord's power and authority, we need not overlook the special relationship that He has to His followers. Moo remarks, "as the metaphor of body and head implies, Christ is in organic relationship to his people in a way that is not true of the creation in general."[92] Maxie D. Dunnam further explains how, "This means *in Christ* is the basic clue for answering all the world's big questions—war, racism, starvation, illiteracy, ecology, pollution—for Christ is the 'heartbeat' of the entire created universe."[93] Yeshua as Head, even in terms of authority, does direct His Divine thoughts that are to control the actions of His followers. A comparison between God as Creator, and the human being who desires to follow Him, as seen in Psalm 19, may be considered:

"The law of the LORD is perfect, restoring the soul; the testimony of the LORD is sure, making wise the simple. The precepts of the LORD are right, rejoicing the heart; the commandment of the LORD is pure, enlightening the eyes. The fear of the LORD is clean, enduring forever; the judgments of the LORD are true; they are righteous altogether. They are more desirable than gold, yes, than much fine gold; sweeter also than honey and the drippings of the honeycomb. Moreover, by them Your servant is warned; in keeping them there is great reward. Who can discern *his* errors? Acquit me of hidden *faults*. Also keep back Your servant from presumptuous *sins*; let them not rule over me; then I will be blameless, and I shall be acquitted of great transgression. Let the words of my mouth and the meditation of my heart be acceptable in Your sight, O LORD, my rock and my Redeemer" (Psalm 19:7-14).

1:18b Similar to what has been previously described (v. 15), Yeshua the Messiah is once again labeled "firstborn," but here "the firstborn from the dead," *prōtotokos ek tōn nekrōn* (πρωτότοκος ἐκ τῶν νεκρῶν). Yeshua being considered "firstborn" means that He possesses a very high and preeminent status, as previously described (vs. 17-18a). This is seen in Revelation 1:5, where Yeshua is "the firstborn of the dead, and the ruler of the kings of the earth." In 1 Corinthians 15:20, Yeshua is called "the first fruits of those who are asleep," not only an emphasis on His completed work for us, but that His resurrection assures us that there will be a resurrection in the future for all (cf. Daniel 12:2-3).[94] Following His resurrection, Yeshua was exalted to the Father's right hand (Philippians 2:9), and it is from there that we await His return "with all His saints" (1 Thessalonians 3:13) who have died in faith.

---

[91] Witherington, 135.

[92] Moo, 128.

[93] Maxie D. Dunnam, *The Preacher's Commentary: Galatians, Ephesians, Philippians, Colossians, Philemon*, Vol 31 (Nashville: Thomas Nelson, 1982), 346.

[94] Yeshua being "firstborn from the dead" is a title of His status as the preeminent among those who will be resurrected. It is **by no means** an attestation that being "born again" occurs at the resurrection. Being born again or spiritually regenerated is something that is to take place now, in the current age, among His people who receive salvation (1 Peter 1:3, 23). It was first an ancient Jewish designation for proselytes, who would turn their back on their previous way of life in paganism (b.*Yevamot* 48b).

19 **For it was the *Father's* good pleasure for all the fullness to dwell in Him, 20 and through Him to reconcile all things to Himself, having made peace through the blood of His cross; through Him, *I say*, whether things on earth or things in heaven.**

1:19 The hymn that Paul has been quoting from makes a very significant claim about Yeshua the Messiah: "For God was pleased to have all his fullness dwell in him" (NIV) The clause *en autō eudokēsen pan to plērōma* (ἐν αὐτῷ εὐδόκησεν πᾶν τὸ πλήρωμα) is actually rendered by YLT as "in him it did please all the fulness to tabernacle." *Plērōma* here communicates the totality of God with all His powers (cf. 2:9), or what the NEB calls "the complete being of God." The Septuagint employs cognates of *plērōma* to depict the Father in all His power and glory:

> "And one cried to the other, and they said, Holy, holy, holy *is the* Lord of hosts: the whole earth is full [adjective *plērēs*, πλήρης] of his glory" (Isaiah 6:3, LXE).

> "Shall any one hide himself in secret places, and I not see him? Do I not fill [verb *plēroō*, πληρόω] heaven and earth? saith the Lord" (Jeremiah 23:24, LXE).

> "And he brought me in by the way of the gate that looks northward, in front of the house: and I looked, and, behold, the house was full [adjective *plērēs*] of the glory of the Lord: and I fell upon my face" (Ezekiel 44:4, LXE).

> "And blessed is his glorious name for ever, even for ever and ever: and all the earth shall be filled [verb *plēroō*] with his glory. So be it, so be it" (Psalm 72:19, LXE).

O'Brien, considering these descriptions of God from the Tanach, describes how this "draws attention to the immanence of God and his personal involvement in the world," something "not to be understood along either pantheistic or dualistic lines."[95] Neither is Yeshua the Messiah some force, or even just an agent sent by God. Yeshua is not a place like the Temple that was filled with God's presence. Even though Temple language may be used to describe the Messiah from time to time, as a person the Messiah is *not* the Temple. Yeshua is, rather, God the Son, possessing all of His Father's attributes, incarnated in the world of mortals. Dunn concurs how "the wholeness of God's interaction with the universe is summed up in Christ. Here the thought reaches well beyond that of Wisdom or even God 'dwelling in' a good and compassionate person."[96] Yeshua the Messiah is to be the only One where all people look people look for "fullness."

The hymn depicts how the Father actually expresses delight in the Incarnation of His Son (John 1:14; cf. Luke 3:22). This is similar to how the Lord was pleased to dwell on Mount Zion (Psalm 67:17), or demonstrate His good pleasure (Psalm 44:3; 147:11; 149:4). Yet, in contrast to God's presence being manifest in *a place* on Earth, Yeshua the Messiah is an actual *person* who will bring redemption not only to humanity, but all Creation. Via the Incarnation, Yeshua is later specified by Paul to the One in whom "all the fullness of Deity dwells in bodily form" (2:9). Wright makes the point, "The full divinity of the man Jesus is stated without any implication that there are two Gods. It is the one God, in all his fullness, who dwells in him."[97] Yeshua was not just one of many mediatorial beings between humanity and God; He is God dwelling as a human among sinful humans to redeem humans from their transgressions. *This goes beyond God's presence manifest in His Temple or upon Mount Zion.* Bowman and Komoszewski excellently summarize,

"What Paul says about Christ...is that all the fullness of what constitutes God dwells bodily in Christ. The presence and nature of God is totally or *wholly* ('all' or 'whole') found in Christ; it is *fully* ('fullness') found

---

[95] O'Brien, *Colossians-Philemon*, 52.
[96] Dunn, 101.
[97] Wright, pp 75-76.

in Christ; it is found in him *personally* ('in him'); and it is found in him *bodily*. It is difficult to imagine a more forceful, emphatic affirmation that Jesus Christ literally embodies God's very being."[98]

The very reason that Paul would use *plērōma* language in praising God for His Son, other than for various connections seen in the LXX, may be to immediately discount what the false teachers in Colossae were promoting. The fullness of everything that the Father is can only be found in Yeshua the Messiah, and not in whatever mediatorial beings or angels the Colossians were considering. Moo summarizes how "since the Gnostics used 'fullness' language quite a lot, it has been suggested that this phrase betrays the fact that the 'original' hymn was in praise of a gnostic redeemer figure. A more plausible variation of this thesis suggests that the hymn may have picked up the language from the Colossian false teachers and turned it against them."[99] The hymn, then, simply provided Paul with the ammunition that he needed to discredit them, and we should easily disregard the proposal that the hymn itself was Gnostic in origin. Hurtado further states, "the proposal that 1:15-20 may represent a Christianization of a hymn to a heavenly redeemer from pre-Christian 'gnostic' circles has suffered a considerable decline in recent decades."[100]

What the Colossians are looking for can only be found in Yeshua—as the "fullness" or *plērōma* of God involves something that no other mediatorial agent can be said to have done.

1:20 The uniqueness of Yeshua the Messiah is that "through him God was pleased to reconcile to himself all things, whether on earth or in heaven, by making peace through the blood of his cross" (NRSV). **Yeshua is the One who provides final redemption**—and not only to individual people, but ultimately to all Creation. This does not at all speak of a universal salvation for all people with sinners not consigned to eternal punishment (Matthew 25:46), but rather establishes the principle that all people can be redeemed to communion with the Father via Yeshua's atoning sacrifice. Within the rubric of how God will be "all in all" (1 Corinthians 15:28), is how even though unredeemed, things "under the earth" (Philippians 2:10) will bow their knees and recognize Yeshua as LORD (Isaiah 45:23). Via the work of Yeshua, one day, things will be set right in the universe (Romans 8:19-22).

Coming to the end of the Colossians 1:15-20 hymn, the fascinating description it offers of Yeshua the Messiah, and the likely subversion of ideas that had errantly influenced the Colossians, Hurtado summarizes for us how "drawing upon a traditional vocabulary of devotion to Jesus, the author of Colossians 1:15-20 produced a fresh and memorable declaration of Christ's glorious status. Those who first heard this celebration of Jesus probably recognized basically familiar convictions expressed freshly and eloquently."[101] While some of the descriptions we see of Yeshua in Colossians 1:15-20 might not be those that people today would immediately use regarding Him, they held some key importance in relation to halting the influence of the false teaching in Colossae. Yeshua is far more than just some agent or force of God; He is the One in whom and for whom all of Creation must give an account. In the larger discussions surrounding the nature of Yeshua and Christology, it should be obvious that Colossians 1:15-20 is not the only passage that informs us about who the Messiah is, and as such Colossians 1:15-20 should not be read isolated.

21 And although you were formerly alienated and hostile in mind, *engaged* in evil deeds, 22 yet He has now reconciled you in His fleshly body through death, in order to present you before Him holy and blameless and beyond reproach— 23 if indeed you continue in the faith firmly established and steadfast, and not moved away from the hope of the gospel that you have heard, which was proclaimed in all creation under heaven, and of which I, Paul, was made a minister.

1:21 Having just expressed a prayer on the Colossians' behalf (vs. 3-14), and a hymn that exalts Yeshua the Messiah and subverts any false teachings about Him they have encountered (vs. 15-20), Paul now begins to teach his audience. Paul reminds them of who they are to be in the Lord, and the role that He has had him

---

[98] Bowman and Komoszewski 77.
[99] Moo, 132.
[100] Hurtado, 505.
[101] Ibid., 508.

play in being a designated servant for the gospel. He first speaks of their prior spiritual condition: "Once you were alienated from God and were enemies in your minds because of your evil behavior" (NIV). This is a condition of sinners who are darkened to God's truth and majesty (Romans 1:18-21). As Paul further specifies in his paralleling letter:

"Therefore remember that formerly you, the Gentiles in the flesh...*remember* that you were at that time separate from Messiah, excluded from the commonwealth of Israel, and strangers to the covenants of promise, having no hope and without God in the world" (Ephesians 2:11-12).

"So this I say, and affirm together with the Lord, that you walk no longer just as the Gentiles also walk, in the futility of their mind, being darkened in their understanding, excluded from the life of God because of the ignorance that is in them, because of the hardness of their heart" (Ephesians 4:17-18).

1:22 In spite of such a negative spiritual condition once having dominated the lives of the Colossians, they have now been restored to proper standing with the Creator God. He tells them, "he has now reconciled [you] in his body of flesh by his death, in order to present you holy and blameless and irreproachable before him" (RSV). The Apostle Paul denies any kind of docetism, where Yeshua was not at all a human man. He also denies any kind of Platonism where physical matter was inherently evil. The means by which reconciliation with the Father has been accomplished is by the physical body of Messiah Yeshua, specifically *tō sōmati tēs sarkos* (τῷ σώματι τῆς σαρκὸς) or "the body of flesh." This is a likely Hebraism, reflected in the DSS, which employs *b'geviyat b'saro* (בגוית בשרו), where the Teacher of Righteousness is inflicted "acts of retaliation against his mortal body" (1QpHab 9.3).[102]

This is important to recognize as "body" (Grk. *sōma*, σῶμα) will be an important theme employed throughout ch. 2 (2:11, 17, 19, 23). Paul has previously discussed redemption being accomplished through Yeshua's physical body, asserting in Romans 7:4 how "you also were made to die to the Law through the body of Messiah," *dia tou sōmatos tou Christou* (διὰ τοῦ σώματος τοῦ Χριστοῦ), a reference to the penalties of the Torah being permanently atoned for.[103] He further elaborates, "For what the Law could not do, weak as it was through the flesh, God *did*: sending His own Son in the likeness of sinful flesh and *as an offering* for sin, He condemned sin in the flesh" (Romans 8:3). It was by the actual shedding of the Lord Yeshua's blood that redemption could only come (Hebrews 9:22), and while we may think it strange that today there were people who actually denied that He was a physical person, according to 1 John 4:2, "By this you know the Spirit of God: every spirit that confesses that Yeshua the Messiah has come in the flesh [*en sarki elēluthota*, ἐν σαρκὶ ἐληλυθότα] is from God." Yeshua must truly be a human in flesh in order to redeem humans (1 Timothy 2:5; Hebrews 2:17).

The severity of what it took to reconcile sinful people to the Father is that His Son had to be crucified and had to die for them. The result of this is that the redeemed can be presented before God as blameless and holy. Without doubt, Paul uses themes from the Torah's sacrificial system, and the high quality of various offerings. Animals that were to be sacrificed before God had to be without defect (Exodus 29:37-38; Numbers 6:14; 19:2). And as Paul had instructed the Romans, he wanted them to serve others as a living sacrifice (Romans 12:1-2).

1:23 In order to be presented before the Father holy and blameless, though, Paul gives the Colossians a condition that must be met: "provided that you continue securely established and steadfast in the faith" (NRSV). Paul admonishes the Colossians *epimenete tē pistei* (ἐπιμένετε τῇ πίστει), "continue the faith" (my translation). While staying sure within the sphere of faith is intended, does it mean that the Colossians were to remain in a certain place or locality, or that they were to continue walking on the good and steady path (v. 10)? Keep in mind that the Colossians were likely influenced by the false teachers *precisely because* they proposed to

---

[102] Wise, Abegg, and Cook, 120.

Cf. Bruce, *Colossians-Philemon-Ephesians*, 78 fn #182; Moo, 142, fn #243.

[103] C.E.B. Cranfield concurs, "Their being made dead to the law's condemnation through the body of Christ is a matter of God's merciful decision: they died in His death in that the death which He died was for them" (*International Critical Commentary: Romans 1-8* [London: T&T Clark, 1975], 336).

Also consult the author's article "The Message of Romans."

offer them some answers to their life questions. Paul sees this to be a problem, because the solution to the Colossians' life questions will be found by "not shifting from the hope of the gospel which you heard, which has been preached to every creature under heaven, and of which I, Paul, became a minister" (RSV). As the Colossians mature in this hope provided by the good news, then they will learn to be holy and blameless before God.

Paul's words here do ask us a question about what he means by the gospel being proclaimed "in all creation." Is this another hyperbole, like in v. 6, used to indicate how broad the gospel message had gone out—or how far it was intended to go out? If so, this would be no different than how "every nation under heaven" (Acts 2:9) was present at *Shavuot*/Pentecost when the Holy Spirit was poured out. The intention was that the outpouring that took place would affect every nation. Most significant to all this, not to be overlooked, is how Paul's statement should eliminate any thought that the good news was an exclusive message to any particular people or nationality.[104] While the Apostle Paul considers God's people to be the Commonwealth of Israel (Ephesians 2:11-12), it is nevertheless a people composed of more than just his own Jewish brethren in which *all* can be a part (Ephesians 3:6).

24 Now I rejoice in my sufferings for your sake, and in my flesh I do my share on behalf of His body, which is the [assembly], in filling up what is lacking in Messiah's afflictions.

1:24 The fact that Paul endured sufferings in his ministry service to the Lord is undeniable from the testimony he gives in his letters (2 Corinthians 11:23-27). In Philippians 3:10, he actually expresses the view, "that I may know Him and the power of His resurrection and the fellowship of His sufferings, being conformed to His death." Yet to the Colossians he writes, "I am now rejoicing in my sufferings for your sake, and in my flesh I am completing what is lacking in Christ's afflictions for the sake of his body, that is, the [assembly]" (RSV). Many people, when reading this, are a bit confused. Would it not be true that Yeshua's afflictions—His crucifixion and death—are already completed events? How could this at all be lacking? Bruce indicates, "This remarkable statement can be best understood if we bear in mind the oscillation in Hebrew thought between individual and corporate personality."[105] It is not Yeshua the individual that is in view here, but rather Yeshua the Head of the Body (v. 18).Paul's sufferings for the Colossians are considered to be a part of the Messiah's sufferings for His Body. Consider that on the road to Damascus, the Lord asked him, "why are you persecuting Me?" (Acts 9:4). Similarly in His judgment of the nations, Yeshua taught, "Truly I say to you, to the extent that you did not do it to one of the least of these, you did not do it to Me" (Matthew 25:45). Negative actions committed against the Lord's people are as though they are committed against Him, as "In all their affliction He was afflicted" (Isaiah 63:9). The Messiah, even though having personally resurrected from the dead and having been exalted in Heaven, is *still suffering*. This is because His people, like Paul, suffer for His sake—things that affect the *ekklēsia* as a whole. Vaughan explains how "'What is still lacking' is not an intimation of deficiency in Christ's own sufferings but a reference to what is yet lacking in Christ's suffering *in Paul*."[106] Moo further comments,

"Because Paul's apostolic ministry is an 'extension' of Christ's work in the world, Paul identifies his own sufferings very closely with Christ's. These sufferings have no redemptive benefit for the church, but they are the inevitable accompaniment of Paul's 'commission' to proclaim the end-time revelation of God's mystery."[107]

Some commentators, though, see an eschatological connection to this suffering, where great trial would immediately precede the arrival of the Messiah.[108] They base this view partly on sentiments seen in the Pseudepigrapha (*1 Enoch* 47:1-4; *2 Baruch* 30:2), as well as in some later Rabbinic teaching which speaks of

---

[104] Moo, 160.

[105] Bruce, *Colossians-Philemon-Ephesians*, 82.

[106] Vaughan, in *EXP*, 11:190.

[107] Moo, pp 152-153.

[108] O'Brien, *Colossians-Philemon*, pp 78-79; Wright, pp 87-88; Witherington, 145.

chevlo shel Mashiach or "the afflictions of the Messiah" (b.*Shabbat* 118a; b.*Pesachim* 118a). O'Brien mentions how "they immediately precede the arrival of the anointed ruler of God. They are the travail out of which the messianic age is born."[109] From this vantage point, then, the trial that Paul endures is not just suffering on behalf of the Messiah, but it is actually a significant part of what will culminate in His return. And by extension, when Believers today suffer, it is a necessary part of what will ultimately manifest in His *parousia* (cf. 1 Thessalonians 4:18).

25 **Of** *this [assembly]* **I was made a minister according to the stewardship from God bestowed on me for your benefit, so that I might fully carry out the** *preaching of* **the word of God,** 26 *that is*, **the mystery which has been hidden from the** *past* **ages and generations, but has now been manifested to His saints,** 27 **to whom God willed to make known what is the riches of the glory of this mystery among the Gentiles, which is Messiah in you, the hope of glory.**

1:25 The NASU provides "Of *this church*" in its rendering, although the Greek only has the genitive case (indicating possession) *hēs* (ἧς), not including an accompanying noun or pronoun. The RSV and ESV simply have "Of which…," indicating the calling that God has placed upon the Apostle Paul. A better italicized rendering might be "Of *this body*," a reference to what is first stated in v. 18. Still, the principal aim is that Paul asserts what he is: "I became a minister according to the stewardship from God that was given to me for you, to make the word of God fully known" (ESV). Paul specifically sees himself as an *oikonomia* (οἰκονομία), which specifically regards "**responsibility of management**…of a household, *direction, office*," quite possibly akin to an "estate manager" (BDAG).[110]

Paul is an administrator of the *ekklēsia*, and with such responsibility Paul must be an able steward of what God has entrusted him with in proclaiming His Word. His mission may be summarized by Isaiah 55:11, "So will My word be which goes forth from My mouth; it will not return to Me empty, without accomplishing what I desire, and without succeeding *in the matter* for which I sent it." Paul has testified previously in Romans 15:19, "in the power of signs and wonders, in the power of the Spirit; so that from Jerusalem and round about as far as Illyricum I have fully preached the gospel of Messiah."

1:26-27 What has Paul been commissioned to specifically proclaim? He tells the Colossians that it is "the mystery that has been kept hidden for ages and generations, but is now disclosed to the saints" (NIV). Using the term "mystery" was not an accident for Paul, as it was a word commonly used in ancient pagan religions and cults. He alters the meaning of it significantly for his Colossian audience, moving it away from any secretive rites, and instead gearing it toward God's plans for the ages. This would be similar to how "the mystery was revealed to Daniel in a night vision. Then Daniel blessed the God of heaven" (Daniel 2:19), as the Aramaic *raz* (רָז) corresponded to the Greek *mustērion* (μυστήριον) via the LXX. In the Qumran materials, secrets are revealed to God's chosen teachers. A prayer in the DSS demonstrates, "I have loved Thee freely and with all my heart; [contemplating the mysteries of] Thy wisdom [I have sought thee]" (1QH 4.27-29).[111] Paul has previously mentioned in 1 Corinthians 2:7, "but we speak God's wisdom in a mystery, the hidden *wisdom* which God predestined before the ages to our glory."

That God would issue a great salvation, which would include the nations at large and not just Israel, was something that was foreseen in the Tanach:

"For I say that Messiah has become a servant to the circumcision on behalf of the truth of God to confirm the promises *given* to the fathers, and for the Gentiles to glorify God for His mercy; as it is written, 'THEREFORE I WILL GIVE PRAISE TO YOU AMONG THE GENTILES, AND I WILL SING TO YOUR NAME.' Again he says, 'REJOICE, O GENTILES, WITH HIS PEOPLE.' And again, 'PRAISE THE LORD ALL YOU GENTILES, AND LET ALL THE PEOPLES PRAISE HIM.' Again Isaiah says, 'THERE SHALL COME THE ROOT OF JESSE, AND HE WHO ARISES TO RULE OVER THE GENTILES,

---

[109] O'Brien, *Colossians-Philemon*, 79.
[110] BDAG, 697.
[111] Geza Vermes, trans., *The Complete Dead Sea Scrolls in English* (London: Penguin Books, 1997), 249.

IN HIM SHALL THE GENTILES HOPE'" (Romans 15:8-12; cf. Psalm 18:49; Deuteronomy 32:43; Psalm 117:1; Isaiah 11:10).

To argue that the mystery would be a great worldwide salvation, from which Israel would be the originator, was not something hidden in the Hebrew Scriptures. The mystery is something "which has been hidden from the *past* ages and generations," only becoming known in Paul's day. **So what was hidden**, if salvation to the nations was already known in the Old Testament? Bruce properly indicates that it was "the manner in which that purpose would come to fruition—by the incorporation of Gentile and Jewish believers alike in the common life of the body of Christ."[112] The full equality of Jewish and non-Jewish Believers within the Body of Messiah was something withheld from view (3:11; cf. Galatians 3:28), even though it certainly is in alignment with the message of the Tanach Scriptures.

The mystery is something "God willed to make known what is the riches of the glory" of, "among the Gentiles." The mystery was not something that was intended to exclusively remain among Paul's own Jewish people, but it was to be shared with the nations as well. **This mystery "is Messiah in you, the hope of glory."** Messiah present in our lives is to surely change how we view one another and relate to one another—in an environment saturated by His love!

Are we to view *Christos en humin, hē elpis tēs doxēs* (Χριστὸς ἐν ὑμῖν, ἡ ἐλπὶς τῆς δόξης) as solely being something individualistic, or the Messiah present among His people corporately? Previously, Paul has asserted that Yeshua is the Head of His Body (v. 18), a corporate entity. Later, Paul will specify some things that the Colossians need to put aside, so that they can live their lives for Him (3:1-17), putting off the old self (3:9). It is best for us to understand that individuals *first* with the Messiah present inside their hearts, can only *then* compose the Body of Messiah. Unredeemed individuals without the Messiah's presence cannot make up His corporate Body. It is imperative for individuals to have the presence of the Lord within redeemed and transformed hearts. If this is accomplished, then as Paul has previously summarized, a great hope of expectation awaits the saints:

"For I consider that the sufferings of this present time are not worthy to be compared with the glory that is to be revealed to us. For the anxious longing of the creation waits eagerly for the revealing of the sons of God. For the creation was subjected to futility, not willingly, but because of Him who subjected it, in hope that the creation itself also will be set free from its slavery to corruption into the freedom of the glory of the children of God" (Romans 8:18-21).

The great mystery that Paul speaks about—"do you not recognize this about yourselves, that Yeshua the Messiah is in you..?" (2 Corinthians 13:5)—is not the existence of a separate group of elect called "the Church."[113] The great mystery is that the presence of God, provided by the work of His Son, would indwell human beings. Not only would it redeem hearts, but it would also transform God's corporate people to take upon themselves the grand mission of His salvation being spread to all. The Tanach certainly had anticipated outsiders to be involved within Israel, but it by no means anticipated them being involved to the same degree that God Himself dwelled among Israel (Numbers 35:34).

The mystery withheld is not the existence of "the Church,"—but quite contrary to this—that "the Gentiles are fellow heirs and fellow members of the body, and fellow partakers of the promise in Messiah Yeshua through the gospel" (Ephesians 3:6). For Paul, this is "my gospel and the preaching of Yeshua the Messiah, according to the revelation of the mystery which has been kept secret for long ages past" (Romans 16:25), meaning that it is the good news how he proclaims it and prioritizes it. The salvation of the nations is to involve the final redemption of Israel (Romans 11:25-26), something we still await the completion of in our day.

Reflecting on this as the emerging Messianic movement, how do we consider the mystery of "the Messiah in you, the hope of glory"? Do we strive to form communities where Jewish and non-Jewish Believers are not only filled with the Spirit of God—redeemed individuals—but where we corporately embody the

---

[112] Bruce, *Colossians-Philemon-Ephesians*, 85; cf. O'Brien, *Colossians-Philemon*, 86.

[113] Against: Geisler, in *BKCNT*, 675.

In his words, "The church was unknown in the Old Testament because it **had been kept hidden**."

Lord's presence? Are we a people that emphasizes equality for all, and the grand fulfillment of the mystery Paul spoke of? Are our teachings on the Torah and Tanach focused on accomplishing God's mandate to His people, or on things that take us away from His mandate like the false teachers of Colossae? If I were to ask your congregation or fellowship what some important mysteries of God were, what would the people answer?

28 We proclaim Him, admonishing every man and teaching every man with all wisdom, so that we may present every man complete in Messiah. 29 For this purpose also I labor, striving according to His power, which mightily works within me.

1:28 Paul speaks of the sacred call it is to "proclaim him, admonishing and teaching everyone with all wisdom, so that we may present everyone perfect in Christ" (NIV). The NASU and NIV use "admonishing and teaching," whereas the RSV/NRSV, ESV, and HCSB use "warning...and teaching." Which is to be taken as the better rendering? The verb *noutheteō* (νουθετέω) fully means "**to counsel about avoidance or cessation of an improper course of conduct, admonish, warn, instruct**" (*BDAG*).[114] From a lexical standpoint, either "admonishing" or "warning" is valid. Yet Paul is directly combating some kind of serious, proto-Gnostic, errors here, and so "warning" should be the preferred translation. But perhaps unlike the false teachers in Colossae, he says that he is "warning everyone and teaching everyone in all wisdom" (NRSV), *en pasē sophia* (ἐν πάσῃ σοφίᾳ). The Apostle Paul knows that his words have to be targeted and specific, carefully referring and/or alluding to the things errantly influencing them to get the Colossians back on the proper course of faith—who are again a group of Believers he has never met in person. So while Paul will have some serious rebukes for them, it will be accompanied with practical teaching and encouragement.

The purpose of Paul's warning and teaching is "that we may present everyone as having reached the goal, united with the Messiah" (CJB). Every person who he instructs should be mature and complete, bonded in a close relationship to the Lord Yeshua. This completeness will not be some higher realm of ethereal knowledge, likely what the false teachers in Colossae were advocating, but instead will be substantiated in ch. 3 to be acts of proper conduct becoming of those transformed by God.

The term *teleios* (τέλειος) is used to describe this maturity. In a classical sense it could have meant "*having reached its end, finished, complete*" (*LS*),[115] yet in a more theological sense it "**pert. to meeting the highest standard**" (*BDAG*).[116] Paul uses it in Romans 12:2, instructing, "do not be conformed to this world, but be transformed by the renewing of your mind, so that you may prove what the will of God is, that which is good and acceptable and perfect [*teleios*]." It is used in Matthew 5:48, where Yeshua teaches, "Therefore you are to be perfect [*teleios*], as your heavenly Father is perfect [*teleios*]."

O'Brien describes how "The word was...employed to designate the 'perfect' man in Greek philosophy...but whether it was also a technical term for initiates in the Hellenistic mystery religions is disputed."[117] While one could certainly speculate that Paul might be subverting yet another term used by the false teachers in Colossae, what is more significant by far is how *teleios* was often used in the Septuagint to render the Hebrew *tamim* (תָּמִים). *Tamim*, while often associated with the quality of animal sacrifices in Leviticus and Numbers, also had ethical and moral applications. We see how "Noah was a righteous man, blameless [*tamim*] in his time; Noah walked with God" (Genesis 6:9). Deuteronomy 18:13 admonishes, "You shall be blameless [*tamim*] before the LORD your God." The Apostle Paul warns and teaches so that people can learn to be diligent followers of God (Ephesians 5:1), who can obey Him and fulfill His tasks for the world.

1:29 So significant for Paul was the work God had given him, that he tells the Colossians, "For this I toil, struggling with all his energy that he powerfully works within me" (ESV). Rendered as "striving" in the NASU and RSV, the verb *agōnizomai* (ἀγωνίζομαι) can relate, "*to contend for a prize, esp. in the public games,*"

114 *BDAG*, 679.
115 *LS*, 797.
116 *BDAG*, 995.
117 O'Brien, *Colossians-Philemon*, 89.

although "generally, *to struggle, to exert oneself*" (LS).[118] It is not a far stretch at all to recognize that Paul agonizes over the work he performs, "toiling strenuously" (REB). Even though a great deal of effort, toil, and even pain may be present in the work of the gospel, for the Apostle Paul this all came according to God's power present within him. As is so often quoted, Paul said "I can do all things through Him who strengthens me" (Philippians 4:13). Furthermore, he remarks how "Everyone who competes [*agōnizomai*] in the games exercises self-control in all things. They then *do it* to receive a perishable wreath, but we an imperishable" (1 Corinthians 9:25).

The Apostle Paul recognized how the work he performed would have significant, long-lasting and eternal effects. For those of us in ministry today, we should be encouraged by his words, recognizing that even though we may agonize sometimes—and we may even have doubts and some lonely seasons (cf. Psalm 23:4)—what we do for the Body of Messiah is not at all in vain. But *like* Paul, and *unlike* the false teachers in Colossae—we must properly declare God's mystery. As one who has been in the Messianic movement since 1995, and now in full time Messianic ministry for over six years (since 2003), I know that this is not an easy task. Given enough faith and perseverance, I believe we can see the realization of what James the Just says: "let endurance have *its* perfect [*teleios*] result, so that you may be perfect [*teleios*] and complete, lacking in nothing" (James 1:4).

---

[118] *LS*, 11.

COLOSSIANS 2
COMMENTARY

1 For I want you to know how great a struggle I have on your behalf and for those who are at Laodicea, and for all those who have not personally seen my face, 2 that their hearts may be encouraged, having been knit together in love, and *attaining* to all the wealth that comes from the full assurance of understanding, *resulting* in a true knowledge of God's mystery, *that is*, Messiah *Himself*, 3 in whom are hidden all the treasures of wisdom and knowledge.

2:1 The Epistle to the Colossians did not exclusively affect those at Colossae, but also those at Laodicea (cf. 4:16), which was a mere ten miles away. Paul writes, "I want you to know how great a struggle I have for you, for those in Laodicea, and for all who have not seen me in person" (HCSB). Paul describes that he is specifically experiencing *agōn* (ἀγών), "generally, *any struggle, trial,* or *danger*" (LS),[1] something that concurs with his immediate prior usage of the verb *agōnizomai* in 1:29. While physical danger and distress can certainly be considered, we should also be reminded of how Paul agonized during his time in Ephesus, being evidenced by his up-and-down relationship with the assembly at Corinth (1 Corinthians 4:17; 16:8, 10; 2 Corinthians 1:23-2:4; 7:8; 12:14). This is something that would likely have been known to those in the immediate vicinity of the Lycus Valley.

The ministry work and sacrifices that Paul made on behalf of the Colossians was something they would have to seriously consider in listening to his instruction to them. Paul works diligently, and struggles in the process, for people like the Colossians. These people are those "who have not met me personally" (NIV), or more specifically *hosoi ouch heorakan to prosōpon mou en sarki* (ὅσοι οὐχ ἑόρακαν τὸ πρόσωπόν μου ἐν σαρκί)—"as many as have not seen my face in the flesh" (YLT). Paul does this because he is a true servant of the Lord Yeshua, knowing that wherever he is, the work he performs will have significant results. Contrary to this kind of work and sacrifice, all the false teachers in Colossae can be said to offer is slippery words and vain philosophy (vs. 4, 8).

2:2 Paul expresses how, "I want their hearts to be encouraged and united in love, so that they may have all the riches of assured understanding and have the knowledge of God's mystery, that is, Christ himself" (NRSV). Even though he may not meet all the people affected by his ministry, the Apostle Paul still wishes them the best. While wisdom originating from God, or His Torah, is a great virtue that is seen throughout the Tanach Scriptures,[2] Paul expresses here how the Colossians, Laodiceans, and any others he works for should come to a knowledge of *tou mustēriou tou Theou, Christou* (τοῦ μυστηρίου τοῦ θεοῦ, Χριστοῦ), "the mystery of God, namely, Christ" (NIV). Whatever mystery the false teachers in Colossae may have been serving up, **it is insignificant to who Yeshua is.** Paul's prayer in Ephesians 3:17-18 further says,

"[S]o that Messiah may dwell in your hearts through faith; *and* that you, being rooted and grounded in love, may be able to comprehend with all the saints what is the breadth and length and height and depth [of such love]."

The most significant way, though, that the Colossians will be able to come to understand the mystery of Messiah is by being "knit together in love." The verb *sumbibazō* (συμβιβάζω) most often means "**to bring together into a unit, *unite*,**" but it can also mean "*instruct, teach, advise*" (BDAG).[3] It appears in Acts 9:22

---

[1] *LS*, 10.

[2] Job 28:12-19; Psalm 110:10; 119:14, 72, 127, 162; Proverbs 3:13-15; Isaiah 33:6.

[3] *BDAG*, 956, 957.

where Paul was "proving [*sumbibazo*] that this *Yeshua* is the Messiah," and in 1 Corinthians 2:16, which includes a quotation from Isaiah 40:13 (LXX), "For WHO HAS KNOWN THE MIND OF THE LORD, THAT HE WILL INSTRUCT [*sumbibazo*] HIM? But we have the mind of Messiah." Certainly, Paul expects the Colossians to come together and be properly instructed—and if they follow what he has told them to do then they will be able to understand the mystery of who the Messiah is.

But, given the parallel usage of *sumbibazo* in Ephesians, it would seem that Paul's intent in v. 2 is to emphasize that those he ministers to, directly and indirectly, come together as one in the Lord: "[F]rom whom the whole body, being fitted and held together [*sumbibazo*] by what every joint supplies, according to the proper working of each individual part, causes the growth of the body for the building up of itself in love" (Ephesians 4:16). In coming together as one, placing Yeshua at the center of their faith (v. 19), then mature men and women filled with the Holy Spirit can learn about Him as the true mystery.

2:3 If one can understand that it is Yeshua the Messiah who is God's mystery, then it will naturally be revealed that in Him "are hidden all the treasures of wisdom and knowledge." In referring to *sophias kai gnōseōs* (σοφίας καὶ γνώσεως) or "wisdom and knowledge," there is likely some deliberate subversion of the terms used by the false teachers in Colossae. These were terms used by ancient mystery cults, but were also present in Diaspora Judaism as evidenced in the Septuagint translation of books like Proverbs, or the works of Philo. Peter T. O'Brien describes, "Paul is making an appeal to Jewish sources partly because the false teaching at Colossae on its Jewish side (it was a fusion of Jewish and pagan elements) was insisting that Jesus Christ was only one mediator and one source of revelation among many."[4]

While we are convinced, as are many evangelical exegetes, that the situation in Colossae was a fuse of ancient proto-Gnostic/mystical and Jewish errors, not all are convinced. James D.G. Dunn indicates an alternative view: "No doubt part of the attractiveness of the Christian message regarding Christ was the degree to which Jewish wisdom and apocalyptic traditions were thus combined."[5]

From either angle one takes, **the Messiah is the key to opening all of the hidden treasures that people seek after** (John 1:18; Hebrews 1:2-3). As Paul previously had written, "by His doing you are in Messiah Yeshua, who became to us wisdom from God, and righteousness and sanctification, and redemption" (1 Corinthians 1:30), and so by placing Yeshua as the focus of one's life—understanding what righteousness, sanctification, and redemption are all about can be achieved. While Yeshua had been identified along the lines of Wisdom in the hymn of 1:15-20, when a person makes a sincere effort to understand His ministry and investigate His accomplishments on behalf of humanity, Yeshua is shown to possess qualities and do things that are far beyond Wisdom, as He is the Son of God. O'Brien relates how, "Because he holds this exalted position there is good reason to encourage these Christians [meaning, Believers] of the Lycus valley to turn to him for all God's stores of insight, understanding, wisdom and knowledge."[6]

4 I say this so that no one will delude you with persuasive argument. 5 For even though I am absent in body, nevertheless I am with you in spirit, rejoicing to see your good discipline and the stability of your faith in Messiah.

2:4 Why does the Apostle Paul remind the Colossians about the work he is performing (v. 1), and about how Yeshua the Messiah is God's true mystery (v. 2)? It should seem pretty obvious: "I tell you this so that no one may deceive you by fine-sounding arguments" (NIV) or "beguiling speech" (RSV). We can safely assume by this that a number of the Colossians had already been deceived by the false teachers. The verb *paralogizomai* (παραλογίζομαι), "*to mislead by fallacious reasoning*" (LS),[7] is used only one other time in the Apostolic Scriptures. James the Just says, "prove yourselves doers of the word, and not merely hearers who delude [*paralogizomai*] themselves" (James 1:22). Can it be said that those who are responsible for misleading others with seemingly

---

[4] O'Brien, *Colossians-Philemon*, 96.

[5] Dunn, 132.

[6] O'Brien, *Colossians-Philemon*, 95.

[7] LS, 599.

persuasive arguments—either in ancient times or today—are not out actively accomplishing the imperatives that are upon God's people, as clearly laid out in the Scriptures? Are such people spending more time philosophizing about things they really know nothing about, or trying to be a blessing to others by demonstrating God's wisdom via faithful service and good works?

The reason that the false teachers in Colossae, or any false teachers for that matter, seem to have success for a season—is that they employ *pithanologia* (πιθανολογία). Often, these are arguments that give the impression of being well thought out and considered, but they have dishonorable motives behind them. N.T. Wright comments, "It is by spurious *arguments* that such teachers win the day, and valid arguments, based on the centrality of Jesus Christ, are the proper weapons with which to meet them."[8] When the focus of one's Bible teaching is as Paul's—"but we preach Messiah crucified" (1 Corinthians 1:23)—and the intent is to get others to live like and emulate Him, then things should be in their proper order. But when they are not, and base human motives are involved, then things can go desperately wrong.

Holding to there being an exclusively Jewish issue at work in Colossae, Dunn argues, "the implication here is that the Colossian Jewish community was not lacking in skilled apologists, but was well able to express the appeal of their worship and code of behavior in beguiling terms."[9] His mention of this is well taken, because in all likelihood even when an interpreter holds to there being a syncretistic mix of religious errors in Colossae (unlike Dunn), the false teachers were some kind of Jewish Believers. They were people intrigued by things that according to Paul, would take people away from Messiah Yeshua being at the center of one's faith.

The Messianic community today is not at all immune to there being teachers who promote insidious things with beguiling speech and seemingly persuasive arguments. Most relevant, to us applying Colossians in a modern Messianic setting, would be teachings that place Medieval Jewish mystical errors at their center, claims made about the Hebrew language that are historically unsubstantiated,[10] and also teachings that deliberately take away from who Yeshua is as God Incarnate in human flesh. The kind of teachers we encounter who promote these things are not only charlatans, who have *anything but* helping people understand who Yeshua is to us as people who need redemption (cf. 1 Corinthians 1:21-25), but via their deceptions they are able *to con a great number of people* out of their hard-earned financial resources. Having some seeming financial success, a number of teachers I have encountered in my Messianic experience over the years have thought themselves to be "invincible," and thus able to preach and teach whatever they want. While this phenomenon is by no means something new to religion, **I fear that the array of false teachings present in the Messianic movement will not get better as time moves forward.**

2:5 No one should be disturbed about such false teaching, because the Apostle Paul was not worried about it in the First Century. Paul expresses confidence that the Colossians are going to do the right thing, writing how "though I am absent from you in body, I am present with you in spirit and delight to see how orderly you are and how firm your faith in Christ is" (NIV). Paul is not present with the Colossians in person (cf. 1 Corinthians 5:3), but *tō pneumati sun humin eimi* (τῷ πνεύματι σὺν ὑμῖν εἰμι), "in the spirit I am with you" (YLT). Is this just talking metaphorically about Paul wishing he were with the Colossians, or that Paul's presence among the Colossians is mediated by God's Spirit, as they are all a part of the same Body of Messiah? Not all interpreters are agreed, but it is not a point on which one's overall interpretation of Colossians rises or falls.

There is an indication that although there are false teachers in Colossae, they have not yet had as significant an influence that they could. Paul rejoices "to see your good order and the firmness of your faith" (ESV), employing some ancient military terminology. *Taxis* (τάξις) can relate to "*a drawing up, the order* or *disposition of an army*," but "generally, *an arrangement, order*" (LS).[11] *Stereōma* (στερέωμα), meaning "*a solid body,*

---

[8] Wright, 96.

[9] Dunn, 133.

[10] Note that as problematic as the teaching that the Apostolic Scriptures (New Testament) was written in Hebrew has been for parts of the Messianic movement, the teachings I would be referring to go far beyond this, being closely associated with the Kabbalah and Jewish mysticism.

[11] LS, 792.

foundation: metaph. *steadfastness"* (*LS*),[12] is seen in 1 Maccabees 9:14 where "Judas saw that Bacchides and the strength [*stereōma*] of his army were on the right." So, in spite of there being some insidious teachings and over/undercurrents present in Colossae, Paul is pleased that most of those who will hear his letter possess a very strong and stable faith in Yeshua the Messiah. Indeed, just like the Apostle Paul, it would be the wish of all of us who teach the Scriptures that when circumstances arise where we have to warn others against errors circulating in the assembly, that we can express a similar confidence that our audience is strong and stable in faith!

6 Therefore as you have received Messiah Yeshua the Lord, *so* walk in Him, 7 having been firmly rooted *and now* being built up in Him and established in your faith, just as you were instructed, *and* overflowing with gratitude.

2:6 Recognizing the Colossians as being firm in their faith in Yeshua (v. 5), Paul instructs them, "as you have received Messiah Yeshua the Lord, *so* walk in Him." The Colossians received (Grk. *parelabete,* παρελάβετε) the gospel message as a valid tradition handed down to them, with some commentators noting a possible parallel with m.*Avot* 1:1: "Moses received Torah at Sinai and handed it on to Joshua, Joshua to elders, and elders to prophets."[13] Just as the Torah would have been considered a reliable tradition, handed down and preserved over many generations of Israelite and Jewish leaders, so should the good news of Messiah Yeshua now be considered as just as reliable a tradition.

Noting many of the things the Apostle Paul will be discussing throughout ch. 2—which are manifold—Ben Witherington III indicates, "it is quite characteristic of Asiatic rhetoric to throw a cornucopia of images and metaphors at the audience, trusting that one or the other will lodge in their brains."[14] Paul's purpose is doubtless to reaffirm to the Colossians what Yeshua has accomplished for them, and how their lives are to be focused around Him—lest they even think about being influenced by the false teachers (cf. 2 Corinthians 11:4; Galatians 1:6)! Colossians 2:6-4:6 composes the main body of Paul's letter, and as he expresses, receiving Yeshua is *not enough*—as one must continue forward in Him.

As the identity of Yeshua is a major feature of Colossians, Paul is specific to say that his audience did not just receive Messiah Yeshua, but rather *ton Christon Iēsou ton Kurion* (τὸν Χριστὸν Ἰησοῦν τὸν κύριον)—"the Messiah Yeshua the Lord." This plays directly into the Christological assertions immediately made in vs. 8-9. The Colossians had properly received Messiah Yeshua and recognized Him as Lord (not just "Master")[15]—and now there was a serious danger that some, if not many of them, could be persuaded against this as Yeshua was advocated to just be one of any number of mediatorial beings between humanity and God the Father.

Recognizing Yeshua as Lord is one of the earliest confessions of Messianic faith (Philippians 2:11; Romans 10:9; 1 Corinthians 12:3), because it is a declaration not only that Yeshua is to be the One a man or woman follows after—**but most significantly because a human being must state that God Himself has had to provide salvation.** Even while not being able to fully understand it as a new Believer, it is still nevertheless a requirement that one recognize Messiah Yeshua as Divine to be saved. Having received Messiah properly stands in stark contrast to the human traditions Paul will refer to (v. 8), and then refute (vs. 18-19).

The Jewish character of Colossians' author is once again seen in the requirement for his readers to "walk" (cf. 1:10), speaking of the manner in which they are to live.

2:7 Before addressing some of the major theological issues of the false teachers' philosophy, Paul acknowledges how most of the Colossians have been doing the right thing. They were "rooted and built up in him and established in the faith, just as you were taught, abounding in thanksgiving" (RSV).

---

[12] Ibid., 745.

[13] Jacob Neusner, trans., *The Mishnah: A New Translation* (New Haven and London: Yale University Press, 1988), 672.
Cf. Bruce, *Colossians-Philemon-Ephesians*, 93; O'Brien, *Colossians-Philemon*, 105.

[14] Witherington, 154.

[15] Cf. *BDAG*, 220.
In most English Bibles, the title that is rendered as "Master" in reference to Yeshua is *Despotēs* (δεσπότης).

Sometimes, English translations do not adequately convey the pattern for faith that Paul establishes with the Greek verbs, seen in the clause *errizōmenoi kai epoikodomoumenoi en autō kai bebaioumenoi* (ἐρριζωμένοι καὶ ἐποικοδομούμενοι ἐν αὐτῷ καὶ βεβαιούμενοι), more accurately rendered by the NASU as "having been firmly rooted *and*...being built up in Him and [being] established in your faith." The first verb, *errizōmenoi* or "having been firmly rooted," is a perfect passive participle, describing the past action of God in rooting people properly in faith via His Spirit. The second two verbs, *epoikodomoumenoi* and *bebaioumenoi*, "building" and "establishing," are present tense passive participles, describing current actions of God in seeing that His people are built up and established. It should not be difficult to detect how being rooted in Yeshua *leads* to a Believer being build up and strengthened during the course of life. There is a likely thematic connection between v. 7 and Ephesians 2:20, where the faith of Believers has "been built on the foundation of the apostles and prophets, Messiah Yeshua Himself being the corner *stone.*"

The growth language that Paul uses in v. 7 has been appropriated from the Tanach and the Apocrypha. Jeremiah 17:7-8 could certainly be in mind, as "Blessed is the man who trusts in the LORD and whose trust is the LORD. For he will be like a tree planted by the water, that extends its roots by a stream and will not fear when the heat comes; but its leaves will be green, and it will not be anxious in a year of drought nor cease to yield fruit." The verb *hrizō* (ῥιζόω), "*to make to strike root*: metaph. *to root in the ground, plant*" (LS),[16] employed in v. 7, is used of Wisdom in Sirach 40:15, where "I took root [*hrizō*] in an honored people, in the portion of the Lord, who is their inheritance." Similarly in Psalms of Solomon 14:2-4, "to those who live in the righteousness of his commandments, in the law, which he has commanded to us for our life. The Lord's saints will live by it forever; his saints are the Lord's paradise, the trees of life. Their planting is rooted [*hrizō*] forever; they will not be plucked out all the days of the heavens."

Of most importance, though, would be Paul's wider word to the Believers in Asia Minor, that they might be "rooted and grounded in love" (Ephesians 3:17).

If the Colossians hold onto the tradition (Grk. *paradosis*, παράδοσις) that they have been handed down about Yeshua's Lordship via the Apostle Paul, and via their fellow servant Epaphras (4:12), then they will have no problems. But if they veer from this course, then they will be subject to things which are at best of human origin, and at worst find their origin in paganism.[17]

8 See to it that no one takes you captive through philosophy and empty deception, according to the tradition of men, according to the elementary principles of the world, rather than according to Messiah. 9 For in Him all the fullness of *the Deity dwells in bodily form, 10 and in Him you have been made complete, and He is the head over all rule and authority;

* Grk. *tēs Theotētos* (τῆς θεότητος) includes the definite article "the"

2:8-23 The selection of writing from Colossians 2:8-23 often has various verses, or pieces of verses, quoted from them to today's Torah observant Messianic Believers. If the argument that Paul is making to his ancient Colossian audience is not followed closely, then what he tells them is likely to be misunderstood and taken out of context by people who just read a clip here or there from it. When many Christians tell today's Messianics that no one is to be their judge, for example, in regard to the appointed times (v. 16)—the original setting and circumstances of this word are often never considered. This is even more true of "the elementary principles of the world" and the superstitious rituals which could have affected the Colossians (vs. 20-22). These are sometimes falsely assumed to be the commandments of God's Torah, when religious syncretism is actually the main issue.

---

[16] LS, 718.

[17] I am fully aware of the fact that in certain quarters of today's Messianic movement, the word "tradition" is viewed with a great deal of disdain or disgust. Yet, tradition in all its forms is not at all condemned by the Holy Scriptures—because ultimately the Bible is something that has been handed down and is a tradition in and of itself. F.F. Bruce reminds us,

"Protestants sometimes overlook that 'tradition' in the NT has this better sense as well as a worse one; it is good to recognize and hold fast the true tradition, while rejecting all tradition that runs counter to the gospel" (Bruce, *Colossians-Philemon-Ephesians*, 94).

Thankfully, while many of today's evangelical laypersons may incorrectly assume that 2:8-23 includes a diatribe against the importance of the Torah of Moses, many of today's evangelical commentators correctly recognize that the overarching issue is a proto-Gnostic/mystical and Jewish amalgamation of errors unique to Colossae and the Lycus Valley. Their thoughts will be carefully considered in our examination.

2:8 The opening word, which will address a great deal of the Colossian false teaching (or as some prefer, Colossian heresy), is absolutely loaded with some descriptions that have to be laid forward very carefully, if the larger cotext is to make any sense. Paul admonishes the Colossians, "Be careful that no one takes you captive through philosophy and empty deceit based on human tradition, based on the elemental forces of the world, and not based on Christ" (HCSB). Certainly in a very general sense, this verse could be used in contemporary preaching to warn people against pursuing modern and post-modern strains of thought that will do nothing more than take people away from Yeshua the Messiah and Biblical faith. Suffice it to say, there was an ancient precedent for this among Paul's audience.

Who are the false teachers in Colossae? All v. 8 tells us is *mē tis* (μή τις) or "no one." Sadly, this rather ambiguous description is one of only a few direct references to the false teachers in Colossae. Some think that "no one" in v. 8 could be a reference to their leader. The Colossians are warned against an empty, vain philosophy that could lead them astray. F.F. Bruce, representing the position of many evangelical interpreters, considers that the problem "appears to have been basically Jewish, but to have included features of pagan affinity...The Jewish law certainly figures in it, but it is associated with an asceticism which was not characteristic of the mainstream of Jewish life."[18] As reviewed in the Introduction, Bruce sees possible connections between the Colossian error and later *Merkavah* mysticism, which could be best described as a kind of Jewish Gnosticism.

The Colossians are not to be taken "captive" (NASU), made "a prey of" (RSV), or carried "away as spoil" (YLT) by the false teachers, possibly akin to "kidnap." To convey how serious this is, v. 8 employs the verb *sulagōgeō* (συλαγωγέω), often used in a classical sense to describe people taken away in battle[19]—which would certainly be an indication that Believers are engaged in spiritual warfare (cf. Ephesians 6:10-20). While he is confident in the Colossians' current stability (v. 5), Paul by no means thinks that he can just write to them without giving them some kind of warning. Witherington offers us some important thoughts to consider as Paul composes his main instruction:

"Paul is speaking into a rhetorically and philosophically saturated environment...Paul therefore is in the awkward position of not being able to speak directly and in person to his audience, thus losing a good portion of the rhetorical arsenals (gestures, tone of voice, etc.). Yet still he must offer an even more powerful and philosophically substantive act of persuasion than is given by those who are beguiling the Colossians."[20]

The readers of the letter are warned against being taken captive *dia tēs philosophias kai kenēs apatēs* (διὰ τῆς φιλοσοφίας καὶ κενῆς ἀπάτης), "by philosophy and empty deceit" (RSV). There could be a connection with the parallel word in Ephesians 5:6, "Let no one deceive you with empty words [*kenois logois*, κενοῖς λόγοις], for because of these things the wrath of God comes upon the sons of disobedience." False knowledge or wisdom is an issue that is certainly confronted throughout the Pauline Epistles,[21] and as 1 Timothy 6:20 well-summarizes, "O Timothy, guard what has been entrusted to you, avoiding worldly *and* empty chatter *and* the opposing arguments of what is falsely called 'knowledge.'"

It can be pretty clear from an English reading the kind of thing that Paul wants the Colossians to be on guard against. It is also clear why he wants them to be on guard, as whatever the false teaching or philosophy might be will inevitably lead them away from Messiah Yeshua. But *how* this will manifest itself is an issue that is undoubtedly affected by the presuppositions one brings to the letter. The present participle *sulagōgōn* (συλαγωγῶν), rendered as "takes you captive" (NASU), is not a frequent term used in Greek. It could be easily changed by writing a *nu* (ν) in place of a *lambda* (λ), to the genitive (indicating possession) noun *sunagōgōn*

---

[18] Ibid., 95.

[19] Joseph H. Thayer, *Thayer's Greek-English Lexicon of the New Testament* (Peabody, MA: Hendrickson, 2003), 594.

[20] Witherington, 154.

[21] 1 Corinthians 1:17-31; 8:1; 13:8; 1 Timothy 1:3-11; 4:3-16; 2 Timothy 2:18; 3:5-7.

(συναγωγῶν) or "synagogue." Among a few commentators, Wright is one who proposes "that Paul uses [sulagōgōn] because it makes a contemptuous pun with the word *synagogue*: see to it that no-one snatches you as a prey...from the flock of Christ, to lock you up instead within Judaism."[22] And in Dunn's estimation, "the Colossian Jews included some effective apologists and rhetoricians in their number."[23] Their view is that the warning is "Do not let anyone in-synagogue you."

From this angle, Judaism is just considered to be another philosophy. This would be similar to how the historian Josephus spoke of "that philosophy which is contained in those writings" (*Against Apion* 1.54),[24] and "The Jews had for a great while had three sects of philosophy peculiar to themselves" (*Antiquities of the Jews* 18.11),[25] referring to the Essenes, Sadducees, and Pharisees. Philo would similarly refer to the "philosophy according to Moses" (*On the Change of Names* 223).[26] Commentators like Wright[27] and Dunn are persuaded that the Colossians as former pagans needed to be warned against joining the Jewish Synagogue, as Wright says, "What Judaism might offer to ex-pagan Christians is in fact just another local and, one might say, tribal religion,"[28] similar to the "elementary principles" they were once subject to prior to finding faith.

Is the *philosophia* (φιλοσοφία) that Paul warns the Colossians against really First Century Judaism? Moo actually observes how, "The word provides no help...in identifying the false teaching in Colossae."[29] The only thing that just about all commentators on Colossians can agree about this philosophy was that it was *ou kata Christon* (οὐ κατὰ Χριστόν), "not [in] accord with the Messiah" (CJB).

Other than the minority proposal that the philosophy warned against was Judaism, there are two other possibilities that an interpreter has to consider:
1. Outright pagan philosophy
2. Pagan philosophy that had influenced the Jewish Synagogue, which was particular to Colossae/the Lycus Valley region

While *philosophia* does appear in ancient Jewish literature to refer to Judaism itself, it should be no surprise that *philosophia* was also used to describe various other religions, cults, and mysterious sects particular to the broad First Century. O'Brien indicates, "those who practiced magic called themselves 'philosophers' as they sought by rights, initiations and magical spells to capture the allegiance of men."[30] Dunn has to similarly agree that "philosophy" had a much broader ancient use: "It is a term which many apologists for all sorts of religious and pseudo-religious teaching would use because of its distinguished pedigree, as subsequently in relation to the mysteries."[31]

The Apostle Paul labels this philosophy to be *ta stoicheia tou kosmou* (τὰ στοιχεῖα τοῦ κόσμου) or "the elementary principles of the world." It is not difficult at all to see a connection to his previous word about the Galatians also being subject to "the weak and worthless elemental things" (Galatians 4:9; cf. 4:3) that they should have left behind in paganism.[32] Norman Geisler indicates one view of how the *stoicheia* "may refer to the evil spirits who inspire...heresy and over whom Christ triumphed."[33] The elements or *stoicheia* being wicked things of the world is something certainly attested in ancient Jewish literature. *Testament of Solomon* 8:1-2 in the Pseudepigrapha relays a scene of how King Solomon saw seven distinct angels of darkness: "When

---

[22] Wright, 100.

[23] Dunn, 147.

[24] *The Works of Josephus: Complete and Unabridged*, 777.

[25] Ibid., 477.

[26] *The Works of Philo: Complete and Unabridged*, 360.

[27] Cf. Wright, pp 100-101.

[28] Ibid., 102.

[29] Moo, 186.

[30] O'Brien, *Colossians-Philemon*, 109.

[31] Dunn, 147.

[32] In the author's commentary *Galatians for the Practical Messianic*, he discusses how these "weak and worthless elemental things" cannot specifically be the appointed times of Leviticus 23, but rather are likely proto-Gnostic and mystical Jewish practices associated with them adhered to by the Judaizers/Influencers. If this is not the case, then the good Apostle Paul could actually be found to associating God's ways in the Torah with paganism.

[33] Geisler, in *BKCNT*, 677.

I, Solomon, saw them, I was amazed and asked them, 'Who are you?' They replied, 'We are heavenly bodies [*esmen stoicheia*], rulers of this world of darkness."[34] Wisdom 13:1-2 in the Apocrypha further explains,

"For all men who were ignorant of God were foolish by nature; and they were unable from the good things that are seen to know him who exists, nor did they recognize the craftsman while paying heed to his works; but they supposed that either fire or wind or swift air, or the circle of the stars, or turbulent water, or the luminaries of heaven were the gods that rule the world."

In Ancient Hellenistic Judaism, *stoicheia* sometimes took on its meaning as seen in Platonic philosophy, representing the forces of air, fire, wind, and water. Philo would refer to how "some nations have made divinities of the four elements, earth and water, and air and fire. Others, of the sun and moon, and of the other planets and fixed stars. Others, again, of the whole world. And they have all invented different appellations, all of them false" (*Decalogue* 53; cf. *On the Eternity of the World* 144).[35] In O'Brien's estimation, "It is probable that in the syncretistic teaching being advocated at Colossae these στοιχεῖα were grouped with the angels and seen as controlling the heavenly realm and man's access to God's presence."[36] It was thought that only by appealing to these forces via some kind of physical denial or pain, would one's spiritual needs actually be met (v. 18).

While we are convinced that *ta stoicheia tou kosmou* is used in the letter to the Colossians to refer to either elemental components of the universe, or some kind of angelic/demonic spiritual powers that the Colossians were being told they needed to appeal to, it is true that not all interpreters are agreed. Moo indicates how *stoicheion* "is a 'formal' word, meaning 'fundamental component' or 'element'...It can, for instance, refer to the letters of the alphabet, the notes of a musical scale, or the propositions of geometry."[37] However, it would seem that all are agreed, as D.G. Reid points out, "interpreters of Paul must focus on *ta stoicheia tou kosmou* as a linguistic unit."[38] (With this in mind, I do not think it is inappropriate to conclude that if the issue in Colossians 2:8 are demonic/angelic spirits involved with pagan philosophy, that the *ta stoicheia tou kosmou* in Galatians 4:3 are also involved with ancient pagan practices that affected parts of the First Century Synagogue.)[39]

In v. 8 Paul further describes this philosophy as *kata tēn paradosin tōn anthrōpōn* (κατὰ τὴν παράδοσιν τῶν ἀνθρώπων), that it is "according to human tradition" (RSV). The issue in Colossians 2 is **human tradition and philosophy**, which should primarily be considered things present in ancient pagan religion. Witherington actually renders this as "according to [mere] human traditions."[40] It is often thought that there is a connection purposefully made with Mark 7:8, where Yeshua chastises various Pharisees: "You are experts at setting aside the commandment of God in order to keep your tradition [*tēn paradosin humōn*, τὴν παράδοσιν ὑμῶν]," where various Pharisaic interpretations of God's Torah are derided. How much of the tradition confronted in Colossians actually was Jewish, Hellenistic, and from the mystery cults of the Lycus Valley has not at all been agreed upon by interpreters.

Moo gives us some important thoughts on how the traditions likely refuted by Paul indeed do relate to the material elements of the world and paganism, partially based on the previously quoted Wisdom 13:1-2

---

[34] D.C. Duling, trans., "Testament of Solomon," in *The Old Testament Pseudepigrapha*, Vol 1, pp 969-970.

[35] *The Works of Philo: Complete and Unabridged*, 522.

[36] O'Brien, *Colossians-Philemon*, 132.

[37] Moo, 187.

[38] D.G. Reid, "Elements/Elemental Spirits of the Universe," in *Dictionary of Paul and His Letters*, 229.
This article (pp 229-233) includes a summation of views present in contemporary Pauline scholarship.

[39] A small few, based in a very anti-Torah interpretation of Galatians 3:19-20 (cf. Deuteronomy 33:2, LXX), actually conclude that (demonic) angels delivered the Law to Israel as a form of Divine punishment. From this angle, keeping the Torah had to be conducted in conjunction with angelic mediation and/or approval, meaning that God originally did not want to give humans any kind of Law or commandments. This view of the Torah is often rooted in a Higher Criticism that not only wants to deny any Divine origin of the Pentateuch, but also often denies its Mosaic origin. It is clearly a long way from simply living the way that God has asked of His people in the Holy Scriptures, where "You shall walk in all the way which the LORD your God has commanded you, that you may live and that it may be well with you" (Deuteronomy 5:33; cf. 30:6).

And once again, normative Jewish practice and Torah keeping of the First Century does not appear to be the issue in Colossians.

[40] Witherington, 152.

reference: "[The] tendency to 'spiritualize' or 'divinize' the material elements was a strong cultural current that the people of God had to fight against...The characterization of pagan religion as involving worship of physical elements as well as warnings against it are found throughout Jewish and early Christian apologetics."[41] Moo actually makes a reference to Deuteronomy 4:19, where it is warned, "And *beware* not to lift up your eyes to heaven and see the sun and the moon and the stars, all the host of heaven, and be drawn away and worship them and serve them, those which the LORD your God has allotted to all the peoples under the whole heaven." This only adds to the problem of the Colossian error including asceticism and self-denial (v. 18).

So, in warning the Colossians about vain philosophies and human traditions, we see that Paul takes language used to specifically describe the base elements of the Earth—employed in contemporary Jewish writings to refer to how the pagans have divinized various aspects of God's good Creation. While pagan philosophy and tradition are principally in view, given the fact that Ancient Israel in the Torah is given warnings against them, this pagan philosophy would have impacted the Jewish community in Colossae, which in turn affected the assembly of Messianic Believers. Various external rituals and an ascetic lifestyle would be rigidly imposed as people were seeking after secret or mystical knowledge.

Paul is warning the Colossians not to be deceived by the false and vain philosophies of the heathen Greeks around them, many of whom embraced proto-Gnostic and mystical ideas, who in turn affected the local Judaism. If they accept such a philosophy, then the Colossian Believers would likely be persuaded against the Divinity of the Messiah, and the Biblical practices that they should be following as members of God's people. It is possible, also, that many of the Colossian converts were still being influenced by family members, former friends, and/or associates who advocated errant religious beliefs. And most especially and more specifically, they were influenced by some Jewish Believers who practiced things that mirrored their former life in paganism. **The philosophy advocated by the false teachers was not according to Messiah, meaning that it did not have Him at its center or as its focus.**

2:9 The main reason the Colossians were warned against the contemporary philosophy floating around their region—something "not based on Christ" (v. 8, HCSB)—is because "in Him all the fullness of Deity dwells in bodily form." **This is one of the most direct statements in the entire Bible that points to Yeshua the Messiah being Divine, the LORD God in human flesh.** It also points to a local, pagan-Jewish synthesis of errors being the problem confronted in this letter, and not Judaism in general. V. 9 includes a reiteration of what Paul has asserted previously in 1:19 about the Father's fullness dwelling in Yeshua. The philosophy that Paul refutes would have eventually caused people to deny Yeshua as God.

But is v. 9 just a statement of dogma that we are to accept without question, or was it delivered in a specific context that we are to not overlook—with errant philosophies being refuted? How are we to understand *en autō katoikei pan to plērōma tēs Theotētos sōmatikōs* (ἐν αὐτῷ κατοικεῖ πᾶν τὸ πλήρωμα τῆς θεότητος σωματικῶς)? Does this only mean, as the ISR Scriptures (1998) renders it, "in Him dwells all the completeness of the Mightiness bodily"? There is a big difference between the rendering "Deity" (RSV, NASU, NIV, et. al.) or "Godhead" (KJV), and just "Mightiness."[42]

It is not improper to assume that thoughts such as those seen in Psalm 68:16 are in view: "Why do you look with envy, O mountains with *many* peaks, at the mountain which God has desired for His abode? Surely the LORD will dwell *there* forever." The Hebrew verb *yashav* (יָשַׁב) is rendered with *katoikeō* (κατοικέω) in the Septuagint, the same verb appearing in v. 9 for *to plērōma tēs Theotētos* dwelling in Yeshua. Yet while the Psalmist may be concerned with God's presence dwelling on a mountain, or in a Temple, the Apostle Paul's description is about God actually filling up a human body. Moo indicates how "God in his fullness has not taken up residence in and therefore revealed himself in a building but in a body," and as a result this makes "Christ as the focus for God's presence and as the nucleus of God's people."[43]

---

[41] Moo, 191.

[42] To be fair, the ISR Scriptures (2009) has made a slight improvement with, "Because in Him dwells all the completeness of Elohim-ness bodily."

[43] Moo, pp 193-194.

The source text is very specific with what dwells in Yeshua's body, employing the term *theotēs* (θεότης), or "Deity" (sometimes rendered as "Godhead"), actually appearing with the definite article, making *tēs Theotētos* "the Deity." This is different than the more general term *theiotēs* (θειότης), often just meaning "Divinity." *TDNT* summarizes how *theotēs* "occurs in the NT only in Col. 2:9. The one God to whom all deity belongs, has given this fullness of deity to the incarnate Christ."[44] Contrary to this, *theiotēs* only regards how "something is divine, whether a god or imperial majesty,"[45] perhaps only regarding supernatural forces. Paul uses *theiotēs* in Romans 1:20 to describe God's "eternal power and divine nature."[46] So, while it is not at all incorrect for us to speak about Yeshua's "Divinity"—**Yeshua is Divine in a much greater sense than just being a supernatural entity.** He is *the Deity* manifested in a body—and *the Deity* is everything that makes God out to be God! Witherington properly concludes,

"There is a reason Paul uses the term 'godhead' (*theotēs*), rather than just 'god-likeness' (*theiotēs*). He believes that Christ is not just one among many supernatural creatures like the angels. He believes that in Christ and Christ alone dwells the fullness of the godhead. This is most certainly a claim that Christ is himself divine, not merely that the divine presence dwells in Christ."[47]

But why does Paul make a point to describe Yeshua possessing the fullness of the Deity in a body? Is there a purpose to this? *There is.* Consider how John 1:16 attests, "For of His fullness we have all received, and grace upon grace." Similarly, consider how Moses desired to see the Father's glory and see the greatness of His love and compassion, but was unable to completely do so as no sinful mortal at the time could see God in such radiance and live (Exodus 33:18-20). The fullness of this Deity—not just Divinity—was present in Yeshua's body so that God's fullness could interact directly with humanity. John 1:17 further describes how, "the only begotten God who is in the bosom of the Father, He has explained *Him*." The reason for God being made manifest in the Person of Yeshua was that those obstacles which originally separated people like Moses from His complete presence would now be removed.

While Colossians 2:9 includes a direct refutation against any who might hold Yeshua to just be a human Messiah, or a human Messiah empowered by God—it also refutes the idea that Yeshua was just a spirit and did not possess a body. Recall how in 2 John 7 it is stated, "those who do not acknowledge Yeshua the Messiah *as* coming in the flesh. This is the deceiver and the antimessiah." At least by the end of the First Century, more refined Gnostic ideas had advocated that Yeshua the Messiah was not a physical person. Colossians 2:9 lays out a delicate balance of Yeshua being both God and human, which the *Carmen Christi* hymn of Philippians 2:5-11 (cf. Isaiah 45:23) confessed quite early for the ancient Messianic Believers.

Not at all to be overlooked is how not only was God's fullness expressed "bodily" in interacting with people, **but most importantly via specific acts of redemption.** This meaning is captured in the NEB rendering, "For it is in Christ that the complete being of the Godhead dwells embodied." And we should not casually disregard—even if we do hold to a high Christology of Yeshua being God Incarnate—some of the thoughts of those who might hold to a lower Christology. Dunn describes, "the present tense indicates this function of Jesus as ongoing: Christ in his historical embodiment still brings the character of deity fully to focus."[48] This would mean that it is not esnough for us to simply affirm "fullness" present in Yeshua, we have to see the actions of "fullness" present in the teachings and works of Yeshua, and in the proclamation of the gospel today.

How would the use of *plērōma* subvert any proto-Gnostic or errant mystical teachings circulating in Colossae? Donald Guthrie remarks how "It was believed that the Pleroma was so transcendent that it was necessary for a long succession of intermediaries to connect man with God, of which the last in the succession was Christ."[49] Paul asserts that any other intermediaries between the Colossians and God the Father, most

---

Here, it is useful for us to be reminded how *plērōma* (πλήρωμα) can mean, "**sum total, fullness**" (BDAG, 829).

[44] E. Stauffer, "*theótēs*," in *TDNT*, 330.

[45] H. Kleinknecht, "*theíotēs*," in Ibid., 331.

[46] Grk. *autou dunamis kai theiotēs* (αὐτοῦ δύναμις καὶ θειότης).

[47] Witherington, 170.

[48] Dunn, 152.

[49] "Colossians," in D. Guthrie and J.A. Motyer, eds., *The New Bible Commentary Revised* (Grand Rapids: Eerdmans, 1970), 1147.

notably angels (v. 18), were not necessary to appeal to precisely because the *plērōma* "dwells" in Yeshua. The present active indicative verb *katoikei* (κατοικεῖ) presents this as a current action, meaning that God's fullness did not just come onto Yeshua and then leave and go to some other intermediary. Lincoln states, "Since the totality of deity is embodied in Christ, there can be no grounds for a person who confesses Christ to seek God or fullness elsewhere or to think that the way to this divine fullness is through cosmic intermediaries."[50]

Colossians 2:9 is one of the most direct statements in the Apostolic Scriptures supporting the fact that Yeshua is God. Yeshua being a Divine Messiah, and not just a human Messiah, is a fiercely debated issue in sectors of today's Messianic movement. I commend Messianic Jewish teachers like David H. Stern for affirming the Apostles' teaching on Yeshua's Divinity, as too frequently there is a temptation to try to totally synthesize Apostolic theology with current Jewish concepts of the Messiah. Worse yet, there are those who only want to view Jesus as a good Jewish teacher, but nothing more. As Stern comments, "This verse poses a challenge to non-Messianic Jews who attempt to reclaim Yeshua for Judaism by making him over into a great teacher, a wonderful man, or even a prophet, but yet a merely human figure and nothing more."[51] Perhaps we should once again consider some critical Tanach prophecies of the Messiah, and His close identification with the LORD God?

> "For a child will be born to us, a son will be given to us; and the government will rest on His shoulders; and His name will be called Wonderful Counselor, Mighty God [*El gibor*, אֵל גִּבּוֹר], Eternal Father, Prince of Peace" (Isaiah 9:6).

> "'Behold, *the* days are coming,' declares the LORD, 'When I will raise up for David a righteous Branch; and He will reign as king and act wisely and do justice and righteousness in the land. In His days Judah will be saved, and Israel will dwell securely; and this is His name by which He will be called, "The LORD our righteousness [*ADONAI tzidqeinu*, יְהוָה צִדְקֵנוּ]"'" (Jeremiah 23:5-6).

> "But as for you, Bethlehem Ephrathah, *too* little to be among the clans of Judah, from you One will go forth for Me to be ruler in Israel. His goings forth are from long ago, from the days of eternity [*mimei olam*, מִימֵי עוֹלָם]" (Micah 5:2).

2:10 The most specific evidence of Yeshua as Divine Savior for the Colossians is how "you have been filled in him" (ESV), *este en autō peplērōmenoi* (ἐστὲ ἐν αὐτῷ πεπληρωμένοι). Rather than seeking the *plērōma* via external means, access to *to plērōma tēs Theotētos* and to God's power is something that they have already experienced in recognizing Yeshua as Lord (v. 6). They have been "made complete" (NASU) only by Yeshua! 2 Peter 1:4 may include a parallel explanation: "For by these He has granted to us His precious and magnificent promises, so that by them you may become partakers of *the* divine nature, having escaped the corruption that is in the world by lust." The power of God accessible via faith in Yeshua should enable a person to overcome the temptations of sin.

In Yeshua the fullness of the Deity is present in bodily form: all of the aspects of God, from His great supernatural power to His compassion. Believers do not have the fullness of the Deity present in their bodies like Yeshua, the Son, but instead because of their being redeemed in Him, they can have access to such fullness and power. As Robert M. Bowman and J. Ed Komoszewski explain, "because God's fullness is found in Christ personally, those who are united to Christ (who are 'in him') have the fullness of God's power and love working in their lives."[52] This is a fullness that only comes to regenerated human beings because of the relationship that we have with the Lord Yeshua.

Yeshua's status as the Deity made manifest in a human body is attendant with great power over all, as "the head of all rule and authority" (RSV), including whatever *other* intermediaries the Colossians may have been tempted to try to appeal to. **This is not a claim made of any human.** Viewing the term *kephalē* (κεφαλή) as

---

[50] Lincoln, in *NIB*, 11:623.
[51] Stern, 607.
[52] Bowman and Komoszewski, 77.

akin to "source," makes Yeshua the very origin of all rule and authority. Lincoln aptly describes, "Because of their link with the fullness of deity through Christ, by definition there can be nothing lacking about their relation with God, no deficiency that needs to be filled by further teachings and practices offered by the philosophy."[53]

11 and in Him you were also circumcised with a circumcision made without hands, in the removal of the body of the flesh by the circumcision of Messiah; 12 having been buried with Him in baptism, in which you were also raised up with Him through faith in the working of God, who raised Him from the dead.

2:11 Paul's remarks in vs. 11-12 have definite connections with what he has already taught in Romans 6:1-14, about born again Believers being made dead to sin, yet being made alive via the resurrection power of Yeshua. Paul asserts, "in Him you were also circumcised with a circumcision made without hands, in the removal of the body of the flesh by the circumcision of Messiah." Here, the circumcision that is appealed to is a "spiritual circumcision" (NRSV) that is to transform men and women by dealing with the condemning consequences of their sinful nature, and bringing them into the renewed life of God. There are important precedents to Paul saying this seen in the Tanach, each of which relates to God admonishing the Ancient Israelites to circumcise their hearts, or the promise that He will by His power give them a circumcised heart:

"So circumcise your heart, and stiffen your neck no longer" (Deuteronomy 10:16).

"Moreover the LORD your God will circumcise your heart and the heart of your descendants, to love the LORD your God with all your heart and with all your soul, so that you may live" (Deuteronomy 30:6).

"Circumcise yourselves to the LORD and remove the foreskins of your heart, men of Judah and inhabitants of Jerusalem, or else My wrath will go forth like fire and burn with none to quench it, because of the evil of your deeds" (Jeremiah 4:4).

In the Tanach, an uncircumcised heart is used to describe a sinful person who has erected some kind of barrier, which separates one from God. By circumcising the heart, such a barrier will be removed, and one will be sensitive to His wishes and instruction. Members of the Qumran community were to "circumcise the foreskin of this [sinful] nature, this stiff neck, and so establish a foundation of truth for Israel" (1QS 5.5).[54] Similarly, a sinner is depicted as one who "had not circumcised his heart's foreskin, and he lived extravagantly to bring to naught those who had but little" (1QpHab 11.13).[55]

How difficult is it for a person to "circumcise" his or her heart? A *mohel* can certainly circumcise a male child (or even adult), but that is only a physical operation. People can *try* to circumcise their hearts, meaning that they can *try* to remove spiritual and emotional barriers formed between themselves and God, which have made one callous to sin. But only the Lord Himself can accomplish the kind of permanent circumcision seen here. To describe the "circumcision made without hands," Paul uses the term *acheiropoiētos* (ἀχειροποίητος), clearly depicting a Divine action. Yeshua Himself is the Temple "made without hands" (Mark 14:58). Contrary to this, *cheiropoiētos* (χειροποίητος), "with hands," is seen in the Greek Septuagint to denote the making of idols (Leviticus 26:1, 30; Isaiah 2:18) and false images (Isaiah 21:9). If we think that we are the only ones who can provide ourselves with the permanent heart circumcision God desires, then is such an action just as vain as an idolater fashioning an image?

How does this appeal to circumcision relate to the issues going on in Colossae? In his paralleling letter, the Apostle Paul criticizes some Jewish pride in the rite of circumcision, which in the First Century often kept out many non-Jewish God-fearers from wanting to become full members of the community of Israel (Ephesians 2:11), something which he says is now primarily determinant on Yeshua's atoning sacrifice

---

[53] Lincoln, in *NIB*, 11:623.
[54] Wise, Abegg, and Cook, 132.
[55] Ibid., 122.

(Ephesians 2:13). Likewise, Paul admonished the Jewish Believers in Rome to remember, "But he is a Jew who is one inwardly; and circumcision is that which is of the heart, by the Spirit" (Romans 2:29a). Could there have been some inclusion debates present within the assembly at Colossae, requiring Paul to target circumcision of the heart as more important than physical circumcision, or circumcision as the ritual of a Jewish proselyte?

In the view of Dunn, "Such language cannot be explained on the assumption that the rite of circumcision had been abstracted from Judaism and thrown as a separate item into some proto-Gnostic, syncretistic melting pot of ideas and rites."[56] Yet, even while considering the issue in Colossae as non-Jewish Believers lured into the Synagogue, he must go on and observe, "At the same time the contrast with Galatians at this point cannot be ignored. Here there is no polemic against circumcision as such...We cannot deduce, therefore, a form of vigorous Jewish or Christian-Jewish proselytizing in Colossae."[57] So, it is his conclusion that "in view of the lightness of the polemic...all that may be implied or envisaged here is some debate with the Jews in Colossae...on the spiritual significance of circumcision."[58]

How do we weigh these opinions into our examination of v. 11? The issue here is really not whether physical circumcision is now unimportant. The issue is **the great significance of heart circumcision.** There is no polemic at all seen in Colossians against circumcision as a medical procedure, and Dunn is correct in recognizing that making proselytes to Judaism is not an issue seen. Rather, as Lincoln describes, "the use of the metaphor of circumcision enables the writer to deal once more with the philosophy's view of what has to be done with humans' body of flesh."[59] The circumcision made without hands is *tē peritomē tou Christou* (τῇ περιτομῇ τοῦ Χριστοῦ), "the circumcision of Messiah." This is a circumcision offered by the Messiah, in union with Him and the transforming work of the gospel. This is a transposition of the heart from one of stone to one of flesh (Ezekiel 36:26). As Paul has previously explained it:

"Therefore we have been buried with Him through baptism into death, so that as Messiah was raised from the dead through the glory of the Father, so we too might walk in newness of life" (Romans 6:4).

"[F]or we are the *true* circumcision, who worship in the Spirit of God and glory in Messiah Yeshua and put no confidence in the flesh" (Philippians 3:3).

About as far as we can go in pushing the circumcision motif of v. 11 is simply recognizing that circumcision of the heart is accomplished only by the salvation available in Yeshua. Moo concurs, "Paul takes this concept, claiming that it is the circumcision of the heart, performed by the Spirit—not physical circumcision as such—that marks a person as belonging to the people of God."[60] But, it is not at all impossible that physical circumcision could have been an external ritual, rigidly imposed by the false teachers of Colossae, to seek greater spirituality in order to enter into their ethereal trances. If circumcision were at all being misused by the false teachers, as is seen elsewhere in the Pauline letters (Galatians 6:16; Philippians 3:2), then Paul is telling the Colossians that it is not at all necessary for them to partake of what they were offering, as Yeshua Himself had already principally brought what they needed.

2:12 What is the result of the Colossians receiving the circumcision of Messiah? "[Y]ou were buried with him in baptism, in which you were also raised with him through faith in the working of God, who raised him from the dead" (RSV). The ritual of water immersion, which the new Believers would undertake, is their identification in not only the death of Yeshua, but also His resurrection. The same power that resurrected Yeshua, is the same power that regenerates Believers and circumcises their hearts! Paul's emphasis to the Colossians is that they have been raised with Messiah into newness (3:1), and so their lifestyle and behavior should follow suit with this reality. Their identity and focus is to be centered around His atoning sacrifice,

---

[56] Dunn, pp 156-157.
[57] Ibid., 157.
[58] Ibid.
[59] Lincoln, in *NIB*, 11:623.
[60] Moo, 197.

death, resurrection, and all the things He has accomplished for them! *The resurrection power should enable them to overcome ungodliness.* Moo offers an excellent explanation:

"...Paul is deploying his typical redemptive-historical theology to counter the false teaching in Colossae, false teaching that appeared above all to be insisting on adherence to ascetic-oriented rules as a means of conquering the fleshly impulse, appeasing the hostile powers, and thereby securing final forgiveness for sins. All these, Paul insists, are provided for the believer 'in Christ.'"[61]

13 When you were dead in your transgressions and the uncircumcision of your flesh, He made you alive together with Him, having forgiven us all our transgressions, 14 having canceled out the certificate of debt consisting of decrees against us, which was hostile to us; and He has taken it out of the way, having nailed it to the cross. 15 When He had disarmed the rulers and authorities, He made a public display of them, having triumphed over them through Him.

2:13 Continuing his words about how the power of Yeshua has changed their lives, Paul tells the Colossians, "When you were dead in your transgressions and the uncircumcision of your flesh, He made you alive together with Him, having forgiven us all our transgressions." He actually uses the more anatomically specific, and to us today a bit more offending, *akrobustia* (ἀκροβυστία) or "foreskin."

The Tanach depiction of death is one that goes far beyond just physical death, as a person's life in the realm of death is shown to be one dominated by and marked by sin (i.e., Psalm 13:1-3; 30:3; 31:12; 88:3-6). In the Pseudepigraphal *Joseph and Aseneth*, when Aseneth is presented to Joseph as his bride, it is said "they were amazed at her beauty and rejoiced and gave glory to God who gives life to the dead" (20:7),[62] as she would be joined to him. Paul considers the realm of death to be something that has affected all of humanity, a status common to both Jews and non-Jews alike (Romans 1:18-3:20). In his paralleling letter, Paul reminds his non-Jewish readers that prior to knowing Messiah Yeshua they were separated from membership in Israel (Ephesians 2:12), engulfed by an existence dominated by death and sin.

Yeshua Himself, in His parable of the Prodigal Son, spoke of how "this son of mine was dead and has come to life again; he was lost and has been found" (Luke 15:24). The older brother, who had not left for the waycountry and a life of sin, is told, "this brother of yours was dead and *has begun* to live" (Luke 15:32). Even in Yeshua's teachings we see confirmation that "death" is something multifaceted. For the Colossians, *tē akrobustia tēs sarkos humōn* (τῇ ἀκροβυστίᾳ τῆς σαρκὸς ὑμῶν), paraphrased by the CJB as "your 'foreskin,' your old nature," represented their pre-salvation state. The same power that resurrected Messiah Yeshua, has now forgiven them and has given them all circumcised hearts and minds. The Colossians have been brought into a realm of life and restored communion with God.

2:14 Making the Colossian Believers alive—bringing them to redemption via the work of His Son—God has done something very important on their behalf. As the ESV renders v. 14, He "cancel[ed] the record of debt that stood against us with its legal demands. This he set aside, nailing it to the cross." What is this "certificate of debt," and what are the "decrees against us, which were hostile to us" (NASU)? All readers of Paul's letter can agree that v. 14 represents a damning indictment against people that needed to be dealt with via the sacrifice of Yeshua on the cross. But as we Messianics are quite abundantly aware, it is Colossians 2:14 that is commonly used to assert that "the Law of Moses has been nailed to the cross." However, with the Greek *nomos* (νομός) or "law" noticeably absent from this verse, what is Paul really communicating? Furthermore, how do we stay away from non-literal or extrapolated renderings of *to kath' hēmōn cheirographon tois dogmasin* (τὸ καθ' ἡμῶν χειρόγραφον τοῖς δόγμασιν)? This is literally rendered as "the handwriting in the ordinances that is against us" (YLT).

There are three main views of what "the certificate of debt" represents, which one is likely to encounter in studying Colossians:

---

[61] Ibid., 201.

[62] C. Burchard, trans., "Joseph and Aseneth," in James H. Charlesworth, ed., *The Old Testament Pseudepigrapha*, Vol 2 (New York: Doubleday, 1985), 234.

1. The debt or penalties incurred from human sin toward God, condemning people without a permanent sacrifice
2. Some kind of a book or record in Heaven that kept a roll of condemned people
3. The Law of Moses, which if not kept perfectly, condemns all people who break it

Traditional views of Colossians 2:14 dating back to the Protestant Reformation often associated the certificate of debt as either the record of human sin, or the guilt of human sin incurred before God.[63] Another common view of Colossians 2:14, similar to this, sees this certificate of debt as the pronouncement of condemnation that hung over Yeshua as He was dying on the cross (Matthew 27:37; Mark 15:26; Luke 23:38; John 19:19). Both would fit within the scope of what is seen in the lexical definition of *cheirographon* (χειρόγραφον): "**a hand-written document, specif. a certificate of indebtedness,** *account, record of* debts" (*BDAG*).[64]

One suggestion among some interpreters is that the "certificate of debt" is somehow similar to a Jewish apocalyptic view in which a book recording all of one's evil deeds was to be remitted. The existence of this book is derived principally from passages seen in the Tanach. Moses appeals to God after the Israelites worshiped the golden calf, "But now, if You will, forgive their sin—and if not, please blot me out from Your book which You have written!" and is told by the LORD, "Whoever has sinned against Me, I will blot him out of My book" (Exodus 32:32, 33). The Psalmist indicates how sinners should "be blotted out of the book of life and may they not be recorded with the righteous" (Psalm 69:28). And Daniel prophesies how in the end, "everyone who is found written in the book, will be rescued" (Daniel 12:1). Furthermore in the Book of Revelation, Yeshua promises those in Sardis, "He who overcomes will thus be clothed in white garments; and I will not erase his name from the book of life" (Revelation 3:5). So, the "certificate of debt" includes a record of human sin that has now been erased or blotted out (Grk. *exaleiphō*, ἐξαλείφω)[65] by the sacrifice of Yeshua at Golgotha (Calvary).

The most common view of the "certificate of debt" that one will find today among lay readers of Colossians is that it represents the Law of Moses nailed to the cross of Yeshua. It proposes that the Torah as *cheirographon* was a note of indebtedness that required cancellation. Sometimes, scholars who argue for this view provide external evidence from Jewish literature to support this proposal. *Testament of Job* 11:9-12 from the Pseudepigrapha is one reference to be considered:

"Sometimes they would succeed in business and give to the poor. But at other times, they would be robbed. And they would come and entreat me saying, 'We beg you, be patient with us. Let us find how we might be able to repay you.' Without delay, I would bring before them the note and *read it* granting cancellation *as the crowning feature* and saying, 'Since I trusted you for the benefit of the poor, *I will take nothing back from you.*' Nor would I take anything from my debtor."[66]

Today's Messianic Believers are of the conviction that God's Torah is still relevant Instruction for His people. While many contemporary Christians have concluded that Colossians 2:14 relates to the Law of Moses being nailed to the cross, it is important for us to survey a wide array of interpreters' opinions. Many are not, in fact, convinced that the Law in its totality was nailed to the cross. The chart below has summarized some of the various views present:

---

[63] For one example, see John Wesley, *Explanatory Notes Upon the New Testament*, reprint (Peterborough, UK: Epworth Press, 2000), 747 says: "This was not properly our sins themselves (they were the debt), but their guilt and cry before God."

Many Protestant churches today hold services on Good Friday where people can write their sins or transgressions on small pieces of paper, and then actually nail them to a cross in the sanctuary, representative of how the record of human sin has been taken care of by Jesus' sacrifice. This concurs with Colossians 2:14 representing the condemnation upon human sin.

[64] *BDAG*, 1083.

[65] In a classical context, the verb *exaleiphō* means "*to wipe out, obliterate,*" or "metaph., like Lat. delere, *to wipe out, destroy utterly*" (*LS*, 269).

[66] R.P. Spittler, trans., "Testament of Job," in *The Old Testament Pseudepigrapha*, Vol 1, 844.

COLOSSIANS 2:14 AND VIEWS OF THE TORAH OF MOSES	
FAVORABLE, OR AT LEAST NEUTRAL, TOWARD THE TORAH OF MOSES	NEGATIVE TOWARD THE TORAH OF MOSES
Paul dwells on God's method of forgiveness. He uses the metaphor of a *bond*...a 'statement of indebtedness' which had to be signed by the debtor as an acknowledgment of his debt. The debt was impossible to pay. Moreover it was backed by *legal demands*, since every trespass is a violation of the law of God....Paul imagines God taking the statement of debts and nailing it to the cross of Christ.[67] Donald Guthrie	Legalism is wrong because believers are dead to the Law in Christ. He fulfilled its demands in His life and by His death, and Christians are *in* Him.[68] Norman Geisler
The image in 2:14 is of a legal document which lists the charges against us: its cancellation is emphasized—it has been erased, set aside, and nailed to Christ's cross. The last phrase suggests that Paul might be thinking of the accusation nailed to the cross (Mark 15:26 and pars.). With Christ's death and resurrection, the power of the charges against us has been nullified (cf. Gal 3:13-14).[69] Morna D. Hooker	The Jews had contracted to obey the law, and in their case the penalty for breach of this contract meant death (Deut 27:14-26; 30:15-20). Paul assumes that the Gentiles were committed, through their consciences, to a similar obligation, to the moral law in as much as they understood it (cf. Rom 2:14, 15). Since the obligation had not been discharged by either group the "bond" remained against us (καθ' ἡμῶν).[70] Peter T. O'Brien
The metaphor is probably adapted to the earlier Jewish idea of a heavenly book of the living...as developed in apocalyptic circles into that of books whereas deeds of good and evil were recorded with a view to the final judgment...This is most obviously the background of thought here, with καθ' ἡμῶν ("against us") confirming that the document in question was one of condemnation, that is, presumably the record of their "transgressions"....[W]e should note that it is not the law which is thought of as thus	It would be in keeping with the ironic tone we find at various points in this chapter that Paul should refer to the Mosaic Law as a mere IOU note, or perhaps as a book which does nothing but keep a tally of one's sins....The Mosaic Torah did not, we should note, stand over against Jews and Gentiles...In Paul's view, it shut *up* the Jews under sin and shut out the Gentiles from the hope and promise of membership in God's people.[72] N.T. Wright

---

[67] Guthrie, in *NBCR*, 1147.

[68] Geisler, in *BKCNT*, 678.

[69] Hooker, in *ECB*, 1408.

Galatians 3:13 speaks how "Messiah redeemed us from the curse of the Law." This is not to be construed to as to mean that having to obey the Torah is actually some kind of curse. Rather, the curse of the Law is the condemnation decreed upon those who violate it.

[70] O'Brien, *Colossians-Philemon*, 125.

destroyed, but rather its particular condemnation (χειρόγραφον) of transgressions, absorbed in the sacrificial death of the Christ (cf. Rom. 8:3).[71]
James D.G. Dunn

In causing him to be nailed to the cross, God (the subject of the verb) has provided for the full cancellation of the debt of obedience that we had incurred. Christ took upon himself the penalty that we were under because of our disobedience, and his death fully satisfied God's necessary demand for due punishment of that disobedience.[74]
Douglas J. Moo

V. 14 says Christ's death wiped out the IOU (a record of debts owed written by the hand of the debtor; cf. Phlm 19; *Testament of Job* 11.11) which stood against believers. While *cheirograph* is used of a receipt in Tob[it] 5.3 and 9.5, it is not found elsewhere in the NT. Here it seems to be a reference to the heavenly book of deeds in which a record of one's wrongdoings is kept. In fact in *Apocalypse of Zephaniah* 3.6-9; 7.1-8 the same word is used for that book (cf. *Apocalypse of Paul* 17; Rev. 5.1-5; 20.12).[75]   Ben Witherington III

To sum up, the great principle asserted in v.14 is the destruction of the law in and by the cross of Christ. The law, however, is viewed in a certain character (i.e., as a bond of indebtedness or as an instrument of condemnation, something that "stood opposed to us").[73]
Curtis Vaughan

In reviewing the above opinions, it may surprise you to see that some of the theologians that we would think to be very anti-Torah in their approach to v. 14, are actually those who rightfully recognize that **the principle issue is God dealing with human sin.** Disturbing to me, those who would classify as being a bit more conservative in their theology, are the ones who immediately jump into claiming that the Torah is precisely what was nailed to the cross. And, one of the most conservative of all the voices, Curtis Vaughan, has a statement that is especially noted: "the great principle asserted in v.14 is the destruction of the law in and by the cross of Christ."[76] This is most worrisome because it goes against Yeshua's own word, "Do not think that I came to destroy the Law or the Prophets" (Matthew 5:17, NKJV).[77]

Also to be noted is that while Witherington correctly acknowledges how the issue in v. 14 is human wrongdoings—and in this way he can be considered to be "neutral" toward the Torah—he later argues that the debt canceled is not a record of sins, but rather is actually the agreement to follow (or even obey?) God's commandments. Rather than concluding that the "certificate of debt" composes the penalties incurred from

---

[71] Dunn, pp 164, 165, 166.
[72] Wright, pp 112, 113.
[73] Vaughan, in *EXP*, 11:202.
[74] Moo, pp 211-212.
[75] Witherington, 158.
[76] Vaughan, in *EXP*, 11:202.
[77] The quote here from the NKJV is poignant, as Vaughan served on its New Testament translation committee. For a summary, consult the Bible Researcher article on the New King James version, available online at <http://www.bible-researcher.com/nkjv.html>.

disobeying God, his conclusion is "that believers need not keep paying a debt to those sorts of records of sin or indebtedness or to such laws and rules that say they still owe something."[78] So, looking at this from one angle, the righteous principles of the Ten Commandments would just be viewed as parts of a bill to be paid, and obedience to them is no longer required now that the Messiah has been crucified. **Has this approach helped a modern Christendom with all of the moral and ethical controversies it faces?** Note how when people are told that they no longer have to be concerned with keeping any of God's commandments, they often never take the time to study or examine what they have to say.

Lincoln's view also cannot go without mentioning. In his estimation, "to argue that what is in view is not the law per se but only the law in its condemnatory function is to have read too fine a distinction into the verse." This he has to say to recognize that there have been many throughout Christian history considering Colossians 2:14 to only speak of condemnation upon sinners, a debt that has been incurred. Perhaps this was caused by human disobedience to the Torah, but the Torah itself as intended by God was not the cause (i.e., Deuteronomy 4:1; 5:33; 8:1; et. al.). In contrast to this, Lincoln concludes, "The document itself is said to be opposed to humanity and, when one brings into play the ascetic regulations mentioned later, the clear implication is that it is condemnatory of humans because of their body of flesh."[79] But why would the Torah be opposed to people if God gave it for the benefit of people? It is only opposed to people when they violate it—not when they follow it! So, Lincoln is correct when claiming that the Torah condemns people because of their uncircumcised body of flesh (v. 11), or their sin nature, but is incorrect when claiming that the Torah as a whole was just given to condemn. And, the promise of the New Covenant is God writing the Torah onto the hearts of His people (Jeremiah 31:31-34; Ezekiel 36:16-36) needs to be seriously considered here.

Moo, interestingly enough, points out that the view of "certificate of debt" being the Torah in totality, has some problems. He says "that the word [*cheirographon*] may refer to the Mosaic law, viewed by Paul as a record of human obligation that has not been met...fits a bit awkwardly with the basic sense of the word, since, of course, an IOU is written not by the one to whom the obligation is due (God, the author of the law), but by the one who is in debt (human beings)."[80] The Lord did not give His people the Torah as a record of what they had done, but rather what they should do to live properly: "All these blessings will come upon you and overtake you if you obey the LORD your God" (Deuteronomy 28:2). Severe violation of His Instruction incurred penalties, and so those penalties—which were backed up by certain stipulations that required capital punishment—needed to be dealt with.

The Apostle Paul asserts that this "certificate of debt" was *cheirographon tois dogmasin*. This is invariably rendered as "the bond which stood against us with its legal demands" (RSV), "the record that stood against us with its legal demands" (NRSV), or "the charge of our legal indebtedness" (TNIV). Dunn notes the crucial clause here to be the "unarticulated dative, τοῖς δόγμασιν," which "leaves the precise relationship obscure."[81] Many interpreters of v. 14 immediately connect *dogmasin* to its parallel usage in Ephesians 2:15,[82] where by Yeshua's sacrifice He has abolished *ton nomon tōn entolōn en dogmasin* (τὸν νόμον τῶν ἐντολῶν ἐν δόγμασιν). They incorrectly assume this to be the termination of the Mosaic Torah, which supposedly divided Jews and non-Jews from each other and had to be removed, and similarly in v. 14 conclude that the "certificate of debt" was backed up by the Torah and that all of the Torah was nailed to the cross.[83]

The challenge, with this interpretation, is recognizing that in Ephesians 2:15 *dogma* (δόγμα) likely pertains to "**a formal statement concerning rules or regulations that are to be observed**" (BDAG), or an opinion,[84] meaning man-made ordinances that were responsible for erecting the dividing wall seen in the Jerusalem Temple (Josephus *Antiquities* 15.417; *Jewish War* 5.194). Anyone who was not a Jew or a proselyte was

---

[78] Witherington, 158.

[79] Lincoln, in *NIB*, 11:625.

[80] Moo, pp 209-210.

[81] Dunn, 165.

[82] In Lincoln's view, though, "The use of the later term in Eph 2:15...cannot be determinative for this earlier usage in Colossians" (in *NIB*, 11:625).

[83] Cf. Wright, 114.

[84] *BDAG*, 254; further stated as "something that is taught as an established tenet or statement of belief, *doctrine, dogma.*"

prohibited from entering the inner court of the sanctuary on threat of death. Paul uses this analogy to describe how via His sacrifice, Yeshua has nullified "the *religious* Law of commandments in dogmas" (my translation), anything that would pass itself off as "Torah" or "commandments," and be inappropriately used—just as the dividing wall—to keep others unnecessarily separated from God's people. (This would notably include things like 1QS 1.9-11, where the Qumran community actually said it was justified to hate outsiders.)[85] So, if the *dogma* seen in Ephesians 2:15 is what caused people in the Temple complex to be separated out on threat of death, are we at all unjustified to conclude that the *dogma* referred to in v. 14 are those things which would similarly require death? **Could earlier generations of Christians indeed be right in concluding that the condemnation and/or record of sin is the whole issue of what was nailed to the cross in Colossians 2:14?**

The two classical definitions of *dogma* we have to consider are "*that which seems to one, an opinion, dogma,*" and "*a public decree, ordinance*" (LS).[86] It is not inappropriate for us to consider how in Colossians 2:14, Paul first could have used *dogma* (as *public decree, ordinance*) to describe the condemning aspects of the Torah that have been erased via the shed blood of the Lord. Later in composing Ephesians, *dogma* (as *opinion*) could have been used to describe condemning injunctions passing themselves off as Torah, keeping people separated from God's purpose, but were by no means Biblical law.[87] The *dogma* that separated the nations in the Temple complex carried with it the threat of death, just as the *dogma* that composed the "certificate of debt" are what ultimately nailed Yeshua to the cross on our behalf. In approaching *dogma* this way—with *dogma* representing something that incurs execution—we eliminate any significant interpretational problems that exist between Yeshua's claim about His work of fulfilling, not abolishing the Torah (Matthew 5:17-19). We can appropriately uphold the foundational principle of how in nailing the Torah's condemnation to the cross of Yeshua, "I [the Lord], even I, am the one who wipes out your transgressions for My own sake, and I will not remember your sins" (Isaiah 43:25).

Dunn actually holds to *dogmasin* being *halachic* rulings that are later condemned in vs. 16, 21-22. He believes this to be valid because the verb rendered "submit[ting]...to decrees," is *dogmatizō* (δογματίζω).[88] Here, we can see how a record of human sin was nailed to the cross of Yeshua, whereas the Colossian errorists were being "dogmatized." They were in error because they did not have to physically abase themselves, as Yeshua had already undergone the most extreme pain imaginable in death.

Dispensationalists, the one group of conservative Christians that Messianics will probably encounter or have to interact with most frequently, must especially argue that the Mosaic Law was nailed to the cross (as opposed to just the record or condemnation of sin). According to them, the Age of Law is now over, and the Age of Grace/Church Age has been inaugurated. When Yeshua said "it is finished" in John 19:30, the Torah came to an end—as opposed to complete reconciliation being made available between God and humanity.[89]

What does the work of Yeshua as depicted in Colossians 2:14, with *something* nailed to the cross, describe for us? Is it the Torah of Moses in its entirety? Or, is it the condemnation upon sinners that He has taken away for us, receiving upon Himself the death that is required of us all? Please consider how of all animal sacrifices specified in the Torah, there is no sacrifice available for intentional sins. Roger Bullard accurately summarizes how, "By forgiving our sins...God erased the record of those sins. What happened on the cross...abolished it and freed us from the grasp of the angelic beings"[90] (v. 18). **The record of sin has been abolished! For this we should all rise in great praise!** With the record of sin nailed to Yeshua's cross and the penalties now remitted, all people have to do is acknowledge this, confessing their sins, and asking the Lord

---

[85] Consult the author's commentary *Ephesians for the Practical Messianic* for a further description.

[86] *LS*, 207.

[87] As evidence of how *dogma* is not always used in reference to Biblical law itself, and can have some wider implications, note how in the Apocrypha an apostate Jew is said to leave all of *tōn patriōn dogmatōn* (τῶν πατρίων δογμάτων) or "the ancestral traditions" (3 Maccabees 1:3). Similarly, a brother who is martyred testifies to have been raised on *dogmasin* or various "teachings" (4 Maccabees 10:2).

[88] Dunn, 165.

[89] Note how the Greek *tetelestai* (τετέλεσται) can be translated as "It is accomplished!" (CJB), or perhaps even "It has been brought to the goal!" (my translation).

[90] Roger Bullard, "The Letter of Paul to the Colossians," in Walter J. Harrelson, ed., et. al., *New Interpreter's Study Bible*, NRSV (Nashville: Abingdon, 2003), 2111.

for forgiveness and reconciliation. The Torah has not been abolished, but the capital penalties that stand over those who break it (making unredeemed sinners "under the Law") have now been paid in full.

I do not disagree with Vaughan when he comments, "The bond...has been removed permanently, that is, removed so that its claims against us can never again alienate us from God."[91] Sadly, though, Vaughan has to define the bond as "the Mosaic law,"[92] and not simply as the condemnation decreed upon sinners as defined by the Law.

The significance of Yeshua suffering and dying is to highlight to the Colossians, in Lincoln's words, that they do not need to feel "a sense of guilt" where "some are undergoing rigorous ascetic requirements."[93] Where various people in Colossae may think that they need to suffer more in order to access the Heavenly realm, by His sacrifice Yeshua has removed those things which have condemned human sin. Yeshua has already suffered the required physical pain that they are trying to inflict upon themselves, and Believers need not seek such pain. As is seen throughout Paul's own ministry experiences, suffering and persecution *will just come* as one accomplishes God's work—and no one has to seek it!

It is perfectly legitimate to recognize how the "certificate of debt" that has been paid by Yeshua's sacrifice, **is the condemnation and record of human sin.** The power of this condemnation was found in various "decrees against us," the stated death penalties for high crimes as specified in the Torah. It is not at all incorrect to recognize that *by His death and shed blood*, our relationship to the Torah has certainly been changed, but that does not mean that the Torah is to be thrown by the wayside and never studied or meditated upon (Psalm 119:15, 27). The Torah remains relevant instruction that is to be upheld and taught as a standard of God's righteousness and holiness (Romans 3:31), but the problem of a permanent sacrifice for sin has now been taken care of (Hebrews 10:11-12).

With this in mind, though, I have still encountered people in today's Messianic movement who would argue for a kind of theonomy.[94] They think that the death penalty decreed upon sinners for various crimes in the Torah should still be enacted—*even with* Yeshua's sacrifice permanently atoning for the human sin problem. This would mean, at least in principle, that if one were to discover adulterers or homosexuals in the assembly, they should be tried and executed. This does make many, most especially myself, **feel very uncomfortable.** In 1 Corinthians 5, rather than demanding that the sexually immoral be executed for their sins, the Apostle Paul rules that they be excommunicated from the assembly. This is not because there was no proper Jewish court for them to be condemned by, but as he states it, their sin will get the better of them and they will die as a consequence if they fail to repent (1 Corinthians 5:5). Paul knew the gravity of the cross, and would never promote stoning people as a method of handling sins after the resurrection—since he himself was responsible for errantly stoning or overseeing the deaths of many Jewish Believers (Acts 7:58; Galatians 1:13; 1 Corinthians 15:9) prior to encountering the Lord on the Damascus Road!

History is replete with post-crucifixion examples of where various societies and religious movements have tried to, albeit unsuccessfully, enact capital punishment for every high crime specified in the Torah. There is perhaps no worse example of this then the complicated record of the English Reformation, where Catholic and Protestant monarchs alike would try those of the other side as heretics, believing them to be in violation of God's Law, and burning many at the stake. About the only significant exception for executing a

---

[91] Vaughan, in *EXP*, 11:201.

[92] Ibid.

[93] Lincoln, in *NIB*, 11:629.

[94] D. Thomas Lancaster indicates, "the strict measures of Torah justice—stoning and the like—are not applicable unless one is in the land of Israel under the authority of a duly ordained Torah court of law like the Sanhedrin." While he admits that a Sanhedrin court in Israel would be able to stone someone, he thankfully says, "As much as we might sometimes like to stone someone, the Torah forbids us from vigilante justice of that sort" (*Restoration: Returning the Torah of God to the Disciples of Jesus* [Littleton, CO: First Fruits of Zion, 2005], 76), recognizing how only authorized people could do this. But in holding to this opinion, he does overlook the great significance of Yeshua's sacrifice for the covering of such sin and how these penalties have now largely been remitted. (Furthermore, even with the possibility of a Sanhedrin court reestablished in Israel sometime in the future, it seems unlikely that the Israeli government would give up control of the criminal justice system.)

Perhaps the only exception, this side of Yeshua's resurrection, would be the death penalty for murder as a Creation ordinance (cf. Genesis 9:5-6)—and even this should be used quite *infrequently*.

criminal would be for murder, the death penalty for murderers being a Creation ordinance (cf. Genesis 9:6). **And even that has to be done very, very carefully.**[95]

Even with the Torah's death penalty upon sinners now remitted via the sacrifice of Yeshua, **this does not at all mean that it is unimportant to know those sins in the Torah that prescribe the death penalty.** While all of our collective human sin is what nailed the Lord to the cross, it is those very specific sins that carry capital punishment which ultimately condemned Him. When we review the weekly Torah portions and examine those regulations, which if violated caused ancient persons to be stoned or hanged until dead, we should stop for a moment and recognize that the Messiah came so that those penalties would not need to be enacted any more (cf. Romans 10:4, Grk.). *They have all been wiped away by His suffering for us.* With final redemption now available, we need to remember how "the kindness of God leads you to repentance" (Romans 2:4). If we should ever suffer for Him, it should only come as we serve Him and are possibly persecuted—not that we have to suffer as He did to attain eternal life.

2:15 In His work for the Colossians, Yeshua has accomplished something—by removing the condemnatory record of sin—that the spiritual forces the false teachers were appealing to could not do. Paul writes, "He disarmed the principalities and powers and made a public example of them, triumphing over them in him" (RSV). This regards any intermediary forces, such as the angels, that the Colossians were being tempted to either worship or entreat. They were stripped of any authority they might have claimed over people by the Father resurrecting His Son, the Messiah later ascending to His right hand. **Yeshua stands as superior over them.** As Paul says in his paralleling letter,

"He brought [this] about in Messiah, when He raised Him from the dead and seated Him at His right hand in the heavenly *places*, far above all rule and authority and power and dominion, and every name that is named, not only in this age but also in the one to come" (Ephesians 1:20-21; cf. Romans 1:3-4; 1 Peter 3:19-22).

What role does understanding Yeshua's superiority over spiritual beings, such as the different orders of angels and demons, play in examining the rest of Paul's warning to his audience? According to Geisler, "believers are delivered from these evil powers which inspire legalistic rules about foods and festivals,"[96] referring to vs. 16-17. Even though some kind of Gnosticism is the overarching issue, Geisler still must insist that the only correct interpretation is that the Lord's appointed times have been abolished.[97] Contrary to this, though, one can certainly see how the appointed times of the Torah may have played a role in the false philosophy—*being hijacked from their original purposes*—and how the Colossians could have easily forgotten that by His triumph "to each one of us grace was given according to the measure of Messiah's gift" (Ephesians 4:8), the sufficient power to overcome sinful temptations and to succeed in God's mission for their lives.

16 Therefore no one is to act as your judge in regard to food or drink or in respect to a festival or a new moon or a Sabbath day—17 things which are a *mere* shadow of what is to come; but the substance belongs to Messiah.

2:16 Every Messianic Believer (Jewish or not) at one point in his or her faith experience has been quoted Colossians 2:16-17, often by a well-meaning Christian friend or family member who wonders why we attend worship services on Saturday (*Shabbat*), remember special times of year like Passover, or abstain from pork and shellfish. Too many of our Christian brethren, by us simply doing these things and not necessarily saying anything about them, think that we are judging them for not being similarly convicted. So, they quote

---

[95] For a further discussion, consult Walter C. Kaiser's remarks in Wayne G. Strickland, ed., *Five Views on Law and Gospel* (Grand Rapids: Zondervan, 1996), pp 155-156.

[96] Geisler, in *BKCNT*, 678.

[97] As a dispensationalist, he must further denounce those "who would bring Christians under the bondage of the Law [and] make artificial distinctions between the 'ceremonial' and 'moral' law," claiming "This Colossian passage explicitly condemns those who command Sabbath obedience" (Ibid.). He says this, even though the issue in Colossians is some kind of Gnosticism and errant human philosophy, and not Sabbitarianism.

Colossians 2:16-17 and do not accept this "judgment."[98] Almost every time, Colossians 2:16-17 is taken out of context from the larger message seen in the surrounding verses and the actual issues Paul is having to address in his letter.

What has the Apostle Paul just said before referring to things like eating, drinking, a festival, the New Moon, or the Sabbath? He has just said that via Yeshua's sacrifice, the "certificate of debt" or the penalties of Torah violation have been erased (v. 14), and that through Yeshua the cosmic powers have been disarmed (v. 15). Now, Paul can move forward with some important elaboration on the false teaching circulating in Colossae. The identity of the false teachers is again described as *Mē...tis* (Μη....τις) or "no one," only adding to the fact that we need to read his statements very carefully.

When Paul says, "do not let anyone judge you by what you eat or drink, or with regard to a religious festival, a New Moon celebration or a Sabbath day" (NIV), it is difficult to avoid how the Colossians were being, or would be, judged for their relationship to various aspects of the Torah. Many Christian lay readers simply conclude that the false teachers in Colossae were judging Paul's readers for not observing these various rituals. But is there more to consider? Should we not wonder what role or significance these religious practices had as a part of the false philosophy, before deciding that Paul says that all people should not be remembering these things any more?

We need to remember how in the past, Colossians 2:16 would often be quoted to Christians who observed a rigid Sunday Sabbath. But today, very few Christians even care about a Sunday Sabbath. Too frequently, Colossians 2:16 is turned on its head by those quoting it, who feel they are somehow being judged by the actions of a Messianic Believer who says nothing about his or her faith practice, to then judge the person supposedly passing judgment! Bruce takes the view, "Had the lesson [taught by this verse] been kept in mind in post-apostolic generations, there might have been less friction than there was in the church over the divergent calculations of the date of Easter (whether during the quartodeciman controversy or later)."[99] There will be some Christians today, who may not think that some of the things of Torah that we Messianics are convicted about, are important for them. Yet, they will consider them individual issues of conscience, left for a person who chooses to follow them to work through them in his or her relationship with God.[100] **Unfortunately, though, this includes too few people.** Many of the Christian family and friends you have will take Colossians 2:16 and inappropriately use it to judge *you* for your obedience to God's commandments.

It is difficult for many to even consider *the possibility* that in instructing the Colossians not to accept judgment in regard to various aspects of the Torah—the judgment spoken of may relate *to something other* than "the Colossians not keeping the Jewish law." In telling the Colossians not to be judged according to eating, drinking, a Sabbath day, or a festival, we should all be agreed that this relates to the false teachers (and/or any pagan Greeks in Colossae) judging the Colossian Believers. But rather than the Colossians being judged for not keeping these things, is it at all possible that the Colossians were told not to accept judgment for not keeping these things in the manner that the false teachers did? If so, **this would make things like kosher eating, the appointed times, and the Sabbath** *mainline practices* **of the Colossian Believers living in accordance with God's Word.** This would be in alignment with how James the Just anticipated that the non-Jews coming to faith would access the local synagogue and learn the Torah (Acts 15:19-21), and accept it at a steady and gradual pace as a part of their maturation in faith, in accordance with "the words of the Prophets" taking shape (Acts 15:15ff; cf. Amos 9:11-12, etc.).[101] *Let us see where the evidence takes us.*

Why does Paul say that the Colossians are not to accept judgment "in regard to food or drink or in respect to a festival or a new moon or a Sabbath day"? Is it because these things have been abolished by the work of Yeshua? (The previous reference in v. 14 only speaks of the penalties of the Torah being remitted—not

---

[98] This is not to say that there are not Messianic people out there who harshly condemn Christians who do not observe *Shabbat*, the appointed times, or eat kosher. There are, and they have frequently brought a great deal of discredit to our faith community.

For a further examination of this, consult the relevant volumes of the *Messianic Helper Series* by Messianic Apologetics.

[99] Bruce, *Colossians-Philemon-Ephesians*, 115.

The Quartodeciman issue is explored in more detail in the *Messianic Spring Holiday Helper* by Messianic Apologetics.

[100] Cf. Ibid., 114.

[101] For a further discussion, consult the author's commentary *Acts 15 for the Practical Messianic*.

God's expectations of how His people are to live.) Or, were these things being connected by the false teachers to their "philosophy and empty deception...to the elementary principles of the world" (v. 9)? Moo points out how, "On the whole...it seems best to view the practices in v. 16 as basically Jewish in origin and perhaps even orientation while still recognizing that they have been taken up into a larger mix of religious ideas and practices."[102]

It is not difficult to see that there are *more* than just Torah-prescribed practices listed by Paul: *en brōsei kai en posei ē en merei heortēs ē neomēnias ē sabbatōn* (ἐν βρώσει καὶ ἐν πόσει ἢ ἐν μέρει ἑορτῆς ἢ νεομηνίας ἢ σαββάτων), "in eating or in drinking, or in respect of a feast, or of a new moon, or of sabbaths" (YLT). Only a few aspects of Torah observance feature prominently in the false teachers' philosophy. Also, do note how the first practices listed are food **and** drink—an important clue that ascetic issues are principally at work. The Torah says very little about drinking alcohol, and by no means prohibits it as a part of daily life. Abstaining from alcohol only affected those taking a Nazirite vow (Numbers 6:3), or priests ministering in the Tabernacle (Leviticus 10:9), but not the normal person having wine with a meal. The fact that the Torah says almost nothing about drinking alcohol, should clue us in **to the issue in Colossae being a bit different than just standard Jewish observances.** Noting how drinking alcohol has been thrown into the mix of observances that the Colossians are not to take judgment by, Moo details,

"We should therefore at least keep open the possibility that the Colossian false teachers' abstinence from food and drink had its origins elsewhere, since many ancient Greco-Roman philosophical and religious traditions also featured prohibitions of meat and wine."[103]

Witherington, significantly clouded by an anti-Torah bias, has to immediately discount the possibility that the issue in v. 16 is not doing the things *in the manner* that the false teachers were doing: "It is evading the point to say that Paul meant that believers no longer keep the Sabbath in the way that the false teachers were suggesting."[104] Yet in having to say this, he at least has to recognize that it is not totally far-fetched to suggest that *how to* keep things like the Sabbath, appointed times, or kosher could be a way of interpreting the passage—and Paul tells the Colossians not to accept judgment for doing these things differently than the false teachers.

Lincoln's conclusions about the false philosophy, and how various Torah practices may have played a role, are quite intriguing:

"[T]here is no indication here that the motivation for abstinence from food and drink was due to observance of Torah....There is no hint that such special days are being observed because of the desire to obey Torah as such or because keeping them was a special mark of Jewish identity. Instead, it is probable that in the philosophy they were linked to a desire to please the cosmic powers."[105]

This is a fair explanation of how the statements made in v. 16, connect to v. 15. O'Brien further describes the kind of significance that the false teachers may have given the observances, Torah-based or otherwise, listed in v. 16:

"There are various reasons why abstinence from food and drink was practiced in the ancient world: the belief in the transmigration of souls might prevent a person from eating meat. Some practiced asceticism since it was bound up with their views of purity. Others thought that by fasting one served the deity, came closer to him or prepared oneself for receiving a divine revelation, a point that is important in the light of verse 18."[106]

Considering these things, **why were the Colossians not to accept judgment?** The false teachers observed things like the Sabbath, or gave the appointed times various esoteric meanings, which were all specifically related to their "self-abasement and...worship of the angels" (v. 18). Who knows what kinds of rituals they performed on the New Moon? Who knows what their Sabbath service would have been like? In encountering the false teachers, Paul tells the Colossians not to take any judgment from any person they may

---

[102] Moo, 221.
[103] Ibid., 220.
[104] Witherington, 160.
[105] Lincoln, in *NIB*, 11:361; cf. Bruce, *Colossians-Philemon-Ephesians*, 114.
[106] O'Brien, *Colossians-Philemon*, 138.

encounter—as within the false philosophy these rituals of Torah were hijacked and used in an effort to appeal to the cosmic powers Yeshua was superior over and had disarmed (v. 15). Sabbath observance for the sake of simple rest, or keeping the appointed times to remember God's works of salvation history, **is not the issue.** O'Brien continues, astutely concluding,

"For Israel the keeping of these holy days was evidence of obedience to God's law and a sign of her election among the nations. At Colossae, however, the sacred days were to be kept for the sake of the 'elemental spirits of the universe,' those astral powers who directed the course of the stars and relegated the order of the calendar. So Paul is not condemning the use of sacred days or seasons as such; it is the wrong motive involved when the observance of these days is bound up with the recognition of the elemental spirits."[107]

Moo also makes some important observations:

"Only Sabbath observance that is connected inappropriately to a wider religious viewpoint is here being condemned. These interpreters [who agree] are quite right to emphasize the importance of interpreting contextually and historically. And they are also right, we have suggested, to argue that Sabbath was taken up into a larger, syncretistic mix."[108]

While interpreters like O'Brien correctly read the issue in v. 16 in relation to how various Torah-based practices were being inappropriately used—as a part of the false philosophy to appease the cosmic powers—we should not be surprised to know that not all Colossians' commentators feel this way. Wright considers the Torah-based practices listed to be things that excluded outsiders from God's people, only to be kept by the Jews for a time, and by necessity they had to be removed with the expanse of the gospel among the nations.[109] But far be it from Wright wanting to encourage any kind of anti-Semitism, as though things like the Sabbath or dietary laws have never possessed any value, he is correct to assert, "what Paul does *not* say in opposition...here, or in Galatians, [is] that Christianity has nothing to do with Judaism...[as] it would have cut off the branch upon which his whole argument rests, namely, the belief that Christianity is the *fulfillment* of Judaism."[110]

From this point of view, the Torah-based practices listed by Paul should certainly be studied as they will teach us things about who God is and His previous plan for Ancient Israel, but they belong to a prior order. Unfortunately, even when emphasized this way—with respect encouraged for Judaism—many of today's standard Christian people do not bother studying the Torah even as Biblical history, too frequently consigning it to the dustbin of the past.

You need to remember that there is often a difference between the Christian layperson who takes snippets from Colossians 2:16, and the pastor or teacher who is engaged with properly applying Paul's words and who is sincerely concerned with showing tolerance and love for people of different points of view (Ephesians 4:2-3). Guthrie's observations are, "In view of Christ's triumph over all spiritual adversaries, it would be foolish to allow anyone to pass judgment over matters as *food* and *festivals*." His conclusion is, "Paul is here referring to any system which makes salvation dependent on the observance of certain food taboos or rigid adherence to the observance of certain days as sacred."[111]

Certainly for the false teachers of Colossae, unless one followed their philosophy and its emphasis on certain Torah practices, one was not considered enlightened, spiritual, or perhaps even "saved." Today's Messianic Believers should not give similar significance to things like the Sabbath or appointed times. They teach us about God's plan of redemption, **but they do not provide redemption.** Keeping these things is not to make us arrogant in our interactions with our fellow brothers and sisters in evangelical Christianity, who do not keep them (at present).

---

[107] Ibid., 139.
[108] Moo, 221.
[109] Wright, 119.
[110] Ibid.
[111] Guthrie, in *NBCR*, 1148.

When understanding the strong likelihood of Paul instructing the Colossians to not allow themselves to be judged for not failing to keep things like the Sabbath or appointed times, but rather for *how* they were not observed in the same manner as the false teachers—contemporary examples of how these things are misused by various people in today's Messianic community can certainly be considered. Is the *Shabbat* service a place to come together as fellow brothers and sisters, praise the Lord with song and liturgy, and be instructed from the Word? Or is it a time to beat others who are not "doing it the way we are"? Are there any syncretistic elements observed during *Shabbat* or the *moedim* that are designed to appease the elemental spirits (v. 8), which you may have seen or heard of? If so, what is the attitude of those who practice them toward those who do not? If there has been any negativity issued, **Paul's word is to not accept their judgment.**

When understood in light of Paul's overall message and warning in his letter, his message in Colossians 2:16 is for the Colossians not to take judgment in what they did with eating, drinking, the appointed times, New Moon, or Sabbath by the false teachers. These things had a significance for the false teachers, which was contrary to the significance they were to have for those who were faithful to the gospel and to Messiah Yeshua. They were normative practices of faith for God's people, not abolished, but kept improperly by the Colossian errorists.

2:17a So what did the Colossian errorists think about various Torah-based practices, and what would Paul consider to be a proper emphasis of them as a standard part of one's faith experience? What he instructs to his audience is, "These are only a shadow of what is to come; but the substance belongs to Christ" (RSV). Colossians 2:17 is seldom quoted by our Christian family and friends, who specifically protest Messianics remembering the Sabbath, appointed times, and kosher, with consideration for the wider issues of the epistle. And also, not enough are aware that there can be some translation issues when v. 17 is brought into English.

The *NIV Study Bible* is about as far as many Christian laypeople go in examining the meaning of Colossians 2:17. Its brief commentary describes, "The ceremonial laws of the OT are here referred to as shadows...because they symbolically depicted the coming of Christ; so any insistence on the observance of such ceremonies is a failure to recognize that their fulfillment has already taken place."[112] Today's Messianics do agree that the practices listed in v. 16, particularly things like the Sabbath and appointed times, teach us important lessons about the Messiah. They teach us about His First *and* His Second Coming, including the Millennium and the eternal rest to come. But in this brief commentary, many Christians will read it not just as "observance of such ceremonies..." **but also** "study of such ceremonies..." Furthermore, if our goal as mature Believers who study the Word is to see how Yeshua has *and will* prophetically fulfill things like the appointed times, how can remembering them—in such an effort to learn—actually subtract from recognizing God's plan of salvation history? Could we not actually appreciate our salvation in Yeshua more *by celebrating* things like the Passover, or even by remembering the rest to come by participating in a weekly rest on *Shabbat*?

In all fairness to the *NIV Study Bible*, its remarks do go on to say, "This...was combined with a rigid asceticism,"[113] but not enough people will recognize the circumstances requiring Paul to use terms like "shadow" and "substance." To them, asceticism might as well just be "legalism."

The role that various Torah-based practices (v. 16) played, in the false philosophy of the errorists, was to help them appeal to various supernatural forces (v. 18) over which Yeshua triumphed (v. 15). Losing sight of Yeshua as the true mystery (1:27), in their observance of those practices, **all they could grasp at would be shadows.** In classical Greek thought, *skia* (σκιά) often "means 'shadow' in contrast to 'reality' and denotes the worthlessness of things" (*TDNT*).[114] Plato uses it in his image of the cave, describing how the real substance of people is found in their ideas, and not in the shadows that they cast on the wall (*Republic* 514a-518b).[115] While Platonic usage of *skia* could be considered, as the "shadow" the Colossian false teachers were reaching toward, in their misuse of various Torah-based practices, would be worthless—Paul's usage of the term is likely not taken from Plato.

---

112 Kenneth L. Barker, ed., et. al., *NIV Study Bible* (Grand Rapids: Zondervan, 2002), 1856.
113 Ibid.
114 S. Schulz, "skiá," in *TDNT*, 1044.
115 Plato: *The Republic*, trans. Desmond Lee (London: Penguin Books, 2007), pp 240-245.

What would seem more likely is a usage of *skia* concurrent with what we see in Philo. This is where "God's works are *skiá* but move us toward the reality...The world of *skiá* is finally related to that of *sōma* as semblance is to substance" (*TDNT*).[116] In Philo, we see the sentiment expressed, "the former fashions shadows only, like painters do, in which it is not right to form any living thing. For the very name Bezeleel is interpreted to mean, 'working in shadows.' But Moses does not make shadows, but the task is assigned to him of forming the archetypal natures of things themselves" (*Concerning Noah's Work as a Planter* 27).[117] From this point of view, even though Bezalel made the various pieces of Tabernacle furniture (Exodus 31:2-3; Hebrews 9:23), these were only shadows when compared to the Divine substance of the Torah that Moses was responsible for conveying. Both have value to be sure, but the shadow sits as a representation of something much more significant.

Yet what is the substance that Plato, or even Philo, would be looking for? A higher plane of consciousness? More insight into God's wisdom?

It is actually not difficult to see how this all relates to the false teachers in Colossae. It is not as though the Torah-based practices have no value (v. 16). *They actually have great value for God's people that should be appreciated.* But, without understanding the substance to which they point, they might not mean as much as they should for those who practice them. Dunn indicates, "In contrast to Platonic-Philonic thought, it is the Christ in all the concrete bloodiness of the cross who is the true reality."[118] Bullard says, "Dietary laws and calendrical observances point beyond themselves to Christ, the reality."[119] Just consider how when we as Messianic Believers gather to celebrate the Biblical holidays, we gather to not only remember the events they commemorate in the Torah, but also what they represent to us who believe in Yeshua. We keep these things because they point us to Yeshua, and speak volumes to us about who He is, what He has done, and what He will do for us.

Challenges exist not only for Bible readers having the right, appreciative perspective toward the practices of v. 16, but also how v. 17 is rendered in English. The first part of the verse, *ha estin skia tōn mellontōn* (ἅ ἐστιν σκιὰ τῶν μελλόντων), is rendered in YLT as "which are a shadow of the coming things." It is easily detected that *mellontōn* is a present tense active participle—meaning that the Torah-based practices possess a shadow of things still yet to come. But various English translations can unfortunately skew this.

The New American Standard translators took a liberty and placed the word "*mere*" in italics—"a *mere* shadow of what is to come"—meaning that the word was not originally in the Greek text,[120] and could have done so in an effort to downplay the significance that the Torah practices of v. 16 actually do possess. This is fairly easy to see for an English reader, because the NASU preface does indicate "**Italics** are used in the text to indicate words which are not found in the original,"[121] so terms unnecessarily added can be more easily detected. (Please note that some words in *italics* are necessary, especially where in the source language a "to be" verb has been left out but is understood, but where a strict translation into English would be very choppy.)

Not all English versions use *italics*, though, to indicate words that have been added to a passage. The RSV and NRSV have "These are only a shadow of what is to come," and few are aware that "only" does not appear in the source text. The ESV, fortunately, started a positive trend by simply having "These are a shadow of the things to come."[122]

More problematic than adding "*mere*" or "only" to v. 17a, is how the NIV has actually changed the verb tense: "These are a shadow of the things that were to come." The NIV might not add "*mere*" or "only," but

---

[116] Schulz, "skiá," in *TDNT*, 1044.

[117] *The Works of Philo: Complete and Unabridged*, 193.

[118] Dunn, 177.

[119] Bullard, in *New Interpreter's Study Bible*, 2111.

[120] The word *monos* (μόνος), which can appear "as adverb, *alone, only, merely*" (*Thayer*, 418), rendered as "mere" in Mark 6:8 in the NASU, does not appear in the full Greek source text of Colossians 2:17:

ἅ ἐστιν σκιὰ τῶν μελλόντων, τὸ δὲ σῶμα τοῦ Χριστοῦ (*ha estin skia tōn mellontōn, to de sōma tou Christou*).

[121] *NASB Text Edition* (Anaheim, CA: Foundation Publications, 1997), v.

[122] This is also followed by *Lattimore*: "These are the shadows of the things to come."

mellontōn means "things coming."[123] Many people who read the NIV are of the mistaken impression that the various Torah practices of v. 16 have nothing more to teach Believers about God's plan of redemption, when in fact they do. O'Brien is one commentator who argues that the past tense "were to come" is the best understanding. In his words, "The expression 'things to come'...does not refer to what lies in the future from the standpoint of the writer...so pointing, for example, to the time of the Second Coming."[124] The reason that *mellontōn* has to be translated in the past tense for O'Brien, with *skia* not pointing to anything more to come, is that "then the σκιά ('shadow') would not have been superseded and the ordinances referred to would retain their importance."[125] O'Brien's words are actually quite telling here: **if there are still things to come, then *Shabbat*, the appointed times, and even the dietary laws have lessons to teach God's people today.**

None of us should ever deny the fact that Yeshua the Messiah has already come in prophetic fulfillment of things like the sacrificial requirement of Passover. To a degree, the Torah practices of v. 16 have been "fulfilled," *but not completely.* A present tense participle like *mellontōn* is changed to the past tense "were to come" to disregard that future things do await the saints. Great substance is certainly found in Yeshua's sacrifice for us at Golgotha (Calvary), but no one can deny how more redemptive acts are yet to come (Hebrews 9:28). In claiming that things like *Shabbat* or the appointed times have all been "fulfilled," and they possess no more lessons for us to learn about the future of salvation history, has contemporary Christian thought or theology really been aided? Is there absolutely nothing for anyone to learn about the ministry of Yeshua, and the mission He has for His people, by considering the role that the practices listed by Paul in v. 16 can properly play in someone's life? Remember that the issue in Colossae was their *improper use* as a part of a Gnosticized-Jewish philosophy.

It is sad that many Christians, when you mention things like *Yom Kippur* or the Feast of Tabernacles, have no idea what you are talking about. Too many, because of inappropriate past tense renderings like "were to come," fail to even attempt to know what the "shadow" is, so that they might understand the "substance." Consider how prior to salvation, the Torah functions as a person's rigid tutor or schoolmaster (Galatians 3:24), but once one arrives at salvation, do the principles of God's Instruction become irrelevant or invalid?[126] Do prophecies from the Tanach or Old Testament, which speak of the Messiah to come, no longer deserve any examination because they are "fulfilled"? Of course not. We appreciate the prior function that the Torah played in showing us the need for redemption, instilling in us principles of holiness, and we study Messianic prophecies to enrich and confirm our understanding of who Yeshua truly is for us!

Similarly, we can each come to God's place today—and even though they are still shadows—learn about who the Messiah is by honoring the Sabbath, remembering the appointed times, and even eating kosher. Bruce is not incorrect: "Many Jews looked on their festivals and sacred seasons as adumbrations of the messianic age. There are rabbinical texts which treat the Sabbath as a foretaste of that coming time—the time which, for Paul and other Christians, has come already in Christ."[127] It is a very Pauline concept that the age to come is surely to be inaugurated in the lives of God's people now (Galatians 1:4), but that does not mean that it is inappropriate or even sinful to remember the acts of salvation history that have had to, and will finally, bring us to the Messianic Age with Yeshua physically ruling and reigning over the Earth.

If v. 17a is not read carefully, especially in light of the issues that originally faced the Colossians, than not only do various Torah practices face their end, but a contemporary application in today's Christendom would actually see most traditions of formal worship abolished. An extremist could grossly misapply Paul's words and argue that he thinks that all forms of outward worship and "doings" are wrong. Wright, representing a high church Anglican tradition, correctly asserts, Paul "never says that it has nothing to do with

---

[123] Cleon L. Rogers, Jr. and Cleon L. Rogers III, *The New Linguistic and Exegetical Key to the Greek New Testament* (Grand Rapids: Zondervan, 1998), 465.

[124] O'Brien, *Colossians-Philemon*, 140.

[125] Ibid.

[126] Consult the author's McHuey Blog post from 13 September, 2009, "A Low Hamartology," available for access at <http://mchuey.wordpress.com>.

[127] Bruce, *Colossians-Philemon-Ephesians*, 116.

material things, even with outward forms of worship and ritual."[128] Yet for some odd reason or another, while high church Christian ritual is acceptable—eucharist and all—for Believers going back to the Jewish rituals of the Apostles of Yeshua would be like going back to a previous age that has nothing more to teach us about redemption. So do we totally let the shadow go? **Or do we appreciate the role of the shadow that much more,** looking forward to *the things to come* in the future?

2:17b By downplaying Yeshua as superior over the elements (vs. 9, 15), all the false teachers could possess would be a *skia* or shadow of the Torah-based practices that played a role in their philosophy. This is why Paul's statement continues: to de sōma tou Christou (τὸ δὲ σῶμα τοῦ Χριστοῦ), "and the substance [is] of Messiah" (my translation). The *shadow*, that the false teachers only have, is to be contrasted to the *substance* that the Colossian Believers have.

Some think that "but the body...of Christ" (KJV) is a better translation of v. 17b, in that while no outside person is to judge the Colossian Believers about different aspects of the Torah (v. 16), the internal community of faith is allowed to judge them. While it is tempting to conclude that the Body of Messiah is to judge on these matters, this does not really fit the context of what Paul is refuting—with the Colossian false teachers only able to go after shadows with their philosophy of error. (This does not mean, of course, that the Body of Messiah cannot make appropriate *halachic* decisions concerning various issues; it just finds no textual support in Colossians 2:17b, unlike a passage such as 1 Corinthians 5:12-13). While sōma (σῶμα) can mean "body" as in the Body of Messiah, with sōma contrasted to skia, it has to mean "**substantive reality, *the thing itself, the reality*** in imagery of a body that casts a shadow, in contrast to σκιά" (BDAG).[129] The issue is, as properly extrapolated by the NEB, "the solid reality is Christ's."

Knowing that the true substance, meaning, or reality of various Torah practices (v. 16) is found in Yeshua the Messiah, it is incumbent upon those who have been transformed by the gospel to, as Dunn says, "embody the same reality."[130] The work of Yeshua does not eliminate or disperse the shadow, but rather shows the greater reality that the shadow prefigures or outlines. And even though we know that Yeshua is the substance of things such as the Sabbath, Biblical holidays, and kosher laws—does Yeshua as substance "do away" with the benefits of remembering them? Christians who observe communion with bread and wine are remembering *a shadow* of something that has occurred in the past, right? So if that is not unacceptable, what would be the problem of doing something even more to commemorate Yeshua's atoning work for us, like a Passover *seder* with an emphasis on the Last Supper? Or for that same matter, consider His future work of redemption at *Yom Teruah/Rosh HaShanah* and *Yom Kippur*?

Evangelical Believers have swelled the Messianic movement in the past two decades (1990s-2000s) precisely because they have taken hold of the important lessons and spiritual significance in things like the Sabbath, Biblical holidays, and kosher eating. They have seen the substance of Yeshua in the weekly day of rest, the Passover *seder*, the giving of the Law and outpouring of the Spirit at *Shavuot*, the blowing of the *shofar* and future resurrection on *Rosh HaShanah*, tabernacling with the Lord at *Sukkot*, and even (although it is extra-Biblical) lighting the *menorah* at *Chanukah*. In eating kosher they have learned how God wishes us to separate holy and unholy things, even in our diet, and how it can benefit our health. These Messianic Believers have not embraced these important aspects of God's Torah to appease the elemental spirits (v. 9) or worship angels (v. 18), **but to do things that Jesus did.**

Things have been made complicated in recent days because the Messianic Jewish movement has become somewhat unwelcoming of non-Jews in their midst. Some of today's Messianic Jewish leaders do not really want Jewish and non-Jewish Believers to be united as the "one new humanity" (Ephesians 2:15, NRSV/CJB) that Paul desired. They do not see things like *Shabbat* or the appointed times as a part of the spiritual heritage of non-Jewish Believers who have put their trust in the Jewish Messiah. Even Stern's opinion is, "For Gentiles...[these] Jewish practices are in most cases nothing more than a shadow, insofar as they do not arise

---

[128] Wright, 120.
[129] *BDAG*, 984.
[130] Dunn, 177.

out of their own national experience."[131] Some might take such a statement to mean that things like the Exodus really cannot teach anyone who is not Jewish that much about their salvation.

Stern's exegesis of Colossians 2:16-17 is actually not that much better than your average Christian layperson, as he totally forgets the larger issues that concern the false philosophy of 2:8-23. He does not even address the role that the Torah-based practices in v. 16 might have played for the Colossian errorists, and that all they had were shadows because they forgot Yeshua (v. 8). He does think, however, that the Torah-based practices *only* have any real significance for Jewish Believers. He actually says that "these shadows are irrelevant to Gentiles, since God did not give these commands to Gentiles, [and] Sha'ul [Paul] urges the Colossians not to bound legalistically to them."[132] From this point of view, Yeshua is only the substance of Judaism's cultural identity markers. Contrary to this—and with significantly more Biblical support—Yeshua is the climax of the Sabbath, appointed times, kosher laws, **and the focus of further acts of redemption to come.** How Messianic Judaism continues to act toward non-Jewish Believers embracing their Hebraic Roots, and wanting to be a part of the Commonwealth of Israel (Ephesians 2:11-12; 3:6), will be a continuing issue to monitor in the years to come.

By far, Colossians 2:17b—the substance or reality found in Messiah—has been used to promote the idea that the appointed times speak to a prophetic plan of redemption. Each of the appointed times has specific Messianic importance that either has played itself out via His First Coming, or will play itself out via His Second Coming. While there have been many voices, *both* Messianic *and* Christian, who have taught from this vantage point (and our ministry is no exception), it is notable that this is a trend now going back well over thirty years. Much of it can actually be traced to a short, 31-page booklet in 1979 by the late Zola Levitt, entitled *The Seven Feasts of Israel*. Evangelical Christians seeing "Jesus in the feasts" has probably been the single largest factor contributing to the growth of today's Messianic movement. With a significant rise of interest by today's Christians in studying the Old Testament, **it will only get larger.**

If the issue in Colossians 2:16-17 pertains to the errorists' false philosophy, and their misuse of various Torah practices, then what do we need to take note of so that these same Torah practices *are not misused?*

If we believe that the Sabbath, appointed times, and kosher are still to be followed today, then as Messianic Believers we have to understand that the true meaning or substance of them is found in the Messiah. We honor the Lord every year by observing His appointed times, and by remembering what Yeshua has done for us. The true meaning and fulfillment of the seventh-day Sabbath, the Biblical appointments, and indeed all of the Torah's practices are found in Messiah Yeshua, and the example that He lived for us!

Looking through the list given to us in Leviticus 23, Passover represents Yeshua's sacrifice for our sin and His covering as the perfect Lamb of God. Unleavened Bread represents the hardships and pain He had to endure for us, for *matzah* is flattened bread with "scourges" on it. At Pentecost we remember the Holy Spirit being poured out at the Upper Room, just as the Torah had been given to Ancient Israel. The Feast of Trumpets prophetically represents Yeshua's Second Coming and our gathering to meet Him in the clouds. The Day of Atonement causes us to become somber as we turn to God and are reminded of the future Day of the LORD when Yeshua defeats His enemies at Armageddon. The Feast of Tabernacles encourages us to look forward to the establishment of His Millennial Kingdom on Earth, *and* it should likewise remind us of the birth of Yeshua who tabernacled among us. *Shemini Atzeret* is a picture of God wanting to spend "one more day" with us and foreshadows eternity with Him.

Also to be considered, and an element worthy of future studies, is how some of the appointed times that have been seemingly "fulfilled" by Yeshua's First Coming, still may teach us some lessons about Yeshua's Second Coming.

The importance of keeping the Lord's appointments for Believers cannot be overstated, because when speaking of the Exodus and events in the wilderness, the Apostle Paul wrote, "Now these things happened to

---

[131] Stern, 611.
[132] Ibid., pp 611-612.
Daniel C. Juster, *Jewish Roots* (Shippensburg, PA: Destiny Image, 1995), pp 130-131 offers a much better Messianic Jewish approach, which does weigh in some place for the Colossian false teaching.

them as an example, and they were written for our instruction, upon whom the ends of the ages have come" (1 Corinthians 10:11). The RSV says that "these things happened to them as a warning." If we find ourselves being the last generation "upon whom the ends of the ages have come," or we at least are nearing that last generation—how are we expected to understand God's redemptive plan for humanity and the end-times if we do not keep the appointments He has specified for us? How are we supposed to properly understand what is to befall Planet Earth?

If we do not keep the appointed times as God has told us, are we liable to misunderstand His prophetic plan for the ages? The "fixed times" (Leviticus 23:3, NJPS) of the Lord tell us when He plans to meet with us, especially regarding the Messiah's Second Coming. By keeping the appointed times and knowing their significance, can concepts such as the any-moment, random pre-tribulation rapture be theologically supported? Or, will we understand that there is a definitive pattern in the set seasons of the God of Israel, that we can only fully understand by keeping, as opposed to just studying, the *moedim*?[133]

My friends, let us properly understand the role that the *shadow* plays in us recognizing the *substance*!

18 Let no one keep defrauding you of your prize by delighting in self-abasement and the worship of the angels, taking his stand on *visions* he has seen, inflated without cause by his fleshly mind, 19 and not holding fast to the head, from whom the entire body, being supplied and held together by the joints and ligaments, grows with a growth which is from God.

2:18 It is unfortunate that those who quote Colossians 2:16-17, in refutation or condemnation of today's Messianics keeping the Sabbath, appointed times, and kosher, have very little consideration for the larger cotext and setting for what is communicated to those in First Century Colossae. The remarks Paul makes about various Torah-based practices and the substance they possess in Messiah Yeshua (vs. 16-17), are sandwiched in-between his assertion that He has disarmed the cosmic powers (v. 15) and that the false teachers are engaged in both self-abasement and some kind of "worship of angels" (v. 18). **Misuse of these Torah practices has to be the issue.** Delighting in the Sabbath as the Scriptures envision it (i.e., Isaiah 58:13-14), for example, is not the issue. Paul is concerned how various Torah-based practices have been caught up in a very worrisome form of asceticism that severely downgraded Yeshua's supremacy over the cosmos.

Why are the Colossian Believers not to take judgment from the false teachers? Paul's instruction is, "Let no one disqualify you, insisting on self-abasement and worship of angels, taking his stand on visions, puffed up without reason by his sensuous mind" (RSV). The delight of the false teachers is not found in the simple rest offered by the Sabbath, but rather *en tapeinophrosunē kai thrēskeia tōn angelōn* (ἐν ταπεινοφροσύνῃ καὶ θρησκείᾳ τῶν ἀγγέλων), in "self-mortification and angel worship" (NEB). This is the Colossian error at its worst, that not only perverted God's appointed times, but where people would submit themselves to physical rigor so as to induce visions. O'Brien observes,

"It was Jewish mixed with pagan elements. The angels determined the course of the cosmos and with it man's circumstances. Men submitted to angels in the cult by performing the prescribed acts and by fulfilling the regulations laid down."[134]

The instruction Paul has just given (vs. 15-17) relates to how the Colossian Believers are to be on serious guard concerning "what they have seen" (TNIV), a reference to the so-called visions and revelations of the false teachers. All of the things they advocated were designed to give them ecstatic hallucinations. The words of Jeremiah 23:32 could certainly be in view: "'Behold, I am against those who have prophesied false dreams,' declares the LORD, 'and related them and led My people astray by their falsehoods and reckless boasting; yet I did not send them or command them, nor do they furnish this people the slightest benefit,' declares the LORD."

---

[133] Note that while there are many Christian books written on the prophetic significance of the appointed times, almost all of them are written by those *who do not keep them* as a standard element of the praxis of their faith. Should we accept prophetic interpretations related to the *moedim* by those who do not keep them, and hence do not understand them as fully as one who does keep them? What about those who consider these to only be a part of the spiritual heritage of the Jewish people, and not for all of God's people who have placed their trust in the Messiah?

[134] O'Brien, *Colossians-Philemon*, 143.

Even Qohelet's word, "For in many dreams and in many words there is emptiness. Rather, fear God" (Ecclesiastes 5:7), may be considered.

Appeals made by people to angels is certainly something that is found in Jewish literature,[135] with some ancient Jewish sects possessing a rather advanced angelology. The *Dictionary of Judaism in the Biblical Period* actually notes how "During the Second Temple period and afterward, developed angelologies appear showing interest in angels' names and functions; these functions include revelation (Ezek. 43:13-14; Zech. 1:19; Dan. 8:15-17; 1 Enoch 7-8; 4 Ezra 4:1-2; Rev. 1:1), mediation (1 Enoch 15:2), guarding of the heavens (1 Enoch 71:7-8; 3 Enoch), controlling meteorological phenomena (Jub. 2:2; 1 Enoch 7, 60:22), and making war (LAB 61:5). Because of their important role in the universe, angels are invoked in mystical and magical texts to produce effects such as healing (Test. Sol., Sefer ha-Razim)."[136] Any kind of angel worship present in Colossae was undoubtedly a pagan import to Judaism. While the Biblical canon does depict angels used as servants of God, superior to human beings, mainline Jews did not worship the angels.

How do you make contact with the angels? How do you pierce the veil of communicating with another dimension? Paul says that the false teachers were advocating *tapeinophrosune* (ταπεινοφροσύνη), a "*lowliness, humility*" (LS)[137] most often related to fasting—or in this case, an extreme fasting. The NASU translation of "self-abasement" is quite appropriate. This is the kind of physical self-torture that would have presumably enabled the false teachers to enter into a trance, whereby they could presumably communicate with the elemental spiritual forces. Seeking to find some contemporary application for the instruction in v. 18, Lincoln argues,

"The loose network of attitudes and beliefs that is often labeled as 'new age' spirituality provides some analogies to the philosophy opposed by Colossians. A wide variety of interests flows into it, including an emphasis on human potential, a fascination with extraterrestrial beings and UFOs, astrology, magic, witchcraft, ecological concerns, and channeling of spirits from the beyond. However, a major aspect of the phenomenon is a syncretistic spirituality that stresses experiences of a transcendence in the attempt to go beyond the limitations of everyday life in the visible world."[138]

The Apostle Paul was never against having genuine supernatural experiences. As he indeed writes in Romans 8:16, "The Spirit Himself testifies with our spirit that we are children of God." Yet let us not also forget how the promise of Yeshua the Messiah is something the Father "promised beforehand through His prophets in the holy Scriptures" (Romans 1:2). The Bereans were those who were "examining the Scriptures daily *to see* whether these things were so" (Acts 17:11). Genuine supernatural experiences will be validated by a thorough support from the Word of God, not subjective physical self-abuses that make one feel superior to others, because one has been able to communicate with the angels. And, especially if the angels are just subordinates of the Messiah!

Not all commentators are agreed that the clause *thrēskeia tōn angelōn* (θρησκείᾳ τῶν ἀγγέλων) is to be taken as an objective genitive (denoting possession), where "worship of angels" speaks of worship *directed to* the angels in some kind of religious cult. Rather than the Colossians worshipping the angels, *thrēskeia tōn angelōn* should be taken as a subjective genitive, representing the worship that the angels *perform before God*.[139] Of course, as the author of Hebrews attests, there is an ongoing worship service in Heaven present with myriads of angels and saints who have died in faith awaiting resurrection (Hebrews 12:22-24). It is not impossible to think that the Colossian false teachers may have tried to develop a legalistic discipline of trying to actually access this via some kind of trance—something that goes way beyond recognizing normal worship on Earth as paralleling worship in Heaven.

---

[135] Bruce, *Colossians-Philemon-Ephesians*, 119.

[136] "angel worship," in Jacob Neusner and William Scott Green, eds., *Dictionary of Judaism in the Biblical Period* (Peabody, MA: Hendrickson, 2002), 36; cf. Dunn, pp 150-151.

[137] LS, 792.

[138] Lincoln, in *NIB*, 11:636.

[139] Cf. O'Brien, *Colossians-Philemon*, pp 142-143; Dunn, pp 179-181.

The fact that a contingent of angels would have been worshiping before God in His Heavenly court, while something testified in Scripture, is certainly a feature of literature like the Dead Sea Scrolls. The Qumran community saw itself participating in the activities of the angels, as it was said, "May you [abide forever] as an Angel of the Presence in the holy habitation, to the glory of the God of host[s. May you] serve in the temple of the kingdom of God, ordering destiny with the Angels of the Presence, a society of the *Yahad* [with the Holy Ones] forever, for all the angels of eternity!" (1QSb 4:24-26).[140]

If the Colossian false teachers were simply desiring to minister before God in Heaven, like the angels worship before Him, this still does not get them off the hook for promoting error. Dunn describes, "more to the point here is the evidence of a desire particularly within apocalyptic and mystical circles of first-century Judaism to join in with the worship of angels in heaven."[141] Ancient error, mysticism, and trying to inappropriately access another dimension would have still been going on without direct worship of angels. Witherington concurs, "Clearly the desire for participation in the heavenly worship of angels is a prominent motif in mystical Judaism of this period,"[142] giving a number of examples from the Pseudepigrapha to consider:

"And they showed me from a distance the LORD, sitting on his throne. And all the heavenly armies assembled, according to rank, advancing and doing obeisance to the LORD. And then they withdrew and went to their places of joy and merriment, immeasurable light, but gloriously serving him" (2 *Enoch* 20:3-4[A]).[143]

"He enlightened my eyes and my heart to utter psalm, praise, jubilation, thanksgiving, song, glory, majesty, laud, and strength. And when I opened my mouth and sang praises before the throne of glory the holy creatures below the throne of glory and above the throne of glory responded after me, saying, Holy, holy, holy, and Blessed be the glory of the Lord in his dwelling place" (3 *Enoch* 1:12).[144]

"Then the other one also, name Amaltheia's Horn, bound on her cord. And her mouth spoke ecstatically in the dialect of those on high, since her heart also was changed, keeping aloof from worldly things. For she spoke in the dialect of the cherubim, glorifying the Master of virtues by exhibiting their splendor. And finally whoever wishes to grasp a trace of 'The Paternal Splendor' will find it written down in 'The Prayers of Amaltheia's Horn'" (*Testament of Job* 50).[145]

While the Pseudepigrapha includes examples of how people were shown, or attempted to participate, in the activities of angels in the Heavenly realm, perhaps more relevant to the situation in v. 18 are some sentiments expressed in the DSS. Here, we see a Sabbath prayer issued where angels are lauded, and you can tell that the Qumran covenanters could be trying to actually praise the angels themselves, or certainly join into what they were doing:

"Praise [the God of...,] you godlike beings of utter holiness; [rejoice] in his divine [kingdom. For He has established] utter holiness among the eternally holy, that they might become for Him priests [of the inner sanctum in His royal temple,] ministers of the Presence in His glorious innermost chamber. In the congregation of all the [wise] godlike beings, [and in the councils of all the] divine [spirits], He has engraved His precepts to govern all spiritual works, and His [glorious] laws [for all the] wise [divine beings], that sage congregation honored by God, those who draw near to knowledge" (4Q400 1.1-6).[146]

Certainly while the angels form an important part of God's Heavenly host, and the Forces of Light not only serve as God's agents in the universe—but also frequently protect humans without their knowledge—

---

[140] Wise, Abegg, and Cook, 149.

[141] Dunn, pp 180-181.

[142] Witherington, 162.

[143] F.I. Andersen, trans., "2 (Slavonic Apocalypse of) Enoch," in *The Old Testament Pseudepigrapha*, Vol 1, 135.

[144] P. Alexander, trans., "3 (Hebrew Apocalypse of) Enoch," in Ibid., pp 256-257.

[145] Spittler, in Ibid., 866.

[146] Wise, Abegg, and Cook, 367.

humans are not to try to find them. Consider how the author of Hebrews instructs, "Do not neglect to show hospitality to strangers, for by this some have entertained angels without knowing it" (Hebrews 13:2). Angels simply appear. Furthermore, similar to how the witch of Endor was able to call up Samuel from Sheol (1 Samuel 28:13-15), **something prohibited in the Torah** (Leviticus 20:27; Deuteronomy 18:11), so would trying to communicate with angelic intermediaries **also be prohibited.**

What do the errors of self-abasement and this "worship of angels" tell us about the false philosophy in Colossae? In Dunn's estimation, "It is quite possible...to envisage a Jewish (or Christian Jewish) synagogue in Colossae, which was influenced by such ideas and which delighted in their worship Sabbath by Sabbath as a participation in the worship of the angels in heaven."[147] Similar to this, Witherington believes it is justified for us to consider "that the issue is not just participation in heavenly worship through visions but that the errorists are seeking information, revelation from above, wisdom from the heavenly realm. Paul then is undermining their insistence on the need for visionary ascent to receive such revelation and the felt need to participate in angelic worship in order to draw closer to God."[148]

Whether "worship of angels" is viewed as actually worshipping the angels as intermediaries for deliverance, or trying to join in with angels in an attempt to access the Heavenly realm, the false philosophy advocated that it had to be preceded or attended by some kind of physical mortification. This would have gone far beyond simple recognition of the fact that there are angels worshipping before God's throne (Isaiah 6:1-4; Revelation 5:11-13).

While the false philosophy of Colossians can be rightfully applied today in refutation of various mystical and Kabbalistic errors that have errantly influenced sectors of the Messianic community, there is also another application of the "worship of angels" which can hit a little too close to home. Consider the many Messianic conferences where young women dress up in white gowns, and then dance as though they are angelic beings. Sometimes this occurs with mock up Tabernacle/Temple furniture like the Ark of the Covenant. I think that this classifies as a kind of "worship of angels"—trying to join into something that is off limits for humans—and regardless of how popular it is, we do need to seriously reconsider some of the artistic dances that take place in our faith community. Too frequently, whether it is dance or song, the messages conveyed have not been subjected to theological critique.

(Another view of angel worship is that rather than worshipping angels, per se, the Jews of Paul's day spent so much time focusing on the giving of the Torah to them, that their attention was given to the angels who helped deliver it [cf. Galatians 3:19] and this had become a form of idolatry.[149] But this view makes assumptions about what role the angels actually performed in the giving of the Torah, and can downplay the Torah as Divinely inspired.)

2:19 How did the false teachers of Colossae get to the point where "worship of angels" would even become a facet of their philosophy and/or theology? For Paul, the answer is very simple. **The main error advocated by the false teachers was that they forgot Yeshua as the center of their faith.** He says, "They have lost connection with the head, from whom the whole body, supported and held together by its ligaments and sinews, grows as God causes it to grow" (TNIV). Just as Yeshua Himself taught, "I am the vine, you are the branches; he who abides in Me and I in him, he bears much fruit, for apart from Me you can do nothing" (John 15:5).

Yeshua was certainly forgotten as the center of the faith for the Colossian errorists. They put their spiritual emphasis and motives on other things. But how are we to specifically understand that they have "lost connection with the Head" (NIV)? Is it that they have failed to recognize Yeshua as Divine (v. 9)? The false teachers in Colossae were certainly looking for means *other than Yeshua* to access the presence of God. In not recognizing Yeshua properly, the false teachers in Colossae were likely going to wither away and die—even though not realizing it—as they were not being nourished from Him. Wright's thoughts are well taken:

---

[147] Dunn, 181.
[148] Witherington, 166.
[149] Wright, 122.

"The true test of whether or not one belongs to God's people is neither observance of dietary laws and Jewish festivals, nor the cultivation of super-spiritual experiences, but whether one belongs to Christ, alive with his life."[150]

Today's Messianic movement (at least as to my knowledge) does not have anyone worshipping angels. We might have some people trying to pierce through the inter-dimensional veil and attempting to access realms they have no business accessing, though, often through Jewish Kabbalah and Medieval Jewish writings (that fall well off the scope of ancient religious literature employed in contemporary New Testament scholarship). We certainly do have people who have advocated false theologies and philosophies which deride Yeshua as the Divine Savior, who reigns supreme over all (vs. 8-10). Even while some of the circumstances we face today here and there, may not be exactly the same as they were in Ancient Colossae, they still nevertheless can be very similar. We need to pay more attention to Colossians than we have been.

Another application of v. 19 to consider, being disconnected from Yeshua as the Head, is how our prime connection and interaction with God occurs through our thoughts. Most of us when we pray, talk to God with silent thoughts expressed in our brain. When we reason with God, either through reading His Word or through meditation with Him, we use our brains. But have you ever had a headache or physical pain that has disrupted the spiritual connection? I know that I have had times, either because of external environmental changes (like the hay fever season or changing barometric pressure) or negative spiritual energies—when my connection to God has been disrupted. Such is the time when we need to just pray for healing, and not concern ourselves with complicated issues of theology or God's universe. I have not by any means felt "unsaved," but these are low spiritual times when we encounter a variety of factors that can disrupt communication with God.

20 If you have died with Messiah to the elementary principles of the world, why, as if you were living in the world, do you submit yourself to decrees, such as, 21 "Do not handle, do not taste, do not touch!" 22 (which all *refer to* things destined to perish with use)—in accordance with the commandments and teachings of men? 23 These are matters which have, to be sure, the appearance of wisdom in self-made religion and self-abasement and severe treatment of the body, *but are* of no value against fleshly indulgence.

2:20 Paul proceeds to ask the Colossians some questions that relate to the various practices advocated by the false teachers, which do indicate that some who will be reading his letter have adopted them, even if in piecemeal. He starts off this section by saying, "If you died with Christ to the elemental forces of this world, why do you live as if you still belonged to the world? Why do you submit to regulations...?" (HCSB). It is important to recognize what the issue is the Colossians are submitting to *tōn stoicheiōn tou kosmou* (τῶν στοιχείων τοῦ κόσμου), which the NRSV renders as "the elemental spirits of the universe." These are things that ultimately do not originate with God.

Too frequently when encountering v. 20, lay readers will focus their attention upon "submit yourself to decrees," and then assume that God's commandments in the Torah are being spoken against. Do the elementary principles really compose God's standard of holiness in the Tanach, or do they compose the false philosophy Paul has warned the Colossians about (v. 8)? How are we to understand the verb *dogmatizō* (δογματίζω), and its relation to the condemning dogmas that have been wiped clean by Yeshua's sacrifice (v. 14)? Vaughan gives us some clues as to the potential origins of what is warned against:

"Some may have been reenactments of the Mosaic law; others were doubtless prohibitions stemming from pagan asceticism. There is a descending order in the terms, the climax being reached in the last word—i.e., 'Don't even touch.'"[151]

A cursory reading of v. 21 makes it clear that the various things that could have "dogmatized" the Colossians were not that significant so as to nullify their salvation. They were various opinions about ritual

---

[150] Ibid., 124.
[151] Vaughan, in *EXP*, 11:207.

purity and/or attaining to the false philosophy that the errorists advocated. The connection with Yeshua nullifying the "certificate of debt," which had dogmas attendant with the death penalty (v. 14), may simply be that if the death penalty for high crimes in the Torah has been atoned for—then whatever lesser dogmas and opinions the Colossians may be attempted to adopt via the superstitious ideology of the false teachers, have also surely been taken care of by the Lord. A rigid adherence to these insignificant principles, which are ultimately ways of the world, will not bring one spiritual satisfaction if the Messiah has been forgotten. These are principles that belong to "the rulers and authorities" (v. 15) over whom He has triumphed. Moo reminds us,

"...Paul's claim that the rules involved here are closely related to 'the elemental forces,' and that they are 'worldly' in orientation (v. 20), also suggests that these Jewish-oriented or –oriented rules have been taken up into a larger and syncretistic religious philosophy."[152]

2:21 Some examples about the kind of worldly, superstitious principles are given: "Do not handle, do not taste, do not touch!" It is very tempting for readers to conclude that various aspects of the Torah are specifically being targeted against here, especially regulations that regard touching an unclean person (Leviticus 15; Numbers 19:11-13) or unclean animals/meat (Leviticus 5:2-3; 11). But then again, it may be that the reasoning behind these various superstitious attitudes is not too dissimilar from how Adam and Eve had exaggerated God's original instruction to them (Genesis 2:16-17; 3:3). Certain touching and handling may also be a word against having sexual intercourse. There may be a basis for some of this found in the Torah, but if so it has been stretched beyond the original meaning, and in the false philosophy's case, applied in order for its initiates to access a prohibited spiritual realm. The *NIV Study Bible* is not incorrect to suggest, "These prohibitions seem to carry OT ceremonial laws to the extreme."[153]

Various ancient Jewish regulations do seem to be in view in v. 21, but we cannot assume that these superstitions were unique or exclusive to Judaism. These worldly, elemental principles are tied to the "self-abasement and worship of angels" (v. 18), physical self-torture and attempting to access the realm of angels either by worshipping them or trying to join into their activities. These same kinds of superstitions were also present among the mystery cults of the day, so it is inappropriate to assume an exclusive Jewish context of this.

2:22 According to the Apostle Paul, the superstitions of the false philosophy in Colossae do not have great value for what they attempt to do for people. "These are all destined to perish with use, because they are based on human commands and teachings" (NIV). They have the capacity to be significantly influential, possessing the appearance of an impressive religious philosophy, promoting some kind of humility, and its adherents perform various physical things that are supposed to make them "spiritual." Yet in spite of what can appear to be positive, the principles advocated are ultimately of human origin: *kata ta entalmata kai didaskalias tōn anthrōpōn* (κατὰ τὰ ἐντάλματα καὶ διδασκαλίας τῶν ἀνθρώπων).

These principles or "commandments" are not considered by Paul to be of Divine origin. Definitely in view is Isaiah's word about "this people draw near with their words and honor Me with their lip service, but they remove their hearts far from Me, and their reverence for Me consists of tradition learned *by rote*" (Isaiah 29:13), something picked up by Yeshua in Mark 7:6-7 in His rebuke of some Pharisees. **The fact that the issue here is human principles enforced as though they are God's commandments often gets overlooked by some readers.** The Apostle Paul recognized the Torah as inspired by God, and considered *its commandments* "holy and righteous and good" (Romans 7:12). Somehow associating God's commandments as only human principles would also seem unthinkable for a disciple of Paul, as Lincoln, who holds to pseudonymous authorship of Colossians, attests, "A Pauline disciple would scarcely have dismissed what, in fact, had been commanded by God in the Torah as merely human commandments."[154]

2:23 What value is there in following the superstitious discipline of the false teachers? Paul comments to the Colossians, "These have indeed an appearance of wisdom in promoting rigor of devotion and self-

---

[152] Moo, 236.
[153] *NIV Study Bible*, 1856.
[154] Lincoln, in *NIB*, 11:634.

abasement and severity to the body, but they are of no value in checking the indulgence of the flesh" (RSV). According to Paul, their ascetic regulations, while giving a veneer of piety to those who practice them, and perhaps even presenting to those who encounter them an aura of spirituality, cannot ultimately curb the temptations of sinful human flesh. In his instruction to Timothy, Paul will later criticize those who practice ascetic regulations that forbid eating meat and marriage (1 Timothy 4:3). Certainly, the physical body of a person should be disciplined (1 Corinthians 9:27), but not at the expense of recognizing that there are good things to benefit from in God's Creation. Qohelet was right to have said,

"Enjoy life with the woman whom you love all the days of your fleeting life which He has given to you under the sun; for this is your reward in life and in your toil in which you have labored under the sun" (Ecclesiastes 9:9).

The claim to fame of later Gnosticism was that what a person did physically did not have any effect spiritually, and vice versa. Did this attitude play a role in the false philosophy circulating in Colossae? To what extent did the false teachers apply their principles "Do not handle, do not taste, do not touch!" (v. 21) to all of their conduct? Are these just ad-hoc categories listed by Paul, or do they compose a selective asceticism practiced? Later in 3:5 some significant fleshly sins are listed. So in saying that their philosophy has "a shew of wisdom" (KJV), might we conclude that it ultimately did not help those who practiced it, as the false teachers would still fall into sin without the aid of Yeshua's transforming power?

The Colossians, who have recognized Yeshua as Lord (vs. 6-7), are not to fall into sin, placing Him at the center of their faith.

COLOSSIANS 3
COMMENTARY

1 Therefore if you have been raised up with Messiah, keep seeking the things above, where Messiah is, seated at the right hand of God. 2 Set your mind on the things above, not on the things that are on earth.

3:1 The main doctrinal section of Paul's letter to the Colossians has just ended, and the practical, or exhortative section now begins. This part of Paul's message serves as a positive counterpart to the previous negative critique of the false philosophy. Instruction is specifically delivered on how Yeshua the Messiah offers power to Believers, enabling them to overcome sinful temptations—a power that the false teaching of the Colossian errorists cannot provide. The ability to live properly before God cannot be attained by the ascetic practices circulating in Colossae, but instead *only* by the Colossians being united with Yeshua. The Apostle Paul teaches the Colossians about their new identity in the Messiah (3:1-4), that they are to put off their old sinful ways (3:5-11) and put on new godly ways (3:12-17), and about some of the responsibilities that those who live properly have, in order to demonstrate right service to the Lord (3:18-4:1).[1]

Compared to what has thus far been written, the tone of the remainder of the epistle is relatively positive (simply see the contrast between 2:20 and 3:1). The emphasis is, "So if you have been raised with the Messiah, seek what is above, where the Messiah is" (HCSB). Some claim that the Epistle to the Colossians must be pseudonymous as Colossians, and similarly Ephesians (2:6), speak of people being "raised up" with Yeshua, and this is a thought that is foreign to Pauline theology. Yet, this is a concept alluded to in the non-disputed Pauline letters (Romans 6:4, 11-12; Philippians 3:10), as only the choice of vocabulary (Grk. *Ei oun sunēgerthēte*, Εἰ οὖν συνηγέρθητε) is unique. The Apostle Paul indeed does treat the resurrection of the dead as a future event (Romans 6:5, 8; 1 Corinthians 15:22-23; 1 Thessalonians 4:16), whereas in this section of Colossians (cf. Galatians 2:19-20) he discusses the life of faith directed *by the Divine power that resurrected Yeshua*. This power is to transform people to live differently, and stands in stark contrast to the ascetic rules of the false teachers that really cannot help the Colossians.

In order for his readers to truly understand the profundity of who the Messiah is, Paul admonishes "keep seeking the things above," specifically employing *zēteite* (ζητεῖτε), a present active imperative verb. The NIV understands this to be "set your hearts on things above," as v. 2 will specifically admonish the Colossians to use their minds *to think* about Yeshua. We can be reminded of how Paul similarly instructed the Philippians, "brethren, whatever is true, whatever is honorable, whatever is right, whatever is pure, whatever is lovely, whatever is of good repute, if there is any excellence and if anything worthy of praise, dwell on these things" (Philippians 4:8).

The Colossians, in considering the Lord Yeshua, are to live the life of the realm of Heaven—where Yeshua is sovereign (Psalm 110)—**while living on Earth.** Born again Believers are connected to Heaven (1 Corinthians 15:47-49; Galatians 4:26; Philippians 3:20), but not in some kind of an ethereal way. The life of Heaven will be manifested in concrete, righteous actions of faith in the saints. Andrew T. Lincoln observes, "In the face of the insistence on ascetic observances in order to participate in heavenly life, [the author] asserts that through God's gracious initiative the readers have already been brought into such life."[2] Similarly, N.T.

---

[1] Interpreters like James D.G. Dunn, who would advocate that the Colossians were being persuaded against entering into the Jewish Synagogue, claim that this section of verses "provide[s] a counterweight to the evident attractiveness of the more traditional Jewish lifestyle" (Dunn, 203).

[2] Lincoln, in *NIB*, 11:637.

Wright reminds us, "The Bible does not say much about heaven. But its central feature is clear: it is the place where the crucified Christ already reigns, where his people already have full rights of citizenship."[3]

3:2 In some ways, Paul actually agrees with the false teachers, in that the attention of the Colossians needs to be directed toward another dimension. He instructs, "mind the things above, not the things on the earth" (LITV), as the verb *phroneō* (φρονέω) means **"to give careful consideration to someth., set one's mind on, be intent on"** (BDAG).[4] But rather than focus on angels or any other spiritual intermediaries (2:18), the focus of the Colossians is to be on Yeshua seated at the Father's right hand (cf. 2:9). Certainly to be considered is Paul's previous teaching on "the Jerusalem above" (Galatians 4:26) and the "upward call" (Philippians 3:14) that Believers possess. *IVPBBC* summaries how "The Jewish mystics creating problems at Colossae were probably seeking these upper realms through mystical experiences (2:18), but Paul only mentions one thing specifically in heaven: Christ."[5]

The affections and thoughts of the Colossians are to be focused on Yeshua the Messiah, "seated at the right hand of God" (v. 1). Psalm 110:1, "The LORD says to my Lord: 'Sit at My right hand until I make Your enemies a footstool for Your feet," formed a major part of early Apostolic theology regarding the exaltation and Divinity of Yeshua (Acts 2:33-35; 5:31; 7:55-56; Romans 8:34; Ephesians 1:20; Hebrews 1:3, 13; 8:1; 10:12; 12:2; 1 Peter 3:22; Revelation 3:21). These are concurrent with Yeshua's own claims about Himself (Matthew 26:64; Mark 12:36-37; Luke 20:41-44), and the Son of Man vision the Prophet Daniel was able to see (Daniel 7:9-14). Interestingly enough, the Talmud records how the Jewish Rabbi Aqiba was rebuked for arguing that a second throne was placed in Heaven for the Messiah:

"One verse of Scripture states, 'His throne was fiery flames' (Dan. 7:9), but elsewhere it is written, 'Till thrones were places, and one that was ancient of days did sit' (Dan. 7:9)! *No problem, the one is for him, the other for David, in line with what has been taught on Tannaite authority:* 'One is for him, the other for David,' the words of R. Aqiba. Said to him R. Yosé the Galilean, 'Aqiba, how long are you going to treat in a profane way the Presence of God?'" (b.*Hagigah* 14a).[6]

If Yeshua the Messiah sits at His Father's right hand, then it is obvious that the Colossians' attention needs to be directed to and focused around Him, seen in the imperative verb *phroneite* (φρονεῖτε). In the Tanach, the imagery of the right hand is one that expresses great power and authority (Exodus 15:6, 12; Psalm 16:11; 17:7; 20:6; 44:3; 60:5; 73:23; 98:1; 118:15-16). Beyond this, Yeshua possesses the highest of power "far above all the heavens" (Ephesians 4:10), and is to be the One to whom all Creation will one day bow as LORD (Philippians 2:10-11; cf. Isaiah 45:23). *This is to all be sure motivation to live properly.* Douglas J. Moo describes, "We are not to strive for a 'heavenly' status, since that has already been freely given us in Christ. Rather, we are to make that heavenly status the guidepost for all our thinking and acting."[7]

In directing his audience to think on Heavenly things, there is a definite subversion of the false philosophy's thought that things of the Earth were evil. Paul concurs that the attention of the Colossians needs to be focused on Heaven, but in so doing he masterfully turns what the false teachers advocate against themselves. Peter T. O'Brien summaries how Paul "outclasses his opponents on their own ground, not completely disparaging their concern with the heavenly realm but rather redirecting it, at the same time exposing its false premises about contacting this realm through legalistic observances."[8]

In 2 Corinthians 4:18, Paul had observed how "we look not at the things which are seen, but at the things which are not seen; for the things which are seen are temporal, but the things which are not seen are eternal." In instructing people to focus on eternal things in the realm of Heaven, no good theologian honestly argues that Paul opposes physical things—like the later Gnostics of the Second Century—but was instead often using the contrast of worldly/Heavenly as a warning about how possessing a physical body can often

---

[3] Wright, 132.
[4] BDAG, 1065.
[5] Craig S. Keener, *The IVP Bible Background Commentary: New Testament* (Downers Grove, IL: InterVarsity, 1993), 578.
[6] *The Babylonian Talmud: A Translation and Commentary.* MS Windows XP. Peabody, MA: Hendrickson, 2005. CD-ROM.
[7] Moo, 246.
[8] O'Brien, *Colossians-Philemon*, 161.

lead to physical sins. Paul wants people to live their lives on Earth in accordance with what exists above. F.F. Bruce further indicates,

"The Gnostics also believed in aiming at what was above...But Paul has in mind a higher plane than theirs...Don't look at life from the standpoint of these lower planes; look at them from Christ's exalted viewpoint. Judge everything by the standards of that new creation to which you belong, not by those of the old order to which you have said a final farewell."[9]

3 For you have died and your life is hidden with Messiah in God. 4 When Messiah, who is our life, is revealed, then you also will be revealed with Him in glory.

3:3 In instructing the Colossians to live righteously, Paul picks up the previous theme of how they have "died" with the Messiah (2:12, 20), meaning that His sacrificial death on their behalf affects how they are to die to the power of sin. He says, "For you died to this life, and your real life is hidden with Christ in God" (NLT). The only real hidden, or secret things, that the Colossians need to be concerned about, are already found with the life that they possess in the Messiah—something God has purposed. The usage of "hidden" here is perhaps about as close to speaking of anything secretive or mystic that Paul gets in his letter. He refers to the fact that the Colossian Believers are to live within God's realm, untouchable by anyone. Yeshua is the One in whom true knowledge and wisdom is to be found (2:3), things that born again Believers raised with Him into a new life are to demonstrate. Dunn describes, "Paul and Timothy were evidently wholly confident that this perspective, this hidden resource, would provide all the wisdom needed to cope with the challenges and problems of daily living."[10]

Another view of the Colossians having a hidden life in the Messiah, is how the language of "hidden" is used in the Tanach regarding safety. 1 Samuel 13:6 records how, "When the men of Israel saw that they were in a strait (for the people were hard-pressed), then the people hid themselves in caves, in thickets, in cliffs, in cellars, and in pits." Psalm 27:5 also exclaims, "For in the day of trouble He will conceal me in His tabernacle; in the secret place of His tent He will hide me; He will lift me up on a rock."[11]

What are the ramifications of dying with the Messiah? Paul has previously expressed how "that I may know Him and the power of His resurrection and the fellowship of His sufferings, being conformed to His death" (Philippians 3:10). He also had previously taught how Believers are to "always [be] carrying about in the body the dying of Yeshua, so that the life of Yeshua also may be manifested in our body" (2 Corinthians 4:10). To one degree or another, the sufferings that the Messiah experienced on our behalf, are to be emulated in the way that we conduct ourselves. This does not mean that we are to physically torture ourselves, similar to the ascetic regulations of the false teachers (2:21-23), but ethically our character is to be one of self-less service and love to each other. Dying to our sinful selves will enable us to understand the magnificence of the Messiah's exaltation. Maxie D. Dunnam considers this to be how, "The risen and exalted Lord conquered death. We do not wait for eternal life; it is ours now. Risen with Christ, the glorious privilege of beginning now the life with Christ which will continue eternally is ours."[12]

The resurrection of the dead surely awaits us in the future—**but the life of the resurrection is to be a present experience now.** Wright observes, "There is a perfect balance here between the 'already' and the 'not yet' that are so characteristic of Paul's teaching...The new age has dawned, and Christians already belong to it. The old age, however, is not yet wound up, and until they die (or until the Lord 'appears' again in his second coming) their new life will be a secret truth."[13] Paul taught in Romans 8:18, "For I consider that the sufferings of this present time are not worthy to be compared with the glory that is to be revealed to us." John also says,

[9] Bruce, *Colossians-Philemon-Ephesians*, 134.

Dunn disagrees that a Pauline subversion of some kind of Jewish-Gnostic philosophy is in view in vs. 1-2, instead arguing that subversion of an apocalyptic Jewish view is seen throughout ch. 3, perhaps as evident in literature like *2 Baruch* 48:42-52:7 (Dunn, 202).

[10] Dunn, 207.
[11] Cf. Moo, 250.
[12] Dunnam, 372.
[13] Wright, 132.

"Beloved, now we are children of God, and it has not appeared as yet what we will be. We know that when He appears, we will be like Him, because we will see Him just as He is" (1 John 3:2).

Lincoln offers a good summary of what the "hidden" life of Believers entails: "This passage can serve...as a reminder that the real new age began with the resurrection of Jesus—not with a planetary shift from the Age of Pisces to the Age of Aquarius."[14] While Heavenly, the life of Believers is to be lived out on an Earth marred by sin—specifically so others can be impacted with the transforming power of the gospel!

3:4 So serious is the life of Believers, that the Apostle Paul actually asserts "When Messiah, who is {y}our life, is revealed, then you also will be revealed with Him in glory." The key statement here is *ho Christos phanerōthē, hē zōē humōn* (ὁ Χριστὸς φανερωθῇ, ἡ ζωὴ ὑμῶν). There is some strong manuscript evidence that points to *humōn* or "your" (NIV, NRSV, ESV, HCSB) actually being the original reading, as opposed to *hēmōn* (ἡμῶν) or "our."[15] O'Brien notes how any change between *humōn* and *hēmōn* "may have been due to faulty hearing or because a copyist wished to maintain the point that Christ is the life of Christians generally and not simply of those at Colossae."[16] If "Christ, who is your life" (NIV), is the more original reading, it does not significantly change anything—because by extension the Messiah is the life of all Believers. The Apostle Paul himself recognized how Yeshua was *his life*: "it is no longer I who live, but Messiah lives in me" (Galatians 2:20). Rhetorically, "Messiah, who is your life," would have placed a significant responsibility upon the Colossians to make sure that Yeshua was at the center of their faith (1:27).

Hearing "Messiah, who is {y}our life" in Colossians 3:4 is something that today's Messianics need to take very serious note of. This is not often something we hear in our congregations and assemblies—as opposed to the declaration "Torah is life." While Deuteronomy 32:46-47 does indeed say, "Take to your heart all the words with which I am warning you today...all the words of this law. For it is not an idle word for you; indeed it is your life [*ki-hu cha'yeikhem*, כִּי־הוּא חַיֵּיכֶם]," this is speaking of how the Torah's commandments are to be *the sphere of conduct* in which Ancient Israel, and certainly God's people today, are to live and find themselves (materially) blessed.[17] The point made in Colossians 3:1-4 is that having died to sin, and raised to new life with the Messiah, He is to be the source of where **eternal life** is found. There is no problem with today's Messianic movement placing a proper emphasis on the Torah as the high standard of God's holiness; but there is a problem when "Torah is life" equaling the means of inheriting eternal life is emphasized.

For a man like Paul, "to live is Messiah and to die is gain" (Philippians 1:21). Regardless of what happened in his life—even whether he lived or died—he did what he did because of who Yeshua was to him. Placing Yeshua at the center of one's being involves living properly in the current world, and looking forward to a future world where He reigns on Earth. O'Brien considers this to be "the life of the age to come which will be received on the final day and which through the resurrection of Christ from the dead has become for the believer a present reality,"[18] in what we might call an inaugurated eschatology. John's writings employ language that speaks of how those who belong to Yeshua pass from a realm of death to a realm of life (John 5:24-25; 11:25-26; 1 John 5:12).

One day in the future, Believers "will appear with him in glory" (RSV), the verb *phaneroō* (φανερόω) meaning "*to make manifest*" (LS).[19] This speaks of the future glorification of Believers at the resurrection (Romans 8:17; 1 Thessalonians 4:16-18), when the human person is fully restored (Hebrews 9:28), when the Lord "will transform the body of our humble state into conformity with the body of His glory, by the exertion of the power that He has even to subject all things to Himself" (Philippians 3:21). While experiencing great fulfillment in life on Earth with God's Spirit within Believers, there is a future coming and a definite return of the Messiah to Earth. Dunn points out, "Whether the present writers shared this expectation [as very soon]...is

---

[14] Lincoln, in *NIB*, 11:640.

[15] Metzger, *Textual Commentary*, 624.

[16] O'Brien, *Colossians-Philemon*, 157 fn #a.

[17] For further consideration, consult the thoughts expressed in Walter C. Kaiser, "Leviticus 18:5 and Paul: Do This and You Shall Live (Eternally?)" in Journal of the Evangelical Theological Society Vol. 14 No. 1 (1971):19-27, with his conclusions also seen in his book *Toward Old Testament Ethics* (Grand Rapids: Eerdmans, 1983).

[18] O'Brien, *Colossians-Philemon*, 165.

[19] *LS*, 855.

not clear...That the parousia is mentioned only here in Colossians is of ambiguous significance, since so many of the items included in the Pauline letters were determined by the circumstances addressed."[20] Vs. 1-4 place an emphasis on living the life of the world to come *now*, before it is actually manifest.

5 Therefore consider the members of your earthly body as dead to immorality, impurity, passion, evil desire, and greed, which amounts to idolatry. 6 For it is because of these things that the wrath of God will come upon the sons of disobedience, 7 and in them you also once walked, when you were living in them.

3:5 Living the life of the world to come, in the present evil world, requires serious changes to be evident in the lives of born again Believers. In the Torah, Ancient Israel was given a choice between two ways: "See, I have set before you today life and prosperity, and death and adversity; in that I command you today to love the LORD your God, to walk in His ways and to keep His commandments and His statutes and His judgments" (Deuteronomy 30:15-16ff). One choice leads to a life of blessing and close communion with God, and another choice leads to a life of cursing, death, and exile from God. Those who have made the choice to walk the right path, as Paul says, are to "Put to death therefore what is earthly in you" (RSV). *Ta melē ta epi tēs gēs* (τὰ μέλη τὰ ἐπὶ τῆς γῆς) are actually "your members that *are* upon the earth" (YLT), and an emphasis of how, in O'Brien's words,

"Being heavenly minded does not mean living in the clouds! The believer who obeys the apostolic injunction to aim at the things above will be involved in an ongoing spiritual warfare here below as he or she puts to death the sinful propensities and pursuits, and allows the new nature to find outward expression in a godly life."[21]

When examining v. 5, some readers need clarification as to what is intended by the use of "member" or *melos* (μέλος), simply meaning "*a limb*" (LS).[22] More than a few think that "members" is directly related to inappropriate sexual sins, and while this is by no means something to be excluded, *melē* would regard more the faculties of a person than anything else. This is the view reflected by Paul in Romans 6:13: "do not go on presenting the members of your body to sin *as* instruments of unrighteousness; but present yourselves to God as those alive from the dead, and your members *as* instruments of righteousness to God." Dunn comments, "the person's interaction with the wider world as through organs and limbs is what is in view. It was precisely the interaction which had characterized the Colossians' old way of life which is now targeted."[23]

After saying that their members are to be dead, v. 5 continues by listing a number of specific sins: "sexual immorality, impurity, lust, evil desires and greed, which is idolatry" (NIV). Victor Paul Furnish interjects his view, "Nothing specific about moral conditions at Colossae should be deduced from these lists,"[24] **but** is it completely impossible that the false teachers did not practice these sins to some degree or another? The whole purpose of Paul emphasizing that the Colossians are to place their attention on the Messiah, raised up with Him in Heaven, recognizing Yeshua as their life—is precisely because the ascetic philosophy (2:23) of the false teachers could not stop people from committing deeds of the flesh. Paul does not insist that the Colossians' life on Earth is "dead," but rather warns how specific vices are to no longer be present among them because of the resurrection power of Yeshua.

Paul observed previously in his letter to the Romans how there are immature Believers who wrestle with sin: "but I see a different law in the members of my body, waging war against the law of my mind and making me a prisoner of the law of sin which is in my members" (Romans 7:23).[25] The new life of faith in

---

[20] Dunn, 208.

[21] O'Brien, *Colossians-Philemon*, pp 175-176.

[22] LS, 496.

[23] Dunn, 212.

[24] Victor Paul Furnish, "The Letter of Paul to the Colossians," in Charles M. Laymon, ed., *The Interpreter's One-Volume Commentary on the Bible* (Nashville: Abingdon, 1971), 862.

[25] Be aware of how many Romans interpreters today are agreed that the "I" of Romans 7 is a hypothetical sinner, and not necessarily the Apostle Paul giving us autobiographical information. For a summary of this, consult J.M. Everts, "Conversion and Call of Paul," in *Dictionary of Paul and His Letters*, 158; and the author's article "The Message of Romans."

Yeshua requires one to understand, "if by the Spirit you are putting to death the deeds of the body, you will live" (Romans 8:13), something that is not instantaneous, although it should be *a steady process*. Bruce concurs, "The impartation of the new nature by Christ does not effect the immediate annihilation of the old hereditary nature; so long as [people] live in this world, the old nature persists like a dormant force which may spring into activity at any time."[26]

How significant are the sins listed by Paul in v. 5? Four sexual sins will later be followed by five anti-social sins (v. 8). Giving a list of sins is not something uncommon to the Pauline letters (Romans 1:29-31; 1 Corinthians 5:11; 6:9-10; Galatians 5:19-21; Ephesians 5:3-4). One may even see some parallels with what is said of sinners in Wisdom 14:25-26:

"For whether they kill children in their initiations, or celebrate secret mysteries, or hold frenzied revels with strange customs, they no longer keep either their lives or their marriages pure, but they either treacherously kill one another, or grieve one another by adultery, and all is a raging riot of blood and murder, theft and deceit, corruption, faithlessness, tumult, perjury, confusion over what is good, forgetfulness of favors, pollution of souls, sex perversion, disorder in marriage, adultery, and debauchery."

There is certainly discussion among Colossians commentators as to where the vice/virtue lists seen in the epistle likely originated. Did they come from Jewish proselyte requirements, ancient Stoic philosophy, or the Qumran literature? It is not at all difficult to discern how the sins listed in vs. 5, 8-9 are forbidden in the Torah, and a principally Jewish background is invoked for them. A cursory examination of the Apocrypha, Philo, and the DSS show us some further parallels:

In pleasure there exists even a malevolent tendency, which is the most complex of all the emotions. In the soul it is boastfulness, covetousness, thirst for honor, rivalry, and malice; in the body, indiscriminate eating, gluttony, and solitary gormandizing (4 Maccabees 1:25-27).

Know, then, my good friend, that if you become a votary of pleasure you will be all these things: a bold, cunning, audacious, unsociable, uncourteous, inhuman, lawless, savage, illtempered, unrestrainable, worthless man; deaf to advice, foolish, full of evil acts, unteachable, unjust, unfair, one who has no participation with others, one who cannot be trusted in his agreements, one with whom there is no peace, covetous, most lawless, unfriendly, homeless, cityless, seditious, faithless, disorderly, impious, unholy, unsettled, unstable, uninitiated, profane, polluted, indecent, destructive, murderous, illiberal, abrupt, brutal, slavish, cowardly, intemperate, irregular, disgraceful, shameful, doing and suffering all infamy, colourless, immoderate, unsatiable, insolent, conceited, self-willed, mean, envious, calumnious, quarrelsome, slanderous, greedy, deceitful, cheating, rash, ignorant, stupid, inharmonious, dishonest, disobedient, obstinate, tricky, swindling, insincere, suspicious, hated, absurd, difficult to detect, difficult to avoid, destructive, evil-minded, disproportionate, an unreasonable chatterer, a proser, a gossip, a vain babbler, a flatterer, a fool, full of heavy sorrow, weak in bearing grief, trembling at every sound, inclined to delay, inconsiderate, improvident, impudent, neglectful of good, unprepared, ignorant of virtue, always in the wrong, erring, stumbling, ill-managed, ill-governed, a glutton, a captive, a spendthrift, easily yielding, most crafty, double-minded, double-tongued, perfidious, treacherous, unscrupulous, always unsuccessful, always in want, infirm of purpose, fickle, a wanderer, a follower of others, yielding to impulses, open to the attacks of enemies, mad, easily satisfied, fond of life, fond of vain glory, passionate, ill-tempered, lazy, a procrastinator, suspected, incurable, full of evil jealousies, despairing, full of tears, rejoicing in evil, frantic, beside yourself, without any steady character, contriving evil, eager for disgraceful gain, selfish, a willing slave, an eager enemy, a demagogue, a bad steward, stiffnecked, effeminate, outcast, confused, discarded, mocking, injurious, vain, full of unmitigated unalloyed misery (Philo *Sacrifices of Abel and Cain* 32).[27]

The operations of the spirit of falsehood result in greed, neglect of righteous deeds, wickedness, lying, pride and haughtiness, cruel deceit and fraud, massive hypocrisy, a want of self-control and abundant

---

[26] Bruce, *Colossians-Philemon-Ephesians*, 142.
[27] *The Works of Philo: Complete and Unabridged*, 98.

foolishness, a zeal for arrogance, abominable deeds fashioned by whorish desire, lechery in its filthy manifestation, a reviling tongue, blind eyes, deaf ears, stiff neck, and hard heart—to the end of walking in all the ways of darkness and evil cunning (1QS 4.9-11).[28]

All of these vices seen **depict a pagan way of life that is to be gone** in the lives of the Colossians. Dunn considers the most significant parallel to exist with CD 4.15-19 in the DSS, an interpretation of Isaiah 24:27, "Terror and pit and snare confront you, O inhabitant of the earth":

"The true meaning of this verse concerns the three traps of Belial about which Levi son of Jacob said that Belial would catch Israel in...The first is fornication; the second is wealth; the third is defiling the sanctuary. Who escapes from one is caught in the next; and whoever escapes from that is caught in the other."[29]

It cannot be denied how every single one of the sins in vs. 5, 8-9 is spoken against in the Torah (hardly what we would expect if the Law really were nailed to the cross in Colossians 2:14, losing all of its validity and relevance). Even though the false teachers would be insistent in matters like Sabbath, New Moons, various festivals, and eating—as these Torah practices had been hijacked as a part of their philosophy (2:16)—how much did they actually discuss and emphasize ethical and moral matters? Sexual sins are the first listed in v. 5, for the specific reason that most of the new, non-Jewish Believers entered into the *ekklēsia* from a Hellenistic society that had low sexual morals. Greek males, in particular, were often allowed to do many things that Jewish culture would completely disallow. A Jewish sentiment seen in the Pseudepigrapha specifically expresses,

"The majority of other men defile themselves in their relationships, thereby committing a serious offense, and lands and whole cities take pride in it: they not only procure the males, they also defile mothers and daughters. We are quite separated from these practices" (*Letter of Aristeas* 152).[30]

What would have been the purpose of Paul listing the various sins of v. 5? Did these sins have any relationship to what the false teachers were advocating? What we know for certain is that the Colossians were under the threat of being seriously influenced by errant worldly philosophies, many of which seem to be represented by teachings that would later classify as being a part of Gnosticism. One of the gross errors of Gnosticism was the teaching that what one did in the body, physically, did not affect a person spiritually. Obviously, Paul insisted that the Colossians were dead to specific physical sins.[31]

I would consider it possible that these were some of the sins that were being practiced by those who were influenced by the errors of early Gnosticism. Not only did the false philosophy not help curtail fleshly urges, but perhaps being so entrenched by their ascetic rituals, should the false teachers have fallen into these various physical sins—they would have failed to stand convicted. Contrary to this would be how when **the Messiah is your life**, sins committed in one's physical body do affect a person spiritually, and/or rewards (or punishment) experienced in the hereafter. *Conviction from the Holy Spirit to rectify mistakes should also be present.*

3:6 There is an important reason not to have sinful vices present in one's life: "it is because of these things that the wrath of God will come upon the sons of disobedience." Some kind of eschatological judgment on sinners is anticipated by the Tanach (i.e., Isaiah 13; 34:1-4; Zephaniah 1:14-18), although the details are frequently debated as applying to a Day of the LORD when Yeshua returns to the Earth, versus the second resurrection (Revelation 20:6, 11-12) followed by the eternal state. The vantage point of Paul in v. 6 sees *hē orgē tou Theou* (ἡ ὀργὴ τοῦ Θεοῦ) as the wrath of God distributed upon sinners at the final judgment. Yeshua the Messiah "rescues us from the wrath to come" (1 Thessalonians 1:10; cf. Romans 2:5), in that His salvation renders such wrath inoperative for born again Believers. A definite parallel exists between vs. 5-6, and Ephesians 5:5-6:

---

[28] Wise, Abegg, and Cook, 130.

[29] Ibid., 55; cf. Dunn, 213.

[30] R.J.H. Shutt, trans., "Letter of Aristeas," in *The Old Testament Pseudepigrapha*, Vol 2, 23.

[31] Consult Dunn, pp 214-217, for a detailed summary of these sins in an ancient Jewish and Greco-Roman context.

"For this you know with certainty, that no immoral or impure person or covetous man, who is an idolater, has an inheritance in the kingdom of Messiah and God. Let no one deceive you with empty words, for because of these things the wrath of God comes upon the sons of disobedience."

While the wrath of God is something that is to be distributed upon sinners at the final judgment, the Apostle Paul's inaugurated eschatology enables him to see that just as Believers get to participate, at least partially, in the life of the world to come—**so do sinners get to similarly participate in the judgment to come.** While the NASU renders v. 6 with the future tense "will come," *erchetai* (ἔρχεται) is a middle voice, present tense verb, rendered in other versions as "is coming" (RSV, NIV, NRSV, ESV), leaving the arrival of God's judgment as something that need not necessarily wait until the final day. In Romans 1:18ff, Paul expresses how "the wrath of God is revealed from heaven against all ungodliness and unrighteousness of men who suppress the truth in unrighteousness," employing the present tense *Apokaluptetai* (Ἀποκαλύπτεται) for "revealed."

Furthermore, the wrath of God is blind to anyone's pedigree: "to those who are selfishly ambitious and do not obey the truth, but obey unrighteousness, wrath and indignation. *There will be* tribulation and distress for every soul of man who does evil, of the Jew first and also of the Greek" (Romans 2:8-9). Paul's theology of sin requires him to recognize that all of humanity—including his own Jewish people—are subject to the penalties of sin should they fail to repent (Romans 3:9ff).

There is certainly a significant degree of controversy in theological studies over what eternal punishment actually is, with many of us forced to navigate between the extremes of annihilationism (where the condemned are completely snuffed out of existence), universal salvation (where not only will evil men like Hitler or Stalin be redeemed, but even Satan), and even those who hold to a too literal fire and smoke for eternity (which often does not counterbalance itself with descriptions of eternal punishment as "outer darkness" as seen in Matthew 8:12; 22:13; 25:30; etc.).[32] Too many might be overly influenced by thinking of eternal punishment as being locked up in a castle dungeon from the Middle Ages, whereas what it really involves is the unredeemed losing their right to rule beside God as His viceroy (Psalm 8; Hebrews 2:5-8).

In Wright's estimation, "Part of the horror of hell, it appears, is that those who consciously and continually choose sin instead of God become less and less human, until all that ennobles them as creatures made in God's image has, by their own choice, been altogether obliterated, beyond hope or pity."[33] Those who lose God's image (Genesis 1:27-28), in this way then, forfeit their right to enter into His purpose as rulers over the redeemed state.

3:7 How significant was it for the Colossians to know that a life of sin merits God's punishment? Paul actually expresses a positive sentiment for them, writing, "You used to walk in these ways, in the life you once lived" (NIV). The usage of "walk" here is characteristic of a Jewish author (1:10), and the sinful experiences are now—for the most part—behind the Colossians, especially as they now know Messiah as their life (v. 4). Dunn observes how, "Probably it was the revulsion against such [a negative] ethos which attracted many Gentiles to the stronger morality of Judaism."[34] The expanse of the Messianic movement in the future, just like the First Century Messianic movement, should likewise occur because of a wider emphasis upon Torah ethics and morality. Yet this will be quite incumbent upon our future leaders and teachers being well versed in theological conversation.

---

[32] For a further discussion, consult William V. Crockett, ed., *Four Views on Hell* (Grand Rapids: Zondervan, 1996), and the author's article "Why Hell Must Be Eternal."

The author generally adheres to Crockett's own metaphorical view of eternal punishment, which holds to eternal punishment actually taking place and being ongoing for eternity, but interprets images like fire, smoke, brimstone, and darkness as principally being literary images of its severity.

Also useful to consider is Bruce Milne, *The Message of Heaven & Hell* (Downers Grove, IL: InterVarsity, 2002).

[33] Wright, pp 135-136.

[34] Dunn, 218.

8 But now you also, put them all aside: anger, wrath, malice, slander, *and* abusive speech from your mouth. 9 Do not lie to one another, since you laid aside the old self with its *evil* practices, 10 and have put on the new self who is being renewed to a true knowledge according to the image of the One who created him—

3:8-9 It would seem that although some major sexual vices have been put out of the lives of the Colossians (v. 5), some significant social vices still have yet to be fully gone. Paul further instructs, "But now you must rid yourselves of all such things as these: anger, rage, malice, slander, and filthy language from your lips. Do not lie to each other" (vs. 8-9a, NIV). In telling the Colossians to eliminate these sins from their lives, he says "you have put off the old self with its practices" (v. 9b, ESV), *ton palaion anthrōpon* (τὸν παλαιὸν ἄνθρωπον) representing the old, sinful person destined for God's wrath. The concept of putting off sin, and putting on God's righteousness and holiness, is appropriated directly from the Tanach:

"I put on righteousness, and it clothed me; my justice was like a robe and a turban" (Job 29:14).

"I will rejoice greatly in the LORD, my soul will exult in my God; for He has clothed me with garments of salvation, He has wrapped me with a robe of righteousness, as a bridegroom decks himself with a garland, and as a bride adorns herself with her jewels" (Isaiah 61:10).

3:10 As the Colossians are instructed to put off their old selves and the attendant sins, they are to "put on the new self, which is being renewed in knowledge after the image of its creator" (ESV). *Ton neon* (τὸν νέον) describes a new way of existence, with the deeds of sin ripped away. Even more specific, the verb *enduō* (ἐνδύω) can mean **"to put any kind of thing on oneself, *clothe oneself in, put on, wear*"** (BDAG),[35] almost as though redeemed people are to take off old sinful clothes, and put on new righteous clothes. This is a recognition of how "if anyone is in Messiah, *he is* a new creature; the old things passed away; behold, new things have come" (2 Corinthians 5:17). Connections can definitely be seen with Paul's parallel letter, where he further explains,

"[I]n reference to your former manner of life, you lay aside the old self, which is being corrupted in accordance with the lusts of deceit, and that you be renewed in the spirit of your mind, and put on the new self, which in *the likeness of* God has been created in righteousness and holiness of the truth" (Ephesians 4:22-24).

The second clause of v. 10 describes how Believers are to be brought "to a true knowledge according to the image of the One who created him." In saying that they are to come *eis epignōsin* (εἰς ἐπίγνωσιν) or "to knowledge," Paul is subverting the terms used by the false teachers in Colossae. Rather than acquiring knowledge through their philosophy, it instead comes via the power of God changing mature men and women, something seen by the present passive participle *anakainoumenon* (ἀνακαινούμενον), "being renewed"—describing actions that only He can perform in leading people to such knowledge by His Spirit (cf. Romans 8:26-27). And in such renewal—a direct consequence of placing trust in Yeshua—the image of God that was marred by the Fall can be restored to people. Such transformation will be directly evident in the good and upright moral conduct of Believers. Also to be considered is how *tou ktisantos* (τοῦ κτίσαντος), "the creator," as Ben Witherington III notes, possibly "even...refers to Christ in light of ch. 1..."[36] According to Paul, it is, after all, the image of the Son that Believers are to be conformed to (Romans 8:29).

God's renewal work of people who cry out to Him, is something seen throughout the Tanach, as evidenced in multiple passages:

"And I will give them one heart, and put a new spirit within them. And I will take the heart of stone out of their flesh and give them a heart of flesh, that they may walk in My statutes and keep My ordinances and do them. Then they will be My people, and I shall be their God" (Ezekiel 11:19-20; cf. 36:26-27).

---

[35] *BDAG*, 333.
[36] Witherington, 178.

"Cast away from you all your transgressions which you have committed and make yourselves a new heart and a new spirit! For why will you die, O house of Israel?" (Ezekiel 18:31).

"Create in me a clean heart, O God, and renew a steadfast spirit within me" (Psalm 51:10).

In connection with what is seen in v. 11, Moo actually suggests that the new self, which the Colossians are to put on and wear, is not necessarily to be understood in terms of individuals per se, but rather "This language strongly suggests that the 'new self' is not a part of an individual or even an individual as a whole, but some kind of corporate entity."[37] He considers the new self to be the *kainon anthrōpon* (καινὸν ἄνθρωπον) or "one new humanity" (Ephesians 2:15, NRSV/CJB) that Paul will speak about in Ephesians. This is certainly something not to be dismissed, because even if individuals are likely in principal view in vs. 7-10, individuals make up a corporate whole in the Body of Messiah.

11 *a renewal* **in which there is no** *distinction between* **Greek and Jew, circumcised and uncircumcised, barbarian, Scythian, slave and freeman, but Messiah is all, and in all.**

3:11 Quite significant within Paul's instruction to the Colossians is how putting on the new self has universal ramifications. Unlike the false teachers who may have catered only to a select few, Paul asserts that "The new self allows no room for discriminating between [Greek] and Jew[38], circumcised and uncircumcised, foreigner, savage, slave, free man; on the contrary, in all, the Messiah is everything" (CJB). V. 11 parallels his previous word in Galatians 3:28, "There is neither Jew nor Greek, there is neither slave nor free man, there is neither male nor female; for you are all one in Messiah Yeshua," where he deliberately undermined some Rabbinical sentiments of his day (t.*Berachot* 6:18),[39] speaking of the grand equality all (including women!) experience in the gospel.[40] Paul also says in 1 Corinthians 12:13, "For by one Spirit we were all baptized into one body, whether Jews or Greeks, whether slaves or free, and we were all made to drink of one Spirit," an allusion to how the Holy Spirit is blind when it comes to distributing power to redeemed people.

Paul's assertion in v. 11 is that ethnic standing, circumcision standing (likely including whether one was a Jewish proselyte or not), cultural standing, linguistic standing, or social standing does not matter that much when it comes to the work of the Lord within His people. This is because "Messiah is all, and in all," *[ta] panta kai en pasin Christos* ([τὰ] πάντα καὶ ἐν πᾶσιν Χριστός)—**as He is to be the focal point around whom all Believers are united.** This grand equality between all who place their trust in Him (Romans 3:22; 10:12), as Bruce indicates, is something "especially celebrated in the first three chapters of Ephesians,"[41] as the reconciliation of Jewish and non-Jewish Believers toward one another is a foreshadowing of the grand redemption that is to come to the cosmos (Ephesians 3:10).

Colossians 3:11 expands the categories that Paul originally listed in Galatians 3:28, but rather than subverting various Jewish prejudices, he here makes a point to more subvert various Greek and Roman prejudices. All of the groups listed regarded the other as inferior.[42] This is especially seen by the Phillips New Testament rendering of "foreigner or savage," given ancient classical prejudices toward the Scythians. The Scythians were a nomadic people originating from the area to the north and east of the Black Sea, known for herding sheep and goats, but also serving as brutal mercenaries.[43] The Jewish historian Josephus would actually say, "Now, as to the Scythians, they take a pleasure in killing men, and differ but little from brute

---

[37] Moo, 267.

[38] Grk. *Hellēn kai Ioudaios* (Ἕλλην καὶ Ἰουδαῖος).

[39] Cf. Joseph H. Hertz, ed., *The Authorised Daily Prayer Book*, revised (New York: Bloch Publishing Company, 1960), pp 19, 21; cf. Nosson Scherman and Meir Zlotowitz, eds., *Complete ArtScroll Siddur, Nusach Ashkenaz* (Brooklyn: Mesorah Publications, 1984), 19.

[40] For a further discussion, consult the author's exegetical paper on Galatians 3:28, "Biblical Equality and Today's Messianic Movement."

[41] Bruce, *Colossians-Philemon-Ephesians*, 149.

[42] Consult Dunn, pp 223-227, for a more detailed expansion of how this was the case.

[43] For more information, consult Karen S. Rubinson, "Scythians," in *ABD*, 5:1056-1057.

beasts" (*Against Apion* 2.269).[44] **Yet in the Messiah, such prejudices against people needing His salvation are to be erased.**

In addressing the universal effects of how the gospel can change people, neither Paul nor any Colossians commentator today, is going to conclude that various differences between people suddenly go away. *They do not.* But they are not to be present in terms of the working of God in the lives of people, as He shows no prejudices toward those whom He saves. Wright indicates, "differences of background, nationality, colour, language, social standing and so forth must be regarded as irrelevant to the question of the love, honour and respect that are to be shown to individuals and groups."[45] This is especially seen in Paul's companion letter to Philemon, regarding what he is to do with the runaway slave Onesimus, treating him "no longer as a slave, but more than a slave, a beloved brother" (Philemon 16).

So, if national and social identities are not erased in Yeshua, what is the role that they should play in relation to the salvation Yeshua has provided? Bruce observes, "Natural and racial idiosyncrasies may survive, but in such a way as to contribute to the living variety of the people of Christ, not so as to create or perpetuate any difference in spiritual status."[46] Moo further describes, "these earthly identities are no longer what is most important: solidarity in Christ is now the ruling paradigm for the new community."[47] This is not at all an easy lesson for today's Messianic movement, which still often falls into the paradigm of Galatians 2:16—an attention focused around human "works of law" (cf. 4QMMT),[48] rather than on Yeshua's faithfulness demonstrated for us.[49] Messianic Judaism, in particular, runs the serious risk of focusing on Jewish-ness at the expense of Yeshua-ness, and in failing to integrate the virtues that many non-Jewish Messianics bring from their native cultures,[50] which can aid in the mission of God for His "one new humanity." Witherington's thoughts are well taken:

"The basis of any kind of ordering in the [assembly] is according to what one is called and gifted to do, a rather bold break from the way things tended to be determined in the pagan world, and also to a larger degree in the Jewish world."[51]

As important as it is to recognize the grand equality that all Believers in Yeshua are to experience, and especially for Messianics how Jewish and non-Jewish Believers are to be bound by His salvation, it is quite easy to see how some can take Colossians 3:11 a bit too far. Lincoln oversteps the appropriate bounds when asserting,

"What are the contemporary equivalents of the categories listed in 3:11 that ought not to be obstacles to unity and reconciled relationships within the church? Certainly male and female still need to be added, and, in light of contemporary understanding of sexual orientation, gay/lesbian and straight should be included. In a global context, the disparity between 'First World' and 'Two-thirds World' Christians scarcely reflects a universal community displaying the overcoming of differences in a loving and just reconciliation in Christ."[52]

We can certainly agree with Lincoln that there are many unnecessary divisions among Believers today, extending to males and females, and also differences between people in the First World and those who live below poverty. Lincoln goes too far, though, in suggesting that sexual orientation is an inappropriate barrier between Believers—especially when the Apostle Paul himself considered homosexual behavior to be a principal result of the pagan Gentiles turning away from the One True God (Romans 1:26-28), a sure reflection of his Torah ethic (Leviticus 18:22; 20:13). Certainly, both evangelical Christians and Messianic Believers often have a way to go in treating homosexual men and women as human beings to be afforded basic rights—

---

[44] *The Works of Josephus: Complete and Unabridged*, 810.

[45] Wright, 140.

[46] Bruce, *Colossians-Philemon-Ephesians*, 149.

[47] Moo, 272.

[48] Consult the author's article "What Are 'Works of the Law'?"

[49] Consult the author's article "The Faithfulness of Yeshua the Messiah."

[50] One of the most important of these virtues would be the strong integration of the Protestant work ethic, applied to how we approach theological research and Biblical Studies.

[51] Witherington, 179.

[52] Lincoln, in *NIB*, 11:646.

people for whom Yeshua was sacrificed (2:14) and who the Father values and loves greatly. But, their non-Biblical lifestyle should very much prohibit them from serving in the leadership of today's *ekklēsia*. They deserve to be shown the love of the Messiah, but their lifestyle is not something that is approved of in the Scriptures.[53]

Contrary to the false teachers of Colossae, who were desiring ecstatic, ethereal trances of another dimension, the power of Yeshua has the awesome capacity to change people while on Earth. Moo observes how "in opposition to a tendency among the false teachers to exclusivity," the Apostle Paul stresses "that the new humanity is inclusive of every nation and every social class."[54] This is because "Christ is all that matters for Christ lives in all" (Phillips New Testament). Yeshua is to be everywhere within every Believer, and so it is incumbent upon fellow brothers and sisters to recognize the Lord Yeshua in one another, the One who reigns supreme (cf. 1 Corinthians 15:28). Dunn has some excellent thoughts that each of us may have to consider:

"[I]t is precisely [this] thought of Christ in a cosmic role, as embodying the creative power and rationality by which God created and sustains the cosmos...Anyone who recognizes God in Christ to that extent will find such human distinctions and boundaries relatively trivial and unimportant."[55]

12 So, as those who have been chosen of God, holy and beloved, put on a heart of compassion, kindness, humility, gentleness and patience; 13 bearing with one another, and forgiving each other, whoever has a complaint against anyone; just as the Lord forgave you, so also should you.

3:12 The grand spiritual renewal, which knows no ethnic or cultural boundaries, that Yeshua can enact within a person—manifests itself in concrete attitudes of holiness and appropriate conduct. Paul instructs the Colossians, "Put on then, as God's chosen ones, holy and beloved, compassion, kindness, lowliness, meekness, and patience" (RSV). This would have had an important rhetorical effect for people in Asia Minor, as Witherington indicates, "The three synonyms piled up together at the outside—the elect, the holy ones, the beloved—are again an Asiatic trait."[56] Not to be overlooked at all is how in describing born again Believers, Paul appropriates language that is used in the Tanach to originally describe Israel. Simply consider what is summarized of Ancient Israel in Deuteronomy 7:6-8:

"For you are a holy people to the LORD your God; the LORD your God has chosen you to be a people for His own possession out of all the peoples who are on the face of the earth. The LORD did not set His love on you nor choose you because you were more in number than any of the peoples, for you were the fewest of all peoples, but because the LORD loved you and kept the oath which He swore to your forefathers, the LORD brought you out by a mighty hand and redeemed you from the house of slavery, from the hand of Pharaoh king of Egypt."

Dunn validly observes, "the idea of a people 'chosen by God' was wholly and exclusively Jewish, a fundamental feature of Israel's self-perception...More clearly than anywhere else in Colossians it is evident that the Gentile recipients of the letter were being invited to consider themselves full participants in the people and heritage of Israel."[57] To certainly be considered would be how the Colossians would relate to Deuteronomy 4:37: "Because He loved your fathers, therefore He chose their descendants after them. And He personally brought you from Egypt by His great power." Such embedded references to Israel, in describing

---

[53] The issue of homosexuality is planned to be explored in the author's forthcoming book *Honoring One Another: Gender Roles, Sexuality, and Equality in Today's Messianic Movement.*

[54] Moo, pp 272-273.

[55] Dunn, 227.

[56] Witherington, 179.

[57] Dunn, pp 227-228.

Do note Wright's conclusions of a replacement theology spoken of here: "As God's new humanity (3:10) the church is God's true Israel, to whom have been transferred the epithets which formerly belonged to Israel in the flesh" (Wright, 141). In recognizing that the *ekklēsia* is not an entity distinct and apart from Israel, he goes too far in suggesting that the *ekklēsia* has supplanted physical promises originally given to Israel.

groups of largely non-Jewish Believers, is not at all uncommon to Paul (cf. Romans 1:7). It is also seen in the Apostle Peter's writing:

"But you are A CHOSEN RACE, A royal PRIESTHOOD, A HOLY NATION, A PEOPLE FOR *God's* OWN POSSESSION, so that you may proclaim the excellencies of Him who has called you out of darkness into His marvelous light; for you were NOT A PEOPLE, but now you are THE PEOPLE OF GOD; you had NOT RECEIVED MERCY, but now you have RECEIVED MERCY" (1 Peter 2:9-10; cf. Deuteronomy 7:6; 10:15; Exodus 19:6; Isaiah 61:6; 43:21; Deuteronomy 4:20; 14:2; Hosea 2:23).[58]

In O'Brien's estimation, what we see in v. 12 describing Believers—and the *ekklēsia* as Israel—is also important because they serve to identify Yeshua the Messiah. He comments, "These descriptions are important not only because they were used of Israel as God's own possession...but also since they are designated of Christ thereby underlining the point of their similarity in a chosen context where they are encouraged to put on his graces."[59] Yeshua Himself is chosen (1 Peter 2:4, 6), is the Holy One (John 6:69; Acts 4:27, 30), and is supremely loved (Matthew 3:17; Ephesians 1:6). Similar to how the Colossians are to put on the godly traits listed in v. 12, Paul previously wrote the Romans, "put on the Lord Yeshua the Messiah, and make no provision for the flesh in regard to *its* lusts" (Romans 13:14). Also not to be overlooked is the reason for God's choosing Israel: "He chose us in Him before the foundation of the world, that we would be holy and blameless before Him" (Ephesians 1:4).

We can definitely see commonality between Colossians 3:12, Paul's prior writing of the fruit of the Spirit in Galatians 5:22-23, and his paralleling comments in Ephesians 4:2:

GALATIANS 5:22-23	COLOSSIANS 3:12	EPHESIANS 4:2
But the fruit of the Spirit is love, joy, peace, patience, kindness, goodness, faithfulness, gentleness, self-control; against such things there is no law.	So, as those who have been chosen of God, holy and beloved, put on a heart of compassion, kindness, humility, gentleness and patience;	with all humility and gentleness, with patience, showing tolerance for one another in love,

The emphasis on "chosenness" is by no means a being chosen simply for the sake of being "special"; Believers are chosen of God to live proper, upstanding lives that reflect the righteousness of their King. This does notably include *tapeinophrosunē* (ταπεινοφροσύνη) or "humility," but of a much different kind than what was advocated by the Colossian errorists (2:23). Instead, this humility is to be a considerable trait adhered to by those whose "life is hidden with Messiah in God" (v. 3).

3:13 In putting on the proper traits, becoming of those chosen of God, the Colossians are to be "bearing with one another, and forgiving each other, whoever has a complaint against anyone; just as the Lord forgave you, so also should you." This attitude of forgiving is certainly true of those inside the community of Believers, but also stands true toward outsiders causing harm, such as the false teachers. They are to be forgiven for the problems they have wreaked, and if possible, brought to a point of repentance from their false doctrines, and reconciled with the community. Unfortunately, though, in both the First Century and today, false teachers frequently do not repudiate their false teachings in order to actually be reconciled and brought back into good standing.

Paul's parallel letter will expand upon v. 13 further, extending forgiveness to the need to tolerate people, presumably on doctrinal non-essentials:

"Therefore I, the prisoner of the Lord, implore you to walk in a manner worthy of the calling with which you have been called, with all humility and gentleness, with patience, showing tolerance for one another in

---

[58] Cf. Dunnam, 376.
[59] O'Brien, *Colossians-Philemon*, 197.

love...Be kind to one another, tender-hearted, forgiving each other, just as God in Messiah also has forgiven you" (Ephesians 4:1-2, 32; doctrinal essentials: 4:1-6).

14 Beyond all these things *put on* love, which is the perfect bond of unity. 15 Let the peace of Messiah rule in your hearts, to which indeed you were called in one body; and be thankful. 16 Let the word of Messiah richly dwell within you, with all wisdom teaching and admonishing one another with psalms *and* hymns *and* spiritual songs, singing with thankfulness in your hearts to God. 17 Whatever you do in word or deed, *do* all in the name of the Lord Yeshua, giving thanks through Him to God the Father.

3:14 The virtues that have just been listed (vs. 12-13), are now given practical application. Important to recognize is that as critical as they all are, Paul is clear to say, "And over all these virtues put on love, which binds them all together in perfect unity" (NIV). Love is placed as the most preeminent of the godly traits that Believers are to demonstrate, which among contemporary Jewish lists is notably not given as such a high status. In the DSS, we see some appropriate virtues that people of God are to have, but with love or compassion *not* given the top billing:

"This spirit engenders humility, patience, abundant compassion, perpetual goodness, insight, understanding, and powerful wisdom resonating to each of God's deeds, sustained by His constant faithfulness" (1QS 4.3-4).[60]

Also not to be overlooked is how Plato thought that law is what bound a city or society together (*Laws* 921c).[61]

In Paul's estimation, as important as God's Torah may be, love was to be the common denominator that upheld what its true intention was, and what God's people are to be focused around *first:*

"For this, 'YOU SHALL NOT COMMIT ADULTERY, YOU SHALL NOT MURDER, YOU SHALL NOT STEAL, YOU SHALL NOT COVET,' and if there is any other commandment, it is summed up in this saying, 'YOU SHALL LOVE YOUR NEIGHBOR AS YOURSELF.' Love does no wrong to a neighbor; therefore love is the fulfillment of *the* law" (Romans 13:9-10).

"But now faith, hope, love, abide these three; but the greatest of these is love" (1 Corinthians 13:13).

In the application of the supremacy of love, we can also consider connections to Yeshua's parable of the unforgiving servant, where those who fail to forgive are not shown any mercy from the Heavenly Father (Matthew 18:23-25).

3:15 If love is able to reign supreme in the hearts of the Colossians, then they will be able to have peace. Paul instructs, "and let the *shalom* which comes from the Messiah be your heart's decision-maker, for this is why you were called to be part of a single Body" (CJB). This is also seen in his parallel teaching in Ephesians 2:14, where Paul asserts, "For He Himself [Yeshua] is our peace." Peace or *eirēnē* (εἰρήνη) is by no means to be understood just in its classical context, but most specifically in its Hebraic context of *shalom* (שָׁלוֹם). This speaks of not only absence of war, but total peace, harmony, tranquility, and wholeness[62]—something fully promised to God's people in the future eschaton—yet something to be partaken of now in their lives on sinful Earth (Isaiah 9:6-7; 54:10; Ezekiel 34:25-31; 37:26; Micah 5:4; Haggai 2:9; Zechariah 8:12). Paul would write the Philippians that "the peace of God, which surpasses all comprehension, will guard your hearts and your minds in Messiah Yeshua" (Philippians 4:7), a present reality to be experienced. This is the peace that Yeshua promised to leave with His followers: "Peace I leave with you; My peace I give to you; not as the world gives do I give to you. Do not let your heart be troubled, nor let it be fearful" (John 14:27).

Most significantly, the peace of the Messiah is a Heavenly peace (vs. 1-2), and it will enable God's people to settle any disputes that they have among themselves as they love one another (cf. 1 Corinthians 13:5).

---

[60] Wise, Abegg, and Cook, 130.

[61] Plato: *The Laws*, trans. Trevor J. Saunders (London: Penguin Books, 1970), 420.

[62] G. Lloyd Carr, "shālōm," in R. Laird Harris, Gleason L. Archer, Jr., and Bruce K. Waltke, eds., *Theological Wordbook of the Old Testament* (Chicago: Moody Press, 1980), 2:931.

3:16 Similar to how peace is to rule, so also does Paul instruct the Colossians, "Let the word of Christ dwell in you richly; teach and admonish one another in all wisdom; and with gratitude in your hearts sing psalms, hymns, and spiritual songs to God" (NRSV). The "word of Messiah" is likely a reference to either the gospel, or Yeshua's teachings, considered by the TNIV to be "the message of Christ."

There could very easily be a connection intended between v. 16 and the hymn that Paul used previously in 1:15-20, detailing what Yeshua has accomplished. Paul says, "Let the message of Christ continue to live in you in all its wealth of wisdom" (Williams New Testament), the clause *en pasē sophia* (ἐν πάσῃ σοφίᾳ) or "in all wisdom" being a deliberate subversion of the false teachers' philosophy. This wisdom is only brought by the word of the Messiah, or the gospel. Furthermore, this message involves *didaskontes kai nouthetountes* (διδάσκοντες καὶ νουθετοῦντες) or "teaching and admonishing" (NASU). Teaching regards positive instruction, whereas admonishing often involves negative warnings.[63]

As "the word of Messiah" dwells in the hearts of God's people, it will be evident by their character of worship. We see a wide array of worship techniques referred to by Paul in v. 16, including: psalms, hymns, and spiritual songs. Too many people today, perhaps because of extreme influences from the charismatic movement, often think that non-spontaneous worship is not spiritual (or even worse, non-spontaneous preaching), yet it is clear simply from v. 16, that formal styles of worship are to play a primary role to more spontaneous styles.

Today's Messianic Believers need to be quite consciously aware of how the First Century Messianic movement directly inherited a rich liturgical tradition from the Jewish Synagogue. In Romans 9:4, Paul observed that to his Jewish people "belongs the adoption as sons, and the glory and the covenants and the giving of the Law and the *temple* service," with *latreia* (λατρεία) being of notable importance. The early Believers certainly employed many of the Psalms from the Tanach in their worship to God, but they were equally quite adept at producing their own songs and hymns. Many of the early hymns of the First Century Believers expressed key doctrinal confessions about Yeshua, such as Colossians 1:15-20, and also Philippians 2:6-11 and 1 Timothy 3:16.

Our worship today need not be exclusively liturgical, or exclusively cater to the needs of spontaneity. Messianic assemblies and congregations should seek a fair medium, where the three groups of psalms, hymns, and spiritual songs all play an important role—ministering to all people, yet people who may have some unique and different needs.[64]

3:17 Worshipping the Lord is notably something that *is not to end* in corporate meeting times, but extends to how a person functions throughout the normal work week. Paul tells the Colossians, "and all, whatever ye may do in word or in work, *do all things in the name of the Lord Jesus*—giving thanks to the God and Father, through him" (YLT). All things considered pertain directly *en logō ē en ergō* (ἐν λόγῳ ἢ ἐν ἔργῳ), "in word or in work" (YLT/LITV). It could be argued that "in word" is a connection back to "the word of Messiah" (v. 16), although much more likely "in word or in work" regards "whatever you do or say" (NLT).

There are some important Jewish parallels to be considered with v. 17, indicating that Paul is only appropriating concepts in which he had been originally trained, and is now placing a life in Yeshua the Messiah as the prime focus. Sirach 47:8, describing King David, says, "In all that he did he gave thanks to the Holy One, the Most High, with ascriptions of glory; he sang praise with all his heart, and he loved his Maker." An admonition seen in the Mishnah explains, "may everything you do be for the sake of Heaven" (m.*Avot* 2:12).[65]

One can easily see that for a transformed Believer, for whom Messiah is his or her life (v. 4), that good works are required to be evident. The gospel is to enable someone to live differently, motivated by love, where peace can reign and where all things are focused around living like the Lord. Knowing this, however, does not stop some theologians from extrapolating faulty conclusions from Paul. Consider what Bruce says:

---

[63] Moo, 289.

[64] The topic of the proper order of service is explored in the *Messianic Sabbath Helper* by Messianic Apologetics.

[65] Neusner, *Mishnah*, 677.

"The NT does not contain a detailed code of rules for the Christian. Codes of rules, as Paul explains elsewhere, are suited to the period of immaturity when the children of God are still under guardians; but children who have come to years of responsibility know their father's will without having to be provided with a long list of 'Do's' and 'Don't's'."[66]

The text referenced to support this is Galatians 3:23-4:7, which is often read through a lens of the Torah only being a temporary measure for the Jewish people, until the Messiah came. It is often not read from the perspective of the Torah playing a role in revealing the need for an individual's salvation—not only for Paul's Jewish people but also for his non-Jewish Galatian audience, given his Torah-based preaching in Galatia (Acts 13:13-14:28).[67] This would be true of those in Paul's day, and those in our day as well, as God's Torah is to still define what is and what is not sin (Romans 3:20b), and why we need a Divine Savior. Bruce's comments, unfortunately, in dismissing all rules as for a previous time, place himself in a very vulnerable position. He observes, "The Christian...when confronted with a moral issue, may not find any explicit word of Christ relating to its particular details."[68] Any and all rules, at least from this vantage point, are now for Believers only to be replaced with the work of the Holy Spirit.

None of us should at all disagree with the fact that our sensitivities need to be inclined toward the leading of the Spirit, and focused around the will of Yeshua's love. But with such an infilling of the Spirit, what role do the Holy Scriptures play? What is to be our definite standard by which we gauge the leadings of the Spirit? Is the Tanach or Old Testament simply to be left aside when complicated moral issues are to be debated? What about the Torah or the Law of Moses? Was it entirely for an old order, even though Yeshua said that the works of His followers are directly tied to His fulfilling the Law (Matthew 5:16-17)? I would be negligent not to remind you that just as non-spontaneous worship should not be disregarded, so are Yeshua's followers not to disregard the definite standards of holiness and righteousness laid forth in the Scriptures—beginning with the Torah and Tanach.

We will encounter issues in life that the Holy Scriptures do not address, either the Tanach or Apostolic Writings. Even extra-Biblical Jewish and Christian works may fail to address them. This is why being in tune with the character of God *contained in the Scriptures* is so crucial. The Holy Spirit present within us is to give us true wisdom and discernment when we do not have definite answers for modern-day questions. This will be a wisdom and discernment in alignment with the ethos of God's Word, even if the Word does not address the issue directly or indirectly, and extra-Biblical tradition may be silent.

How can Believers adequately perform what they say or what they do? They must invoke the approval of God. Specifically, Paul tells the Colossians that this is to be *en onomati Kuriou Iēsou* (ἐν ὀνόματι κυρίου Ἰησοῦ), "in the name of the Lord Yeshua." We should be steadfastly reminded how the term "name" (Heb. *shem*, שׁם; Grk. *onoma*, ὄνομα) throughout the Scriptures often relates to one's authority or repute,[69] and not principally the pronunciation or spelling of something. What is significant to note in v. 17, is that the Colossians' devotion is to be focused around the Lord Yeshua. How one serves God, the Father, is accomplished through Yeshua, His Son, **with the Son integrated directly into the Divine Identity.** For the Apostle Paul, a life of faith is considered to be *a life of worship*, something emphasized both in v. 17 and in Romans 12:1-2:

"Therefore I urge you, brethren, by the mercies of God, to present your bodies a living and holy sacrifice, acceptable to God, *which is* your spiritual service of worship. And do not be conformed to this world, but be transformed by the renewing of your mind, so that you may prove what the will of God is, that which is good and acceptable and perfect."

To do something through the name of the Lord is spoken affluently throughout the Tanach. In Genesis 12:8, it is recorded that Abraham "built an altar to the LORD and called upon the name of the LORD." In Micah 4:5, it is asserted that Israel is a people who "walk in the name of the LORD our God forever and ever," meaning that they are devoted to Him and to His ways. Richard Bauckham considers passages like Colossians

---

[66] Bruce, *Colossians-Philemon-Ephesians*, 160.

[67] This is examined more fully in the author's commentary *Galatians for the Practical Messianic*.

[68] Bruce, *Colossians-Philemon-Ephesians*, 160.

[69] Consult Walter C. Kaiser, "שׁם," in *TWOT*, 2:934-935; and H. Bietenhard, "ónoma," in *TDNT*, pp 694-700.

3:17 to play a role in "Paul's christological interpretation of scriptural passages about YHWH, taking the name YHWH (*kurios* in LXX) to refer to Jesus Christ."[70] These are places where Yeshua the Messiah directly takes the identity of His Father, YHWH (יהוה) or the LORD, and is served, worshipped, or obeyed as the LORD (often, but not always, connected to some Tanach intertextuality).[71] This goes well beyond the title *Kurios* (κύριος) simply alluding to Yeshua as some kind of "Master" or authority figure, but how He is integrated into the Being of the Lord God of Israel, in an effort to recognize the LORD as the One True God and no other. The reference we see to "in the name of the Lord..." in Colossians 3:17, referring to Yeshua, is thus to be understood as being no different to *b'shem-ADONAI* (בְּשֵׁם־יְהוָה) in the Tanach. Moo concurs,

"[This] is, then, another (less direct) sign of the high Christology of this letter (and of the New Testament in general) that the 'LORD' is now identified with Jesus Christ. The phrase 'in the name of the Lord' takes on a wide variety of nuances, but often the focus is on the nature or character of the Lord. To do all things 'in the name of the Lord Jesus,' then, does not simply mean to utter Jesus' name but to act always in concert with the nature and character of our Lord."[72]

Dunn, who holds to the lowest Christology of the commentators we have been consulting in our study, even has to note the closeness of the Lord Yeshua to YHWH. He validly observes how this means, "Not that Jesus is thought to have taken over, far less usurped, the role of Yahweh...rather...God has shared his sovereign role with Christ."[73] I do not think anyone holding to a high Christology of Yeshua being the Lord God actually believes that Yeshua takes over, or even usurps, His Father's role. Rather, we see devotion for life by people—again, something Paul considers to be "worship"—focused around Yeshua, and through Yeshua it is directed to God the Father. Something done in the name of the Lord Yeshua is done as though it is *b'shem-ADONAI*. It is difficult to overlook how Yeshua is identified as a part of the Godhead here, with Yeshua being recognized as "Lord" and the Father as "God."

18 Wives, be subject to your husbands, as is fitting in the Lord. 19 Husbands, love your wives and do not be embittered against them.

3:18-4:1 A significant part of the instruction that the Apostle Paul delivers to the Colossians concerns the proper ordering of a household of Believers (Ger. *Haustafel*), something paralleled by the more expansive instruction he gives in his parallel letter in Ephesians 5:21-6:9.[74] In reading how this is addressed to husbands, wives, children, **and slaves**, we must be reminded of how these words were originally delivered to an ancient First Century Mediterranean cultural context, where homes were frequently made up of more than just parents and children, and where males often had unchallenged authority. It is specifically the position of the male in ancient times that has come under close scrutiny in recent years by interpreters. Most significant to remember, particularly as it concerned the First Century Messianic movement, is that due to the high position of males, religious groups that attracted large numbers of women and slaves—precisely what the *ekklēsia* did—were often treated with great suspicion. The same negative and distasteful social prejudices, that the Greeks and Romans had shown toward the Jewish Synagogue, were also directed toward those who believed in the Jewish Messiah. The Roman historian Tacitus' words are worth reviewing, especially as it regarded ancient proselytes:

"Whatever their origin, these observances are sanctioned by their antiquity. The other practices of the Jews are sinister and revolting, and have entrenched themselves by their very wickedness. Wretches of the most abandoned kind who had no use for the religion of their fathers took to contributing dues and free-will offerings to swell the Jewish exchequer; and other reasons for their increasing wealth may be found in their stubborn loyalty and ready benevolence towards brother Jews. But the rest of the world they confront with the

---

[70] Richard Bauckham, *Jesus and the God of Israel* (Grand Rapids: Eerdmans, 2008), 186.

[71] Cf. Bauckham's detailed list in Ibid., pp 186-188.

[72] Moo, 291.

[73] Dunn, 240.

[74] For other similar codes in the Apostolic Scriptures, see 1 Peter 2:13-3:12; Titus 2:1-10.

hatred reserved for enemies...Proselytes to Jewry adopt the same practices, and the very first lesson they learn is to despise the gods, shed all feelings of patriotism, and consider parents, children and brothers as readily expendable" (*The Histories* 5.5).[75]

Scholars often consider Colossians 3:18-4:1 to compose the oldest list of household rules in the Apostolic Scriptures. Any instruction delivered by Paul to the Colossians about the home was going to have to be carefully delivered, because the First Century Messianic movement was not intended to spur on massive social upheavals and revolution. It was, rather, to emphasize the great spiritual transformation that is to take place via the gospel, often changing institutional strongholds from within. The series of instructions that we see here, needs to be considered against both the Jewish and Greco-Roman social norms of the day (as probably best seen in Aristotle, which had influenced Diaspora Judaism),[76] and how much of what is said is subversive, but not too radically subversive to what was commonly practiced. The changes that are advocated by this code, to the existing one practiced in many Mediterranean homes, would not have fomented fierce government hostility. Dunnam summarizes his view:

"Paul has often been criticized as being down on women. The truth is, he presented a radically new view of marriage and family which elevated women and children to a hitherto unthinkable level of equality. The Hebrew and Greek understanding of marriage reduced women to 'things' to be used and enjoyed, not loved and cherished. Women were seen as totally subservient to men, not only in society but in the home. It was a man's world in every way."[77]

The Apostle Paul's teachings include a very high emphasis on a mutual submission required by all people who compose the community of faith—and most especially people who compose a home where Yeshua is recognized as Lord. The ethical side of "Whatever you do in word or deed, *do* all in the name of the Lord Yeshua" (v. 17a), means that one's conduct is to be guided by His example of service toward others, even death if need be (John 15:13). **Too often overlooked** for these codes is Paul's instruction, "be subject to one another in the fear of Messiah" (Ephesians 5:21)—as *mutual submission* is to be the overriding rubric for submission that is to take place within marriage, between parents and children, and between whatever other people compose the household. Bruce's thought is,

"That [ancient] structure, hierarchical as it was, was left unaltered, apart from the introduction of the new principle, 'as is fitting in the Lord'—which indeed was to be more revolutionary in its effect than was generally foreseen in the first Christian century."[78]

Strict interpreters of Colossians would insist that the exact same structures which were in place in the First Century Mediterranean world, also need to be observed today. Most interpreters, though, would propose much more caution in that **we must first interpret the code of Colossians 3:18-4:1 for its ancient audience.** Dunn proposes, "we need to recall how much they were conditioned and adapted to the situation of the times. They are not timeless rules...and can no more be transferred directly to the different circumstances of today,"[79] perhaps going to the other side of the spectrum in largely ignoring them as having any bearing on our times. A better approach, navigating the various extremes, would simply be to emphasize what these rules meant to the First Century recipients of Colossians, and then recognize the future intentions they had for Believers. No one today honestly argues that Paul endorsed the practice of slavery. Yet it was a social reality in the First Century that the ancient Believers had to contend with.

Also not to be forgotten is the role that the household code of 3:18-4:1 played in confronting the false teaching circulating in Colossae. It may be that in the philosophy of the false teachers, there was such a high individualistic dynamic, that there was a severe danger to families. In inserting this code, the Apostle Paul would place the main spiritual locus for people within the household, where familiar groups of Believers

---

[75] Cornelius Tacitus: *The Histories*, trans. Kenneth Wellesley (London: Penguin Books, 1992), pp 273-274.

[76] Aristotle: *Politics*, trans. Ernest Barker (New York: Oxford University Press, 1995), pp 12-17.

[77] Dunnam, 386.

[78] Bruce, *Colossians-Philemon-Ephesians*, 163.

[79] Dunn, 246.

encountering one another every day would have to be bonded together in the Messiah's love.[80] In O'Brien's estimation, "Wives, children and slaves are addressed equally with their husbands, fathers and masters. They too are ethically responsible partners who are expected to do 'what is fitting in the Lord' just as the male, the father and the free man."[81]

3:18 Paul's instruction to the household of Believers is first directed to wives: "Wives, be subject to your husbands, as is fitting in the Lord." Take important notice of how wives are addressed here, and not single women. Likewise, both the wife and the husband are assumed to be Believers in Yeshua, as some kind of mixed marriage between a Believer and a pagan is not addressed. Wives are by no means treated as inferior to their husbands, but the role of a godly wife is to submit to the husband "as is appropriate in the Lord" (CJB). The verb *hupotassesthe* (ὑποτάσσεσθε) is a present passive participle, indicating that via the wife knowing the Lord and being led by the Spirit, she will naturally submit to her husband. This kind of submission is by no means to be a forced action. O'Brien observes how,

"The exhortation...is balanced with the instruction to husbands to love their wives: the admonition is an appeal to free and responsible agents that can only be heeded voluntarily, never by the elimination or breaking of the human will, much less by means of a servile submissiveness."[82]

Christian **complementarian** views today, of the husband being somewhat of a superior to his wife, are actually not that extreme. (They probably do not go far enough for some of today's Messianic men and congregational leaders.) The husband is only *slightly* above his wife in the hierarchy, as Norman Geisler describes, "If he may be thought of as the 'president,' she is the 'vice-president.'"[83] Curtis Vaughan further says, the "main thought is that the wife is to defer to, that is, be willing to take second place to, her husband. Yet we should never interpret this as if it implies that the husband may be a domestic despot, ruling his family with a rod of iron. It does imply, however, that the husband has an authority the wife must forgo exercising."[84]

Challenges erupt when it is thought that complementarians advocate that wives are to submit to their husbands, so far that if their husbands tell them to do something immoral or illegal, that the Scriptures bid them to follow their husbands in spite of the error. This goes against the emphasis of remembering that how wives are to submit is reflective of the character of the Lord Yeshua. As The Message renders v. 18, "Wives, understand and support your husbands by submitting to them in ways that honor the Master." Moo, a complementarian, makes the following valid conclusions:

"[S]ubmission to any human is always conditioned by the ultimate submission that each believer owes to God: in any hierarchy we can imagine, God stands at the 'top of the chart.' This means, then, that a wife will sometimes have to disobey a husband (even a Christian one) if that husband commands her to do something contrary to God's will."[85]

An **egalitarian** view of v. 18, which I advocate, is going to more directly emphasize that a wife's willful submission to her husband is something that is to be guided exclusively by the clause *hōs anēken en Kuriō* (ὡς ἀνῆκεν ἐν κυρίῳ), "as is fitting in the Lord." The wife is certainly free to disobey her husband's wishes if they are contrary to the will of God. Yet the wife is to also honor and respect her husband, especially as he will be bigger and stronger than she, and will have the significant responsibility with such strength to make sure that the family is protected and that all are safe and secure. Wright comments how "The wife must forgo the temptation to rule her husband's life, using perhaps one of the many varieties of domestic blackmail; the husband must ensure that his love for his wife, like Christ's love for his people, always puts her interests first."[86]

---

[80] Cf. Witherington, pp 186-187.

[81] O'Brien, *Colossians-Philemon*, 220.

[82] Ibid., 222.

[83] Geisler, in *BKCNT*, 683.

[84] Vaughan, in *EXP*, 11:218.

[85] Moo, 301.

[86] Wright, 148.

It is often overlooked that v. 18 does not include an injunction that wives are to obey their husbands, but simply submit to them as a reflection of the Lord within them. Children are actually told *to obey* (v. 20), an indicator on the differences of age. Also not to be overlooked is how women did play an important role in the leadership of the early *ekklēsia*, as in Paul's closing remarks, he asks the Colossians to extend greetings to Nympha, a Laodicean woman who led a congregation in her home (4:15).

3:19 Living via the character of the Lord Yeshua, and having just told believing wives to submit to their husbands, Paul instructs, "Husbands, love your wives and do not be embittered against them." Entirely absent from this word is the admonition for husbands *to rule* their wives; instead they are *to love* their wives. A godly husband is to be guided by significant devotion and service to his wife. In Paul's paralleling instruction, he asserts, "the husband is the head of the wife, as Messiah also is the head of the [assembly], He Himself *being* the Savior of the body" (Ephesians 5:23). Contrary to common opinion, *kephalē* (κεφαλή) relates more to the husband being *the source* of his wife, than as an authority over her, because recognizing that Eve came from Adam as her source or origin, the husband is required to treat his wife the same as he would treat his own body (Ephesians 5:28).

These were seriously subversive words for a First Century social world where women were often treated no better than slaves.[87] A review of the Book of Sirach (Ecclesiasticus) in the Apocrypha easily reveals how Sirach always takes the side of the husband or father, and not the wife, in his philosophic diatribes (Sirach 25-26; 30:1-13; 42:14). Witherington compares how "While Ben Sira is trying to reinforce a patriarchal authority structure, Paul is not. Paul is, rather, trying to ameliorate the harm the existing structure does and can do."[88]

Guided by Yeshua's example, just as He died in serving His Body, so must if necessary the husband die for his wife. More likely to happen, though, is that a godly husband needs to be reminded not to willfully cause problems or ruptures between himself and his wife. He is to love his wife, and as it is commonly rendered, "do not be embittered against [her]" (NASU) or "never treat [her] harshly" (NRSV). The verb *pikrainō* (πικραίνω) can mean "to provoke" (*TDNT*).[89] Absolutely forbidden for husbands is thinking that they can harshly dominate their wives. And also forbidden for husbands is thinking that in forcing their will upon their wives, they are to automatically expect their wives to respect them.[90] Only by loving their wives will husbands receive their due respect.[91]

20 Children, be obedient to your parents in all things, for this is well-pleasing to the Lord. 21 Fathers, do not exasperate your children, so that they will not lose heart.

3:20 A non-Believing Greek or Roman who would have originally read v. 20 directed to the Colossians, would not have seen anything too subversive about Paul's instruction: "Children, obey your parents in everything, for this is your acceptable duty in the Lord" (NRSV). This is what a pagan would expect from a child. A Jewish reader would similarly see continuity between v. 20 and what the Torah admonishes to children, and possibly even how rebellious children could face capital punishment (Deuteronomy 21:18-21). Paul's parallel letter, in fact, directly appeals to the importance of the Fifth Commandment for children in the households of Believers (Ephesians 6:1-3; cf. Exodus 20:12; Deuteronomy 5:16).

Just as wives would be permitted to disobey their husbands in matters contrary to God's will, no responsible interpreter would take obedience to parents "in all things" as requiring obedience to parents in things resulting in disobedience to God. Yet, a family of Believers is in view within this household instruction (3:18-4:1), so most of the instruction that parents would deliver to their children would seemingly be in line

---

[87] For a much further examination, consult the author's remarks in his commentary *Ephesians for the Practical Messianic*.

[88] Witherington, 191.

[89] W. Michaelis, "*pikraínō*," in *TDNT*, 839.

[90] Dunn, 249.

[91] For further consideration, consult the useful discussion in Philip B. Payne, *Man and Woman, One in Christ* (Grand Rapids: Zondervan, 2009), pp 271-290.

with the character of the Scriptures. In much later life, children should honor their parents, by caring for them in their old age. As Paul would instruct Timothy, "if any widow has children or grandchildren, they must first learn to practice piety in regard to their own family and to make some return to their parents; for this is acceptable in the sight of God" (1 Timothy 5:4). Some have suggested that the thoughts of Philo may be in view, as he elaborated on a significant number of virtues that would not only please people, but ultimately please God:

"[F]or if you honor your parents, or show mercy to the poor, or do good to your friends, or fight in defense of your country, or pay proper attention to the common principles of justice towards all men, you most certainly are pleasing to those with whom you associate, and you are also acceptable in the sight of God: for he sees all things with an eye which never slumbers, and he unites to himself with especial favor all that is good, and that he accepts and embraces" (*On the Change of Names* 40).[92]

3:21 It is difficult to avoid that in an ancient context, Paul does reduce the role the father. But unlike today where fathers can be greatly disrespected, in this case the role of the father is reduced from that of an unchallengeable autocrat. V. 21 says, "Fathers, do not provoke your children, lest they become discouraged" (RSV), or "aggravated" (NLT). The *BDAG* definition of the verb *erethizō* (ἐρεθίζω) is "**to cause someone to react in a way that suggests acceptance of a challenge, *arouse, provoke*** mostly in bad sense *irritate, embitter.*"[93] Paul's parallel instruction will say, "Fathers, do not provoke your children to anger, but bring them up in the discipline and instruction of the Lord" (Ephesians 6:4).

22 Slaves, in all things obey those who are your masters on earth, not with external service, as those who *merely* please men, but with sincerity of heart, fearing the Lord. 23 Whatever you do, do your work heartily, as for the Lord rather than for men, 24 knowing that from the Lord you will receive the reward of the inheritance. It is the Lord Messiah whom you serve. 25 For he who does wrong will receive the consequences of the wrong which he has done, and that without partiality.

3:22 For most readers of Colossians, while there are surely some issues that need to be worked through with the preceding vs. 18-21 in describing wives, husbands, children, and fathers—it is the instruction that deals with slavery that is the most difficult to examine. Too many immediately try to apply these instructions as relating to employer-employee relationships today,[94] downplaying their original context in a Roman Empire where as many as possibly half of the total population were considered "slaves" to one degree or another.

Paul does instruct the slaves in Colossae, "Slaves, obey your earthly masters in everything, not only while being watched and in order to please them, but wholeheartedly, fearing the Lord" (NRSV). While some readers may hastily conclude that this is a blind obedience of slaves to their owners, it is notable that Roman law did allow slaves to disobey their owners, should their owners order them to commit any crimes. Seneca would observe how "nor are slaves compelled to obey us in all things; they will not carry out treasonable orders, or lend their hands to an act of crime" (*On Benefits* 3.20).[95]

The Apostle Paul recognized slavery as simply being a matter of the day, and so it is necessary for a reader to consider what he says often in light of how other First Century people instructed, ordered, or valued their slaves. Paul himself encouraged, that should the circumstances arise, slaves to become free (1 Corinthians 7:21-22). Moo validly remarks, "Paul never hints that he endorses the institution of slavery. He tells slaves and masters how they are to conduct themselves within the institution, but it is a bad misreading of Paul to read into his teaching approval of the institution itself."[96] Various evangelical interpreters, like Donald Guthrie, have simply thought "Paul's advice here is to transform the master-slave relationship from within."[97] Bruce

---

[92] *The Works of Philo: Complete and Unabridged*, 344.
[93] *BDAG*, 391.
[94] Cf. Geisler, in *BKCNT*, 684.
[95] Seneca: *On Benefits*, trans. Aubrey Stewart (Hard Press, 2006), pp 49-50.
[96] Moo, 308.
[97] Guthrie, in *NBCR*, 1152.

takes it even further, suggesting, "If a Christian slave came to be recognized as a leader in the church, he would be entitled to receive due deference from his Christian master."[98]

In a manner befitting the character of Yeshua, the slaves in Colossae were to obey *kata sarka kuriois* (κατὰ σάρκα κυρίοις) or "the lords according to flesh" (LITV). It is important for us to recognize that in this section of text (3:22-4:1), even though most English translations use the rendering "master" in reference to slaveowners, *kurios* or "lord" is used for both slaveowners and the Lord Yeshua. Dunn considers how "the affirmation of Christ as Lord constituted for the first Christians a line of continuity and not breach with their Jewish heritage."[99]

The motivation of slaves properly obeying their masters, for Paul, would be how ultimately their obedience is to be a reflection on the fear they have for the Lord. They are not simply to try to curry favors from their masters by obeying them. A sentiment seen in the Mishnah expresses how "Do not be like servants who serve the master on condition of receiving a reward, but [be] like servants who serve the master not on condition of receiving a reward" (m.*Avot* 1:3).[100]

Similar to what is asserted in v. 17, notice how here that slaves are to fear the Lord. Fearing the LORD (YHWH) is a significant feature of the Tanach (Isaiah 2:10, 19, 21, etc.).[101] Rather than fear being directed to the LORD, per se, it is directed to the Messiah, as a part of His integration into the Divine Identity. Witherington observes, "So much is Christ Lord that even the OT phrase 'fearing the Lord' refers to Jesus rather than Yahweh."[102] Moo further comments, "the high Christology of the letter to the Colossians as a whole is again brought to bear on the ordinary situation of the...household."[103]

What did Paul intend for the proper relationship of slaves and masters, who were both Believers, to be? This is why it is quite important for Colossians to be read in conjunction with his letter to Philemon, to get a fuller picture of Paul's view of slavery (cf. 4:9).

3:23 In the fear of Yeshua, Paul tells slaves "Whatever you do, work at it with all your heart, as working for the Lord, not for human masters" (TNIV). It was not uncommon in ancient times for slaves to be motivated by their masters with the promise of various treats. Xenophon indicated,

"[W]here slaves are concerned, the training which is apparently designed only for lower animals is very effective for teaching obedience; for you'll get plenty of results by gratifying their bellies in accordance with their desires. Those of them with ambitious temperaments can also be motivated by praise: I mean that some have an innate appetite for praise, just as others have for food and drink. Anyway, by using this training method, I think the people I deal with become more obedient, so I use it for those I want to appoint as foremen; I also back them up in situations like the following. You see, I am bound to supply my labourers with clothing and footwear, but I have some of these articles made better than others rather than making them all the same; then I can reward better workers with better articles, and give worse workers the inferior articles" (*The Economist* 13.9-12).[104]

Quite contrary to Xenophon's sentiments, slaves are not to obey their owners solely for the sake of better treatment.

3:24 These slaves, rather than working entirely for some kind of treats, as though they are animals to be rewarded, are to instead recognize that ultimately what they do in life is being monitored by the Lord Himself. Paul says that they need to know "that from the Lord you will receive the reward of the inheritance. It is the Lord Messiah whom you serve." A slave is not to do shoddy work, simply because he is a Believer, and all human beings are equal in the eyes of God. Paul clearly instructs, "be slaves of the Lord Christ" (New American Bible), as Yeshua is the One to whom slaves must answer to for their conduct.

---

[98] Bruce, *Colossians-Philemon-Ephesians*, 168.

[99] Dunn, 255.

[100] Neusner, *Mishnah*, 673.

[101] Also: Leviticus 19:14, 32; Deuteronomy 13:11; 17:13; Psalm 103:11, 13, 17; Proverbs 1:7; 23:17 (cf. O'Brien, *Colossians-Philemon*, 227).

[102] Witherington, 171.

[103] Moo, 311.

[104] Xenophon: *Conversations of Socrates*, trans. Hugh Tredennick and Robin Waterfield (London: Penguin Books, 1990), 336.

3:25 If slaves do not conduct themselves properly, then as Paul says, "the wrongdoer will be paid back for the wrong he has done, and there is no partiality" (RSV). Yeshua will be the judge of the slave who does not live properly, and we can possibly see echoes of Deuteronomy 10:17 in this: "For the LORD your God is the God of gods and the Lord of lords, the great, the mighty, and the awesome God who does not show partiality nor take a bribe." The Jewish character of the author comes through, as a Rabbinical sentiment in the Mishnah is, "know what sort of reward is going to be given to the righteous in the coming time" (m.*Avot* 2:16).[105]

---

[105] Neusner, *Mishnah*, 678.

COLOSSIANS 4
COMMENTARY

1 Masters, grant to your slaves justice and fairness, knowing that you too have a Master in heaven.

4:1 The Apostle Paul closes up his admonishing words to the Colossian Believers, and in ch. 4 finishes his letter with some final instructions and personal greetings. He tells slaveowners, "Masters, provide your slaves with what is right and fair, because you know that you also have a Master in heaven" (NIV). We once again should note that the term rendered "master" here is *Kurios* (κύριος), better rendered as "lord." Even if a slaveowner on Earth may have some authority as a lord over another, that slaveowner has *the Lord* who ultimately sits over him.

The issue of a human being owning another human being is a very difficult one for many readers to encounter in the Bible. Too often, people forget to place themselves within the culture and times of the texts they are reading. Overlooked is the fact that although slavery is a feature of the Torah's instructions, the Torah requires much more favorable treatment of the slaves owned by the Israelites (i.e., Exodus 20:10; Leviticus 25:43, 53) than that required by most contemporary Ancient Near Eastern law codes.[1] And, most of those who were "slaves" (Heb. sing. *eved*, עֶבֶד; Grk. sing. *doulos*, δοῦλος) were not by any means the kind Americans often picture, working on plantations in the Deep South. Many of them were indentured servants, who had no other way to pay off their debts than sell themselves to a master.

Both the Torah, and Paul's instruction here in v. 1, laid stepping stones back to the equality experienced at Creation prior to the Fall—which Yeshua has restored via His sacrifice (Galatians 3:28)—as it was never God's intention for people to *actually own* other people. The Torah's requirements that slaves be treated without any spiteful harm, and now Paul's instruction that slaveowners treat their slaves with justice, **were quite subversive for their times.** In fact, the Greek is even more subversive than what is seen in many English translations: *to dikaion kai tēn isotēta* (τὸ δίκαιον καὶ τὴν ἰσότητα), "that which is righteous and equal" (YLT). Paul's word to slaveowners ran quite contrary to what Aristotle had taught, saying, "There cannot be injustice in an unqualified sense towards that which is one's own" (*Nichomachean Ethics* 5.1134b),[2] speaking of how masters had a broad window of what they could do toward their slaves/property.

Ben Witherington III observes, "[I]f to our ears this advice sounds rather conventional or even conservative and commonplace, the truth is that it was not in that day."[3] Paul's word to the slaveowners in Colossae was clear: "Lords, give what is just and equal to the slaves, knowing that you have a Lord in Heaven also" (LITV). We should be reminded of the possibility that there were *more slaves* than slaveowners in the assembly (as most of the early Believers were taken from the lower classes), meaning that in treating slaves with justice and fairness, proper slaveowners would be contributing to the overall well-being of the *ekklēsia*. The instruction of Sirach 4:30 was, "Do not be like a lion in your home, nor be a faultfinder with your servants."

Slaveowners were to be responsible people, and very much aware of the fact that the Lord Yeshua, ruling and reigning in Heaven, would deal with them if they were unjust or unfair to their slaves. The Jewish philosopher Philo would instruct how there were Biblical commandments "to the masters recommending them to practice that gentleness and mildness towards their slaves, by which the inequality of their respective

---

[1] For a further discussion, consult the author's article "Addressing the Frequently Avoided Issues Messianics Encounter in the Torah."

[2] Aristotle, *Ethics*, 189.

[3] Witherington, 196.

conditions is in some degree equalized" (*Decalogue* 167).[4] This is a reflection of how the Jewish tradition of Paul's day included sentiments to treat slaves with a degree of respect, something reflected in Paul's concurrent letter (Philemon 12-14). The reality, though, is that in v. 1 Paul is mostly having to not build on a Jewish foundation, recognizing the equality of slaves as human beings made in God's image—but that he would have to instruct slaveowners *to go farther* than what popular Greco-Roman philosophers and figures had taught. Notable to be considered from this vantage point could be Plato's teaching,

"The best way to train slaves is to refrain from arrogantly ill-treating them, and to harm them even less (assuming that's possible) than you would your equals" (*Laws* 777d).[5]

2 Devote yourselves to prayer, keeping alert in it with *an attitude of* thanksgiving; 3 praying at the same time for us as well, that God will open up to us a door for the word, so that we may speak forth the mystery of Messiah, for which I have also been imprisoned; 4 that I may make it clear in the way I ought to speak.

4:2 Vs. 2-6 compose the last major instructive section of Paul's letter to the Colossians, then attended by personal greetings (vs. 7-18). Paul gives the Colossians some final responsibilities that they need to be performing, starting with prayer: "Continue steadfastly in prayer, being watchful in it with thanksgiving" (RSV). Asking an audience to pray is something that is seen in the closing sections of some of his other letters (Ephesians 6:18; Philippians 4:6; 1 Thessalonians 5:17), which also includes prayer for his ministry and colleagues (Romans 15:30-32; Ephesians 6:19-20; 2 Thessalonians 3:1-2). The specific verb that Paul uses to describe this action is *proskartereō* (προσκαρτερέω), **"to persist in someth,"** more specifically **"busy *oneself with, be busily engaged in, be devoted to*"** (BDAG).[6] The Colossians will find themselves preserved by God if they "Continue earnestly in prayer, being vigilant in it with thanksgiving" (NKJV).

The instruction seen in Colossians 4:2-4 is paralleled by Ephesians 6:18-20 very closely, an indicator that these two epistles were written at about the same time:

COLOSSIANS 4:2-4	EPHESIANS 6:18-20
Devote yourselves to prayer, keeping alert in it with *an attitude of* thanksgiving; praying at the same time for us as well, that God will open up to us a door for the word, so that we may speak forth the mystery of Messiah, for which I have also been imprisoned; that I may make it clear in the way I ought to speak.	With all prayer and petition pray at all times in the Spirit, and with this in view, be on the alert with all perseverance and petition for all the saints, and *pray* on my behalf, that utterance may be given to me in the opening of my mouth, to make known with boldness the mystery of the gospel, for which I am an ambassador in chains; that in *proclaiming* it I may speak boldly, as I ought to speak.

The instruction for the Colossians to pray, as rudimentary as it may sound, is rooted deeply in the psyche of the Apostle Paul as a servant of the Lord. Paul prays a great deal, just as he opened up his letter with the words, "We give thanks to God, the Father of our Lord Yeshua the Messiah, praying always for you...For this reason also, since the day we heard *of it*, we have not ceased to pray for you and to ask that you may be filled with the knowledge of His will in all spiritual wisdom and understanding" (Colossians 1:3, 9). In Romans 12:12 he lists being "devoted to prayer" as an important virtue evident in mature Believers. In urging the Colossians to be devoted to prayer, there is a likely link to the scene of Gethsemane, when the Disciples were caught sleeping and were unalert. Yeshua instructed them, "Keep watching and praying that you may

---

[4] *The Works of Philo: Complete and Unabridged*, 167.
[5] Plato, *Laws*, 213; Cf. O'Brien, *Colossians-Philemon*, 232.
[6] *BDAG*, 881.

not enter into temptation; the spirit is willing, but the flesh is weak" (Matthew 26:41; cf. Mark 14:38; Luke 18:1). Believers are to be on the alert, because they are people of the day (1 Thessalonians 5:4-11).

4:3 In being watchful to pray, Paul respectfully asks the Colossians to pray for his ministry activity in Rome. He says, "At the same time, pray also for us, that God may open to us a door for the word, to declare the mystery of Christ, on account of which I am in prison" (ESV). The "us" here is to be understood as Paul and Timothy (1:1), and possibly also Epaphras (1:7). Paul has previously spoken of the mystery of "Messiah in you, the hope of glory" (1:26-27), as well as how he received the message he teaches "through a revelation of Yeshua the Messiah" (Galatians 1:12). Paul was specially chosen by the Lord to take His gospel to the nations (Acts 9:15), and being imprisoned, asks the Colossians to intercede that he can declare this gospel in his current circumstances. The description of an open door is used elsewhere in Paul's letters to depict an opportunity to present the good news (1 Corinthians 16:19; 2 Corinthians 2:12).[7]

Douglas J. Moo argues that *to mustērion tou Christou* (τὸ μυστήριον τοῦ Χριστοῦ), "the mystery of Messiah," is to be understood as an epexegetic genitive (case denoting possession), equating to "the mystery which is Christ." Yeshua the Messiah, in all of His glory and all of His majesty—and the unique work that is being accomplished through His vessels like Paul and Timothy—is what the Colossians are to pray is declared and embraced. Moo describes how "God opens the door for the mystery of Christ to be proclaimed."[8]

In Peter T. O'Brien's estimation, not only were the Colossians to be praying for Paul's efforts in declaring the good news, but they were also to be eagerly looking for the Lord's return. He summarizes, "the Colossians are to persevere in prayer with their eyes fixed on the second coming, at the same time interceding for the apostle whose ministry to Gentiles has a salvation historical significance in the purposes of God."[9] Moo somewhat concurs, remarking, "Believers need constantly to be 'awake' to the nature of the times they live in—the 'last days' of eschatological 'fulfillment without consummation'—and to orient their lives accordingly."[10] The need to always be on the alert, whether one sees himself in an eschatological period or not, should be pretty obvious to a Believer. 1 Peter 5:8 reminds us, "Be of sober *spirit*, be on the alert. Your adversary, the devil, prowls around like a roaring lion, seeking someone to devour."

The need for prayer (vs. 2-3) on the Colossians' behalf has many important facets. They are asked to pray for Paul's circumstances, given his special calling by God as apostle to the nations. Yet the Colossians being told to preserve in prayer is another instructive measure issued against the false teachers' philosophy. Whereas the false teachers might be trying to pierce that inter-dimensional veil and access the realm of angels (2:18), the Colossians are told by Paul **to simply pray.** This was to be a regular, consistent discipline where they could intercede before God for a practical, on the ground situation in Paul's imprisonment, expressing their hopes to Him that more would come to saving faith. Doing this would also serve as a benchmark for the Colossians to make sure that their faith is hidden with God (3:3), and that they really are accomplishing His will.

4:4 The more specific reason why the Colossians need to pray for Paul is stated: "Pray that I will proclaim this message as clearly as I should" (NLT). The verb *phaneroō* (φανερόω) means "*to make manifest*" (LS).[11] The scene is most probably Paul's arrest period in Rome (cf. Acts 28:30-31). Not only does he ask that opportunities open up for him to declare the good news, but also that when those opportunities arise, he can speak the message properly given his circumstances. Consistent with this period of arrest, F.F. Bruce observes,

"He would have to answer the charges brought against him, but he desired to do so in such a way that the content and nature of his apostolic preaching would be made plain to all who heard. He was in Rome, under official custody, on account of Christ and the gospel; it was of the highest importance that the interests

---

[7] Cf. Acts 14:27; Revelation 3:8, 20.

[8] Moo, 323.

[9] O'Brien, *Colossians-Philemon*, 240; cf. Dunn, 262.

[10] Moo, 320.

[11] *LS*, 855.

of Christ and the gospel should be promoted by the way in which he made his defense before the supreme court. For this he prayed himself, and asked his friends to pray too."[12]

Paul would later observe, facing imprisonment a second time, that even though he was confined as a criminal, "the word of God is not imprisoned" (2 Timothy 1:9). While it may be easy for us to just gloss over the references to Paul in confinement, and that asking for prayer would be a natural request of him to make of the Colossians, Moo states, "what is of greater relevance for this text is why Paul chose to bring up the matter of his imprisonment at this point in the letter. Probably he does so to illustrate the power of God in opening doors for the gospel even when humans conspire to close them."[13] The Colossians could be encouraged in knowing that their prayers really did work miracles, over and against the false teachers' asceticism which would accomplish very little, if anything, in making a tangible difference.

5 Conduct yourselves with wisdom toward outsiders, making the most of the opportunity. 6 Let your speech always be with grace, *as though* seasoned with salt, so that you will know how you should respond to each person.

4:5 In the last part of his instruction to the Colossians, Paul tells his audience "Walk in wisdom toward outsiders, making the most of the time" (HCSB). The Colossians are required to act toward people outside the community of faith, "those who are not believers" (NLT), in a proper way. We can see a parallel to this sentiment in James the Just's words, "Who among you is wise and understanding? Let him show by his good behavior his deeds in the gentleness of wisdom...But the wisdom from above is first pure, then peaceable, gentle, reasonable, full of mercy and good fruits, unwavering, without hypocrisy" (James 3:13, 17). Andrew T. Lincoln's comments are well taken:

"In the Jewish tradition, wisdom involved not simply right knowledge but skill in living—ethical insight into God's will as revealed in the Torah. For this writer, spiritual wisdom also involves living rightly, but now in displaying conduct worthy or pleasing to Christ as Lord."[14]

It is pretty obvious that living properly, with outsiders to the faith making observations, is a requirement for God's people. With this in mind, every opportunity to demonstrate a proper example to others needs to be taken—and this is something fully based in the imperatives of God's Torah. God's people are a chosen kingdom of priests (Exodus 19:6), serving as His intermediaries between Him and a sinful humanity that needs redemption.

Sometimes Paul's expression "making the most of the time" (NRSV) or "make the most of every opportunity" (TNIV) is read as an expectation of the Lord's soon return. Whether or not the First Century generation of Believers *really did* expect Yeshua to come back in their lifetimes is a fiercely debated issue. Moo suggests that "making the most of every opportunity," be read from the vantage point of salvation history. He says "Believers live after the initial coming of Messiah and the inauguration of the redemptive kingdom. But they also live in expectation of a second coming of Messiah to complete the work of redemption."[15] Living in anticipation of the coming Kingdom of God on Earth is to be sure motivation to make sure that one is performing the necessary actions of faith that edge the world closer and closer to the *parousia*. What you do for Yeshua is not isolated to the here and now.

The specific Greek clause *ton kairon exagorazomenoi* (τὸν καιρὸν ἐξαγοραζόμενοι) was rendered in the KJV as "redeeming the time," or can also be understood as "buying up the time" (*NIGTC*).[16] The verb *exagorazō* (ἐξαγοράζω) is used elsewhere in Paul, in regard to salvation and how "Messiah redeemed [*exagorazō*] us from the curse of the Law" (Galatians 3:13), and how He came "that He might redeem [*exagorazō*] those who were under the Law" (Galatians 4:5), speaking of the penalties laid down upon sinners (cf. 2:14). The reality of

---

[12] Bruce, *Colossians-Philemon-Ephesians*, pp 173-174.

[13] Moo, 234.

[14] Lincoln, in *NIB*, 11:662.

[15] Moo, 329.

[16] Dunn, 261.

redeeming the time can be seen in Paul's later instruction to Timothy, "preach the word; be ready in season *and* out of season; reprove, rebuke, exhort, with great patience and instruction" (2 Timothy 4:2). N.T. Wright considers this to be how "every opportunity is to be snapped up...like a bargain."[17] Maxie Dunnam further comments,

"This word of advice from Paul is connected with how we behave toward outsiders. Among the early [Believers], as among those in the present, were persons whose fanatical behavior prejudiced outsiders against them. Paul wanted persons to be attracted to the gospel, not repelled from it. This is the key to understanding his words."[18]

Curtis Vaughan's thoughts also need to be considered:

"To 'be wise in the way you act toward outsiders' is to show practical Christian wisdom in dealing with secular society. Paul's words imply that believers are to be cautious and tactful so as to avoid needlessly antagonizing or alienating their pagan neighbors. In a positive sense, they also imply that believers should conduct themselves so that the way they live will attract, impress, and convict non-Christians and give the pagan community a favorable impression of the gospel."[19]

I totally agree with what both Dunnam and Vaughan have said here. **Positive ways in which to impact the larger community of people need to be formulated by born again Believers.** This has definite precedent in Paul's previous writing, as in Philippians 2:15 he says that Believers should "prove yourselves to be blameless and innocent, children of God above reproach in the midst of a crooked and perverse generation, among whom you appear as lights in the world." He also admonishes in 1 Corinthians 10:32 how Believers are to "Give no offense either to Jews or to Greeks or to the [assembly] of God." Yeshua Himself instructed His followers, "Behold, I send you out as sheep in the midst of wolves; so be shrewd as serpents and innocent as doves." This is not only true of the Colossians, or modern-day evangelical Christians, but also today's Messianic Believers.

How would the emphasis on this kind of practical wisdom—the Colossians living a different, impactful kind of life on the pagans around them—relate to what Paul had instructed them earlier in his letter? In O'Brien's view, "The wisdom which the apostle sets forth is fundamentally different from that propounded by the false teachers. The latter is but an empty show of wisdom."[20]

4:6 One of the most important ways that outsiders will see the Colossians' life of faith, in them emulating the wisdom of Yeshua, is by their speech. Paul instructs, "Let your conversation be always full of grace, seasoned with salt, so that you may know how to answer everyone" (NIV). Their speech is to be "never insipid" (NEB). In ancient times as is still true today, salt was both a major preservative as well as a seasoning agent, and for the ancient period in particular, salt was also a significant cleansing/sanitizing agent. It is easy to see how the Colossians' speech, "seasoned with salt," pertains to their words being clean and preserved by the will of God. As Paul states in his parallel letter, "Let no unwholesome word proceed from your mouth, but only such *a word* as is good for edification according to the need *of the moment*, so that it will give grace to those who hear" (Ephesians 4:29).

The Colossians' speech "seasoned with salt" definitely also recalls Yeshua's teachings on salt. Yeshua's followers are "the salt of the earth" (Matthew 5:13), and salt is used as a point of reference for their proper behavior (Mark 9:49-50; Luke 14:34). The need to speak properly is also a major feature of James' letter (James 3:5-6). Also to be considered could be Job 4:4: "Your words have helped the tottering to stand..."

As important as these Biblical references are, references to salt and speaking are not without connection in ancient classicism. Plutarch spoke, "For we are not to ease and discharge ourselves of our words, as if they were a heavy burthen that overloaded us; for speech remains as well when uttered as before; but men either speak in behalf of themselves when some necessity compels them, or for the benefit of those that hear them, or else to recreate one another with the delights of converse, on purpose to mitigate and render more savory, as

17 Wright, 153.
18 Dunnam, pp 391-392.
19 Vaughan, in *EXP*, 11:222.
20 O'Brien, *Colossians-Philemon*, 241.

with salt, the toils of our daily employments" (*On Talkativeness* 645f).[21] In Witherington's estimation, "Paul is speaking about rhetorically effective speech"[22]—something that the Colossians are to demonstrate in their interactions with outsiders to the faith. These are exactly the kinds of things the Apostle Peter refers to:

"[B]ut sanctify Messiah as Lord in your hearts, always *being* ready to make a defense to everyone who asks you to give an account for the hope that is in you, yet with gentleness and reverence" (1 Peter 3:15).

Speaking appropriately may include an entire range of necessary activities, from simply showing courtesy to other people, to being articulate in how one communicates, to how one explains and defends the gospel of salvation. James D.G. Dunn offers us some important thoughts:

"When asked about the distinctiveness of their faith and its lifestyle expression, the [Believers] should be ready to give an answer in each case...Again it should be noted how integrated their faith was expected to be with their workaday lives in the city and how rounded the religion that could both charm a conversation partner by its quality and give testimony of faith as part of the same conversation."[23]

Taking vs. 5-6 into account, how much time have today's Messianics not redeemed, but have instead utterly wasted by promoting bad attitudes and inappropriate ways of communicating? Paul told the Colossians to demonstrate their godly wisdom to others through prayer, and through being able to speak properly in their interactions in public. The practical application of this in modern society is not too difficult to see: **people who represent the Lord must speak and act in ways that reflect highly of His love and goodness, and His desire that all should be brought to salvation.** Unfortunately in today's Messianic movement, too many people have gained a reputation of doing *anything but this.* Rather than build on the positive work of our Jewish and Christian forebearers, being a conduit of God's holiness and righteousness, and encourage people to grow in their knowing the Messiah of Israel and appreciate God's Torah—what do we see? We see people tearing down others, insulting others, and not speaking salted words of godly wisdom. We see much of base humanity at its worst, and just as Dunnam said above, some "fanatical behavior" among us.

I have confidence that things will change in the future. But, there will definitely be some damage control in order for us to enact the required change. Learning how to use our time wisely, speaking properly, and finding constructive and edifying solutions to promoting the Torah obedient lifestyle we are convicted of may be a challenge with the current generation. Learning to be people empowered with God's wisdom—which includes when knowing not to speak—is something each one of us needs to be highly conscious of.

7 As to all my affairs, Tychicus, *our* beloved brother and faithful servant and fellow bond-servant in the Lord, will bring you information. 8 *For* I have sent him to you for this very purpose, that you may know about our circumstances and that he may encourage your hearts; 9 and with him Onesimus, *our* faithful and beloved brother, who is one of your *number*. They will inform you about the whole situation here.

4:7 With v. 6, Paul has completed with what he intended to do with his letter. The rest of the epistle includes important greetings, which do tell us a few things about Paul's ministry work, and the demographic makeup of at least one part of the First Century *ekklēsia*. Paul extends personal greetings to his colleagues in Colossae, people who he has known in one way or another. Most of these people are mentioned in Paul's letter to Philemon. According to Witherington, "It is this section in particular which makes it difficult to imagine this letter coming from a post-Pauline situation, for it has a very personal Pauline character to it."[24] Similarly arguing against total pseudonymity for Colossians, Dunn points out that "if it was penned by Timothy while Paul was in prison...all we need envisage is Paul's approval in substance if not in detail,"[25] with Paul himself

---

[21] Plutarch: *Moralia*, by John Thomson, Prebendary of Hereford (1878). Accessible online at <http://www.bostonleadershipbuilders.com/plutarch/moralia/index.htm>.
[22] Witherington, 200.
[23] Dunn, pp 267-268.
[24] Witherington, 201.
[25] Dunn, 269.

delivering the final greeting in the last verse (v. 18). (Note that Dunn does not hold to Pauline authorship of the Pastoral Epistles, the last letters of the Pauline corpus.)[26]

Paul begins in v. 7 by telling the Colossians, "Tychicus will tell you all about my affairs; he is a beloved brother and faithful minister and fellow servant in the Lord" (RSV). There is almost an exact parallel between this and Ephesians 6:21-22, a strong indication that both Colossians and Ephesians were written at about the same time:

"But that you also may know about my circumstances, how I am doing, Tychicus, the beloved brother and faithful minister in the Lord, will make everything known to you. I have sent him to you for this very purpose, so that you may know about us, and that he may comfort your hearts."

Tychicus was a close associate of the Apostle Paul in the latter stages of his ministry, who had accompanied Paul during his Third Missionary Journey (Acts 18:23-21:16), specifically during his time in Macedonia and Greece (Acts 20:4). He was a Greek Believer, and likely a native of Asia Minor. Tychicus was a trusted courier of the Apostle Paul, who had also been commissioned to carry the general letter that would become known as "Ephesians" (Ephesians 6:21-22). Paul tells Titus that he may send Tychicus to him at Crete (Titus 3:12), and in his last recognized epistle, the Apostle says that he had sent him to Ephesus (2 Timothy 4:12). This appears to indicate that Tychicus had an ongoing relationship with Paul beyond the period of his composing Colossians, even if he were not there with him in Paul's final days.

4:8 Tychicus was apparently so trusted by Paul, that he can tell the Colossians, "I am sending him to you for the express purpose that you may know about our circumstances and that he may encourage your hearts" (NIV). Tychicus would be sent to Colossae with Paul's letter, and he would also be able to speak to the Colossians about his personal impression of Paul's circumstances in Rome. There may have been a few things that Paul did not want written down, that only Tychicus could convey in person. Or, Tychicus could have more simply relayed the expected "We really need to pray for our brother Paul, more than he has written!" Witherington describes how "He is not just the postman but will orally deliver the news. In good Asiatic rhetorical fashion we are told three times that he will give the Colossians the news about Paul (vv. 7-9)."[27] Moo further indicates, "As fellow ministers of the gospel, [Paul's couriers] were in a position not only to deliver the letter but also to elaborate on it and fill in blanks,"[28] in a definite effort to "put fresh heart" (NEB) into them.

4:9 Similar to how Tychicus will be going to Colossae, so too will Onesimus be joining him. Paul says, "he is coming with Onesimus, the faithful and beloved brother, who is one of you. They will tell you about everything here" (NRSV). In Philemon 18 we see how Onesimus had apparently stolen from his owner, Philemon. Later in fleeing away, Onesimus had met Paul and came to faith as a Believer in Yeshua (Philemon 10). Paul would encourage Philemon to treat Onesimus as a fellow brother in the Lord.

Take important note of the fact that both Tychicus (v. 7) and Epaphras (1:7), are both considered to be trusted and faithful brothers by the Apostle Paul. In v. 9, the runaway slave—but now born again Believer—Onesimus, is given this same high regard. It is a definite reflection back on 3:11, where the power of Yeshua has the capacity to seriously transform the slave as well as the free. Apparently, Onesimus was going to be sent back to Colossae, or the Lycus Valley, with Tychicus. A personal letter from Paul was going to be sent to Philemon on Onesimus' behalf, to vouch for this transformed slave, who had once wronged his master.

---

[26] James D.G. Dunn, "The First and Second Letters to Timothy and the Letter to Titus," in *NIB*, 11:773-880.
[27] Witherington, 203.
[28] Moo, 334.

10 Aristarchus, my fellow prisoner, sends you his greetings; and *also* Barnabas's cousin Mark (about whom you received instructions; if he comes to you, welcome him); 11 and *also* Jesus who is called Justus; these are the only fellow workers for the kingdom of God who are from the circumcision, and they have proved to be an encouragement to me.

4:10a The final greetings of Paul's letter continue, as they give us not only some important information about Paul's ministry activity in Rome, but also the people who have helped him. The first person mentioned here is Aristarchus, who was present with Paul in the Ephesian riot (Acts 19:29), and would therefore have been known to the Believers in Colossae, only about a hundred miles away. Aristarchus accompanied Paul to Greece, originally being from Thessalonica (Acts 20:4), and later accompanied Paul on his voyage to Rome (Acts 27:2), likely going all the way with him.

Paul designates Aristarchus as *ho sunaichmalōtos mou* (ὁ συναιχμάλωτός μου) or "my fellow prisoner." How are we to understand Aristarchus being a "prisoner"? He either attended to Paul in his confinement, and so "Christ's captive like myself" (NEB) is some kind of an honorific title, **or** Aristarchus was actually locked up with Paul. Moo favors the latter, with Aristarchus being a literal prisoner, although he does have to explain, "We do not know how Aristarchus ended up in prison with Paul, but we can speculate that he volunteered to share the apostle's imprisonment in order to be of help to him."[29]

Advocates of pseudonymity for Colossians note a possible problem, because in Philemon 23 it is Epaphras who is listed as the prisoner, and not Aristarchus. Yet this need not mean that Colossians was not written or authorized by the Apostle Paul. If Aristarchus had to share Paul's imprisonment to assist him, he could have shared these duties with Epaphras, who at the time of Philemon's composition had taken Aristarchus' place.

4:10b The second person who extends greetings to the Colossians here is Mark, the cousin of Barnabas. This is the same man as John Mark, whose mother Mary had a house in Jerusalem where some of the early Believers met (Acts 12:12). Mark accompanied Barnabas and Paul back to Antioch (Acts 12:25), and went with them on their First Missionary Journey (Acts 13:1-14:28). Apparently, during their quest, Mark had abandoned them at Pamphylia (Acts 13:13), and as Paul's Second Missionary Journey (Acts 15:36-18:28) prepares to commence, "Paul kept insisting that they should not take him along" (Acts 15:38a). There had been a prior point of contention with John Mark, so much so that Barnabas split up and went to Cyprus instead of continuing with Paul (Acts 15:39).

John Mark is the traditional author of the Gospel that bears his name (Eusebius *Ecclesiastical History* 3.39.14-16). By the time the Epistle to the Colossians was written, the previously strained relations that Paul and Mark had, were patched up. Later in 2 Timothy 4:11 we see the even more complimentary, "Pick up Mark and bring him with you, for he is useful to me for service." John Mark apparently had some kind of ministry in Rome (1 Peter 5:13), considering that Rome is the traditional location from which the Gospel of Mark was written, from the perspective of the Apostle Peter.[30]

Barnabas being mentioned need not be overlooked, either. He was an important figure in the founding of the Jerusalem assembly (Acts 4:36), and he featured prominently in the assembly at Antioch (Acts 11:22; 13:1; 15:35). Barnabas also helped Paul in the early stages of his ministry (Acts 9:27; 11:25-26). Barnabas appears to have been well known by the Colossians.

Paul's statements about Mark, "about whom you received instructions," are a bit perplexing. This is because the clause *peri hou elabete entolas* (περὶ οὗ ἐλάβετε ἐντολάς) is better translated as "concerning whom ye did receive commands" (YLT). Paul actually uses "commandments" (KJV) or "orders" (LITV) to describe this. These directives may have been authorized by Paul for Tychicus to tell them, or may have already come down via Paul's teaching ministry in Ephesus. This is a good indication that the Colossians were somehow aware of

---

[29] Moo, 338.

[30] Consult the author's entry for the Gospel of Mark in *A Survey of the Apostolic Scriptures for the Practical Messianic*.

the rift that had existed between Paul and Mark in the past, and Paul wanted to make it perfectly clear that this rift was over.[31]

4:11a The greetings to the Colossians continue in v. 11 with a man who has a very intriguing name: "Jesus who is called Justus." This is a prime attestation of how in ancient times, and even frequently today, Jewish people commonly had two names: one from their Jewish heritage, and one from the environment in which they were living. Paul or *Paulos* (Παῦλος), otherwise known as Saul or *Shaul* (שָׁאוּל), also had two names (Acts 13:9). What makes this so intriguing for us as Messianics is that this Jewish man, also with the name Justus (Grk. *Ioustos*, Ἰοῦστος), was actually named *Iēsous* (Ἰησοῦς). The following is what the *ABD* entry has to say about this man:

"Jesus Justus, a Jewish Christian who sent greetings to the Colossians along with Paul from his place of imprisonment (Col 4:11). Jesus (the Greek form of Joshua or Jeshua) was his Jewish name. It was common for Jews to have this name (cf. Acts 13:6) up until the 2d cent. C.E. Justus was his Latin surname, which denoted loyal observance of the law, and was probably given to him because of his reputation."[32]

What makes Jesus Justus significant is that it points to the fact that the name *Iēsous*, the Greek transliteration of the Hebrew name *Yeshua* (יֵשׁוּעַ), was in fact used among Greek-speaking Jews as an acceptable male name. While it is common in some parts of today's Messianic movement to hear that the Greek name *Iēsous* derives from "Zeus," this has no basis in linguistic fact, because *Iēsous* (Ἰησοῦς) and *Zeus* (Ζεύς) have two totally different Greek spellings and pronunciations. *TDNT* further asserts, "a modern theory is that Jesus is a masculine form of *Iasō*, the goddess of salvation, but Eusebius recognizes the Hebrew basis, and the use of *Iēsoús* predates Christian contacts with the Hellenistic world."[33] Surely, if the Greek name *Iēsous* were of pagan origin, and not a Jewish transliteration of a Hebrew name to be employed among Greek speakers, then it would not have been used for the title of the Book of Joshua (appearing as ΙΗΣΟΥΣ) in the Septuagint.[34]

The CJB renders v. 11 with "Yeshua, the one called Justus." Bruce recognizes how "Jesus is the Greek/Latin form of Joshua or Jeshua; Justus was a common Latin cognomen."[35] O'Brien also recognizes that for this man "'Jesus' (Ἰησοῦς) was his Jewish name (the Greek from of 'Joshua' or 'Jeshua') and this was common among Jews (Acts 13:6) until the second century A.D. when it disappeared as a proper name, no doubt because of the conflict between the synagogue and the Church."[36] Moo further observes, "'Jesus' was a popular name among the first-century Jews, fading in popularity only in the second century because of growing Jewish/Christian tensions."[37]

What this all points to is the fact that when people like the Apostle Paul went out into the Greek speaking world, to Greek speaking Jewish synagogues, referring to the Messiah with the name *Iēsous* (Ἰησοῦς) would not at all have been something strange to them—even if they and their adherents knew it was a transliteration of *Yeshua* (יֵשׁוּעַ). The negative reaction that we often find in today's Messianic movement to the English name "Jesus," would not have been mirrored among the First Century Jewish Believers to the name *Iēsous*—because just as there were normal Jewish men in Judea who bore the name *Yeshua*, so were there normal Jewish men in the Diaspora who bore the name *Iēsous*. The name *Iēsous* may not have been the original name that the pregnant Mary was instructed to call her unborn child (Matthew 1:21), but it was by no means

---

[31] The dilemma seen in these statements is a grammatical one. Dunn points out, "In Paul the word ἐντολή ('command') almost always refers to divine commands (Rom. 7:8-13; 13:9; 1 Cor. 7:19; 14:37; also Eph. 2:15; 6:2; 1 Tim. 6:14); only here and in Tit. 1:14 it is used of human 'commands' or 'instructions'" (Dunn, 277). If *entolē* can be used for human instructions, even if only in a few locations in the Pauline letters, could it at all be used this way in Ephesians 2:15? Could man-made commandments be what had separated the nations from the Jewish people, and what required the construction of the dividing wall in the Second Temple complex?

[32] John Gillman, "Justus," in *ABD*, 3:1135.

[33] W. Foerster, "*Iēsoús*," in *TDNT*, 361.

[34] Alfred Rahlfs, ed., *Septuaginta* (Stuttgart: Deutsche Bibelgesellschaft, 1979), 1:354-405.

[35] Bruce, *Colossians-Philemon-Ephesians*, 180.

[36] O'Brien, *Colossians-Philemon*, 251.

[37] Moo, 340.

something concocted in later centuries by Greeks and Romans so that they could somehow continue to worship their pagan deities.

4:11b Paul says that between Aristarchus, Mark, and Jesus Justus, "These are the only men of the circumcision among my fellow workers for the kingdom of God, and they have been a comfort to me" (RSV). Suffice it to say, in understanding Paul's ministry activity in Rome, recognizing what is meant by the clause *hoi ontes ek peritomēs* (οἱ ὄντες ἐκ περιτομῆς) deserves much more attention than the name of the last of these men. The NIV simply renders this as "These are the only Jews." But what is intended by "who are from the circumcision" (NASU)? Is it just speaking of people who were Jewish from the time of birth, being circumcised on the eighth day, or something more? Could it have been a party of early Jewish Believers, as thought by some New Testament theologians, that was more conservative and advocated more Torah observance than others?

Both Dunn and Wright lean toward there being something a little more present than those of the "circumcision" just being Jews. This is concurrent with their view that the false philosophy countered in Colossians is not a Gnosticized Judaism, but rather the non-Jewish Believers in Colossae being persuaded to join the Synagogue. They argue that these three men were a part of a conservative faction of Jewish Believers, which on the whole would have disapproved of Paul's ministry work among the nations, but these three men were the exception. They recognized how the gospel needed to be tailored for the unique needs of Greeks and Romans, and were willing to recognize the special calling upon Paul. In Dunn's view,

"Here it may simply denote Jews, the people marked out by the designating feature of circumcision...but probably with the hint that 'those of the circumcision' were usually active in hostility to Paul's mission. The reference presumably is intended to assure the Colossians that there were such Jews, or at any rate other Jews apart from himself, who, as Jews, were fully approving of and cooperative in the Gentile mission ('fellow workers'), despite, presumably, the disapproval of most of their compatriots."[38]

Even though Dunn concludes that those of the "circumcision" is a reference to a conservative group of Jewish Believers, he goes on to assert how the issue of circumcision was by no means as serious as it was in Paul's writing to the Galatians. He simply refers to Aristarchus, Mark, and Jesus Justus as being of the "circumcision" to highlight how his ministry work was not at odds with the prerogatives of these Jewish Believers:

"[W]hy mention these individuals, less well known to the Colossians...unless he wanted to give particular prominence to them precisely because they were Jews? Furthermore, that the reference is made without any sign of resentment or hostility to 'the circumcision' (contrast Gal. 2:12 and Tit. 1:10) equally strengthens the suggestion that the threat from the Colossian synagogue was not at all so forceful as earlier in Galatia, nor was it making such an issue of circumcision as there."[39]

Wright's conclusions are a bit more plausible. Aristarchus, Mark, and Jesus Justus could have been of a sector of Jewish Believers that required more immediate changes from the non-Jewish Believers in regard to the Torah. Yet, they had to recognize Paul's valid ministry among the nations, how people were really being changed by the gospel, but also how the gospel needed to be proclaimed to those people in a bit different manner than to Jewish people:

"[I]t seems difficult to take the phrase 'those...of the circumcision' to indicate a party within the church without at the same time expressing Paul's disapproval of it. Perhaps a compromise is possible: Paul may be referring not to a party but to people of a particular background: having belonged to a branch of Christianity more concerned than Paul with observing the Jewish law, they were by now happy to proclaim God's sovereign rule alongside Paul with his different emphases."[40]

---

[38] Dunn, 278.

[39] Ibid., pp 278-279.

[40] Wright, 157.

Keep in mind that Paul believed that the most important aspect of the Torah was love (Romans 13:8-9; Galatians 5:14), just as the Lord Yeshua had taught (Matthew 19:19; Mark 12:31; Luke 10:27; cf. Leviticus 19:18). From the basis of love, all other obedience to God will naturally come forth.

Not all commentators, however, are agreed that *hoi ontes ek peritomēs* has anything to do with the mission and emphases of Jewish Believers over and against non-Jewish Believers. Moo simply states,

"Some...think that Paul might be characterizing these three men as Jewish-Christians who were more conservative than Paul on issues of the law and who worked with the apostle in evangelism. But there are insufficient grounds in this context to limit the reference in this way. Paul is probably simply identifying them as Jewish...in terms of their national identity."[41]

I am inclined to agree more with Moo, as basically the fact that these three men "are the only Jews among my fellow workers for the kingdom of God, and they have proved a comfort to me" (NIV). The difficult fact to note here is that, presumably, it was only Aristarchus, Mark, and Jesus Justus who were the only Jews who helped Paul during his imprisonment. Moo suggests that some of Paul's statements in his letter to the Philippians, also written during his confinement,[42] could give us some clues about what was going on in Rome during this time:

"Some, to be sure, are preaching Messiah even from envy and strife, but some also from good will; the latter *do it* out of love, knowing that I am appointed for the defense of the gospel; the former proclaim Messiah out of selfish ambition rather than from pure motives, thinking to cause me distress in my imprisonment. What then? Only that in every way, whether in pretense or in truth, Messiah is proclaimed; and in this I rejoice. Yes, and I will rejoice" (Philippians 1:15-18).

Apparently, some significant factionalism has manifested itself among the Roman Believers,[43] and only three Jewish men being willing to help Paul, was a sad consequence of this. Yet as Bruce is clear to remind us, "in this work he had these men of Jewish birth to assist him at this particular point in the course of those years, and he found great comfort in their presence and help."[44]

12 Epaphras, who is one of your number, a bondslave of Yeshua the Messiah, sends you his greetings, always laboring earnestly for you in his prayers, that you may stand perfect and fully assured in all the will of God. 13 For I testify for him that he has a deep concern for you and for those who are in Laodicea and Hierapolis.

4:12 Epaphras, who has gone all the way to Rome to visit Paul in his confinement, sends his greetings to the Colossians. Paul writes, "Epaphras, who is one of you, a servant of Christ Jesus, greets you, always struggling on your behalf in his prayers, that you may stand mature and fully assured in all the will of God" (ESV). Epaphras is the one who had originally proclaimed the good news to the people in Colossae (1:7-8). Epaphras is the Colossian who had gone to see Paul in Rome, informing him of the false teaching circulating in Colossae, and needing to consult with the Apostle on what was to be done.

V. 12 employs the verb *agōnizomai* (ἀγωνίζομαι), which can mean to "engage *in a contest*" (BDAG),[45] to describe how Epaphras is "wrestling in prayer for you" (NIV) or how he "never stops battling for you" (New Jerusalem Bible). Epaphras can be said to agonize over the Colossians when he prays for them. In Moo's estimation, "it refers to strenuous and consistent intervention with the Lord on behalf of the Colossians— prayer needed especially in light of the danger posed by the false teachers."[46] In some ways, we can be reminded of Luke 22:44, where it is said of Yeshua, "And being in agony [*agōnia*, ἀγωνία] He was praying very fervently; and His sweat became like drops of blood, falling down upon the ground." Epaphras has a special calling for the Believers in the Lycus Valley, those in: Colossae, Hierapolis, and Laodicea, and he does stress out over it a great deal.

---

[41] Moo, 342.

[42] Ibid.

[43] Consult the author's article "The Message of Romans," as factionalism likely existed among the Roman Believers before Paul even arrived in Rome.

[44] Bruce, *Colossians-Philemon-Ephesians*, 181.

[45] *BDAG*, 17.

[46] Moo, 344.

What Epaphras desperately prays for is how the Colossians "may stand perfect and fully assured in all the will of God." This is a perfection or maturity that is able to accomplish the realistic will of God, impacting others with the truth of the gospel, and manifesting itself in works of kindness and goodness (3:12). O'Brien indicates how "The reference to perfection (τέλειος) touches on one of the key issues at Colossae in which members of the congregation were encouraged by the false teachers to seek maturity or perfection through their philosophy (2:8) with its ascetic practices, visionary experiences and special revelations, rather than through Christ."[47] Epaphras shared Paul's concern seen in 1:28, speaking of an ultimate, eschatological perfection of Believers on the final day.

Surely if Epaphras agonized over the false teachings circulating in Colossae of the First Century C.E., should not today's Messianic leaders similarly agonize over the false teachings that too often circulate in our faith community? *I know I do, and probably too frequently.*

4:13 Paul is clear to tell the Colossians of Epaphras, "I vouch for him that he is working hard for you and for those at Laodicea and Hierapolis" (NIV). The actual vocabulary is *echei polun ponon* (ἔχει πολὺν πόνον), with the noun *ponos* (πόνος) generally relating to "*toil, labour,*" as well as "*bodily exertion, exercise*" (LS),[48] used in the Book of Revelation to describe "pain" (16:10-11; 21:4). The verb *echei* is present active indicative, pointing to how Epaphras "**has** much toil" (my translation) for the Colossians. The false philosophy was likely not just affecting those in Colossae, but in the surrounding area. Epaphras would return to his home with Paul's blessing "I testify for him" (NRSV). Dunn notes, "The writer(s) no doubt wished thereby to sustain and boost Epaphras's standing in the eyes of the Colossians, though there is no hint that Epaphras needed to be defended for some failure or loss of authority."[49]

14 Luke, the beloved physician, sends you his greetings, and *also* Demas. 15 Greet the brethren who are in Laodicea and also Nympha and the [assembly] that is in her house.

4:14 Two final people extend greetings from Rome, to the Colossians in v. 14. The first of these is Luke, and it is only in this passage that we actually learn of Luke as a doctor in the Apostolic Scriptures. In time, Luke will become Paul's only consistent companion (2 Timothy 4:11). Luke is the traditional author of both the Gospel of Luke and the Book of Acts (Eusebius *Ecclesiastical History* 3.4.1-7; 3.24.14-15; 5.8.3; 6.25.6). The various "we" passages seen in the Book of Acts are understood to include Luke.[50] Being the only one who stayed along with Paul, he could have served as Paul's amanuensis or secretary in the composition of the Pastoral Epistles (1&2 Timothy, Titus), or even could have played some kind of role in the writing of Paul's final letters.

The second person seen in v. 14 is Demas. Just three to four years later in the mid 60s C.E. (assuming that Colossians was written between 60-62 C.E.), though, Paul observes, "Demas, having loved this present world, has deserted me and gone to Thessalonica" (2 Timothy 4:10). For a season, Demas was a trusted friend, but near the end of Paul's life, he left.

4:15 Vs. 15-17 include some final housekeeping instructions to the Colossians. He tells them, "Give my greetings to the brothers in Laodicea, also to Nympha and the congregation that meets in her home" (CJB). Anyone who reads v. 15 from the KJV will notice a significant difference from what is seen in more modern versions: "Salute the brethren which are in Laodicea, and Nymphas, and the church which is in his house." Some have taken this person to be a man, *Numphas* (Νυμφᾶς), while others a woman, *Numpha* (Νύμφα). Many debates have ensued about this, but as Bruce M. Metzger's *Textual Commentary on the Greek New Testament* indicates, the original reading was likely with "Nympha" and "her":

---

[47] O'Brien, *Colossians-Philemon*, 253.

[48] LS, 661.

[49] Dunn, 281.

[50] Consult the author's entries for the Gospel of Luke and the Book of Acts in *A Survey of the Apostolic Scriptures for the Practical Messianic*.

"Νυμφαν can be accented Νύμφα, from the feminine nominative Νύμφα ('Nympha'), or Νυμφᾶν, from the masculine nominative Νυμφᾶς ('Nymphas'). The uncertainty of the gender of the name led to variation in the following possessive pronoun between αὐτῆς [autēs] and αὐτοῦ [autou]. On the basis chiefly of the weight of B 6 424c 1739 1877 1881 syrh, palms copsa Origen, the Committee preferred Νύμφαν... αὐτῆς [Numphan...autēs]. The reading with αὐτῶν arose when copyists included ἀδελφούς [adelphous] in the reference."[51]

Most commentators today favor Nympha as female,[52] with Moo describing how "the feminine name, with corresponding pronoun, should probably be preferred, since it would be more natural for early scribes to think of a man as the one in whose house a church [or, congregation] met rather than a woman."[53] Ancient copyists were more likely to favor the person being male than female, and given how there were originally no accents in the accusative case (denoting direct object) Numphan (Νυμφᾶν male / Νύμφαν female), it could read as either male or female. One of the most conservative commentators we have been consulting on Colossians, Vaughan, astutely concludes "The feminine pronoun represents perhaps the true reading. Numerically the MS evidence for it is slight, but the overall attestation is very strong."[54] Also important to note is how versions like the NRSV and TNIV recognize how adelphous (ἀδελφούς) can have an inclusive quality to it: "brothers and sisters."

But even if we rightly assume that Nympha was a female, who had a congregation of Believers assemble in her home, what role did she play? Was she simply a female patron, or did she really play an important role in the leadership? It is not unlikely that Nympha was a widow or unmarried, probably a woman of some means via inheritance. In Dunn's estimation, "as the householder and the only one named in connection with the [congregation] in her home, Nympha was probably the leader of the [congregation] there, or at least she acted as host for the gathering and for the fellowship meal...Certainly there is nothing in the New Testament as a whole which would tell against such an inference, though the inference itself is hardly certain."[55] While it might be difficult to argue that Nympha was a full blown congregational leader here, it is not at all difficult to suggest that if this is a female, she did play an important role in this congregation and was not at all put off to the side.

Wherever this home actually was, whether it was Colossae, or adjacent to Colossae and to Hierapolis and Laodicea, this may be an indication that the number of Believers in the area was too small to meet in a larger place. The more important fact to note is how the early Believers often met in homes. History since is replete with how many new moves of God begin when faithful men and women open up their homes to others, in order for Believers to assemble together for worship and teaching. By no means do growing congregations or fellowships *have to stay in homes*, but the pattern is that they often start in homes. Many of today's Messianic congregations have started in someone's home, but as they get larger they find it necessary to begin meeting in some kind of a public place such as a school, share the facilities of a church for a while and/or rent some office space, and then eventually purchase or build their own permanent facilities.

16 When this letter is read among you, have it also read in the [assembly] of the Laodiceans; and you, for your part read my letter *that is coming* from Laodicea.

4:16 It was quite customary for the letters that Paul wrote to be read aloud to the congregations which received them. Much earlier in 1 Thessalonians 5:27, Paul wrote, "I adjure you by the Lord to have this letter read to all the brethren." It is no surprise he similarly instructed the Colossians, "When this letter is read among you, have it also read in the [assembly] of the Laodiceans" (v. 16a). The challenge with this statement is what is to be made with what he means by "and you, for your part read my letter *that is coming* from Laodicea" (v. 16b).

---

[51] Metzger, *Textual Commentary*, 627.
[52] Bruce, *Colossians-Philemon-Ephesians*, 183; O'Brien, *Colossians-Philemon*, 256; Dunn, pp 284-285.
[53] Moo, 349.
[54] Vaughan, in *EXP*, 11:225.
[55] Dunn, 285.

What is the letter that Paul wrote to the Believers at Laodicea? Some would suggest that this is something that has been lost to antiquity, that Paul wrote separately, and was likewise carried by Tychicus. Others suggest, based on the manuscript evidence of Ephesians 1:1 (RSV), which lacks "in Ephesus," that the so-called Epistle to the Laodiceans is actually the circular epistle that became known as "Ephesians." Among the extant Pauline materials, this is probably the best guess that scholars have to choose from. Wright concurs that among all of the hypotheses available, this may be the best one:

> "[N]o major arguments have been specifically advanced against it, and it may be worth while to outline its implications further in terms of a hypothetical reconstruction of events. According to this possibility, Paul...wrote 'Ephesians' as a general letter to the young churches in the surrounding area [of Ephesus]...Tychicus (Eph. 6:21) was despatched with the copy for the churches in the Lycus valley area, with the intention of visiting Colossae after Laodicea, as would be natural...But Paul does not want the Colossian church to be merely another recipient of a circular, any more than he had wanted to include in that majestic and poetic 'circular' the more specific warnings of Colossians 2, relevant though they will be for Laodicea also. So Tychicus takes with him 'Ephesians', Colossians, and— Onesimus; the latter being the shorter letter intended for his erstwhile master Philemon....This hypothesis is, of course, unprovable. But (in my judgment at least) it covers the data well, particularly the close relationship between 'Ephesians' and Colossians."[56]

I would concur with Wright **that the so-called Epistle to the Laodiceans is, in all likelihood, the Epistle of Ephesians.** Moo discounts this, thinking, "Surely Paul simply would have included Colossae in the churches to whom 'Ephesians' was to be circulated,"[57] meaning that the letter which would become "Ephesians" would have gone to Colossae as well, requiring what he wrote to the Laodiceans to be different. Church history bears the record that there was actually an apocryphal Letter to the Laodiceans that had been compiled after the time of Paul, although as early as the Fourth and Fifth Centuries it was being declared inauthentic by Eastern Church authorities. Not until the Council of Trent (1545-1563) did this Letter to the Laodiceans find itself officially removed from the Roman Catholic canon, and Protestants have never found the apocryphal text that interesting, either. "Modern scholars...are unanimous in regarding the apocryphal Laodiceans as a forgery" (ABD).[58]

The plausibility that the so-called Epistle to the Laodiceans is really the circular letter that became known as "Ephesians" is not something to be overlooked when it comes to the disputed authorship of Colossians. Morna D. Hooker notes, "the suggestion that" what was coming from Laodicea "was Ephesians requires that the letters were by the same author."[59] Yet, if Paul really did write a separate, non-extant letter to the Laodiceans, it becomes quite obvious why Paul's letters began being copied and preserved for future generations. Witherington points out, "What we do have a hint of here is how the process of collecting and later canonizing Paul's letters transpired. Letters were exchanged or copied and exchanged, and precisely because they were seen as of ongoing value they were kept and reused."[60]

17 Say to Archippus, "Take heed to the ministry which you have received in the Lord, that you may fulfill it." 18 I, Paul, write this greeting with my own hand. Remember my imprisonment. Grace be with you.

4:17 One final instruction is given to the Colossians by Paul: "Tell Archippus: 'See to it that you complete the work you have received in the Lord'" (NIV). Archippus obviously appears to be an important person within the Colossian congregation, who has an important work to fulfill, but the Greek specifically does have *diakonia* (διακονία), "*attendance on a duty, ministration*" (LS).[61] What this specific "ministry" was we

---

[56] Wright, pp 160-161.
[57] Moo, 351.
[58] Charles P. Anderson, "Laodiceans, Epistle to the," in ABD, 4:231.
[59] Hooker, in ECB, 1411.
[60] Witherington, 206.
[61] LS, 189.

cannot know for certain, as it may have been something like preaching or instructing young Believers.[62] Suffice it to say, whatever Archippus was doing, it was not promoting the false teaching of the Colossian errorists!

The issuing of this kind of a specific, encouraging word to Archippus, does not at all support the Epistle to the Colossians being pseudonymous. Dunn recognizes,

"The character of the request, coming just before the personally written final phrases, makes its invention by a pseudonymous author less plausible and strengthens the impression that Paul himself was standing directly behind the letter."[63]

4:18 The Epistle to the Colossians ends with a standard Pauline salutation: "I, Paul, write this greeting with my own hand. Remember my chains. Grace be with you" (NRSV/ESV). This is a good indication that up to this point, the letter has actually been written by an amanuensis or secretary authorized by Paul, with the final signature penned by the Apostle Paul himself, just as he does in other letters (1 Corinthians 16:21; 2 Corinthians 10:1; Galatians 6:11; 2 Thessalonians 3:17; Philemon 19). Dunn recognizes, "The brevity in this case and its cramped character...suggest that it was added under difficult circumstances, when such a telegraphic note was all that he could (or was allowed to) contribute."[64] Consider the chance that Paul's hands were in chains when this signature was appended, or that he had to write this with the letter being held by someone outside of prison bars.

Much has been made of the fact that the Roman Senator Cicero, even though he commonly wrote his letters himself, always made sure that if a secretary composed a letter for him, he signed it in his own hand, "*hoc manu mea*" (*Letters to Atticus* 13.28).[65] The reason for doing this is obvious: **authentication.** O'Brien points out, "Paul apparently employed the autograph with special nuances: because of a concern that forged letters in his name might be sent to churches or individuals (2 Thes 2:2), to give a quasi-legal commitment which his personal certification (Philem 19), or to add especial emphasis to what has been said (so the reference to 'large letters' in Gal 6:11)."[66]

It is very difficult to argue pseudonymity for Colossians, especially when the claim of the author—Paul—is that the final greeting was written with his own hand. Those holding to pseudonymity for Colossians, such as Victor Paul Furnish, would argue, though, "In conformity with Paul's custom the author concludes with a final apostolic certification of the whole letter."[67]

In Wright's estimation, Paul's salutation of "Grace be with you" is an indication of how this letter should be understood as "a *means* of grace."[68] Surely, if any of us are to take inspiration and meaning from Paul's Epistle to the Colossians, it should be that we are motivated to serve the Lord Yeshua as a means of grace, demonstrating the new life He has given us (3:1-3). We should not find ourselves persuaded by deluding arguments of false teachers (2:8), but instead be those who intercede for the Body of Messiah—local and universal—just like the faithful Epaphras (4:12-13).

[62] Cf. Moo, 352.
[63] Dunn, 288.
[64] Dunn, 289.
[65] Cited in Bruce, *Colossians-Philemon-Ephesians*, 186 fn #79.
[66] O'Brien, *Colossians-Philemon*, 259.
[67] Furnish, in *The Interpreter's One-Volume Commentary on the Bible*, 864.
[68] Wright, 162.

PHILEMON

INTRODUCTION TO PHILEMON

The letter to Philemon[1] (Grk. *Pros Philēmona*, ΠΡΟΣ ΦΙΛΗΜΟΝΑ) is a Biblical text that often draws a blank stare from many people today. Perhaps at twenty-five verses, it is often thought to be too small to demand any serious attention. It is, after all, just a piece of personal correspondence from the Apostle Paul to a friend, right? "Unlike Paul's other letters, Philemon does not deal with theological controversies or ethical difficulties in the lives of his audience" (*EDB*),[2] so what bearing does it really have on our understanding of Scripture, or even just the Apostolic Writings?

It has been my observation that too frequently, it is those small, rather obscure Biblical books that often contain a lesson or two **that are vital** for us understanding something important. A. Patzia observes how the letter to Philemon "offers a fascinating window not only on a corner of the social world of the first century, but on Christian principles at work in a particular setting within the early church."[3] Not enough of today's evangelicals read Philemon, in an effort to understand the transformative power of the gospel. And if this be true of Christians, then how are today's Messianic Believers to learn to appreciate Philemon, and what it shows us in our distinct reading of the Apostolic Scriptures?

It is quite difficult to separate Philemon from the Epistle to the Colossians, as traditionally it is considered to be a part in a series known as the Prison Epistles, also including Philippians and Ephesians. The letter to Philemon would have originally been composed on a single piece of papyrus or ancient parchment (also similar to 3 John), concurrent with ancient letter writing conventions of the day. Philemon's canonicity has scarcely been challenged by mainline theologians, although those who deny Pauline authorship of all his attributed letters will similarly discount Philemon (similar to those of the liberal Tübingen school). But even if Philemon's place in the Biblical canon has been largely assured, that does not mean that the role Philemon plays within the Scriptures has not been questioned.

What is the purpose of Philemon within the Bible? A cursory reading shows how Onesimus encounters Paul, and Paul is writing this letter because he is sending him back to Philemon (v. 10). The letter to Philemon is a difficult text to consider when we really sit down and dissect the issues, because it forces us to deal with the ancient issue of slavery. This is not the slavery once known to the American South or the Caribbean, but a slavery practiced in the Roman Empire where one human being owned the life of another. Did the work of Yeshua on the cross change anything in regard to slavery? Was it still to be a valid practice that born again Believers could use? What does Paul write to Philemon about how he is to treat Onesimus?

PAUL AND HIS RELATIONSHIP TO PHILEMON

The authorship of the letter to Philemon is virtually unchallenged today, as generally all scholars believe Philemon to be genuinely Pauline, following a Pauline style of composition, vocabulary, and theological themes. James D.G. Dunn summarizes, "The style and vocabulary, as judged particularly by the opening and closing (vv. 1-7, 21-25), are characteristically Pauline, and overall the degree of variation lies well within the

---

[1] Please note that in spite of the common reference to Philemon as "the Book of Philemon," I am going to purposefully refer to the text as either the Epistle to Philemon or Paul's letter to Philemon, and not use this reference. By failing to forget that this text is a letter written to a specific audience in a specific setting, we can make the common error of thinking that this was a text written *directly to us*. Our goal as responsible interpreters is to try to reconstruct what this letter meant *to its original audience first*, before applying its message in a modern-day setting.

[2] Marion L. Soards, "Philemon, Letter to," in David Noel Freedman, ed., *Eerdmans Dictionary of the Bible* (Grand Rapids: Eerdmans, 2000), 1046.

[3] A. Patzia, "Philemon, Letter to," in *Dictionary of Paul and His Letters*, 703.

diversity of Paul's epistolary practice as attested by the undisputed letters...reasons for a later pseudepigrapher to bother to invent a letter of this sort and pass it off as Paul's are hard to imagine."[4] The Epistle to Philemon is a personal letter, rather than a theological treatise, but even so it does tell us a great deal about the Apostle Paul. By no means is the letter to Philemon a mere personal note.

The contents of the letter itself state that Paul is the author (vs. 1, 9, 19), although Timothy is listed as a co-sender (v. 1). Given the shortness of Philemon in comparison to Colossians, the entire message probably came from Paul, unlike Colossians where Timothy could have served as a co-author. The style of Philemon is consistent with the non-disputed Pauline Epistles, so in v. 4 where Paul says "I thank my God always, making mention of you in my prayers," it is easy to see a composition parallel with Philippians 1:3-4: "I thank my God in all my remembrance of you, always offering prayer with joy in my every prayer for you all."

The connection between the letter to Philemon, and the much larger Epistle to the Colossians, is pretty obvious to see when examining the list of people who greet the Colossians, and then also greet Philemon. Apparently these individuals were known, in some degree, to both.

PERSONAL REFERENCES AND GREETINGS	
PHILEMON	COLOSSIANS
...Timothy our brother... (1)	...Timothy our brother... (1:1)
Epaphras, my fellow prisoner in Messiah Yeshua, greets you, *as do* Mark, Aristarchus, Demas, Luke, my fellow workers (23-24)	Aristarchus, my fellow prisoner, sends you his greetings; and *also* Barnabas's cousin Mark (about whom you received instructions; if he comes to you, welcome him)...Epaphras, who is one of your number, a bondslave of Yeshua the Messiah, sends you his greetings...Luke, the beloved physician, sends you his greetings, and *also* Demas (4:10-12, 14)
...and to Archippus our fellow soldier... (2)	Say to Archippus, "Take heed to the ministry which you have received in the Lord, that you may fulfill it" (4:17)
I appeal to you for my child Onesimus... (10)	... and with him Onesimus, *our* faithful and beloved brother, who is one of your *number*... (4:9)

Philemon himself was either a member of the Colossian assembly, or was known in the wider community of Believers present in the Lycus Valley triangle of Colossae, Laodicea, and Hierapolis. We can safely surmise that Philemon, similar to Colossians like Epaphras (see Introduction to Colossians), had come to faith in Yeshua as a result of Paul's preaching ministry in Ephesus (Acts 19:10), which saw people in Asia evangelized. Philemon was presumably a wealthy non-Jewish Believer, who owned several slaves, which would have included the runaway Onesimus (v. 16). We have to assume that Paul and Philemon met in person at least at one point, as it would seem doubtful that Paul would have taken the time to write Philemon

---

[4] Dunn, pp 299, 300.

if the two had not met face to face. The two men had formed some kind of bond (v. 7), and one of Philemon's slaves, Onesimus, knew of Paul either by name or by appearance, so as to encounter him in the future.

The relationship between the Apostle Paul and the Greek Philemon had to be cordial enough for Paul to be able to write to him so freely on what to do with his runaway slave Onesimus. Paul was able to tell him, "I appeal to you for my child Onesimus, whom I have begotten in my imprisonment" (v. 10).

WHERE WAS PAUL WHEN HE WROTE THIS LETTER?

Considering the greeting connections seen between Colossians and Philemon, Paul probably wrote Philemon in the same place as the Epistle to the Colossians was composed. But, even if where Philemon was written was in a different location or domicile in the same city, that city would definitely have been where he encountered the runaway Onesimus. The traditional location of Philemon's composition is believed to be Rome. D.A. Carson and Douglas J. Moo indicate, "Onesimus may well have wanted to get as far away from Colossae as possible, and the teeming cosmopolitan population of Rome offered obvious advantages to a person trying to hide from the authorities."[5] It would have been very easy for Onesimus to hide in a city with so many slaves, so much so that it would have been largely futile for someone like a bounty hunter to try to find him.

Paul expresses hopes in his letter to visit Philemon in person soon (v. 22), and so some think it is most unlikely that Paul was confined in Rome when he writes to him. While traditionally Rome is held to be the place of Philemon's composition, other interpreters have concluded that perhaps he was confined in Ephesus, given the short distance between Colossae and Ephesus. Some find it difficult to think that with Paul's ministry activity turning Westward, that he would make the effort to return to the East from Rome, requiring an Eastern imprisonment. Others claim that the best location for the place of writing would be during his Caesarean imprisonment (Acts 24:27).

While on the surface, a Roman imprisonment could seem unlikely, Paul could have traveled from Rome to Colossae in about five weeks time. F.F. Bruce points out that the need for Paul to return to Asia from Rome may have been quite serious. He observes, "The developing situation in the province of Asia as a whole, as he learned of it from Epaphras and other visitors, may well have seemed to him to demand his presence as soon as he regained his freedom...His opponents there were exploiting his absence to gain support for their policy and to undermine his authority."[6] Moo further states, "if we accept the Pastoral Epistles as genuinely Pauline, they pretty clearly indicate that Paul, in fact, did end up traveling back to the Eastern Mediterranean after his release from Roman imprisonment."[7]

Our analysis of Philemon will stand by the traditional view that the letter was written by Paul when he was in Rome.

WHEN DID PAUL WRITE THIS LETTER?

When we rightfully assume that Philemon was composed at the same time as Colossians, an approximate date of 60-62 C.E. seems likely. Not to be overlooked is how Paul describes himself as "the aged" (v. 9), so Philemon was written as Paul was getting old. The letter to Philemon would have been one of Paul's later letters, the latest for those who hold to pseudonymous authorship of other epistles in the Pauline corpus. Many think it likely that Paul wrote the entire letter to Philemon himself, without the aid of an amanuensis.[8]

Due to the close connection between Colossians and Philemon, most interpreters are rightfully agreed that the two letters were sent together. Paul's courier Tychicus would be taking the Epistle of Colossians with him (Colossians 4:4-7), and with Colossians the runaway slave Onesimus would be returning home, with the letter to Philemon. It is also not impossible that the general epistle which became known as "Ephesians" was

---

[5] Carson and Moo, 592.

[6] Bruce, *Colossians-Philemon-Ephesians*, 196.

[7] Moo, 363.

[8] S. Scott Bartchy, "Philemon, Epistle to," in *ABD*, 5:306.

also finished off at this time, for the early communities of Believers in the region of Asia Minor, to which Tychicus was traveling (Ephesians 6:21; cf. 1:1, RSV).

A few have actually suggested that Philemon is the letter that Paul told the Colossians was coming from Laodicea (Colossians 4:16).

WHO WAS THE TARGET AUDIENCE OF THIS LETTER?

The letter to Philemon is addressed "To Philemon our dear friend and co-worker" (v. 1, NRSV). Philemon was an individual who certainly lived in the Lycus Valley, who was a Greek Believer in Yeshua, and who worked in some way in the evangelistic mission. Philemon was likely a person of means, who was perhaps a successful businessman who owned several slaves.[9] Onesimus, the runaway slave, was either from Colossae or the surrounding area as well, as in Colossians 4:9 he is labeled as "one of yourselves." This is naturally taken as though Onesimus was a part of the Colossian assembly, although the people in the surrounding general area could also be intended, indicating that Onesimus was from the region. Epaphras, who had traveled to visit Paul in prison, and for whom the Epistle to the Colossians was composed, extends Philemon his greetings (v. 23).

The letter to Philemon also extends greetings "to Apphia our sister, and to Archippus" (v. 2), with Apphia most probably being Philemon's wife, and Archippus possibly his son, although this cannot be known for certain. These people were members of the congregation that met in Philemon's home. Another possibility, though less likely, is that Philemon was the host of the congregation, and Archippus was its main leader (cf. Colossians 4:17).

The letter to Philemon concerns what to do with Onesimus, who was a runaway slave. In reading through Philemon, we have to remember how we have no extant information on how Onesimus became a slave. Did he become a slave because of an indebtedness he was trying to pay off, or was he a slave because of some military campaign against an oppressed people? Likewise, it is a mistake for us to think that Philemon is an *entirely private* letter from Paul to Philemon, especially as Timothy is included in the opening greeting (v. 1). **The letter to Philemon would eventually be read in the congregation meeting in Philemon's house.**

While the significant majority of commentators recognize that the letter to Philemon concerns the matter of a runaway slave, at least one interpreter has proposed something radical, by suggesting that Onesimus and Philemon were brothers in the flesh.[10] This is concluded on the basis of Paul's word to Philemon in v. 16 to treat Onesimus "no longer as a slave but more than a slave, a beloved brother...both in the flesh and in the Lord" (NRSV). So, Philemon really did not own Onesimus, but just treated him poorly, like he was a slave. This is often viewed to be a stretch of what is written in Paul's letter, and also an over-reaction to not wanting to acknowledge some of the First Century Believers as actually owning slaves.

No scholar, conservative or liberal, has ever proposed a Hebrew or Aramaic origin for the composition of the letter to Philemon.[11] If there would have been any language other than Greek for the letter's composition, then we would have to consider how Philemon's wife, *Apphia* (Ἀπφία), had a Phrygian name[12] and pick one of the dialects particular to the Lycus Valley. And arguing for a Hebrew or Aramaic origin is particularly difficult when we see the wordplay between *Onēsimos* (Ὀνήσιμος), meaning "useful" (BDAG),[13] and *archēstos* (ἄχρηστος) and *euchrēstos* (εὔχρηστος), "useless" and "useful," in vs. 11-12. *ABD* further summarizes how the letter to Philemon followed standard classical conventions, well known to the First Century C.E.:

---

[9] Cf. Dunn, pp 300-301.

[10] Allen Callahan, "The Letter of Paul to Philemon," in *New Interpreter's Study Bible*, pp 2147-2150.

[11] Even self-attested expert Andrew Gabriel Roth, *Ruach Qadim: Aramaic Origins of the New Testament* (Malta: Tushiyah Press, 2005), 329, who strongly advocates an Aramaic origin for the Apostolic Scriptures (notably being completely disengaged with contemporary discussions in conservative New Testament scholarship), has to admit that the letter to Philemon had to eventually reach Philemon in Greek transcription.

[12] Florence Morgan Gillman, "Apphia," in *ABD*, 1:317-318.

[13] *BDAG*, 711.

"The letter is correspondingly brief: 335 [Greek] words encompassing an occasionally specialized vocabulary of 143 words. As such, it is the shortest extant Pauline letter in the NT canon. In its final form, Paul followed more closely than in any of his other writings the pattern of Hellenistic letters known to us, particularly letters of intercession."[14]

WHAT IS THE THEOLOGICAL MESSAGE OF PHILEMON?

The letter to Philemon follows standard First Century convention, but most readers do not examine it to admire Paul's ability to ably communicate to a wealthy Asiatic Believer. Most people read Philemon to see what Paul does with the issue of slavery. In the epistles that were also composed at the same time, Paul instructs, "Masters, grant to your slaves justice and fairness, knowing that you too have a Master in heaven" (Colossians 4:1), and "Slaves, be obedient to those who are your masters according to the flesh, with fear and trembling, in the sincerity of your heart, as to Messiah" (Ephesians 6:5). Does Paul uphold the ancient status quo of slavery just being a part of the Roman economic system, or does he challenge this system in any way? Furthermore, how did the runaway Onesimus actually run into Paul or encounter him, and what were the circumstances surrounding his flight from Philemon?

The traditional view surrounding this letter's circumstances is that Onesimus had done some kind of wrong to his owner Philemon (v. 18), and then he ran away. Onesimus may have not been a very useful or profitable slave,[15] and it is often thought that he stole money from Philemon. And so while it is often thought that Onesimus stole money from Philemon, Dunn is keen to note, while this "most likely indicates robbery or embezzlement...It should be recalled...that Onesimus's physical removal of himself from Philemon's household would itself constitute an act of robbery."[16] Either way we view this, being a runaway slave, Onesimus sought out Paul's help. It is held that Onesimus escaped to Rome, and then through whatever circumstances—which can only be supposed—he either encountered Paul in prison, ran into Paul accidentally, or he encountered other Believers who then directed him to Paul. N.T. Wright simply observes how,

"Onesimus could have joined a band of other ex-slaves, hidden himself in the underworld of a big city, or fled for refuge to a pagan shrine. Instead, whether by design or sheer providence, he had met Paul. And he had become a Christian [meaning, a born again Believer]."[17]

According to Roman law, a runaway slave could be punished by death, even though runaway slaves could have found solace in a temple.[18] Instead, the runaway Onesimus, now coming to faith in Yeshua, sought the Apostle Paul's help in reconciling with his master. The traditional framework of what necessitated Philemon's composition serves to ask the question what the slaveowner Philemon was to do with Onesimus, how he was to reconcile with him, and how he was to treat this slave as a fellow brother in the Lord.

An alternative view behind Philemon's being written, suggests that Onesimus was not at all a runaway slave, but had legally departed from Philemon, in order to seek out some form of mediation from the Apostle Paul, with Onesimus having had a dispute with his master. *ABD* summarizes that for this view, "This means that Onesimus' wrongdoing was neither running away nor stealing from household funds in order to finance his travel. Rather, something that he had done wrong led Onesimus to decide to seek out Paul as his advocate."[19] It is partially based on some Roman legal conventions, which decreed,

"A slave who takes refuge with a friend of his master, in order to obtain his intercession with the latter, is not a fugitive; not even if he has the intention of not returning home if he does not obtain pardon. He is not

---

[14] Bartchy, "Philemon, Epistle to," in *ABD*, 5:305.

[15] Dunn, 302, speculates how Onesimus may have become a slave. He may have sold himself, or had been sold into slavery because of an unpaid debt, but notes "that Phrygian slaves were notoriously unsatisfactory." Yet, Onesimus may have been well trained and educated, being someone of ability who impressed Paul (vs. 11-13).

[16] Ibid., 303.

[17] Wright, 166.

[18] Bartchy, "Philemon, Epistle to," in *ABD*, 5:307.

[19] Ibid., 5:308; also summarized by Patzia, "Philemon, Letter to," in *Dictionary of Paul and His Letters*, 705.

yet a fugitive, for the reason that the term 'flight' does not merely apply to design but also to the act itself" (*Digest* 21.1.17.5).[20]

From this view, the slave Onesimus was not a Believer in the Lord, but he was going to persuade Paul, who was a Believer, to influence another Believer, Philemon. In writing the return letter to Philemon, Paul expresses how he is responsible for Onesimus' conversion of faith, and that Philemon should deal with him generously (v. 19). The debt that Paul intends to pay for Onesimus (vs. 18-21), was not something that Onesimus necessarily stole, but would have been lost income from the lack of Onesimus' services in Philemon's household. Advocates of a traditional Roman location for Paul's imprisonment, such as Carson and Moo, think that even though an appealing alternative view, "it is unlikely that Onesimus would have gone as far as Rome to find a mediator."[21]

Another alternative view behind Philemon's composition is that it was not Philemon, but actually Archippus (v. 2), who was the owner of Onesimus. Philemon would have been the overseer of the congregation which met in his home. The unspecified ministry, that Archippus is encouraged by Paul to fulfill (Colossians 4:17), is actually to release Onesimus and send him back to Paul for him to use.[22]

Not all are agreed that the traditional view of Onesimus' flight as a runaway slave can be easily determined, and that it is best for us to try to not figure out all of the details that preceded Paul's writing to Philemon. Instead, in Morna D. Hooker's estimation, "It is best to begin with what the letter actually tells us."[23] This vantage point prefers not to really speculate on what happened before Onesimus showed up to encounter Paul, but prefers to focus more on what happened after. Still, Hooker suggests that Onesimus had indeed been a slave in some way, somehow encountering Paul in prison, and now as a new Believer, Philemon was required to welcome Onesimus as a brother in faith. This would hint that Philemon manumitted Onesimus, treating Onesimus with graciousness and compassion.

Presumably, whatever the original circumstances of this letter's composition, Onesimus was able to return to Philemon, and Onesimus was released from his bond of slavery, being set free so he could fulfill some kind of ministry work. The historical record does indicate that there was an Onesimus who became bishop of Ephesus at the beginning of the Second Century (Ignatius *Letter to the Ephesians* 1.3),[24] and various commentators have suggested that this is the same Onesimus who was a young man at the time the Apostle Paul wrote to Philemon. Donald Guthrie notes how "There seems to be no positive reason for rejecting the theory that Onesimus the slave later became bishop of the Ephesian church, but merely the similarity of name cannot of itself confirm the identity."[25] Contrary to this suggestion, Wright expresses some doubts as "the name 'Onesimus' was not uncommon."[26] But, if the Second Century Bishop Onesimus were the same Onesimus featured in the Epistle to Philemon, then Peter T. O'Brien's thoughts are not far-fetched:

"If the latter did subsequently become bishop of Ephesus and knew about the collection and publication of the Pauline corpus of letters, then he may have made sure that *his* Pauline letter found a place in the collection."[27]

Even though the traditional view of Onesimus being a runaway slave, making his way to Rome, encountering Paul and becoming a Believer, **certainly is something we can accept**—what is most important is not the backstory behind the letter to Philemon, but how we interpret and apply it. V. 16, where Paul instructs Philemon to regard Onesimus "no longer as a slave, but more than a slave, a beloved brother," was especially subversive for the First Century. This is a distinct manifestation of the equality that the work of Yeshua has

---

[20] *The Civil Law*, trans. S.P. Scott (Cincinnati: Central Trust Company, 1932). Accessible online at <http://www.constitution.org/sps/sps.htm/>.

[21] Carson and Moo, 591.

[22] This view is summarized by Guthrie, *New Testament Introduction*, 661; BY O'Brien, *Colossians-Philemon*, 266.

[23] Hooker, "Philemon," in *ECB*, 1447.

[24] "I received, therefore, your whole multitude in the name of God, through Onesimus, a man of inexpressible love, and your bishop in the flesh, whom I pray you by Jesus Christ to love, and that you would all seek to be like him. And blessed be He who has granted unto you, being worthy, to obtain such an excellent bishop" (Ignatius *Letter to the Ephesians* 1.3).

[25] Guthrie, *New Testament Introduction*, 665.

[26] Wright, 165.

[27] O'Brien, *Colossians-Philemon*, 268.

brought to all people (Galatians 3:28; Colossians 3:11). The fact that Paul could ask Philemon to forgive Onesimus of any prior wrong would have been most serious, as Roman law allowed a slaveowner to inflict whatever punishment he wanted on a runaway, usually death.

Paul urges Philemon to be beneficent toward Onesimus, working on the meaning of Onesimus' name as "useful" (v. 11). Much has been made by some interpreters of a Roman letter written about forty years later, by Pliny the Younger, which is thought to use a similar language and style seen in Philemon. A freedman of Pliny's friend Sabinianus comes to him for help, and so in writing, Pliny says things like "praise for forbearance is especially due when the grounds for anger are more justified...you pain yourself when your mild disposition turns to anger," and "having rebuked him more sharply and severely, having threatened that I shall never plead with you again after this" (*Epistle* 9.21).[28]

Aside from the kinds of external data we can piece together, Dunn is probably correct in asserting, "it may not matter much that we know so little about Onesimus himself; what [is important is what] the letter reveals as a witness to an early Christian attitude to slavery."[29] A direct confrontation to abolish the institution of slavery in the First Century Roman Empire would have been nothing short of fomenting revolution for the early Believers.[30] The Apostle Paul was not a revolutionary, and so what we can detect from a letter like Philemon is that he proposed a transformation from within, against its evil. Even if Paul did choose to openly protest slavery as some kind of ancient abolitionist, what would it have really done? Wright observes,

"What alternatives were actually open to him? He was committed to the life, and the standards, of the new age over against the old (Col. 3). But a loud protest, at that moment in social history, would have functioned simply on the level of the old age: it would have been heard only as a criticism by one part of society."[31]

Paul says to Philemon in v. 21, "Having confidence in your obedience, I write to you, since I know that you will do even more than what I say," and this is about as close as he gets to describing an utter disdain for slavery. In Colossians 3:22-23, Paul instructs slaves to demonstrate proper behavior, which would include avoiding the deeds of the flesh (Galatians 5:19-21). What Paul sought in changing the institution of slavery was not a violent slave uprising, but rather a slaveowner-by-slaveowner encounter with how this was not what God originally intended from Creation. *IDB* concludes,

"In its very nature...slavery is antithetical to the heart of the Christian gospel; but so are political revolution and bloody warfare. Only a bloody revolution could at that time have changed the institution, and Paul chose the method of working for brotherhood within the prevailing social pattern. As many have pointed out, he was sowing the seeds of a more spiritual type of revolution—that of the transformation of relationships."[32]

Had the Christian Church of later centuries taken Paul's letter to Philemon more seriously, it is thought that the institution of slavery would have been undermined much sooner in history. (And not to be overlooked is the still-ongoing exploitation of the poorer classes in various "Christian" countries.) Guthrie concludes that "It is clearly incongruous for a Christian master to 'own' a brother in Christ in the contemporary sense of the word, and although the existing order of society could not be immediately changed by Christianity without a political revolution (which was contrary to Christian principles), the Christian master-slave relationship was so transformed from within that it was bound to ultimately lead to the abolition of the system."[33]

Some disagree, though, claiming that there is no clear abolitionist tenor in either the letter to Philemon, or similarly in Pauline passages like 1 Corinthians 7:20-24. Arthur A. Rupprecht thinks, Paul "strongly hinted that the slave would be useful to him in the work of evangelism. Nowhere does Paul openly state that

---

[28] Pliny the Younger: *Pliny the Younger: Complete Letters*, trans. P.G. Walsh (Oxford: Oxford University Press, 2006), 227.

[29] Dunn, 302.

[30] Moo, pp 371-372, points out how we cannot read the more recent experiences of slavery in North America, ending in the Nineteenth Century, as a grid to fully understand ancient slavery in the Roman Empire—even though both practices were equally abhorrent.

[31] Wright, 169.

[32] M.E. Lyman, "Philemon, Letter to," in *IDB*, 3:784.

[33] Guthrie, *New Testament Introduction*, pp 665-666.

Philemon should set Onesimus free. Nor is it necessary to assume that Onesimus would be freed if he were to join Paul in his missionary work."[34] But can the idea that Onesimus would never be freed from slavery by Philemon be truly supported from the tone of Paul's letter? Did Paul expect Onesimus to just be treated as an equal brother in the Lord, but still be a slave?

Other than Paul addressing, even indirectly, the issue of slavery, the Epistle to Philemon also includes within it a definite theology of fellowship. Paul writes, "*I pray* that the fellowship of your faith may become effective through the knowledge of every good thing which is in you for Messiah's sake" (v. 6), and "If then you regard me a partner, accept [Onesimus] as *you would* me" (v. 17). Paul asks Philemon to forgive Onesimus of whatever he has done to wrong him, and for him to be reconciled to the congregation of Believers that meets in his home (at least indicating that Onesimus had already been exposed to the gospel before encountering Paul in Rome). The transformation that takes place when one comes to faith in Messiah Yeshua is to change relationships between people, which in Onesimus' case meant that his owner Philemon would have needed to treat him differently (vs. 16-17). Both Onesimus (v. 10) and Philemon (v. 19) owed their salvation to Paul's ministry.

One challenge that cannot be overlooked is that past interpretations of Philemon actually used Paul's letter *as a support* for the institution of slavery. Some Nineteenth Century American theologians considered Philemon to include a "Pauline mandate" for slavery, even for the requirement of runaway slaves to return home to their masters.[35] It is quite difficult, if not utterly absurd, to argue that First Century Roman slavery is the same as the plantation slavery that was witnessed in the American South and Caribbean. Roman slaves could be of any ethnic background, they could work to earn their freedom, and they had opportunities—even if difficult ones—to become wealthy once such freedom was attained. Some slaves, within a wealthy household, had better living conditions than free, rural peasants.[36]

As much as Paul probably did not personally like slavery, there would have been problems with him throwing down his fist and requiring immediate release of all of Philemon's, or anyone else's, slaves. Moo discusses the various problems that exist when such instantaneous change is required:

"A Christian slave owner who immediately released all his or her slaves might be condemning many of them to poverty and starvation. Perhaps the contemporary problem of polygamy among new converts is something of a parallel. Should a man who has converted to Christianity and come to recognize monogamy as a biblical principle immediately send all but one wife away—even if, in doing so, he condemns those women to a life of outcasts and economic hardship? While going some way toward answering the problem, this factor still does not go all the way; for we still might have expected Paul to have encouraged Christians to release their slaves in a timely and compassionate way."[37]

Moo, surprisingly, does not think that Paul really advocated the early Believers who owned slaves to release them, given the social implications of the First Century. Fortunately though, he does think, "we rightly draw from Paul's principle [in Galatians 3:28 and Colossians 3:11] the conclusion—that Christians not own slaves—that he did not explicitly draw in his day."[38] So from this perspective, Paul continued to lay stepping stones back to the equality of all human beings—a trajectory forward which would see to the eventual death of slavery in later centuries.

While we should not have expected all slaves to be released by their owners who were Believers, specifically dependant on whether or not these people could economically make it on their own—the letter to

---

[34] Arthur A. Rupprecht, "Philemon," in *EXP*, 11:454.

[35] Cain Hope Felder's words are entirely correct:

"There is no basis whatsoever for thinking of Onesimus as a progenitor of the African American slave, especially since the Roman Empire did not have a race-based policy for the institution of slavery, neither in the first century nor at any other time" ("The Letter to Philemon," in *NIB*, 11:885; cf. Dunn, pp 306-307).

[36] For a further review, consult S. Scott Bartchy, "Slavery (Greco-Roman)," in *ABD*, 6:65-73.

[37] Moo, pp 376-377.

The author discusses the issue of polygamy in his article "Is Polygamy for Today?", refuting any Messianics today who would argue that it is a valid principle.

[38] Ibid., 377.

Philemon certainly encourages that First Century slaveowners treat their slaves with a great deal more respect and kindness than their contemporary culture did. Manumission should be encouraged, but it would probably not have happened in every single instance where a slave was owned by a Believer. Yet in Onesimus' case, it would be most unlikely that the Epistle to Philemon was included among the books of the New Testament, **if he had not been released from his slavery.**

HOW DOES PHILEMON RELATE TO MESSIANIC BELIEVERS TODAY?

Moo begins his introduction to Philemon with the word, "Most Christians have never studied Philemon; many have never heard it taught or preached."[39] If this is true of most of today's evangelical Believers, what is to be said of today's Messianic Believers? In our Messianic faith community, we have enough problems with trying to get people to study more than the weekly Torah portion, so small books of the Bible like Philemon never get noticed. Yet even within their Torah studies every week, today's Messianics almost always avoid the issue of slavery. (And if Torah questions about slavery ever do come up, people often just irresponsibly allegorize the passages, like Exodus 21:1-6, and say that it describes "my relationship to Yeshua.")

When the Apostle Paul encountered Onesimus, he was certainly stuck with the difficult question of what to do. As a faithful Jew, Paul would have known that the Torah allows for a runaway slave to not have to go back to his master (Deuteronomy 23:15-16), yet as a Roman citizen, harboring a runaway slave, or helping one escape, could have meant further problems for Paul in prison. A Jewish community functioning within the confines of the Roman Empire would certainly have had to develop *halachah* in order to deal with the authorities. While Paul's preference was no doubt to keep Onesimus for himself, having helped bring him to faith in Yeshua, the law of Rome required Onesimus to be sent back to Philemon (v. 12). Fortunately, though, Philemon was a Believer just like Paul—and so Paul could instruct him on how to be kind and gentle with Onesimus (vs. 15-17).

Our exegesis of Philemon must be tempered by the fact that Onesimus was not a slave like the Ancient Israelites were in Egypt. Rather than helping to run the Egyptian Empire, Onesimus was probably a household servant or field laborer, and his master saw that all of his needs were met. Paul had actually desired to keep Onesimus with him as a useful associate in his ministry work, but knew that he would have to be returned to Philemon.

Knowing the Torah, Paul realized that slaves could be released in the year of jubilee (Exodus 21:2-13), slaveowners who killed their slaves could be executed (Exodus 21:12), and harsh punishment of slaves would mean that the slaves could immediately go free (Exodus 21:26-27). These were casuistic laws in the Pentateuch, originally designed to regulate Ancient Israel's economy in the Ancient Near East—not the Roman province of Judea, nor a widespread Diaspora Jewish community in the Mediterranean basin. So Paul was *informed* from these Torah commandments on how Philemon needed to act toward Onesimus, but he also had to deal with the necessities of Roman law, and most importantly how the gospel of salvation is blind to one's status as either slave or free.

How important is it, really, for today's Messianic movement to understand the Epistle to Philemon? **The Epistle to Philemon is a testament to the social realities of the First Century Mediterranean.** When we read the Apostolic Scriptures, we often forget that as much as one-third of the Roman Empire in the First Century C.E. was made up of some kind of slaves. When we study the Apostolic Scriptures, the social diversity of the Mediterranean—Jewish, Greek, Roman, slave, poor, etc.—is often not considered. This is a problem, because large numbers of people from the slave class and/or lower class were Believers in Yeshua.

Understanding a letter like Philemon could aid us significantly for remembering the kinds of ethical and moral controversies faced by the early *ekklēsia*. Onesimus was a runaway slave who could very easily have stolen money, escaped, but then encountered the Apostle Paul. Onesimus realized what he did wrong, and he was changed by the good news. We are often at a disadvantage, because even though we think we are trying to understand the Scriptures in their ancient context, we do forget that while the needs of people to be loved

---

[39] Ibid., 361.

and treated with respect have not changed—the demographics of the First Century assembly were quite diverse. Patzia is correct in asserting, "When read together with Colossians 3:22-4:1, we begin to appreciate how conversion to the Christian faith broke down all social, racial and economic barriers."[40] Rupprecht's remarks are also well taken:

"Each [main person in the letter] has heard the claims of [the gospel] from totally different backgrounds. Paul was once a rigorous Jew of the Dispersion who advanced in Judaism beyond all his contemporaries. Philemon was a wealthy Asiatic Gentile. Onesimus was the most despicable of all creatures, a runaway slave. They find themselves united in the gospel of Christ."[41]

Carson and Moo also point out how (1) Philemon shows us a significant picture of the love and respect shown toward others in the early Body of Messiah, and (2) how Believers should approach the issue of slavery.[42] Today's evangelical Christian theology is much further along in appreciating the role of Philemon within the canon than today's Messianic movement. If we are truly a faith community that desires to be "fully Biblical," I think it is fair to say that a reconsideration of Philemon is in order. This is most especially true if when reading the Torah, we scratch our heads at what to do over the issue of slavery. The Epistle to Philemon shows us where the trajectory was headed: **the ultimate elimination of the practice.**

In reconsidering Philemon, Messianic Believers will also be able to understand a little more about why Torah issues like *Shabbat* or the dietary laws are really not addressed in the Pauline letters, when compared to issues like how to treat one's slaves, or why not to fornicate. Too many of today's Messianics, even some of the professionally trained teachers among us, forget the complicated social dynamics present in the ancient world. The First Century world *was not* the same world as the Twenty-First Century. Today's Messianic movement simply does not have to deal with the issue of runaway slaves, much less all of the baggage that goes along with those who were really raised in Greco-Roman pantheism.

We also get a detailed look into the personal traits of the Apostle Paul, who was a man who was willing to pay another's debts (v. 18).

It is my hope that each of us, in examining this short letter in the Apostolic Scriptures, can learn something vital for our reading of the whole Bible.

ABBREVIATED OUTLINE OF PHILEMON

    I.   Greeting (vs. 1-3)
    II.   Commendation of Philemon (vs. 4-7)
    III. An Apology or Defense for Onesimus (vs. 8-22)
        a.   Paul's condition in prison (vs. 8-9)
        b.   Onesimus as Paul's "son" in faith (v. 10)
        c.   Paul is sending back Onesimus as "profitable" (vs. 11-14)
        d.   Philemon should receive back Onesimus as a dear brother, and no slave (vs. 15-16)
        e.   Paul offers to pay back Onesimus' debts (vs. 17-20)
        f.   Paul expects Philemon to honor his requests, and asks him to prepare a lodging for him when he arrives for a visit (vs. 17-20)
    IV. Conclusion (vs. 23-25)[43]

BIBLIOGRAPHY FOR INTRODUCTION TO PHILEMON
Bartchy, S. Scott. "Philemon, Epistle to," in *ABD*, 5:305-310.
Blaiklock, Edward M. "Philemon, Letter to," in *NIDB*, pp 780-781.
Bruce, F.F. "Introduction to Philemon," in *NICNT: Colossians, Philemon, Ephesians*, pp 191-202.

---

[40] Patzia, "Philemon, Letter to," in *Dictionary of Paul and His Letters*, 706.
[41] Rupprecht, in *EXP*, 11:456-457.
[42] Carson and Moo, pp 593-594.
[43] Adapted from Guthrie, *New Testament Introduction*, pp 666-667.

Carson, D.A., and Douglas J. Moo. "Philemon," in *An Introduction to the New Testament*, pp 588-595.

Callahan, Allen. "The Letter of Paul to Philemon," in *New Interpreter's Study Bible*, pp 2147-2150.

Deibler, Edwin C. "Philemon," in *BKCNT*, pp 769-775.

Dunn, James D.G. "Introduction," in *NIGTC: The Epistles to the Colossians and to Philemon*, pp 299-309.

Dunnam, Maxie D. "Introduction to Philemon," in *PreachC: Galatians, Ephesians, Philippians, Colossians, Philemon*, 31:397-398.

Felder, Cain Hope. "The Letter to Philemon," in *NIB*, 11:883-888.

Furnish, Victor Paul. "The Letter of Paul to Philemon," in *The Interpreter's One-Volume Commentary on the Bible*, pp 894-896.

Gundry, Robert H. "Plea for a Runaway Slave," in *A Survey of the New Testament*, pp 391-392.

Guthrie, Donald. "Philemon," in *NBCR*, pp 1187-1190.

_____. "The Epistle to Philemon," in *New Testament Introduction*, pp 660-667.

Hemer, C.J. "Philemon," in *ISBE*, 3:830-831.

_____. "Philemon, Epistle to," in *ISBE*, 3:831-832.

Hooker, Morna D. "Philemon," in *ECB*, pp 1447-1450.

Kaiser, Jr., Walter C. "Philemon: The Fellowship Found in the Gospel," in *The Promise-Plan of God*, pp 290-293.

Lyman, M.E. "Philemon, Letter to," in *IDB*, 3:782-784.

Moo, Douglas J. "Introduction to Philemon," in *Pillar New Testament Commentary*, pp 361-378.

O'Brien, Peter T. "Introduction to Philemon," in *WBC: Colossians-Philemon*, 44:265-270.

Patzia, A. "Philemon, Letter to," in *Dictionary of Paul and His Letters*, pp 703-707.

Rollins, W.G. "Philemon, Letter to," in *IDBSup*, pp 663-664.

Rupprecht, Arthur A. "Philemon," in *EXP*, 11:453-457.

Soards, Marion L. "Philemon, Letter to," in *EDB*, pp 1046-1047.

Stern, David H. *Jewish New Testament Commentary*, pp 658-659.

Watson, Duane F. "Philemon," in *EDB*, pp 1045-1046.

Wright, N.T. "Philemon: Introduction," in *TNTC: Colossians and Philemon*, pp 164-171.

Witherington III, Ben. "Introduction," in *The Letters to Philemon, the Colossians, and the Ephesians: A Socio-Rhetorical Commentary on the Captivity Epistles*, pp 1-40.

PHILEMON
COMMENTARY

---

1 Paul, a prisoner of Messiah Yeshua, and Timothy our brother, To Philemon our beloved *brother* and fellow worker, 2 and to Apphia our sister, and to Archippus our fellow soldier, and to the [assembly] in your house: 3 Grace to you and peace from God our Father and the Lord Yeshua the Messiah.

1 Paul's letter begins following standard ancient letter writing techniques. He identifies himself as "Paul, a prisoner of Messiah Yeshua," Timothy is listed as a co-sender, and Philemon is considered to be "our beloved *brother* and fellow worker." This is very important to notice, because Paul makes no reference to his apostolic authority as he typically does in the opening of his other letters.[1] The Epistle to Philemon is the only one of Paul's letters where he begins by describing himself as "a prisoner for Christ Jesus" (RSV). For one who has been imprisoned for the cause of Messiah, Paul deserves to be heard, as he has an important message to Philemon about his runaway slave Onesimus. Paul does not have to assert his apostleship, because there is no question of it being challenged.

In the view of Maxie D. Dunnam, "The letter to Philemon resonates with an understanding of life Jesus set forth in the Sermon on the Mount and gives dynamic witness to the meaning of faith in the marketplace."[2] Paul's reference to himself as a prisoner, as opposed to an apostle, is an assertion of a unique kind of authority. This kind of authority is one which Douglas J. Moo considers is related "to pursue a particular argumentative strategy...Paul's imprisonment is a subtle reminder of his own sacrifices for the sake of the gospel and should lead Philemon to look on his request with sympathy."[3]

Timothy is listed as a co-sender of the letter to Philemon, just like he is in Colossians, but Paul refers to himself as "I" throughout the letter, devoid of any real usage of "we." Timothy is listed in the opening greeting because he stands by Paul as a close ministry associate. Ultimately, though, the letter to Philemon is the account of one man communicating to another man.

V. 1 also gives us some important clues into who Philemon was, including the only explicit reference to him as *tō agapētō* (τῷ ἀγαπητῷ), meaning "the beloved," indicating that he was valued by Paul, Timothy, and other Believers. Knowing the connection between Philemon and Colossians (see Introduction), we can deduce that Philemon was a recipient of Paul's ministry work in Ephesus (Acts 19:9-10), who could have encountered his preaching ministry during a business trip to Ephesus. Philemon as a fellow worker (*sunergos*, συνεργός) would suggest that he helped build up the community of Believers in various acts of service. It could be suggested that Philemon was some kind of itinerant minister in Colossae and the Lycus Valley,[4] but we cannot know this for certain.

2 Paul's opening greeting continues, with him expressing goodwill "to Apphia the beloved, and to Archippus our fellow-soldier, and to the assembly in your house" (LITV). We can safely assume that Apphia was Philemon's wife, with James D.G. Dunn even noting that there is "a serious attempt made...to treat women as individuals."[5] She is recognized as a fellow "sister" (*adelphē*, ἀδελφή) in the Lord, after all. Some have

---

[1] Romans 1:1; 1 Corinthians 1:1; 2 Corinthians 1:1; Galatians 1:1; Ephesians 1:1; Colossians 1:1; 1 Timothy 1:1; 2 Timothy 1:1; Titus 1:1.

[2] Dunnam, 402.

[3] Moo, 380.

[4] O'Brien, *Colossians-Philemon*, 272.

[5] Dunn, 321.

speculated that Archippus was Philemon's son, but we cannot know this for certain. All three of them were a part of the congregation that met in Philemon's home.

Archippus did have a special ministry, which Paul alludes to in the closing salutation of his letter to the Colossians (4:17), being a good indication that he was a leading member of the assembly that met in Philemon's home. Like Epaphroditus (Philippians 2:25), Archippus is considered to be a "fellow soldier" (*sustratiōtēs*, συστρατιώτης) or "comrade-in-arms" (NEB).

V. 2 is yet another confirmation of how the early congregations of Believers most always met in homes. The implication for reading Paul's letter is that Philemon was probably wealthy, and that Onesimus was one of several slaves that he owned.

3 Common to his letters, Paul issues grace and peace to Philemon: "Grace to you and peace from God our Father and the Lord Yeshua the Messiah." Issuing grace and peace was a combination of both Greek and Jewish greetings. V. 3 includes the plural "you" (*hēmōn*, ἡμῶν) as a matter of courtesy to Apphia and Archippus, even though Philemon is the addressee of the letter. Also common to the opening Paul's letters, "God" is a reference to the Father and "Lord" represents Yeshua. But, Yeshua as "Lord" or *kurios* (κύριος) does not solely pertain to Him being Divine, but also serves to underscore the issue that Philemon as a master who owns a slave, has himself a Master to whom he must submit. Ben Witherington III indicates, "Philemon himself has a Master, who provides him with a model as to how he should behave in this situation."[6]

4 I thank my God always, making mention of you in my prayers, 5 because I hear of your love and of the faith which you have toward the Lord Yeshua and toward all the saints; 6 *and I pray* that the fellowship of your faith may become effective through the knowledge of every good thing which is in you for Messiah's sake.

4 Vs. 4-7 in Paul's letter to Philemon serve to establish not only Paul's appreciation for his friend, but also help build Paul's credibility to Philemon, as he will be informing him about what has become of the runaway Onesimus. He informs him how "I always thank my God as I remember you in my prayers" (NIV). Paul's reference to God as "my God" (cf. Romans 1:8; 1 Corinthians 1:4; Philippians 1:3) is not an implication that he somehow worships or serves a different deity than Philemon, but is rather a reflection on his own relationship and experience with God. According to Dunn, this "does not denote Paul's God as distinct from Philemon's, but rather underlies the personal character of Paul's devotion."[7] Paul's usage likely parallels various references we see in the Psalms to the interactions people have with God (Psalm 3:8; 5:3; 7:2, 4, 7; 12:4; 17:3; 21:2; etc.)

In order to pray for Philemon, Paul had to consciously make the effort to remember him and the relationship that the two of them had. One of the most important things a good Jew like Paul would have known, was how Exodus 13:3 admonished Ancient Israel, "Remember[8] this day in which you went out from Egypt, from the house of slavery; for by a powerful hand the LORD brought you out from this place." Whether there are echoes of God requiring His people to remember how He delivered them from slavery, and how Paul remembers Philemon—with this being a distant clue about what will be discussed further on about the slave Onesimus—we can only speculate. Remembering Philemon in prayer, though, would have been important to express how valuable he was to Paul. Moo states, "'Remembering' people in prayer, then, involves not only the mental activity of considering their needs but also calling on God to consider them and act for their benefit."[9]

5 The main reason Paul is able to really pray for Philemon is "because I hear of your love and of the faith which you have toward the Lord Jesus and all the saints" (RSV). It is reasonable to assume that Paul has heard

---

[6] Witherington, 56.

[7] Dunn, 316.

[8] Heb. *zakar* (זָכַר); Grk. LXX *mnēmoneuō* (μνημονεύω).
   Philemon 4 employs the noun form of *mnēmoneuō, mneia* (μνεία).

[9] Moo, 386.

something about Philemon via Epaphras (Colossians 1:4, 8). Yet, as mundane as we might consider this expression of gratitude to be, there is some slight disagreement about what it is intended to convey. The NASU, RSV, and ESV all follow the Greek pretty closely, which reads *sou tēn agapēn kai tēn pistin, hēn echeis pros ton Kurion Iēsoun kai eis pantas tous hagious* (σου τὴν ἀγάπην καὶ τὴν πίστιν, ἣν ἔχεις πρὸς τὸν κύριον Ἰησοῦν καὶ εἰς πάντας τοὺς ἁγίους)—"your love and faith which you have toward the Lord Jesus, and toward all the saints" (YLT). The reason that there is disagreement is that "love **and** faith" are directed toward *both* the Lord Yeshua and toward the saints.

How can faith be directed not only toward the Lord, but also toward the saints? F.F. Bruce suggests that "loyalty" is the best rendering for *pistis* (πίστις).[10] Philemon demonstrates loyalty to the Lord and to the saints, which is something to be slightly differentiated from "faith in Messiah Yeshua"[11] (Colossians 1:4; cf. Ephesians 1:15). Peter T. O'Brien, however, lists how *pistis* might be taken to mean "reliability."[12] Moo suggests that any option other than *pistis* as "faith" is difficult, primarily because he cannot see *pistis* as relating to anything other than faith in the Lord. He argues that v. 5 is to be read chiastically, with faith in the Lord Yeshua, and then love toward all of God's people, being spoken of.[13] This view is reflected in both the NIV and NRSV renderings of v. 5:

> "[B]ecause I hear about your faith in the Lord Jesus and your love for all the saints" (NIV).

> "[B]ecause I hear of your love for all the saints and your faith toward the Lord Jesus" (NRSV).

Still, another view of *pistis*, fully at our disposal,[14] is that Philemon demonstrates "love and faithfulness" to both the Lord and the saints. This may be our best option, simply because Paul is trying to express appreciation to Philemon for the good service that he has demonstrated as a worker (v. 1) in the *ekklēsia*.

6 What Paul actually prays for, on Philemon's behalf, is now detailed: "*I pray* that the fellowship of your faith may become effective through the knowledge of every good thing which is in you for Messiah's sake" (NASU). Believe it or not, this is the most difficult verse in the entire letter, in terms of evaluating what Paul is trying to convey to Philemon, how it is to be translated, and the overall theological purpose of it.[15]

How is the clause *hē koinōnia tēs pisteōs sou* (ἡ κοινωνία τῆς πίστεώς σου) to be translated? The NIV has this as "in sharing your faith," followed by the NRSV which has "the sharing of your faith." A common view is that the knowledge of one's faith leads a person to be more active in sharing it, and this must be the case with Philemon. Philemon has a proper faith in the Lord, is experiencing the Lord's goodness, and Paul is desiring that "the sharing of [his] faith" via the proclamation of the good news becomes more effective.

Also to be considered is how the *koinōnia*, viewed to be "sharing" by many, could regard the sharing of one's resources that comes from an active faith in Yeshua. From this vantage point, 2 Corinthians 9:6, 8 would be appropriate to note: "Now this *I say*, he who sows sparingly will also reap sparingly, and he who sows bountifully will also reap bountifully...And God is able to make all grace abound to you, so that always having all sufficiency in everything, you may have an abundance for every good deed."

Yet is it an assumption that *koinōnia* means "sharing"? Could "the fellowship of your faith" regard coming together with other Believers, and in the process of being built up together in the Lord, properly express oneself as changed by Him? The options before us, in Dunn's estimation, are how "The puzzle is whether κοινωνία is something objective (the fellowship brought by faith) or subjective (the experience of shared faith), and likewise whether πίστις is objective (the fellowship of a shared confession) or subjective (the shared experience of believing)."[16]

---

[10] Bruce, *Colossians-Philemon-Ephesians*, 208.

[11] Grk. *tēn pistin humōn en Christō Iēsou* (τὴν πίστιν ὑμῶν ἐν Χριστῷ Ἰησοῦ); "your faith in Christ Jesus" (RSV).

[12] O'Brien, *Colossians-Philemon*, 278.

[13] Moo, 388.

[14] Cf. *LS*, 641.

[15] Consult Moo, pp 389-394 for an evaluation of views.

[16] Dunn, 318.

N.T. Wright further observes, "*Koinōnia* cannot mean 'sharing' in the sense of dividing something up or parcelling it out. Nor is the language primarily of business. The key idea is 'mutual participation'. The whole phrase then means 'the mutual participation which is proper to your faith.'"[17] The NLT rendering of v. 6 tries (although perhaps not as well as it could) to capture this option with, "I am praying that you will put into action the generosity that comes from your faith as you understand and experience all the good things we have in Christ."

Sharing or "fellowship" in terms of Philemon being generous with his finances, distributed to other Believers, does not appear to be the issue in v. 6. Rather, *koinōnia* appears to pertain to what occurs when one participates in fellowship with Believers, and the implications of that fellowship as demonstrated in faith. This would fit the theme of Paul's letter quite well. Moo summarizes, "When people believe in Christ, they become identified with one another in an intimate association and incur both the benefits and responsibilities of that communion. Philemon is fundamentally all about those responsibilities, as Paul, Onesimus, and Philemon, bound together in faith, are forced by circumstances to think through the radical implications of their *koinōnia*."[18]

If the "fellowship of your faith" is understood to mean the shared experiences of one's faith, helping build up one another to become more effective Believers in the Lord, then for what purpose is this to take place? Paul says that is to occur *en hēmin eis Christon* (ἐν ἡμῖν εἰς Χριστόν), literally "in us to/toward Christ." The NASU having "for Christ's sake" (also TNIV) seems a rather ambiguous and general rendering, and the HCSB having "for *the glory of* Christ" makes a value judgment. Also not to be overlooked are the textual variants between *hēmin* (ἡμῖν) or "us" (ESV), and *humin* (ὑμῖν) or "you," both of which seem to have some good evidence among mss.,[19] although "us" should be preferred as it would include Paul in this mix. Given the specificity of the Greek clause *eis Christon*, either "in Messiah" or "unto Messiah" would be the clearer rendering. The implication of how one's shared experiences of faith make us be more effective Believers is certainly done for the Lord's sake, but more specifically is done unto the Lord for the further establishment of His Body. In Ephesians 4:12-13 Paul details how this works,

"[F]or the equipping of the saints for the work of service, to the building up of the body of Messiah; until we all attain to the unity of the faith, and of the knowledge of the Son of God, to a mature man, to the measure of the stature which belongs to the fullness of Messiah."

Philemon's fellowship of faith, that Paul prays for, is involved with this important process. And, the textual evidence favoring "in us unto Messiah," points to how Paul, Philemon, *and* Onesimus are all participants in this faith. They are all involved in the Body of Messiah.

7 For I have come to have much joy and comfort in your love, because the hearts of the saints have been refreshed through you, brother. 8 Therefore, though I have enough confidence in Messiah to order you *to do* what is proper, 9 yet for love's sake I rather appeal *to you*—since I am such a person as Paul, the aged, and now also a prisoner of Messiah Yeshua—

7 V. 7 serves as a transition point, as Paul has just expressed his appreciation for Philemon, by telling him how he is in his prayers, and how he is mindful of his involvement in the Body of Messiah. He says, "Your love has given me great joy and encouragement, because you, brother, have refreshed the hearts of the saints" (NIV). This is not too different than how Paul reports to the Colossians how Epaphras "also informed us of your love in the Spirit" (Colossians 1:8). We can assume that given how the Believers have been refreshed by Philemon, that he has demonstrated benevolence toward the community of saints in his home, but possibly also Colossae and/or the Lycus Valley. In Bruce's estimation, "Philemon, it appears, was fairly well-to-do, and used his means to help his fellow-Christians. But he showed grace not only in the fact of his generosity but in the manner in which he practiced it: those who benefited were not made to feel

---

[17] Wright, 176.
[18] Moo, 392.
[19] Cf. Metzger, *Textual Commentary*, 657.

embarrassed."[20] So, while v. 6 may not directly allude to any kind of financial sharing, it can be implied from v. 7.

The most notable parallel with v. 7 actually appears in 3 John 3, when the Apostle John writes to Gaius, "For I was very glad when brethren came and testified to your truth, *that is*, how you are walking in truth."

What has just been compiled in vs. 4-7, where Paul expresses goodwill toward Philemon, issuing a word of appreciation for his service in the Lord, is thought by Witherington to be part of a very distinct rhetorical approach to his addressing the issue concerning Onesimus. He remarks, "He does not attack the problem head on, but rather builds rapport with Philemon, praises his character and previous behavior, appeals to the deeper emotions, and then shows how the requested action gives Philemon an opportunity to continue to behave in such gracious Christian ways."[21]

8 The reason why Paul expresses such appreciation, for Philemon's faith experience, is indicated in his careful words, "Accordingly, though I am bold enough in Christ to command you to do what is required..." (RSV). Paul would very much be able to order Philemon to do something—but this he does not do. Being an elder in the faith, and one who has served in the Lord in ministry work, Paul wants to see what Philemon will do of his own free will, not asserting the authority that he could.

This is actually pretty serious when you think about it, because in a classical sense, *parrēsia* (παρρησία) or "*freespokenness, openness, frankness*" (*LS*),[22] did concern where a citizen could speak his candid opinion as a part of the democratic process. Witherington points out, "In Paul's immediate milieu *parrēsia* had come to refer to the kind of speech that was characteristic between true friends."[23] Paul, because of his ministry service and now imprisonment, has very much earned the right to say whatever he feels to Philemon: "I might feel free to dictate..." (REB). The term *parrēsia* similarly appears in John 18:20, where Yeshua says "I have spoken openly [*parrēsia*] to the world..."

In addition to his faithful ministry service, which requires Philemon to respect Paul, O'Brien notes how also, "No doubt Paul has in view their personal intimacy...which probably began at the time of Philemon's conversion when Paul was the instrument God used."[24] Paul could very much "command" (RSV, NRSV, ESV, HCSB; Grk. *epitassō*, ἐπιτάσσω) Philemon as to what his proper duty was. He does not do this because instead he has confidence that Philemon will do what is necessary according to the imperative of love (v. 9), and that being assertive to Philemon regarding Onesimus (who he still has not mentioned) he will not have to issue any stringent dictate. Also not to be overlooked is how even while Paul expects Philemon to be guided by love, completely concurrent with his track record of faith, using direct language might have caused some problems for the good Apostle in prison. Dunn reminds us,

"A further factor not to be ignored is the possibility that Paul's letters would have been read by the authorities before being allowed to be taken out of prison. A concern not to arouse suspicion or give unfriendly officials excuse to accuse him of disrupting the social fabric could also have weighed in Paul's choice of words and use of what was in effect Christian code language."[25]

When the subject would shortly come up about what Philemon was to do with Onesimus, Philemon could have thought that enforcing the Roman slave code regarding runaways was his appropriate duty. But Paul, writing to Philemon, expresses how he has confidence that Philemon will consider what will be right for him to do in the Messiah, **without him having to be demanding of it.**

9 Appealing to love, Paul reminds his friend Philemon of who he actually is: "I appeal to you on the basis of love. I then, as Paul—an old man and now also a prisoner of Christ Jesus—" (NIV). Paul chooses not to order Philemon, but instead act *dia tēn agapēn* (διὰ τὴν ἀγάπην), "because of love" (LITV).[26] Paul is an old man when writing this letter, but for someone of the First Century C.E., a *presbutēs* (πρεσβύτης) was probably

---

[20] Bruce, *Colossians-Philemon-Ephesians*, 210.

[21] Witherington, 61; detailed further on pp 62-64.

[22] *LS*, 611.

[23] Witherington, 66.

[24] O'Brien, *Colossians-Ephesians*, 288.

[25] Dunn, 324.

[26] Cf. Romans 13:8-10; Galatians 5:13-15.

someone in his fifties, concurrent with Philo's sentiment "He is a middle aged man till he is fifty-six" (*On the Creation of the World* 105).[27]

Some versions like the RSV render v. 9 with "Paul, an ambassador." This judgment is made on the basis of *hōs Paulos presbutēs* (ὡς Παῦλος πρεσβύτης) being almost identical to the word for ambassador, *presbeutēs* (πρεσβευτής), and wishing to conform the translation to the sentiment he expresses in Ephesians 6:20, "I am an ambassador in chains." Wright favors this view, commenting, "If it is as *Christ's* ambassador, and prisoner, that he is writing, then the appropriate method for him to use is that of Christ himself, namely, the setting aside of right in order to bring salvation to others."[28]

Dunn is one, among various interpreters, who argues that the mss. evidence is not convincing in favor of *presbeutēs* being intended by v. 9,[29] and the rendering "old man" is followed by other modern versions like the NIV and NRSV. The reasoning behind wanting to render *presbutēs* as "ambassador" and not "old man," is to try to connect it to the later wordplay seen in v. 11 between "useless" and "useful." While Paul is doubtlessly an ambassador for the Lord, he does not really appeal to that role here, and instead appeals to Philemon on a personal basis.

Older people are required to be treated with respect, given their life experience and accumulation of wisdom. Leviticus 19:32 explains, "You shall rise up before the grayheaded and honor the aged, and you shall revere your God; I am the LORD." Also informing us would be Sirach 8:6, "Do not disdain a man when he is old, for some of us are growing old." In the estimation of Witherington, "This letter is not an ambassadorial letter but an emotive appeal using Asiatic rhetoric."[30] If Paul had yet to reach his fifties, then perhaps he could have used "ambassador," but given the nature of his message to Philemon, "old man" is best.

10 I appeal to you for my child Onesimus, whom I have begotten in my imprisonment, 11 who formerly was useless to you, but now is useful both to you and to me.

10 Having now gone through his words of commendation to Philemon (vs. 4-7), and knowing that in the Lord and on the basis of love he will do the right thing (vs. 8-9), Paul now addresses the main issue of his letter. He says, "I appeal to you for my child, Onesimus, whose father I have become in my imprisonment" (RSV). But do take note of the actual word order in the Greek, and how Onesimus is the last word of the sentence:

Parakalō se peri tou emou teknou, hon egennēsa en tois desmois, **Onēsimon** (παρακαλῶ σε περὶ τοῦ ἐμοῦ τέκνου, ὃν ἐγέννησα ἐν τοῖς δεσμοῖς, Ὀνήσιμον).

We are looking at this letter and are trying to probe the various reasons Paul says what he does in vs. 4-9 preceding, knowing that they are building up to the subject of the runaway Onesimus. *Philemon did not know this.* The Greek of v. 10 is clearer than English translations, as Paul states what had happened first, and then he mentions Onesimus by name. O'Brien points out to us how "This was probably the first news Philemon had received of his slave since he ran away and he might be expected to react negatively to the mention of his name."[31] Being the first time that Philemon had heard of Onesimus, Cain Hope Felder poses a list of poignant questions that are deserving to be asked of whose who recognize that he had run away:

"Why did Onesimus leave in the first place? Where did he go, and where could he expect refuge? If Onesimus had committed some crime, had Philemon published a reward notice regarding him? If so, then how widely would that reward notice have been circulated and known? If there was a reward notice, then Onesimus would have had increased need to remove himself as far from that master's arena of influence (Colossae) as resources and opportunity would allow."[32]

[27] *The Works of Philo: Complete and Unabridged*, 16.
[28] Wright, 181.
[29] Dunn, 322 fn #3.
[30] Witherington, 67.
[31] O'Brien, *Colossians-Philemon*, 290.
[32] Felder, in *NIB*, 11:898.

We will probably never know all of the answers to why or how Onesimus fled from Philemon, and then how he encountered Paul. The reality of the letter to Philemon is that he did encounter Paul, and that Onesimus was converted to saving faith by the ministry activity of Paul. Paul referring to Onesimus as a child that he had begotten is not something inconsistent with his other letters, where he also has spiritual "children" (1 Corinthians 4:15; Galatians 4:19; 1 Timothy 1:2; Titus 1:4). Not unimportant to also be aware of is what comes with being a spiritual "father" to such a child. It is sometimes noted that there might be a connection to the Rabbinical opinion, "Whoever teaches Torah to the son of his neighbor is credited by Scripture as if he had made him" (b.Sanhedrin 99b).[33]

11 Being born again as a result of Paul's ministry service, even with Paul in prison, has manifested itself in something quite serious. Paul reports to Philemon, "Formerly he was useless to you, but now he is indeed useful to you and to me" (RSV). There is a wordplay present in the Greek between "useless" and "useful":

Ton pote soi **achrēston** *nuni de [kai] soi kai emoi* **euchrēston** (τόν ποτέ σοι ἄχρηστον νυνὶ δὲ [καὶ] σοὶ καὶ ἐμοὶ εὔχρηστον).

The wordplay is seen between the adjectives *achrēstos* (ἄχρηστος) and *euchrēstos* (εὔχρηστος). Surprisingly, David H. Stern is one who really does make note of this, commenting, "The Greek name *Onēsimos* (v. 10) is another word for 'useful.' The JNT makes explicit the Greek text's implicit wordplay."[34] Stern's version paraphrases v. 11 with, "His name means 'useful,' and although he was once useless to you, he has now become most useful—not only to you but also to me" (CJB). This kind of wordplay was common to both Jewish and classical literature,[35] and in Witherington's opinion, "The wordplay is more than just clever verbal pyrotechnics. It helps the argument along."[36] The same kind of wordplay seen in v. 11 is seen in the Second Century Hermas *Vision* 3.6.7, "When you were rich, you were useless; but now you are useful and fit for life. Be ye useful to God; for you also will be used as one of these stones."

12 I have sent him back to you in person, that is, *sending* my very heart, 13 whom I wished to keep with me, so that on your behalf he might minister to me in my imprisonment for the gospel; 14 but without your consent I did not want to do anything, so that your goodness would not be, in effect, by compulsion but of your own free will.

12 Informing Philemon that his runaway slave Onesimus is now "useful" (v. 11), Paul tells him "I have sent him back to you in person, that is, *sending* my very heart." While sending back Philemon's runaway slave, Paul considers Onesimus to be his "bowels" (KJV), as *splagchnon* (σπλάγχνον) can mean **"inward parts"** (BDAG),[37] which is tried to be captured with renderings like "very heart" (RSV/NIV/ESV). Witherington observes, "Paul therefore means that the slave has become a profound part of himself, taken into his heart, life, and ministry. Sending him away is very difficult. How Philemon treats Onesimus will be how he treats Paul's heart, or very self."[38]

In returning Onesimus to Philemon, it could be thought that Paul is endorsing the practice of slavery, sending a runaway slave back to his owner. In actuality, though, Paul is simply being tactful. He will proceed to express how he really did not want to send back Onesimus to Philemon, but did recognize it to be necessary.

13 Paul actually has a very good reason as to why he did not want to send Onesimus back to Philemon, reflecting on the fact that Onesimus really did get saved: "I wanted to keep him with me, so that in my imprisonment for the gospel he might serve me in your place" (HCSB). Rather than Philemon coming to Rome to help Paul, Onesimus could help Paul. Onesimus could be very useful in attending to Paul in his personal needs, while in prison, unlike Timothy who needed to attend to Paul's ministerial needs as an evangelistic

---

[33] *The Babylonian Talmud: A Translation and Commentary.*
[34] Stern, 658.
[35] O'Brien, *Colossians-Philemon*, 291.
[36] Witherington, 74.
[37] *BDAG*, 938.
[38] Witherington, 75.

agent. Paul retaining Onesimus and not sending him back to Philemon would have been consistent with the Torah's instruction regarding runaway slaves:

"You shall not hand over to his master a slave who has escaped from his master to you. He shall live with you in your midst, in the place which he shall choose in one of your towns where it pleases him; you shall not mistreat him" (Deuteronomy 23:15-16).

Unlike the Torah, Roman law required Onesimus to be sent back, and being someone who was already in prison—and aiding a runaway slave—could have severely hurt Paul. But not all are agreed that Paul really considered the Torah's instruction on slaves to be that important, as it largely pertained to foreign, and not Israelite slaves. Moo's opinion is that "Paul's decision to send Onesimus back to Philemon is based on neither Jewish nor Roman law, but on the higher law of love."[39] Regardless of which way one looks at it, Paul had to send Onesimus back to Philemon, because he was Philemon's property.

14 Vs. 14-21 summarize the issue of what Paul expects Philemon to do with Onesimus, based on their relationship as friends to one another, and the confidence that Paul places in Philemon. Paul informs Philemon that Onesimus is being sent back because "I did not want to do anything without your consent, so that any favor you do will be spontaneous and not forced" (NIV), or "that your good deed might be voluntary and not something forced" (NRSV). Notable is that nowhere so far is this favor or good deed defined by Paul. While many of us want to leap ahead and automatically assume that Paul is requesting that Onesimus be released from slavery, Paul could just as well be referring to Philemon sparing Onesimus' life for him having run away. Slaveowners in the Roman Empire did have the responsibility to take good care of their slaves, as the practice of slavery was an important part of the economy, and that could have been a "good deed."

Paul did not plan to just do anything with Onesimus without Philemon's consent, taking improper advantage of the cordial relationship that these two men had. The term *gnōmē* (γνώμη), rendered as "consent," can have legal implications meaning *"a proposition, motion"* (LS).[40] Paul wants Philemon to make decisions regarding Onesimus of his own free will, not because he feels like he is being compelled to do it by force. The good deed that Philemon would perform would be consistent with what he has thusfar done with the other saints in fellowship service (vs. 6-7). Dunn states, "In the social relationships of a church [meaning, a congregation of Believers] existing in an unequal society there is a particular responsibility on the part of the powerful to act toward others in a spirit of goodness rather than standing on their rights."[41] **The good deed would be highly reflective on Onesimus' new status as a born again Believer.**

15 For perhaps he was for this reason separated *from you* **for a while, that you would have him back forever, 16 no longer as a slave, but more than a slave, a beloved brother, especially to me, but how much more to you, both in the flesh and in the Lord. 17 If then you regard me a partner, accept him as** *you would* **me.**

15 Vs. 15-17 actually detail what Paul expected Philemon to do regarding Onesimus, and while we may think it likely that they allude to his release from slavery, we need not come to this conclusion too quickly as no direct statement is made regarding Onesimus' physical status compared to his spiritual status.

Having just told Philemon about Onesimus' conversion of faith (v. 10) and how he has become useful (v. 11), Paul tells him "Perhaps this is why he was parted from you for a while, that you might have him back for ever" (RSV). The passive aorist verb *echōristhē* (ἐχωρίσθη) is employed for "separated," which many are inclined to think is a Divine passive, detailing the sovereign work of God. Was the separation of Onesimus from Philemon really Onesimus' doing—or God's doing? Joseph's sentiment to his brothers, "As for you, you meant evil against me, *but* God meant it for good in order to bring about this present result..." (Genesis 50:20), could certainly be in view. Yet Paul tempers his words with *Tacha gar dia touto* (Τάχα γὰρ διὰ τοῦτο), "for perhaps because of this" (YLT), as it is not his intention to directly state whether God did this or not.

---

[39] Moo, 411.

[40] *LS*, 166.

[41] Dunn, 333.

The larger point made is that Onesimus was separated from Philemon *pros hōran* (πρὸς ὥραν), only "for an hour" (YLT), to later be received back by Philemon *hina aiōnion* (ἵνα αἰώνιον), "forever" or "permanently" (HCSB).

16 How was Philemon to receive back Onesimus? If Philemon really is a mature, generous, born again Believer, then Paul's request of him will be easily fulfilled: "have him back...no longer as a slave, but more than a slave, a beloved brother, especially to me, but how much more to you, both in the flesh and in the Lord." He first says that Philemon is to no longer consider Onesimus *hōs doulon*, but continues by adding, *all' huper doulon* (ὡς δοῦλον ἀλλ᾽ ὑπὲρ δοῦλον), meaning no longer "as a slave, but above a slave" (my translation).[42] We are not required to read this verse in the context of Onesimus being manumitted, but rather in the relationship that Philemon and Onesimus would have. For certain, in treating Onesimus as being above a slave, Philemon would need to give him greater love and warmth as he returned.[43] Some echoes of 1 Corinthians 7:21-23 could be considered, but perhaps more applicable would be how in the Lord a born again Believer is to be considered "no longer a slave, but a son; and if a son, then an heir through God" (Galatians 4:7).

In the salutation of his letter to the Colossians, Paul does label Onesimus to be "*our* faithful and beloved brother, who is one of your *number*" (Colossians 4:9). Onesimus has come to faith, and he is considered to be faithful and beloved in the Lord. The Colossians were certainly going to know this, meaning that the personal word to Philemon to value Onesimus highly, would have had an effect on the community of Believers in the region.

Paul tells Philemon to regard Onesimus as a beloved brother *en sarki kai en Kuriō* (ἐν σαρκὶ καὶ ἐν κυρίῳ), "in the flesh and in the Lord." Paul's usage of "in the flesh" probably does not relate to Onesimus remaining as a slave, but rather speaks of Philemon recognizing him person-to-person or man-to-man. Bruce does note, though, how it would not have been irregular if Onesimus were somehow Philemon's son, should Philemon have fathered him via a slave-girl, which would make Onesimus a slave child. Yet, as he concludes, "nothing in Paul's language suggests that this was the situation."[44] Paul's reference to "in the flesh" could also be regarded along the lines of "in your earthly relationship" (*NICNT*)[45] or "on the natural plane" (New Jerusalem Bible).

While the work of the gospel itself was to radically change the relationship of people to one another (Galatians 3:28; Colossians 3:11), not to be overlooked is how Stoic philosophy had already advocated some kind of an equality for all people (Seneca *Epistles* 44.1). While Philemon would be motivated by how Messiah Yeshua had changed his heart, in his approach to Philemon, commentators are often keen to note how in a classical context Paul's statements do have some parallels, as seen Seneca's writing, "Be kind and courteous in your dealings with a slave; bring him into your discussions and conversations and your company generally" (*Epistles* 47.10).[46] Paul's assertions are, of course, far more profound than anything pagans could say about slavery, but they are not inconsistent. Witherington further concludes,

"Paul certainly believes that all persons in Christ are new creatures and of equal sacred worth. This clearly has implications for the way he treats Jews and Gentiles and men and women, and there is no reason to doubt it would have social implications for his views about relationships between Christian slaves and masters."[47]

Notable to be considered is that Philemon 16 is the only place in the Apostolic Scriptures where a slave is actually labeled as a "brother." While Philemon could receive Onesimus back, and retain his ownership of him, this would be very difficult to envision if he were to treat him as a fellow "brother." While Moo emphasizes how we need to weigh the different ancient options of continuing a master-slave relationship, and

---

[42] I have chosen here to render the preposition *huper* (ὑπέρ), appearing with the accusative case (denoting direct object) *doulon*, as "above" (LS, 833; option B.II.).

[43] Dunn, 336.

[44] Bruce, *Colossians-Philemon-Ephesians*, 218.

[45] Ibid., 216.

[46] Seneca: *Letters from a Stoic*, trans. Robin Campbell (London: Penguin Books, 2004), 93.

[47] Witherington, 80.

the legitimate challenges that could present themselves should Onesimus be manumitted, he also has to say how "Paul is not yet technically asking Philemon to do anything...But by suggesting that this might indeed be God's purpose, Paul is, of course, putting considerable pressure on Philemon."[48] It really would be hard to argue that Paul envisions Philemon to treat Onesimus as an equal, yet keep him as a slave.

17 In considering Onesimus a beloved brother, Paul is clear to emphasize, "if you consider me your partner, receive him as you would receive me" (RSV). Philemon is to "welcome" (NIV) Onesimus. The verb *proslambanō* (προσλαμβάνω) is used by Paul in Romans 15:7 to describe the mutual welcoming of all people toward one another in the Body of Messiah: "Therefore, accept [*proslambanō*] one another, just as Messiah also accepted [*proslambanō*] us to the glory of God." If Philemon highly regards the Apostle Paul, then he will similarly regard the returned slave Onesimus. He will also (have to) learn to act toward him as though he were Paul, forgiving him of having run away, and we can safely assume, manumitting him from his bonds.

But v. 17 is less about Onesimus and Philemon, and is more about Paul and Philemon. Paul and Philemon were fellow brothers in the Lord, and even though separated, they were in fellowship together. Their fellowship could be compared to a business partnership, as Onesimus' expenses will be discussed (v. 18), but spiritual ties were far more important. Dunn comments, "its implication [is] that Philemon like Paul put the work of the gospel and care of the churches [or, assemblies] among his highest priorities, [and] that gave Paul the stronger confidence that Philemon would know how to put the righting of Onesimus's wrong in its proper perspective."[49] He further observes how serious it would be for Philemon to actually welcome Onesimus back as a partner, as though Onesimus were Paul:

"[I]t was a traditional assumption in Greco-Roman society that such a relationship was possible between equals, and certainly not between master and slave."[50]

Paul has directly subverted some of the sentiments seen in Platonic and Aristotelian philosophy:

"[E]ven if you proclaim that a master and his slave shall have equal status, friendship between them is inherently impossible. The same applies to the relations between an honest man and a scoundrel" (Plato *Laws* 757a).[51]

"Friendship between brothers is like that which unites the members of a social club, because the parties are equal in standing and age...but there can be no friendship or justice towards inanimate things, and not even towards a horse or an ox, nor yet towards a slave *qua* slave; because there is nothing common to both parties: the slave is a living tool in the same way that a tool is an inanimate object" (Aristotle *Nicomachean Ethics* 8.11.6-7).[52]

We can agree with Moo, "The focus throughout this verse...is on the need to receive Onesimus as a Christian, with all the revolutionary implications of that action."[53] Such a welcoming of Onesimus, the same way that Paul would be welcomed, would serve as a significant testimony against the prevailing views of First Century Greco-Roman society.

18 **But if he has wronged you in any way or owes you anything, charge that to my account; 19 I, Paul, am writing this with my own hand, I will repay it (not to mention to you that you owe to me even your own self as well).**

18 The clue that is used to imply that Onesimus likely stole something from Philemon, either money or goods, is found in Paul's willingness to pay back any debt: "If he has wronged you at all, or owes you anything, charge that to my account" (RSV). Noting that he will personally incur any financial penalties that

---

[48] Moo, 425.
[49] Dunn, 337.
[50] Ibid., 338.
[51] Plato, *Laws*, 184.
[52] Aristotle, *Ethics*, 278.
[53] Moo, 427.

Onesimus has accrued is fairly serious, especially given how in his larger letter to the Colossians he says, "For he who does wrong will receive the consequences of the wrong which he has done, and that without partiality" (Colossians 3:25), and "Masters, grant to your slaves justice and fairness, knowing that you too have a Master in heaven" (Colossians 4:1). The Apostle Paul is willing, in many ways, to take as much of the place of Onesimus as he can.

It is, of course, possible that Onesimus did not steal money from Philemon, but instead the debt is some kind of lost income that would be derived from Onesimus' service to his owner. Paul recognized Philemon as an able businessman, and here uses his language.

Of course, how would Paul have been able to repay such a debt? He probably had no money as a prisoner. Moo asks, "Did he have his own private funds that he could draw upon? Did he have financial backers, or 'patrons,' willing to help? We simply cannot know."[54] Philemon would have had to suspect that Paul had no money, and so would have to take this as a point of how serious Paul was about Onesimus being treated properly. *The Apostle with no money was willing to pay for Onesimus' debt.*

19 So serious is Paul about paying Onesimus' debt, that he actually says, "I, Paul, write this with my own hand, I will repay it" (RSV). We can tell from this that at least part of Paul's letter was not written by an amanuensis (the secretary possibly being Timothy), and so Paul, possibly handcuffed, made the deliberate point to at least write this sentence.[55] Writing an important statement should have impressed Philemon, no different than how in 1 Corinthians 16:21 we see, "The greeting is in my own hand—Paul."

The thought could very well be that not only is Paul taking upon himself an unpayable debt to himself, but that he really is striving to emulate his Lord, whose sacrifice paid for the sin debt of humanity (Isaiah 53:6; John 1:29; Hebrews 7:27; 9:26, 28). Writing a note with his own hand, Paul is making a legal obligation to pay Onesimus' debt.

Yet in asking Philemon to charge Onesimus' debt to himself, Paul slips in a short reminder to him: "not to mention to you that you owe to me even your own self as well." Paul reminds Philemon that *he is responsible* for bringing him to saving faith, which is something that Philemon could never by any amount of money ever pay back. Philemon was a new man in Messiah Yeshua because of Paul's ministry. Even releasing Onesimus from slavery, and/or sending him back to the Apostle Paul, would never pay back what Philemon could be thought to actually "owe" Paul.

20 **Yes, brother, let me benefit from you in the Lord; refresh my heart in Messiah.** 21 **Having confidence in your obedience, I write to you, since I know that you will do even more than what I say.** 22 **At the same time also prepare me a lodging, for I hope that through your prayers I will be given to you.**

20 A very critical clue about what Paul wants Philemon to do is seen in his word, "I do wish, brother, that I may have some benefit from you in the Lord; refresh my heart in Christ" (NIV). The verb translated benefit is *oninēmi* (ὀνίνημι), an obvious cognate to the name *Onēsimos*. By doing something important with Onesimus, Paul will be refreshed in the Lord.

About fifty years later, Ignatius bishop of Antioch, would highly acclaim the bishop of Ephesus, Onesimus.[56] While Ignatius is a rather controversial figure for today's Messianics (including proposals of him being among the false prophets of Revelation 2:2), in no small part because of his negative statements about the Torah,[57] if this is the same Onesimus as appears in the letter to Philemon, **then what kind of a reflection would this be upon those who knew of his spiritual character?** Even if we might consider Ignatius to not be

[54] Ibid, 428.

[55] Bruce, *Colossians-Philemon-Ephesians*, 220.

[56] "But as touching my fellow servant Burrhus, who by the will of God is your deacon blessed in all things, I pray that he may remain with me to the honor of yourselves and of your bishop. Yea, and Crocus also, who is worthy of God and of you whom I received as an ensample of the love which ye bear me, hath relieved me in all ways—even so may the Father of Jesus Christ refresh him—together **with Onesimus** and Burrhus and Euplus and Fronto; in whom I saw you all with the eyes of love" (*Epistle to the Ephesians* 2.2; cf. Bruce, *Colossians-Philemon-Ephesians*, 221).

[57] Cf. "Law, Mosaic," in David W. Bercot, ed., *A Dictionary of Early Christian Beliefs* (Peabody, MA: Hendrickson, 1998), 393.

the kindest of people to the Jews and the Law of Moses, Ignatius would have been able to laud Onesimus because of the impact that Paul had left on him.

21 Paul did not explicitly ask Philemon to release Onesimus, but very much tells him, "I am confident as I write this letter that you will do what I ask and even more!" (NLT). From Paul's expectation *huper ha legō* (ὑπὲρ ἃ λέγω), "even more than I say" (RSV) or "above what I say" (my translation), **is an excellent indicator that he desires Onesimus to be manumitted.** Paul certainly expected Philemon to do more than just welcome Onesimus as he himself would be welcomed, but still maintain Onesimus' slave status. Witherington notes how "manumission was not opposed in the Roman world, even by social conservatives, because it was in fact a way of maintaining the ongoing existence and stability of the system."[58] Many slaves could expect to be released at one point or another in their tenure of service, as a normal part of this ancient social practice. Moo summarizes the First Century realities:

"[I]t is most likely that Onesimus, like most slaves in the ancient world, could have looked forward to being manumitted at some point; it is therefore possible that what Paul is really asking is that Philemon not use Onesimus's absence as a reason to delay his manumission or, alternatively, that Philemon should free Onesimus immediately...Still, while perhaps not the focus of Paul's concern, the emancipation of Onesimus, we feel, is an action indivisible from what Paul hopes Philemon will do."[59]

Paul considers whatever Philemon will do regarding Onesimus—*beyond* what he has asked him—to constitute "obedience." Witherington indicates, "There was in any case a cost for manumission, it appears that Paul was asking Philemon to bear it, though he offered to pay for Onesimus's wrongdoing and for what Onesimus owed Philemon."[60] How Paul would have paid for any of this is, of course, unsolvable. Philemon, because he was a mature and generous Believer in Messiah Yeshua, would simply have to write off the financial loss, and recognize how the power of the gospel had changed Onesimus. In so doing, freeing Onesimus from slavery would be an appropriate gesture of their new brotherhood in the Lord.

22 Paul communicates to Philemon as a very close friend, with whom he really can speak directly. He expects some kind of soon release from his imprisonment, informing Philemon that as he does more than what he has asked regarding Onesimus (v. 21), "At the same time, prepare a guest room for me, for I am hoping through your prayers to be granted to you" (RSV). The Apostle Paul recognizes how Philemon and his home congregation ("your" [*humōn*, ὑμῶν] is plural) has been praying for him, being in prison, and he asks him to have a "lodging" (NASU) ready for him, a very good indication that Philemon was wealthy.

Some think that by asking Philemon to have a guest room ready, that it was most likely for Paul to be confined in Ephesus, given the fact that a trip from Rome to Colossae could have taken around two months. Furthermore, Paul's ministry orientation from Rome had turned Westward toward Spain (Romans 15:23-24), and it is thought that this would make a return visit Eastward unlikely. But if the Pastoral Epistles are genuinely Pauline (as we believe), then the circumstances in Asia may very well have required him to return from Rome to the East.[61] The Apostle Paul was very much able to alter his travel schedule for the will of the Spirit (i.e., Acts 16:6-10), or the needs of the *ekklēsia*.

Not wanting to read too much into v. 22, some would simply take this as a courtesy remark. O'Brien indicates, "It has been suggested that this feature at the close of the epistle, called a 'travelogue,' is no courtesy remark but a deliberately phrased convention, known from letter forms in the Greco-Roman world."[62] V. 22 could be considered as an allusion simply to Paul's apostolic presence, implying that Paul may never actually have to go visit Philemon in order for his authority to reach there. Yet Paul probably did desire to visit the East again, similar to how he wanted to visit his close friends in Philippians 2:24, and so having a place to stay in the home of a good friend like Philemon would have been important. Not to be overlooked is how Dunn describes, "hospitality played a much larger role in traveling than today; inns were generally places to be

---

[58] Witherington, 88.

[59] Moo, 436.

[60] Witherington, 89.

[61] Moo, 438.

[62] O'Brien, *Colossians-Philemon*, 306.

avoided if at all possible, so that householders would generally expect to provide hospitality for their compatriots."[63]

23 Epaphras, my fellow prisoner in Messiah Yeshua, greets you, 24 *as do* Mark, Aristarchus, Demas, Luke, my fellow workers. 25 The grace of the Lord Yeshua the Messiah be with your spirit.

23-24 The letter to Philemon ends with some greetings extended by Philemon to the same people who extend greetings to the Colossians (4:10-14). The only person missing from this list is Jesus Justus (Colossians 4:11), who was probably just not present when the letter to Philemon was written.[64] Epaphras, labeled by Paul to be his "fellow prisoner in Messiah Yeshua," served here as his personal attendant, similar to how Aristarchus had performed this function when Colossians was composed. The rest of the people are Paul's "fellow laborers" (NKJV), just like Philemon (v. 1). No matter how all of these people are separated, they are all connected in the Lord, and are all working for His objectives.

25 In Paul's closing word to Philemon, he says "The grace of the Lord Yeshua the Messiah be with your spirit," with *tou pneumatos humōn* (τοῦ πνεύματος ὑμῶν) appearing in the plural. This is not only a reference back to Philemon, Apphia, and Archippus (vs. 1-2), but now all the Believers meeting in Philemon's home. Why would they all need to have grace be present among them? Moo astutely answers, "here he might especially be aware of how much the whole community would need a strong measure of grace in order to respond well to the Onesimus affair."[65]

It stands reasonable for us to believe that when Onesimus returned, he was manumitted from his slavery. The historical record could very well indicate that this is the same Onesimus who served as bishop of Ephesus. Even if this were a different man, Onesimus the runaway slave became "useful" (v. 11) for the Kingdom of God. The letter to Philemon makes all Twenty-First Century Believers look back in time to a period when slavery was a normal practice, and should cause us to consciously be aware of the ancient social and demographic settings of the Holy Scriptures. This is even more important for us as a Messianic movement, that is trying to not only bridge a huge gulf between the past and present, but reconnect all of God's people to their Hebraic Roots and heritage in Israel.

---

[63] Dunn, 346.
[64] Bruce, *Colossians-Philemon-Ephesians*, 224; Wright, 192; Dunn, 348.
[65] Moo, 442.

EPILOGUE

Do the Epistles of Colossians and Philemon need to be things that today's Messianic movement overlooks any more? It has been my experience that we really do not appreciate these letters to the degree that we should. We know that they are in the Bible, and we may quote bits and pieces from Colossians at times. But we often do not sit down like we should, read Colossians and Philemon in their entirety, and really consider the ramifications of not only the ancient issues addressed, but how they may be paralleled today in our faith community.

As I survey the Messianic movement in 2009,[1] I know that Christology and who Yeshua is, are very big issues. Because our overall theology is behind the curve of where it needs to be, and due to a great deal of skepticism toward our Christian theological and spiritual heritage, many people in leadership really are not sure as to whether or not Yeshua is God. They were certainly taught that He was God, but such teaching was more in the form of dogma rather than well reasoned doctrine. Nobody has really sat down, explained how the false philosophy in Colossae degraded Yeshua as just another intermediary, and how the hymn of Colossians 1:15-20 directly subverted the false teaching by affirming that Yeshua is more than just Wisdom. The Epistle to the Colossians certainly affirms that Yeshua is the Deity, made manifest to us in bodily form (Colossians 2:9), and does so in a context whereby not only is His work for us uplifted (Colossians 1:20; 2:11-14), but also His supremacy over the cosmic powers (Colossians 2:15).

There are some reasons why Colossians is not examined that frequently by today's Messianic Believers. Obviously, many Messianics are so conditioned to having Colossians 2:16-17 thrown at them by Christian family or friends—criticizing them for remembering *Shabbat* or eating kosher—that people easily disregard how these things were taken up into the false philosophy. Not enough really pause and consider what the appointed times meant to the false teachers, and how improper observance of various Torah practices is really what is being spoken of. The Colossians were not to take judgment over how these things were hijacked into the false philosophy. While Colossians chs. 3 and 4 might be thought to have some general instruction for Believers, such instruction can be found elsewhere, and so why not examine those other places instead? Yet I would have to say that the main reason why many Messianics today avoid considering Colossians is because of its criticism of the ascetic practices refuted in Colossians 2:18-23.

If one holds to Colossians being a refutation of a false philosophy that was an amalgamation of proto-Gnostic, pagan, and mystical Jewish errors—**then it really does find relevance for refuting some aberrant teachings in today's Messianic movement.** Just this past Summer (2009) I had to read a commentary from a Messianic ministry that was trying to reconcile and synthesize Chassidic Jewish views of God, to what the Apostolic Scriptures affirm about Yeshua.[2] A generous amount of quotations were provided from Medieval Jewish, mystical sources,[3] that mainline scholars considering the broad Biblical period do not consult (unlike say, the Mishnah or Talmud). Considering some of this ministry's other materials on the Torah and the New Testament from a Jewish perspective, which are often not as detailed, I was naturally quite disturbed as it was clear what their teachers had really been investing their time and energies to research. Suffice it to say, I do not

---

[1] The Colossians-Philemon study was conducted between April-September, 2009.

[2] Toby Janicki, "The Exalted Rebbe," in *Love and the Messianic Age: Study Guide and Commentary* (Marshfield, MO: Vine of David, 2009), pp 143-154.

For an alternative approach, I would recommend Bauckham, *Jesus and the God of Israel*, which is actually concerned with the various Jewish views of monotheism germane to the broad First Century period, and how Yeshua is integrated into the Divine Identity—*not* with Jewish views of God and the Messiah from a millennia or more later.

[3] Cf. Ibid., pp 165-169.

believe that today's Messianics examine Colossians enough, because it really does speak against many of the "nuggets" floating around our faith community that originate in the mystical Jewish tradition. Speaking about the ins-and-outs of Second Temple Judaism, and Jews in the wider Mediterranean world, is often thought to be too boring compared to what one can learn from things like Kabbalah. But trying to learn from something like Kabbalah will often lead people to downgrading the supremacy of Yeshua (Colossians 2:9), and cause people to develop a sense of false spirituality (Colossians 2:23).

Colossians does not only hit too close to home as it concerns the errors of Jewish mysticism present in the Messianic movement. Consider also Paul's words against "worship of angels" (Colossians 2:18). While the false teachers were likely worshipping angels to some degree, the alternative view of them trying to join into the worship of angels in Heaven—accessing a spiritual dimension to which they were not granted permission—is a view that is well taken. This is different than recognizing that worship on Earth parallels worship in Heaven, for as Ben Witherington III concludes, "Paul in Colossians is dealing with a specific sort of spiritual problem—aberrant forms of worship."[4] Consider for a moment whether or not Messianic conferences that have young women dress up as angelic beings in white, dancing around a mock-up Ark of the Covenant, is a proper or aberrant form of worship. Dancing in the joy of the Lord might be one thing, but reproducing Temple vessels, even out of plywood or cardboard, probably goes too far.

Paul's letter to the Colossians in one way is a hard slap in the face to today's Messianic movement. It is not a criticism of observing the Sabbath or appointed times, but rather of false philosophies and worship styles that are allowed to go on with little question **and which need to be halted.** It is a reminder that Yeshua the Messiah is *the Intermediary* between God the Father and humankind, who we entreat with our problems, being the Deity Himself and supreme over the universe. It definitely tells us not to be superstitious with how we follow the Torah, as though it is some "Step on a crack and break your mother's back" necessity for a good standing with God. Unlike those who may overanalyze things a bit, like the false teachers who practiced self-abasement (Colossians 2:23), if we falter we can simply ask the Lord for forgiveness because the penalties of sin have been remitted (Colossians 2:14). Mind you, we are to set our minds on things of the Lord (Colossians 3:1-3), and be committed to a life of obedience. Yet should unintentional sin be committed, then we should ask for forgiveness and "let the peace of Messiah rule in your hearts" (Colossians 3:15) because of what He has done for us.

Like just about everyone who reads the Bible, today's Messianics do not know what to do with Paul's letter to Philemon. Because it is only twenty-five verses, it is overlooked. Philemon is necessarily addressed in concert with Colossians because it was written at the same time, and the same people who greet the Colossians, also greet Philemon (Colossians 4:10-14; Philemon 23-24)—even though it has much more to teach us. The very reason that Philemon, a personal letter from Paul regarding the runaway slave Onesimus, could be in the Bible, is to remind people to read the Scriptures in their ancient historical context before jumping ahead and applying things for today. Twenty-First Century people do not have the problem of runaway slaves like First Century people did. And so, if we are forced to read a text like Philemon for its ancient setting and background, would not the same be true of Colossians, its paralleling letter of Ephesians, and just about any other text of Scripture?

I have always believed and taught that today's Messianic movement, a faith community where Jewish and non-Jewish Believers are brought together as a single people in the Messiah of Israel, has a huge amount of potential to be a force of holiness and righteousness in the world. If I know this, then we can be confident that the Adversary knows it as well. Just like the false philosophy which was disturbing the Colossians, so will false philosophies enter into our congregations and fellowships today, taking us away from the mission that God has given us. This mission is to proclaim that in Messiah Yeshua is found "*a renewal* in which there is no *distinction between* Greek and Jew, circumcised and uncircumcised, barbarian, Scythian, slave and freeman," where we can discover how "Messiah is all, and in all" (Colossians 3:11). This involves loving others

---

[4] Witherington, 209.

(Colossians 3:12) and making sure that "Whatever you do in word or deed, *do* all in the name of the Lord Yeshua, giving thanks through Him to God the Father" (Colossians 3:17).

Only a diligent and consistent discipleship in the Holy Scriptures, and constant vigilance, will ensure that the Messianic community can fulfill this, with people who have put on the new self, reflecting the goodness of our Creator (Colossians 3:9-10). My friends, let us take Colossians and Philemon more seriously, and be a people who will one day "be revealed with Him in glory" (Colossians 3:4)!

THE MESSAGE OF COLOSSIANS AND PHILEMON

a summary for Messianic teaching and preaching

The Epistle of Paul to the Colossians, and most especially his letter to Philemon, are two of the most elusive texts of the Apostolic Scriptures for today's Messianic community.[1] Our current level of engagement with Colossians is often with having to respond to Christian colleagues who quote Colossians 2:16-17 at us for being Torah observant, and we have to scramble to try to understand what is really being said. *Beyond this, we really do not read Colossians.* I actually find Colossians and Philemon—which were written at the same time as the same people are listed in the closing greetings (Colossians 4:10-14; Philemon 23-24)—to be very easy to follow. We just have to read them in their entirety, and remind ourselves that Paul is not writing to Twenty-First Century Believers.

Colossians is a part of the series commonly called the Prison Epistles (also including Ephesians and Philippians), traditionally believed to have been written during the Apostle Paul's confinement in Rome (Acts 28:30). Epaphras, one of the Colossian Believers who had likely come to faith by Paul's preaching tenure in Ephesus (Acts 19:9-10), which was only about 100 miles away from Colossae, had traveled all the way to visit the Apostle. A complicated circumstance had arisen in Colossae. Epaphras, who had been one of the main people to share the gospel of Yeshua with his hometown, was disturbed so much that he journeyed 1,500 miles all the way to see Paul, who could then craft a letter to send back to a congregation of Believers for whom he served as a kind of "grandfather."

Many commentators are widely agreed that the circumstance which had arisen in Colossae was that a strange mix of religious and philosophical errors—Greco-Roman, mysterious, proto-Gnostic, and even Jewish—was infecting the assembly. False teachers had promoted the idea that Yeshua the Messiah was but one of many intermediaries between God the Father and humankind. These errorists promoted a false philosophy, involving some kind of angel worship and asceticism. While there were Jewish elements within this error, we cannot at all assume that it was exclusively Jewish, as history does show how in the Diaspora the local paganism could influence the local Judaism. Throughout his letter, Paul uses terms like *gnōsis*, *plērōma*, and *sophia*—knowledge, fullness, and wisdom—to directly subvert the false teaching that was denigrating the Lord. The good Apostle must carefully choose his words, showing how the work of Yeshua completely trumps the false philosophy, and how He is supreme over all spiritual forces.

Paul and Timothy extend greetings to the Colossians (Colossians 1:1-2), and after doing so express how they are not only thankful for them (Colossians 1:3), but how "we have heard of your faith in Messiah Yeshua and of the love you have for all the saints" (Colossians 1:4). This is a word of confidence that regardless of what is going on in Colossae, the Believers there are going to do the right thing, as they are beneficiaries of the good news and have understood it well (Colossians 1:5-6). Epaphras, who has traveled to see Paul, has spoken well of their faith (Colossians 1:7-8).

Paul really is quite gracious to express how much the Colossians mean to him, and how "we have not stopped praying for you and asking God to fill you with the knowledge of his will through all spiritual wisdom and understanding" (Colossians 1:9). The Colossians are Believers who will be able to lead lives pleasing to the Lord, bearing good fruit, being strengthened, and being able to have endurance (Colossians

---

[1] Unless otherwise noted, Biblical quotations in this article are from the New International Version (NIV).

1:10-11). They make up a part of the Father's inheritance of the saints, having been rescued from darkness and brought into light, the Kingdom of His Son (Colossians 1:12-13). Paul asserts to them that in the Messiah "we have redemption, the forgiveness of sins" (Colossians 1:14).

How serious is it to recognize who Yeshua is? Interpreters are largely agreed that Colossians 1:15-20 composes some kind of an early hymn used by the First Century *ekklēsia*. Within this hymn, some of the terms used such as "image of...God," "firstborn over all creation," and "the beginning" are likely appropriated from the figure of Wisdom, seen in Proverbs, the Apocrypha, and Philo.[2] In ancient Jewish literature, Wisdom was an impersonal force that emanated from God, often acting behind the scenes in history, and so the false teachers might have simply thought that the Messiah was a similar (created) force. While Yeshua is identified as possessing these same qualities of Wisdom, Yeshua is ultimately *much more* than Wisdom, being a person. Yeshua the Messiah was the Agent used by the Father to create the universe, yet He is also the fullness of the Deity (cf. Colossians 2:9) in human flesh, crucified so that peace and redemption might come to sinners, and was resurrected from the dead. Yeshua stands supreme as the One for whom all things in the universe were made, standing as the ultimate. **No such claim is ever made of Wisdom.** *Yeshua desires a personal relationship with us, after all!* The hymn affirms,

"He is the image of the invisible God, the firstborn[3] over all creation. For by him all things were created: things in heaven and on earth, visible and invisible, whether thrones or powers or rulers or authorities; all things were created for him and by him. He is before all things, and in him all things hold together. And he is the head of the body, the [assembly]; he is the beginning and the firstborn from among the dead, so that in everything he might have the supremacy. For God was pleased to have all his fullness dwell in him, and through him to reconcile to himself all things, whether things on earth or things in heaven, by making peace through his blood, shed on the cross" (Colossians 1:15-20).

Yeshua is no mere minor force sent by God. The Colossians had once been sinners, but thanks to the sacrifice of Yeshua they can now stand holy, "without blemish and free from accusation" (Colossians 1:21-22). Yet this requires the Colossians to continue in their faith, "not moved from the hope held out in the gospel" (Colossians 1:23a), a message that has significant worldwide importance (Colossians 1:23b).

While Paul knows Colossian Believers like Epaphras and Philemon (discussed further) personally, and probably a few others, he does not know most of the Colossian Believers personally. He reminds the Colossians about his ministry service for the Lord (Colossians 1:24-25), specifically the great mystery of "Messiah in you, the hope of glory" that equalizes all people—Jewish and non-Jewish—in Him (Colossians 1:26-27). Paul says, "We proclaim him, admonishing and teaching everyone with all wisdom, so that we may present everyone perfect in Messiah. To this end I labor, struggling with all his energy, which so powerfully works in me" (Colossians 1:28-29). The Apostle Paul is by no means someone just trying to gain a following or impress people with some slick teaching; he is a servant of Yeshua empowered by Him to see that lives are changed **and that the great mystery of the ages be manifest to all.** Paul desires all to know Yeshua's salvation, and for all to be empowered by Him!

Paul has had to endure much for the gospel, things that will benefit those in Colossae, Laodicea, and the surrounding Lycus Valley—people he has not seen in person (Colossians 2:1). Paul states, "My purpose is that they may be encouraged in heart and united in love, so that they may have the full riches of complete understanding, in order that they may know the mystery of God, namely, Messiah, in whom are hidden all the treasures of wisdom and knowledge" (Colossians 2:2-3). These words are surely uplifting words for any Believer to hear or read, but the purpose for Paul making these claims would have been quite significant for those under the influence of the false teachers: "I tell you this so that no one may deceive you by fine-sounding arguments" (Colossians 2:4). Paul might not be with the Colossians in person, but he knows what

---

[2] Image of God (Wisdom 7:26; Philo *Allegorical Interpretation* 1.43); firstborn (Philo *Questions and Answers on Genesis* 4.97); beginning (Proverbs 8:23; Wisdom 6:22).

[3] The title "firstborn" is used in the Tanach to speak of one who possesses a high, preeminent status, even if one is not the first actually born in a family line (Genesis 49:3-4; Exodus 4:22; Psalm 89:27; Jeremiah 31:9).

has been going on because of Epaphras. He also knows that the Colossians have a firm faith in the Lord, and will not be led astray if they take his instruction seriously (Colossians 2:5).

As human beings, we tend to often think that admonishing people has to be an entirely negative experience. While there are certainly letters from Paul like Galatians or 1 Corinthians, where some severe negative tones can be easily detected, such is not the case with Colossians. Confidence is expressed in the Colossians, as Paul instructs them, "So then, just as you received Messiah Yeshua as Lord, continue to live in him, rooted and built up in him, strengthened in the faith as you were taught, and overflowing with thankfulness" (Colossians 2:6-7). While the false philosophy will not really influence the Colossians, they still need to know why it is wrong, and why they should not feel "unenlightened" because they have chosen not to embrace it.

The Apostle Paul is clear to tell the Colossians, "See to it that no one takes you captive through hollow and deceptive philosophy, which depends on human tradition and the basic principles of the world rather than on Messiah" (Colossians 2:8). The false teaching circulating in Colossae, then, originates in human ideas and not ideas consistent with who Yeshua is. Paul summarizes for the Colossians what Yeshua has done for all of them, as the Deity in bodily form, who has provided redemption by His crucifixion and resurrection—having to assert **what is not of vain human tradition.** Only by knowing Him can a person partake of salvation:

"For in Messiah all the fullness of Deity lives in bodily form, and you have been given fullness in Messiah, who is the head over every power and authority. In him you were also circumcised, in the putting off of the sinful nature, not with a circumcision done by the hands of men but with the circumcision done by Messiah, having been buried with him in baptism and raised with him through your faith in the power of God, who raised him from the dead" (Colossians 2:9-12).

Yeshua the Messiah, as the Deity, reigns supreme and provides a circumcision of the heart unto salvation. Paul reminds the Colossians, "When you were dead in your sins and in the uncircumcision of your sinful nature, God made you alive with Messiah" (Colossians 2:13)—speaking of how the same power that resurrected the Lord also changes sinful people! By the work of Yeshua the *cheirographon* or "certificate of debt" (Colossians 2:14, NASU) has been nailed to the cross and paid for. While this is commonly thought by some to be the Torah of Moses, it is actually the record of human sin, perhaps also to be viewed as the pronouncement of condemnation that hung over Yeshua as He was dying on the cross (Matthew 27:37; Mark 15:26; Luke 23:38; John 19:19)—penalties that stood against sinners which have now been remitted.

One of the most important effects of Yeshua's atoning sacrifice is that any of the lesser spiritual powers, which could once claim dominance over people, are now powerless to do so for those who are in Him. The Messiah has "disarmed the powers and authorities" (Colossians 2:15; cf. Ephesians 1:20-21). To try to appeal to those forces, **when Yeshua as the Deity and as Redeemer was supreme over them,** would make little sense. The Colossians were to easily reject any false philosophy that subtracted from whom Yeshua was, and His accomplished work.

Paul will continue by summarizing other features of the false philosophy. The most difficult verses of Colossians, for today's Messianics, are found in how Paul instructs his audience to not allow themselves to be judged about various features of the Torah. He says, "do not let anyone judge you by what you eat or drink, or with regard to a religious festival, a New Moon celebration, or a Sabbath day" (Colossians 2:16). Many think that Paul has just said that these things are unimportant for all Believers, failing to recognize what these things meant *to the false teachers in Colossae.* How were these Torah practices integrated into the false philosophy? Is Paul speaking against *Shabbat*, the appointed times, and kosher eating as a normal part of obedience to God? Or is he speaking against these things connected to how the false teachers might have associated them with their ascetic practices and angel worship (Colossians 2:18ff)? If the latter is the case, then Paul is speaking against the misuse of these Torah practices, and for the Colossians not to take judgment because they might not share the same opinions about them as the false teachers.

The Apostle Paul does not downgrade the significance of Torah practices like *Shabbat*, the appointed times, or kosher eating. Yet he does point out, "These are a shadow of the things to come,[4] but the substance belongs to Christ" (Colossians 2:17, ESV). If some areas of Torah observance were caught up into the false philosophy of the errorists, the most that the errorists could see would be shadows. But if these things are observed properly, as a part of the sanctification process and in demonstrating good works (Matthew 5:16ff), then the shadows that they possess can easily be seen to point to the substance of the Messiah. The Sabbath, appointed times, and even dietary laws teach God's people important things about His holiness, as well as of His plan of salvation history for the world. Understanding the shadow allows Believers to more greatly appreciate the substance.

It is sad that many Christian laypersons reading Colossians 2:16-17 forget to read the surrounding cotext, because immediately Paul warns the Colossians about the dangerous features of the false philosophy. This was an error that advocated "self-abasement and the worship of the angels" (Colossians 2:18, NASU) in an effort to induce visions. Even if one views "worship of angels" as not being actual worship directed *to angels*, but people trying to participate *with* angelic worship in Heaven—things off limits for normal people were still being accessed. People trying to appeal to angels for spiritual help, rather than going to the Lord Himself, according to Paul, have "lost connection with the Head, from whom the whole body, supported and held together by its ligaments and sinews, grows as God causes it to grow" (Colossians 2:19).

The Colossians are not to be like the fickle people of the world, allowing themselves to be influenced by the ascetic superstitions of the false teachers like "Do not handle! Do not taste! Do not touch!" (Colossians 2:21), which ultimately have no use in curtailing sinful urges (Colossians 2:23). And while some may be tempted to associate these things with regulations seen in the Torah, they are labeled as being "based on human commands and teachings" (Colossians 2:22), an indication that they are not of Divine origin. The Sabbath, appointed times, and dietary laws were taken up into this whole mess of ideas—being improperly used—and the Colossians were not to let the false teachers intimidate them.

The second half of Paul's letter to the Colossians is spent addressing the lives of those who "have been raised with Messiah," who should set their "hearts on things above, where Messiah is seated at the right hand of God" (Colossians 3:1), reigning supremely. Believers have their lives found in Him, and will experience much greatness when the Messiah returns (Colossians 3:2-4). He lists a number of serious sins that are not to be found in the lives of his audience (Colossians 3:5-9), precisely because they "have put on the new self, which is being renewed in knowledge in the image of its Creator" (Colossians 3:10). The power of the Messiah to change people is so magnificent, because "Here there is no Greek or Jew, circumcised or uncircumcised, barbarian, Scythian, slave or free, but Messiah is all, and is in all" (Colossians 3:11). What Paul tells the Colossians to manifest in their lives—by the transforming power of Yeshua—is something that the false philosophy of the errorists cannot bring:

"Let the peace of Messiah rule in your hearts, since as members of one body you were called to peace. And be thankful. Let the word of Messiah dwell in you richly as you teach and admonish one another with all wisdom, and as you sing psalms, hymns and spiritual songs with gratitude in your hearts to God. And whatever you do, whether in word or deed, do it all in the name of the Lord Yeshua, giving thanks to God the Father through him" (Colossians 3:15-17).

Paul issues some important instructions to the Colossians on the home life of Believers, and some of the roles that husbands, wives, children, and slaves all play (Colossians 3:18-4:1; cf. Ephesians 5:22-6:9). The fact that slaves are mentioned should immediately remind us that this word was indeed given against a First Century C.E. background. What would these instructions have meant to ancient people? Only by acknowledging this first, can we properly apply its principles today.

The final request Paul asks of the Colossians is to continue to pray for him, as he is in jail and will need to discern the opportunities when he can declare the gospel message (Colossians 4:2-5). He similarly

---

[4] Note how the NIV has improperly translated the present tense participle *tōn mellontōn*, with the past tense "things that were to come."

Also be aware of how "*mere*" has been added to the NASU, and "only" to the RSV, renderings.

encourages them, "Let your conversation be always full of grace, seasoned with salt, so that you may know how to answer everyone" (Colossians 4:6).

Paul's letter to the Colossians ends with a series of greetings from the mixed group of Jewish and non-Jewish Believers helping him in Rome (Colossians 4:7-15). These include the courier Tychicus, who also took with him the general epistle that would become "Ephesians" (Colossians 4:7; Ephesians 6:21). Onesimus, the runaway slave who features prominently in Paul's letter to Philemon, is considered to be "our dear and faithful brother," and he will be traveling with him (Colossians 4:9). The Jewish Believers are Aristarchus, John Mark, with whom Paul had patched up previous differences (cf. Acts 13:13; 15:39), and a man named Jesus Justus (Colossians 4:10-11). Take important notice of the fact that a normal Jewish man of the Diaspora would indeed have the Greek name *Iēsous*. This is not only proof that *Iēsous* is a legitimate Jewish transliteration of *Yeshua* and not the name of a pagan god, but also that when the Apostles proclaimed salvation in the name of *Iēsous*, it was a normal name that Greek-speaking Jewish men had.

Epaphras, who has yet to return home to Colossae, is attested by Paul to be "one of you and a servant of Messiah Yeshua...He is always wrestling in prayer for you, that you may stand firm in all the will of God, mature and fully assured" (Colossians 4:12). Paul gives Epaphras some approving words, for the ministry work he has performed in the Lycus Valley (Colossians 4:13), which would be quite helpful when he did finally return home. Also extending greetings to the Colossians are Luke the doctor and Demas (Colossians 4:14). Paul wants the Colossians to greet the congregation that meets in the home of Nympha, a woman, on his behalf (Colossians 4:15). He also commends the special ministry of Archippus (Colossians 4:17), whatever that might have been.

Paul requests that this letter he has sent to the Colossians be read in the congregation of the nearby Laodiceans as well. He also tells them that they will be receiving a letter that he wrote to the Laodiceans (Colossians 4:16). Although many proposals have been made, there are some good reasons for us not to think that this is a non-extant "Epistle to the Laodiceans." Given the evidence of the oldest manuscripts of Ephesians 1:1 lacking "in Ephesus" (see RSV), the letter coming from Laodicea could very well be the general epistle that became known as "Ephesians," which had been circulated in the same vicinity of Asia Minor.

The imprisoned Paul is sure to write the final part of his message to the Colossians, with his own hand: "Remember my chains. Grace be with you" (Colossians 4:18).

When examining Paul's letter to the Colossians, we would be at a complete loss to not also examine Paul's letter to Philemon. Philemon was written at the same time, by simple virtue of the fact that the people who extend the Colossians greetings, also extend Philemon greetings (Philemon 23-24).[5] Most Bible readers avoid considering Philemon because of its small size at just twenty-five verses. Most others avoid considering Philemon because they do not know what to do with the issue of slavery in the Bible, and how Paul is sending back Onesimus, a runaway slave *but* a Believer, to his owner Philemon. What was Philemon to do with Onesimus? Philemon is a unique epistle in the Pauline corpus, actually being a personal letter between Paul and a fellow Believer in Messiah Yeshua. We get a unique glimpse into not only First Century Mediterranean culture, but also Paul as a man.

The opening of Philemon includes greetings consistent with the other Pauline letters (Philemon 1-3), with Philemon not only addressed, but also acknowledgements of his wife Apphia, and Archippus as a member of their home congregation. Philemon is lauded by Paul because of his faith in the Lord, and his goodness toward others (Philemon 4-6). Paul is sure to tell his friend, "Your love has given me great joy and encouragement, because you, brother, have refreshed the hearts of the saints" (Philemon 7). Everything that Paul tells Philemon is leading up to him explaining what has happened regarding the runaway Onesimus.

Paul carefully says, "although in Messiah I could be bold and order you to do what you ought to do, yet I appeal to you on the basis of love" (Philemon 8-9a). He reminds Philemon that he is "an old man and now also a prisoner of Messiah Yeshua" (Philemon 9b). Somehow in that prison confinement he encountered the runaway Onesimus, who had fled to Rome to get away from his master and hide. Onesimus is one "who

---

[5] The greetings to Philemon do notably exclude Jesus Justus (Colossians 4:11), who was probably just not present when Paul's letter was written.

became my son while I was in chains. Formerly he was useless to you, but now he has become both useful to you and to me" (Philemon 10-11). While we might not know all the details of why Onesimus fled from Philemon, and how he encountered Paul in Rome, **this runaway slave had become a born again Believer.** What was Philemon going to do now that he was returning home?

Paul says, "I am sending him—who is my very heart—back to you" (Philemon 12). Paul has a great amount of love and affection for Onesimus, and so should Philemon. Paul would have liked to keep Onesimus in Rome for some ministry service (Philemon 13), yet he had to respect Philemon as his owner (Philemon 14). He tells Philemon how, "Perhaps the reason he was separated from you for a little while was that you might have him back for good—no longer as a slave, but better than a slave, as a dear brother" (Philemon 15-16a). Maybe it was God who had Onesimus run away, so that when he returned Philemon could show him a great kindness. The referral to "no longer as a slave" is as close as Paul gets to suggesting that Philemon manumit Onesimus from his slave status. Paul indicates how "He is very dear to me but even dearer to you, both as a man and a brother in the Lord" (Philemon 16b).

It would seem quite unlikely that given how Onesimus is a fellow Believer now, a brother of Philemon in the Lord, that Paul would want him to remain a slave. Paul informs Philemon, "if you consider me a partner, welcome him as you would welcome me" (Philemon 17). Paul expects Philemon to treat Onesimus as an equal, a clear indication that he would have to release him. So serious is Paul, that any expenses Onesimus has accumulated—either in having stolen money from Philemon, or lost earnings from Philemon's estate because of his absence—Paul himself is willing to pay, with a note in his own handwriting (Philemon 18-19a). Yet Paul is also able to tell Philemon how "you owe me your very self" (Philemon 19b), in that Philemon was a direct beneficiary of Paul's ministry service just as Onesimus.

Paul is confident that this instruction he has delivered to Philemon will be followed (Philemon 20-21), and he expresses hope that he can come and visit him soon, being released from prison (Philemon 22). After his associates in Rome greet Philemon and his home congregation (Philemon 23-24), Paul closes by wishing them all grace (Philemon 25)—something they would surely need to show as Onesimus was returning. We can be rest assured that Philemon released Onesimus, because not only did the Epistle to Philemon get collected into the Biblical canon, but there was even a bishop of Ephesus named Onesimus who served in the early Second Century. *This could have been the Onesimus featured in Philemon.*

Neither Colossians nor Philemon need to be avoided by Messianic Believers any more. These are not difficult letters to understand, although they do sometimes remind us that we need to read texts of Scripture for what they meant to their *original audiences* first. Messianics needs to recognize how Colossians 2:16-17 appears in a rebuke about the false philosophy circulating in Colossae, and directly pertains to how *Shabbat*, the appointed times, and dietary laws were caught up in the errorists' asceticism. Similarly, Philemon does portray a scene of a runaway slave returning home, something which Twenty-First Century people admittedly read with difficulty. I think that today's emerging Messianic movement can actually learn much from both of these epistles, as we consider not only the broad religious diversity of the First Century *ekklēsia*, but the broad religious diversity we face today, with all of its complex issues.

EPISTLES OF PAUL TO THE COLOSSIANS AND TO PHILEMON

adapted from the 1901 American Standard Version,
incorporating the conclusions made and defended in this commentary

EPISTLE OF PAUL TO THE COLOSSIANS

1

Salutation

1 Paul, an apostle of Messiah Yeshua by the will of God, and Timothy our brother,

2 to the saints and faithful brothers and sisters in Messiah *who are* at Colossae: Grace to you and peace from God our Father.

Paul Thanks God for the Colossians

3 We give thanks to God, the Father of our Lord Yeshua the Messiah, praying always for you,

4 having heard of your faith in Messiah Yeshua, and of the love which you have toward all the saints;

5 because of the hope which is laid up for you in Heaven, of which you heard before in the word of the truth, the gospel,

6 which has come to you, just as in all the world also it is bearing fruit and increasing, as *it has* in you also, since the day you heard and came to know the grace of God in truth;

7 just as you learned it *from* Epaphras, our beloved fellow servant, who is a faithful minister of Messiah on our behalf,

8 who also declared to us your love in the Spirit.

The Person and Work of Messiah

9 For this reason we also, since the day we heard *it*, do not cease to pray and make requests for you, that you may be filled with the knowledge of His will in all spiritual wisdom and understanding,

10 to walk in a manner worthy of the Lord, in everything pleasing *to Him*, bearing fruit in every good work, and increasing in the knowledge of God;

11 strengthened with all power, according to the might of His glory, for all patience and longsuffering with joy,

12 giving thanks to the Father, who qualified us to be partakers of the inheritance of the saints in light.

13 He delivered us out of the power of darkness, and transferred us to the Kingdom of His beloved Son;

14 in whom we have redemption, the forgiveness of sins.

15 He is the image of the invisible God, the firstborn over all creation.

16 For in Him all things were created, in Heaven and upon the Earth, things visible and things invisible, whether thrones or dominions or principalities or powers; all things have been created through Him and for Him.

17 And He is before all things, and in Him all things hold together.

¹⁸ And He is the head[a] of the body, the assembly; He is the beginning, the firstborn from the dead; so that in all things He might have the preeminence.

¹⁹ For it was the good pleasure *of the Father* that in Him should all the fullness dwell,

²⁰ and through Him to reconcile all things to Himself, having made peace through the blood of His cross; through Him, *I say*, whether things upon the Earth, or things in Heaven.

²¹ And you, having once been alienated and hostile in your mind, in evil works,

²² yet He has now reconciled in the body of His flesh through death, to present you holy and without blemish and irreproachable before Him—

²³ if indeed you continue in the faith, grounded and steadfast, and not moved away from the hope of the gospel which you heard, which was preached in all creation under Heaven, of which I Paul was made a minister.

Paul's Ministry to the Assembly

²⁴ Now I rejoice in my sufferings for your sake, and fill up on my part that which is lacking of the afflictions[b] of Messiah in my flesh for His body's sake (which is the assembly).

²⁵ Of *this body* I was made a minister, according to the administration of God which was given to me for you, to fulfill the word of God,

²⁶ the mystery which has been hidden for ages and generations; but now has been manifested to His saints,

²⁷ to whom God willed to make known what is the riches of the glory of this mystery among the nations, which is Messiah in you, the hope of glory.

²⁸ We proclaim Him, admonishing every person and teaching every person in all wisdom, that we may present every person complete[c] in Messiah;

²⁹ for which I also labor, striving according to His energy, which operates in me, in power.

2

¹ For I would have you know how greatly I strive for you, and for those at Laodicea, and for as many as have not seen my face in the flesh,

² that their hearts may be comforted, they being knit together in love, and *attaining* to all riches of the full assurance of understanding, that they may know the mystery of God, *the* Messiah *Himself,*

³ in whom are hidden all the treasures of wisdom and knowledge.

⁴ I say this, in order that no one may delude you with persuasiveness of speech[d].

⁵ For though I am absent in the flesh, yet am I with you in the spirit, rejoicing and seeing your good order, and the steadfastness of your faith in Messiah.

Fullness of Life in Messiah

⁶ As therefore you received Messiah Yeshua the Lord, *so* walk in Him,

⁷ rooted and being built up in Him, and being established in your faith, just as you were taught, abounding in thanksgiving.

⁸ Beware that no one takes you captive through philosophy and empty deceit, according to human tradition, according to the elementary principles of the world, and not according to Messiah.

⁹ For in Him all the fullness of the Deity dwells embodied[e],

---

[a] Grk. *kephalē* (κεφαλή); or, "source."

[b] Or, "tribulations" (YLT).

[c] Grk. *teleios* (τέλειος); "perfect" (ASV, NIV); "mature" (RSV/NRSV/ESV); "reached the goal" (CJB).

[d] Grk. *pithanologia* (πιθανολογία); "enticing words" (KJV); "beguiling speech" (RSV); "fine-sounding arguments" (NIV).

[e] Grk. *hoti en autō katoikei pan to plērōma tēs Theotētos sōmatikōs* (ὅτι ἐν αὐτῷ κατοικεῖ πᾶν τὸ πλήρωμα τῆς θεότητος σωματικῶς).

¹⁰ and you have been filled in Him^a, who is the head^b of all principality and power;

¹¹ in whom you were also circumcised with a circumcision not made with hands, in the putting off of the body of the flesh, in the circumcision of Messiah;

¹² having been buried with Him in immersion, in which you were also raised with Him through faith in the working of God, who raised Him from the dead.

¹³ And you, being dead in your trespasses and the foreskin^c of your flesh, He made you alive together with Him, having forgiven us all our transgressions,

¹⁴ having canceled the certificate of debt in dogmas^d that was against us, which was hostile to us; and He has taken it out of the way, nailing it to the cross.

¹⁵ *When* having disarmed the principalities and the powers, He made a public show of them, triumphing over them in Him^e.

¹⁶ Therefore let no one judge you in regard to food or drink or in respect to a festival day or a new moon or Sabbaths^f —

¹⁷ things which are a shadow of the things to come; and the substance is of Messiah^g.

¹⁸ Let no one disqualify you, insisting on self-abasement and worship of the angels, taking his stand on the things which he has seen^h, vainly puffed up by his fleshly mind,

¹⁹ and not holding fast to the headⁱ, from whom all the body, being supplied and held together through the joints and ligaments, grows with a growth that is from God.

The New Life in Messiah

²⁰ If you died with Messiah to the elementary principles of the world, why, as if you were living in the world, do you allow yourself to be dogmatized *by decrees*^j, *such as*,

²¹ "Do not handle, do not taste, do not touch!"

²² (things which all perish with use), according to human precepts and doctrines?

²³ These things indeed have an appearance of wisdom in self-imposed religion and self-abasement and severe treatment of the body, *but are* of no value against the indulgence of the flesh.

3

¹ If then you were raised together with Messiah, seek the things that are above, where Messiah is, seated at the right hand of God.

² Set your mind on the things that are above, not on the things that are upon the Earth.

³ For you died, and your life is hidden with Messiah in God.

⁴ When Messiah, *who is* our life, is manifested, then you also will be manifested with Him in glory.

⁵ Put to death therefore your earthly members^k: fornication, uncleanness, passion, evil desire, and covetousness, which is idolatry.

---

^a Grk. verb *plēroō* (πληρόω); "come to fulness of life" (RSV); "made complete" (NASU).

^b Grk. *kephalē* (κεφαλή); or, "source."

^c Grk. *akrobustia* (ἀκροβυστία); more commonly rendered as "uncircumcision."

^d Grk. *to kath' hēmōn cheirographon tois dogmasin* (τὸ καθ' ἡμῶν χειρόγραφον τοῖς δόγμασιν); "the certificate of debt consisting of decrees against us" (NASU); " the handwriting in the ordinances that is against us" (YLT).

^e Grk. *en autō* (ἐν αὐτῷ); rendered by the ASV as "in it," taken by some to be a reference to the cross rather than God the Father.

^f Grk. plural *sabbatōn* (σαββάτων); while this is the plural "Sabbaths," there is every reason to think that the weekly "Sabbath day" (NASU) which regularly occurs is in view.

^g Grk. *ha estin skia tōn mellontōn, to de sōma tou Christou* (ἅ ἐστιν σκιὰ τῶν μελλόντων, τὸ δὲ σῶμα τοῦ Χριστοῦ).

^h The NASU extrapolates this as, "taking his stand on *visions* he has seen," which is probably justified if self-abasement with the intention to induce a trance is in view.

ⁱ Grk. *kephalē* (κεφαλή); or, "source."

^j Grk. verb *dogmatizō* (δογματίζω); "of persons, *to submit to ordinances*" (LS, 207).

^k Grk. *ta melē ta epi tēs gēs* (τὰ μέλη τὰ ἐπὶ τῆς γῆς); more literally "your members which are upon the earth" (ASV).

⁶ For it is because of these things that the wrath of God comes upon the children of disobedience,

⁷ and in them you once walked, when you were living in these things.

⁸ But now you also, put them all away: anger, wrath, malice, blasphemy[a], abusive speech from your mouth.

⁹ Do not lie to one another, seeing that you have put off the old self with its practices[b],

¹⁰ and have put on the new self, which is being renewed in knowledge after the image of its Creator,

¹¹ where there is no Greek and Jew[c], circumcision and foreskin[d], barbarian, Scythian, slave, free; but Messiah is all, and in all.

¹² Put on therefore, as God's elect, holy and beloved, inward compassion[e], kindness, humility, gentleness, longsuffering;

¹³ forbearing one another, and forgiving each other, if one has a complaint against another; even as the Lord forgave you, so you *should* also do.

¹⁴ And above all these things *put on* love, which is the bond of perfection.

¹⁵ And let the peace of Messiah rule in your hearts, to which also you were called in one body; and be thankful.

¹⁶ Let the word of Messiah dwell in you richly, in all wisdom teaching and admonishing one another, *and* with psalms *and* hymns *and* spiritual songs, singing with grace in your hearts to God.

¹⁷ And whatever you do, in word or in work, *do* all in the name of the Lord Yeshua, giving thanks to God the Father through Him.

Social Duties of the New Life

¹⁸ Wives, be submissive to your husbands, as is fitting in the Lord.

¹⁹ Husbands, love your wives, and do not be bitter against them.

²⁰ Children, obey your parents in all things, for this is well-pleasing in the Lord.

²¹ Fathers, do not provoke your children, so that they will not lose heart.

²² Slaves, in all things obey those who are your lords according to the flesh[f], not with eyeservice, as people-pleasers, but in singleness of heart, fearing the Lord.

²³ Whatever you do, work heartily, as for the Lord and not for people;

²⁴ knowing that from the Lord you will receive the reward of the inheritance; you serve the Lord Messiah.

²⁵ For the one doing wrong will be paid back for the wrong that he has done, and there is no partiality.

---

[a] Grk. *blasphēmia* (βλασφημία); most often rendered as "slander" (RSV/NASU).

[b] The NASU is probably justified to have "its *evil* practices," even though "*evil*" does not appear in the clause *tais praxesin autou* (ταῖς πράξεσιν αὐτοῦ).

[c] Grk. *Hellēn kai Ioudaios* (Ἕλλην καὶ Ἰουδαῖος); a Messianic version like the CJB has improperly rendered this as "Gentile and Jew," but the TLV, also working from the ASV, properly has "Greek and Jew," as two proper nationalities are listed.

[d] Grk. *akrobustia* (ἀκροβυστία); more commonly rendered as "uncircumcision."

[e] Grk. *splagchna oiktirmou* (σπλάγχνα οἰκτιρμου); "bowels of mercies" (KJV).

[f] Grk. *tois kata sarka kuriois* (τοῖς κατὰ σάρκα κυρίοις); "those who are your masters on earth" (NASU) or "earthly masters" (RSV).

The rendering of "lord" for *kurios* (κύριος) here should be obvious, as there is a greater Lord or *Kurios* to whom both the slaveowner and slave must give an account.

4

¹ Lords[a], give to your servants that which is just and equal, knowing that you also have a Lord in heaven.

Exhortations

² Continue steadfastly in prayer, being watchful in it with thanksgiving;

³ praying at the same time for us also, that God may open to us a door for the word, to speak the mystery of Messiah, for which I have also been imprisoned;

⁴ that I may make it clear, as I ought to speak.

⁵ Walk in wisdom toward outsiders, redeeming the time[b].

⁶ Let your speech be always with grace, seasoned with salt, so that you may know how you ought to answer everyone.

Final Greetings

⁷ Tychicus will inform you *about* all my affairs, *our* beloved brother and faithful minister and fellow servant in the Lord.

⁸ I have sent him to you for this very purpose, that you may know *about* our affairs and that he may comfort[c] your hearts,

⁹ together with Onesimus, the faithful and beloved brother, who is one of you. They will inform you *about* all that *is going on* here.

¹⁰ Aristarchus, my fellow prisoner, greets you, and Mark, the cousin of Barnabas (about whom you received commands[d]: if he comes to you, receive him);

¹¹ and Jesus who is called Justus[e]; these are the only fellow workers for the Kingdom of God who are from the circumcision[f], *and* they have been a comfort to me.

¹² Epaphras, who is one of you, a slave of Messiah Yeshua, greets you, always striving for you in his prayers, that you may stand perfect and fully assured in all the will of God.

¹³ For I bear him witness that he has much toil for you, and for those in Laodicea, and for those in Hierapolis.

¹⁴ Luke, the beloved physician, and Demas greet you.

¹⁵ Greet the brothers and sisters who are in Laodicea, and Nympha and the assembly that is in her house.

¹⁶ And when this letter has been read among you, make sure that it is read also in the assembly of the Laodiceans; and that you also read the letter from Laodicea.

¹⁷ And say to Archippus, "Take heed to the ministry which you have received in the Lord, that you fulfill it."

¹⁸ The greeting of me, Paul, with my own hand. Remember my imprisonment. Grace be with you.

---

[a] Grk. *kurioi* (κύριοι); most often rendered as "Masters."

[b] Grk. *ton kairon exagorazomenoi* (τὸν καιρὸν ἐξαγοραζόμενοι); "making the most of the opportunity" (NASU).

[c] Grk. verb *parakaleō* (παρακαλέω); also commonly rendered as "encourage."

[d] Grk. *entolas* (ἐντολάς); this is most properly "commandments" (KJV/ASV), but other versions tend to render it more as "instructions" (RSV/NASU/NRSV/ESV et. al.) or "orders" (YLT).

[e] Grk. *Iēsous ho legomenos Ioustos* (Ἰησοῦς ὁ λεγόμενος Ἰοῦστος).

[f] A version like the NIV extrapolates this simply as, "These are the only Jews."

EPISTLE OF PAUL TO PHILEMON

Salutation

[1] Paul, a prisoner of Messiah Yeshua, and Timothy our brother, to Philemon our beloved *brother* and fellow worker,

[2] and to Apphia our sister, and to Archippus our fellow soldier, and to the assembly in your house:

[3] Grace to you and peace from God our Father and the Lord Yeshua the Messiah.

Philemon's Love and Faith

[4] I thank my God always, making mention of you in my prayers,

[5] hearing of your love, and of the faith which you have toward the Lord Yeshua, and toward all the saints;

[6] *and I pray* that the fellowship of your faith may become effective, in the knowledge of every good thing which is in you, unto Messiah.

[7] For I had much joy and comfort in your love, because the hearts of the saints have been refreshed through you, brother.

Paul Pleads for Onesimus

[8] Therefore, though I have much confidence in Messiah to order you *to do* that which is proper,

[9] yet for love's sake I rather appeal—being such a one as Paul, the aged, and now also a prisoner of Messiah Yeshua—

[10] I appeal to you for my child, whom I have begotten in my bonds, Onesimus,

[11] who once was useless to you, but now is useful to you and to me,[a]

[12] whom I have sent back to you in person, that is, my very heart,

[13] whom I wished to keep with me, that on your behalf he might minister to me in my imprisonment for the gospel;

[14] but without your consent I did not want to do anything, so that your goodness would not be, in effect, of compulsion, but of free will.

[15] For perhaps he was for this reason parted *from you* for a season, that you would have him forever,

[16] no longer as a slave, but more than a slave, a beloved brother, especially to me, but how much rather to you, both in the flesh and in the Lord.

[17] If then you count me a partner, receive him as *you would* me.

[18] But if he has wronged you at all, or owes *you* anything, charge that to my account;

[19] I, Paul, write this with my own hand, I will repay it (not that I say to you that you even owe to me your own self also).

[20] Yes, brother, let me benefit from you in the Lord; refresh my heart in Messiah.

[21] Having confidence in your obedience, I write to you, knowing that you will do even beyond what I say.

[22] And at the same time also prepare a lodging for me; for I hope that through your prayers I will be granted to you.

---

[a] The Greek of v. 11 reads with a discernible wordplay: *Ton pote soi **achrēston** nuni de [kai] soi kai emoi **euchrēston*** (τόν ποτέ σοι ἄχρηστον νυνὶ δὲ [καὶ] σοὶ καὶ ἐμοὶ εὔχρηστον). The ASV rendered this as, "who once was unprofitable to thee, but now is profitable to thee and to me." Here, the renderings "useless" and "useful," follow more contemporary translations of *achrēstos* (ἄχρηστος) and *euchrēstos* (εὔχρηστος), respectively, seen in versions such as the RSV, NASU, NIV, NRSV, and ESV.

This is directly connected to the meaning of the proper name *Onēsimos* (Ὀνήσιμος), "*useful, profitable, beneficial*" (*LS*, 559).

Final Greetings

23 Epaphras, my fellow prisoner in Messiah Yeshua, greets you,

24 *and so do* Mark, Aristarchus, Demas, Luke, my fellow workers.

25 The grace of our Lord Yeshua the Messiah be with your spirit. Amen.

ABOUT THE AUTHOR

John Kimball McKee is an integral part of Outreach Israel Ministries, and serves as the editor of Messianic Apologetics, an Internet website that specializes in a wide variety of Biblical topics. He has grown up in a family which has been in constant pursuit of God's truth, and has been exposed to things of the Lord since infancy. Since 1995 he came to the realization of the post-tribulational return of the Messiah for His own and the importance of the Jewish and Hebraic Roots of our faith. He is a graduate of the University of Oklahoma (Class of 2003) with a B.A. in political science, and holds an M.A. in Biblical Studies from Asbury Theological Seminary (Class of 2009). He is a 2009 recipient of the Zondervan Biblical Languages Award for Greek. John holds memberships in the Evangelical Theological Society, the Evangelical Philosophical Society, and Christians for Biblical Equality, and is a longtime supporter of the perspectives and views of the Creationist ministry of Reasons to Believe.

John is an apologist for the Creator God and in helping people understand their faith heritage in Ancient Israel and Second Temple Judaism. Much of his ministry in the past has been campus based to the multitudes in evangelical Christianity who are associated with a wide variety of Protestant denominations and persuasions. John has introduced college students to things that are Messianic such as the original Hebrew name of our Savior, Yeshua HaMashiach (Jesus the Messiah), a name that he has known since 1983.

John's testimony before his Christian friends at college challenged much of their previous thinking about the whole of the Holy Scriptures and the need to follow the commandments of the Most High. His college peers asked him many varied questions: Why do you not believe in the pre-trib rapture? What do you think of the *Left Behind* books? Why do you observe the seventh-day Sabbath? Why do you eat kosher? Why do you wear a beard? Why do you celebrate the feasts of Israel? Why will you use a *tallit* and wrap *tefillin*/phylacteries during private prayer? Why do you consult original Hebrew and Greek language texts of the Bible? Why don't you come to church with us on Sunday? This led John into Messianic apologetics and the defense of our faith. John strives to be one who is committed to a life of holiness and methodical Bible study, as a person who has a testimony of being born again and who sincerely desires to obey the Lord.

Since the 1990s, John's ministry has capitalized on the Internet's ability to reach people all over this planet. He has spoken with challenging, probing, and apologetic articles to a wide Messianic audience, and those Christians who are interested in Messianic beliefs. In the past decade (2005-2014), John has positioned himself as a well-needed, moderate and Centrist voice, in a Messianic movement which is trying to determine its purpose, relevance, and mission to modern society—a voice striving to sit above much of the posturing, maneuvering, and religious politics of the broad Messianic spectrum. Given his generational family background in evangelical Christian ministry, as well as in academics and the military, John carries a strong burden to assist in the development and maturation of our emerging Messianic theology and spirituality, so that we might truly know the mission of God. John has had the profound opportunity since 1997 to engage many in dialogue, so that they will consider the questions he postulates, as his only agenda is to be as Scripturally sound as possible. John believes in demonstrating a great deal of honor and respect to both his evangelical Christian, Wesleyan and Reformed heritage, as well as to the Jewish Synagogue, and together allowing the strengths and virtues of both Judaism and Christianity to be employed for the Lord's plan for the Messianic movement in the long term future.

J.K. McKee is author of numerous books, dealing with a wide range of topics that are important for today's Messianic Believers. He has also written many articles on theological issues, and is presently focusing his attention on Messianic commentaries of various books of the Bible.

J.K. McKee is the son of the late K. Kimball McKee (1951-1992) and Margaret Jeffries McKee Huey (1953-), and stepson of William Mark Huey (1951-), who married his mother in 1994, and is the executive director of Outreach Israel Ministries.

John has a very strong appreciation for those who have preceded him. His father, Kimball McKee, was a licensed lay minister in the Kentucky Conference of the United Methodist Church, and was a very strong evangelical Christian, most appreciable of the Jewish and Hebraic Roots of the faith. Among his many ministry pursuits, Kim brought the Passover *seder* to Christ United Methodist Church in Florence, KY, was a Sunday school teacher, and was extremely active in the Walk to Emmaus, leading the first men's walk in Madras, India in 1991. John is the grandson of the late William W. Jeffries (1914-1989), who served as a professor at the United States Naval Academy in Annapolis, MD from 1942-1989, notably as the museum director and founder of what is now the William W. Jeffries Memorial Archives in the Nimitz Library. John is the great-grandson of Bishop Marvin A. Franklin (1894-1972), who served as a minister and bishop of the Methodist Church, throughout his ministry serving churches in Georgia, Florida, Alabama, and Mississippi. Bishop Franklin was President of the Council of Bishops from 1959-1960. John is also the third cousin of the late Charles L. Allen (1913-2005), formerly the senior pastor of Grace Methodist Church of Atlanta, GA and First Methodist Church of Houston, TX, and author of numerous books, notably including *God's Psychiatry*. Among all of his forbearers, though, he considers his personality to be most derived from his late paternal grandfather, George Kenneth McKee (1903-1978), and his maternal grandmother, Mary Ruth Franklin Jeffries (1919-).

J.K. McKee is a native of the Northern Kentucky/Greater Cincinnati, OH area. He has also lived in Dallas, TX, Norman, OK, Kissimmee-St. Cloud, FL, and Roatán, Honduras, Central America. He presently resides in Dallas, TX, and is a member in good standing at Eitz Chaim Messianic Jewish Synagogue.

On social media, J.K. McKee can be friended on Facebook at **facebook.com/JKMMessianic**, and followed on Twitter **@JKMMessianic**.

BIBLIOGRAPHY

Articles

Anderson, Charles P. "Laodiceans, Epistle to the," in *ABD*.

Arnold, Clinton E. "Colossae," in *ABD*, 1:1089-1090.

Banks, E.J. "Colossae," in *ISBE*, 1:732.

Barabas, Steven. "Colossae," in *NIDB*, 227.

_____. "Colossians, the Letter to," in *NIDB*, 227.

Bartchy, S. Scott. "Philemon, Epistle to," in *ABD*, 5:305-310.

Blaiklock, Edward M. "Philemon, Letter to," in *NIDB*, pp 780-781.

Bruce, F.F. "Colossians, Epistle to the," in *ISBE*, 1:733-735.

Carr, G. Lloyd. "shālôm," in *TWOT*.

Chan, Frank. Review of *The Letters to the Colossians and to Philemon* in <u>Journal of the Evangelical Theological Society</u> Vol. 52 No. 2 (2009).

Filson, F.V. "Phrygia," in *IDB*.

Foerster, W. "Iēsoús," in *TDNT*.

Francis, F.O. "Colossians, Letter to the," in *IDBSup*, pp 169-170.

Furnish, Victor Paul. "Colossians, Epistle to the," in *ABD*, 1:1090-1096.

Gillman, John. "Justus," in *ABD*.

Hay, David M. "Colossians, Letter to the," in *EDB*, pp 270-271.

Hemer, C.J. "Philemon," in *ISBE*, 3:830-831.

_____. "Philemon, Epistle to," in *ISBE*, 3:831-832.

Johnston, G. "Colossians, Letter to the," in *IDB*, 1:658-662.

Kleinknecht, H. "theíotēs," in *TDNT*.

Lyman, M.E. "Philemon, Letter to," in *IDB*, 3:782-784.

Mellink, M.J. "Colossae," in *IDB*, 1:658

Michaelis, W. "pikraínō," in *TDNT*.

Nash, Scott. "Colossae," in *EDB*, pp 269-270.

O'Brien, Peter T. "Colossians, Letter to the," in *Dictionary of Paul and His Letters*, pp 147-153.

Patzia, A. "Philemon, Letter to," in *Dictionary of Paul and His Letters*, pp 703-707.

Reid, D.G. "Elements/Elemental Spirits of the Universe," in *Dictionary of Paul and His Letters*.

Rollins, W.G. "Philemon, Letter to," in *IDBSup*, pp 663-664.

Schulz, S. "skiá," in *TDNT*.

Soards, Marion L. "Philemon, Letter to," in *EDB*, pp 1046-1047.

Stauffer, E. "theótēs," in *TDNT*.

Watson, Duane F. "Philemon," in *EDB*, pp 1045-1046.

Bible Versions and Study Bibles

Abegg, Jr., Martin, Peter Flint, and Eugene Ulrich, trans. *The Dead Sea Scrolls Bible* (New York: HarperCollins, 1999).

American Standard Version (New York: Thomas Nelson & Sons, 1901).

Barker, Kenneth L., ed., et. al. *NIV Study Bible* (Grand Rapids: Zondervan, 2002).

Berlin, Adele, and Marc Zvi Brettler, eds. *The Jewish Study Bible* (Oxford: Oxford University Press, 2004).

Bratcher, Robert G., ed. *Good News Bible: The Bible in Today's English Version* (New York: American Bible Society, 1976).

Esposito, Paul W. *The Apostles' Bible, An English Septuagint Version* (http://www.apostlesbible.com/).

Garrett, Duane A., ed., et. al. *NIV Archaeological Study Bible* (Grand Rapids: Zondervan, 2005).

Green, Jay P., trans. *The Interlinear Bible* (Lafayette, IN: Sovereign Grace Publishers, 1986).

God's Game Plan: The Athlete's Bible 2007, HCSB (Nashville: Serendipity House Publishers, 2007).

Harrelson, Walter J., ed., et. al. *New Interpreter's Study Bible*, NRSV (Nashville: Abingdon, 2003).

Harris, W. Hall, ed. *The Holy Bible: The Net Bible*, New English Translation (Dallas: Biblical Studies Press, 2001).

Holman Christian Standard Bible (Nashville: Broadman & Holman, 2004).

Holy Bible, King James Version (edited 1789).

Holy Bible, New International Version (Grand Rapids: Zondervan, 1978).

LaHaye, Tim, ed. *Tim LaHaye Prophecy Study Bible*, KJV (Chattanooga: AMG Publishers, 2000).

Lattimore, Richmond, trans. *The New Testament* (New York: North Point Press, 1996).

May, Herbert G., and Bruce M. Metzger, eds. *The New Oxford Annotated Bible With the Apocrypha*, RSV (New York: Oxford University Press, 1977).

Meeks, Wayne A., ed., et. al. *The HarperCollins Study Bible*, NRSV (New York: HarperCollins, 1993).

Newman, Barclay M., ed. *Holy Bible: Contemporary English Version* (New York: American Bible Society, 1995).

New American Standard Bible (La Habra, CA: Foundation Press Publications, 1971).

New American Standard, Updated Edition (Anaheim, CA: Foundation Publications, 1995).

New English Bible (Oxford and Cambridge: Oxford and Cambridge University Presses, 1970).

New King James Version (Nashville: Thomas Nelson, 1982).

New Revised Standard Version (National Council of Churches of Christ, 1989).

Packer, J.I., ed. *The Holy Bible, English Standard Version* (Wheaton, IL: Crossway Bibles, 2001).

Peterson, Eugene H. *The Message: The Bible in Contemporary Language* (Colorado Springs: NavPress, 2002).

Phillips, J.B., trans. *The New Testament in Modern English* (New York: Touchstone, 1972).

Ryrie, Charles C., ed. *The Ryrie Study Bible*, NASB (Chicago: Moody Press, 1978).

Scherman, Nosson, and Meir Zlotowitz, eds. *ArtScroll Tanach* (Brooklyn: Mesorah Publications, 1996).

Siewert, Frances E., ed. *The Amplified Bible* (Grand Rapids: Zondervan, 1965).

Suggs, M. Jack, and Katharine Doob Sakenfeld, and James R. Mueller, et. al. *The Oxford Study Bible*, REB (New York: Oxford University Press, 1992).

Stern, David H., trans. *Jewish New Testament* (Clarksville, MD: Jewish New Testament Publications, 1995).

_____, trans. *Complete Jewish Bible* (Clarksville, MD: Jewish New Testament Publications, 1998).

Tanakh: The Holy Scriptures (Philadelphia: Jewish Publication Society, 1999).

The Holy Bible, Revised Standard Version (Nashville: Cokesbury, 1952).

The Jerusalem Bible (Jerusalem: Koren Publishers, 2000).

Today's New International Version (Grand Rapids: Zondervan, 2005).

Williams, Charles B., trans. *The New Testament: A Private Translation in the Language of the People* (Chicago: Moody Publishers, 1937).

Young, Robert, trans. *Young's Literal Translation.*

Zodhiates, Spiros, ed. *Hebrew-Greek Key Study Bible*, NASB (Chattanooga: AMG Publishers, 1994).

Books

Bauckham, Richard. *Jesus and the God of Israel* (Grand Rapids: Eerdmans, 2008).

Berkowitz, Ariel and D'vorah. *Torah Rediscovered* (Lakewood, CO: First Fruits of Zion, 1996).

_____. *Take Hold* (Littleton, CO: First Fruits of Zion, 1999).

Bowman, Jr., Robert M., and J. Ed Komoszewski. *Putting Jesus in His Place: The Case for the Deity of Christ* (Grand Rapids: Kregel, 2007).

Bruce, F.F. *New Testament History* (New York: Doubleday, 1969).

Carson, D.A., and Douglas J. Moo. *An Introduction to the New Testament*, second edition (Grand Rapids: Zondervan, 2005).

Crockett, William V., ed. *Four Views on Hell* (Grand Rapids: Zondervan, 1996).

Dillard, Raymond B., and Tremper Longman III. *An Introduction to the Old Testament* (Grand Rapids: Zondervan, 1994).

Fee, Gordon D., and Douglas Stuart. *How to Read the Bible for All Its Worth* (Grand Rapids: Zondervan, 2003).

Friedman, David. *They Loved the Torah* (Baltimore: Lederer Books, 2001).

Gundry, Robert H. *A Survey of the New Testament*, third edition (Grand Rapids: Zondervan, 1994).

Guthrie, Donald. *New Testament Introduction* (Downers Grove, IL: InterVarsity, 1990).

Harrison, R.K. *Introduction to the Old Testament* (Grand Rapids: Eerdmans, 1969).

Hegg, Tim. *Interpreting the Bible* (Tacoma, WA: TorahResource, 2000).

_____. *The Letter Writer: Paul's Background and Torah Perspective* (Littleton, CO: First Fruits of Zion, 2002).

_____. *Introduction to Torah Living* (Tacoma, WA: TorahResource, 2002).

_____. *It is Often Said: Comments and Comparisons of Traditional Christian Theology and Hebraic Thought*, 2 vols. (Littleton, CO: First Fruits of Zion, 2003).

_____. *The Messiah: An Introduction to Christology* (Tacoma, WA: TorahResource, 2006).

Horrell, David G. *An Introduction to the Study of Paul* (London: T&T Clark, 2006).

Hurtado, Larry W. *Lord Jesus Christ: Devotion to Jesus in Earliest Christianity* (Grand Rapids: Eerdmans, 2003).

Juster, Daniel C. *Jewish Roots* (Shippensburg, PA: Destiny Image, 1995).

Kaiser, Walter C. *Toward Old Testament Ethics* (Grand Rapids: Zondervan, 1983).

_____. *The Promise-Plan of God: A Biblical Theology of the Old and New Testaments* (Grand Rapids: Zondervan, 2008).

Kaiser, Walter C., and Moisés Silva. *An Introduction to Biblical Hermeneutics* (Grand Rapids: Zondervan, 1994).

Keener, Craig S. *Paul, Women & Wives: Marriage and Women's Ministry in the Letters of Paul* (Peabody, MA: Hendrickson, 1992).

Lancaster, D. Thomas. *Restoration: Returning the Torah of God to the Disciples of Jesus* (Littleton, CO: First Fruits of Zion, 2005).

Levitt, Zola. *The Seven Feasts of Israel* (Dallas: Zola Levitt Ministries, 1979).

McGrath, Alister E. *Christian Theology: An Introduction* (Oxford: Blackwell Publishing, 2001).

McKee, J.K. *Torah In the Balance, Volume I* (Kissimmee, FL: TNN Press, 2003).

_____. *The New Testament Validates Torah* (Kissimmee, FL: TNN Press, 2004).

_____. *James for the Practical Messianic* (Kissimmee, FL: TNN Press, 2005).

_____. *Hebrews for the Practical Messianic* (Kissimmee, FL: TNN Press, 2006).

_____. *A Survey of the Apostolic Scriptures for the Practical Messianic* (Kissimmee, FL: TNN Press, 2006).

_____. *Philippians for the Practical Messianic* (Kissimmee, FL: TNN Press, 2007).

_____. *Galatians for the Practical Messianic*, second edition (Kissimmee, FL: TNN Press, 2007).

_____. *Ephesians for the Practical Messianic* (Kissimmee, FL: TNN Press, 2008).

_____. *A Survey of the Tanach for the Practical Messianic* (Kissimmee, FL: TNN Press, 2008).

Moseley, Ron. *Yeshua: A Guide to the Real Jesus and the Original Church* (Baltimore: Lederer Books, 1996).

Patzia, Arthur G. *The Making of the New Testament: Origin, Collection, Text & Canon* (Downers Grove, IL: InterVarsity, 1995).

Payne, Philip B. *Man and Woman, One in Christ* (Grand Rapids: Zondervan, 2009).

Piper, John, and Wayne Grudem. *Recovering Biblical Manhood and Womanhood* (Wheaton, IL: Crossway, 1991).

Strickland, Wayne G., ed. *Five Views on Law and Gospel* (Grand Rapids: Zondervan, 1996).

Thompson, David L. *Bible Study That Works* (Nappanee, IN: Evangel Publishing House, 1994).

Westerholm, Stephen. *Perspectives Old and New on Paul: The "Lutheran" Paul and His Critics* (Grand Rapids: Eerdmans, 2004).

Wilson, Marvin R. *Our Father Abraham* (Grand Rapids: Eerdmans, 1989).

Wright, Christopher J.H. *The Mission of God: Unlocking the Bible's Grand Narrative* (Downers Grove, IL: IVP Academic, 2006).

Wright, N.T. *Paul in Fresh Perspective* (Minneapolis: Fortress Press, 2005).

Christian Reference Sources

Alexander, T. Desmond, and David W. Baker, eds. *Dictionary of the Old Testament Pentateuch* (Downers Grove, IL: InterVarsity, 2003).

Arnold, Bill T., and H.G.M. Williamson, eds. *Dictionary of the Old Testament Historical Books* (Downers Grove, IL: InterVarsity, 2005).

Bercot, David W., ed. *A Dictionary of Early Christian Beliefs* (Peabody, MA: Hendrickson, 1998).

Bromiley, Geoffrey, ed. *International Standard Bible Encyclopedia*, 4 vols. (Grand Rapids: Eerdmans, 1988).

Buttrick, George, ed. et. al. *The Interpreter's Dictionary of the Bible*, 4 vols. (Nashville: Abingdon, 1962).

Cairns, Alan. *Dictionary of Theological Terms* (Greenville, SC: Ambassador Emerald International, 2002).

Crim, Keith, ed. *Interpreter's Dictionary of the Bible: Supplementary Volume* (Nashville: Abingdon, 1976).

Evans, Craig A., and Stanley E. Porter, eds. *Dictionary of New Testament Background* (Downers Grove, IL: InterVarsity, 2000).

Freedman, David Noel, ed. *Anchor Bible Dictionary*, 6 vols. (New York: Doubleday, 1992).

_____, ed. *Eerdmans Dictionary of the Bible* (Grand Rapids: Eerdmans, 2000).

Geisler, Norman L., ed. *Baker Encyclopedia of Christian Apologetics* (Grand Rapids: Baker, 1999).

Green, Joel B., Scot McKnight, and I. Howard Marshall, eds. *Dictionary of Jesus and the Gospels* (Downers Grove, IL: InterVarsity, 1992).

Grenz, Stanley J., David Guretzki, and Cherith Fee Nordling. *Pocket Dictionary of Theological Terms* (Downers Grove, IL: InterVarsity, 1999).

Harrison, Everett F., ed. *Baker's Dictionary of Theology* (Grand Rapids: Baker Book House, 1960).

Hawthorne, Gerald F., Ralph P. Martin, and Daniel G. Reid, eds. *Dictionary of Paul and His Letters* (Downers Grove, IL: InterVarsity, 1993).

Longman III, Tremper, and Peter Enns, eds. *Dictionary of the Old Testament Wisdom, Poetry & Writings* (Downers Grove, IL: InterVarsity, 2008).

Martin, Ralph P., and Peter H. Davids, eds. *Dictionary of the Later New Testament & its Developments* (Downers Grove, IL: InterVarsity, 1997).

McLay, R. Timothy. *The Use of the Septuagint in New Testament Research* (Grand Rapids: Eerdmans, 2003).

Patzia, Arthur G., and Anthony J. Petrotta. *Pocket Dictionary of Biblical Studies* (Downers Grove, IL: InterVarsity, 2002).

Roberts, Alexander, and James Donaldson, eds. *The Apostolic Fathers*, American Edition.

Schaff, Philip. *History of the Christian Church*, 8 vols. (Grand Rapids: Eerdmans, 1995).

Tenney, Merrill C., ed. *The New International Dictionary of the Bible* (Grand Rapids: Zondervan, 1987).

The Book of Common Prayer (New York: Oxford University Press, 1990).

Commentaries

Bruce, F.F. *New International Commentary on the New Testament: The Epistles to the Colossians, to Philemon, and to the Ephesians* (Grand Rapids: Eerdmans, 1984).

Cranfield, C.E.B. *International Critical Commentary: Romans 1-8* (London: T&T Clark, 1975).

Deibler, Edwin C. "Philemon," in John F. Walvoord and Roy B. Zuck, eds. *The Bible Knowledge Commentary: New Testament* (Wheaton, IL: Victor Books, 1983), pp 769-775.

Dunn, James D.G. *New International Greek Testament Commentary: The Epistles to the Colossians and to Philemon* (Grand Rapids: Eerdmans, 1996).

Dunnam, Maxie D. *The Preacher's Commentary: Galatians, Ephesians, Philippians, Colossians, Philemon*, Vol 31 (Nashville: Thomas Nelson, 1982).

Felder, Cain Hope. "The Letter to Philemon," in Leander E. Keck, ed., et. al. *New Interpreter's Bible* (Nashville: Abingdon, 2000), 11:883-905.

Geisler, Norman M. "Colossians," in *BKCNT*, pp 667-686.

Guthrie, Donald. "Colossians," in D. Guthrie and J.A. Motyer, eds. *The New Bible Commentary Revised* (Grand Rapids: Eerdmans, 1970), pp 1139-1153.

_____. "Philemon," in Ibid., pp 1187-1190.

Hooker, Morna D. "Colossians," in James D.G. Dunn and John W. Rogerson, eds. *Eerdmans Commentary on the Bible* (Grand Rapids: Eerdmans, 2003), pp 1404-1412.

_____. "Philemon," in Ibid., pp 1447-1450.

Lincoln, Andrew T. "The Letter to the Colossians," in *NIB*, 11:553-669.

Keener, Craig S. *The IVP Bible Background Commentary: New Testament* (Downers Grove, IL: InterVarsity, 1993).

Keil, C., and F. Delitzsch, eds. *Commentary on the Old Testament*, 10 vols.

Furnish, Victor Paul. "The Letter of Paul to the Colossians," in Charles M. Laymon, ed. *The Interpreter's One-Volume Commentary on the Bible* (Nashville: Abingdon, 1971), pp 856-864.

_____. "The Letter of Paul to Philemon," in Ibid., pp 894-896.

Moo, Douglas J. *Pillar New Testament Commentary: The Letters to the Colossians and to Philemon* (Grand Rapids: Eerdmans, 2008).

O'Brien, Peter T. *Word Biblical Commentary: Colossians, Philemon*, Vol. 44 (Nashville: Thomas Nelson, 1982).

Rupprecht, Arthur A. "Philemon," in Frank E. Gaebelein, ed. et. al. *Expositor's Bible Commentary* (Grand Rapids: Zondervan, 1978), 11:453-464.

Stern, David H. *Jewish New Testament Commentary* (Clarksville, MD: Jewish New Testament Publications, 1995).

Vaughan, Curtis. "Colossians," in *EXP*, 11:163-226.

Walton, John H., and Victor H. Matthews and Mark W. Chavalas. *The IVP Bible Background Commentary: Old Testament* (Downers Grove, IL: InterVarsity, 2000).

Walvoord, John F., and Roy B. Zuck, eds. *The Bible Knowledge Commentary: Old Testament* (Wheaton, IL: Victor Books, 1985).

Wesley, John. *Explanatory Notes Upon the New Testament*, reprint (Peterborough, UK: Epworth Press, 2000).

Witherington III, Ben. *The Letters to Philemon, the Colossians, and the Ephesians: A Socio-Rhetorical Commentary on the Captivity Epistles* (Grand Rapids: Eerdmans, 2007).

Wright, N.T. *Tyndale New Testament Commentaries: Colossians and Philemon* (Grand Rapids: Eerdmans, 1986).

Greek Language Resources

Aland, Kurt, et. al. *The Greek New Testament, Fourth Revised Edition* (Stuttgart: Deutche Bibelgesellschaft/United Bible Societies, 1998).

Brenton, Sir Lancelot C. L., ed & trans. *The Septuagint With Apocrypha* (Peabody, MA: Hendrickson, 1999).

Bromiley, Geoffrey W., ed. *Theological Dictionary of the New Testament*, abridged (Grand Rapids: Eerdmans, 1985).

Brown, Robert K., and Philip W. Comfort, trans. *The New Greek-English Interlinear New Testament* (Carol Stream, IL: Tyndale House, 1990).

Danker, Frederick William, ed., et. al. *A Greek-English Lexicon of the New Testament and Other Early Christian Literature*, third edition (Chicago: University of Chicago Press, 2000).

Liddell, H.G., and R. Scott. *An Intermediate Greek-English Lexicon* (Oxford: Clarendon Press, 1994).

Metzger, Bruce M. *A Textual Commentary on the Greek New Testament* (London and New York: United Bible Societies, 1975).

Nestle, Erwin, and Kurt Aland, eds. *Novum Testamentum Graece, Nestle-Aland 27th Edition* (New York: American Bible Society, 1993).

Nestle-Aland Greek-English New Testament, NE27-RSV (Stuttgart: United Bible Societies/Deutche Bibelgesellschaft, 2001).

Newman, Jr., Barclay M. *A Concise Greek-English Dictionary of the New Testament* (Stuttgart: United Bible Societies/Deutche Bibelgesellschaft, 1971).

Rahlfs, Alfred, ed. *Septuaginta* (Stuttgart: Deutsche Bibelgesellschaft, 1979).

Rogers, Cleon L., Jr., and Cleon L. Rogers III. *The New Linguistic and Exegetical Key to the Greek New Testament* (Grand Rapids: Zondervan, 1998).

Thayer, Joseph H. *Thayer's Greek-English Lexicon of the New Testament* (Peabody, MA: Hendrickson, 2003).

Vine, W.E. *Vine's Expository Dictionary of New Testament Words* (Nashville: Thomas Nelson, 1968).

Wallace, Daniel B. *Greek Grammar Beyond the Basics* (Grand Rapids: Zondervan, 1996).

Zodhiates, Spiros, ed. *Complete Word Study Dictionary: New Testament* (Chattanooga: AMG Publishers, 1993).

Hebrew Language Resources

Arnold, Bill T., and John H. Choi. *A Guide to Biblical Hebrew Syntax* (New York: Cambridge University Press, 2003).

Baker, Warren, and Eugene Carpenter, eds. *Complete Word Study Dictionary: Old Testament* (Chattanooga: AMG Publishers, 2003).

Brown, Francis, S.R. Driver, and Charles A. Briggs. *Hebrew and English Lexicon of the Old Testament* (Oxford: Clarendon Press, 1979).

Davidson, Benjamin. *The Analytical Hebrew and Chaldee Lexicon* (Grand Rapids: Zondervan, 1970).

Dotan, Aron, ed. *Biblia Hebraica Leningradensia* (Peabody, MA: Hendrickson, 2001).

Elliger, Karl, and Wilhelm Rudolph, et. al., eds. *Biblica Hebraica Stuttgartensia* (Stuttgart: Deutche Bibelgesellschaft, 1977).

Gabe, Eric S., ed. *New Testament in Hebrew and English* (Hitchin, UK: Society for Distributing the Hebrew Scriptures, 2000).

Harris, R. Laird, Gleason L. Archer, Jr., and Bruce K. Waltke, eds. *Theological Wordbook of the Old Testament* (Chicago: Moody Press, 1980).

Holladay, William L., ed. *A Concise Hebrew and Aramaic Lexicon of the Old Testament* (Leiden, the Netherlands: E.J. Brill, 1988).

Jastrow, Marcus. *Dictionary of the Targumim, Talmud Bavli, Talmud Yerushalmi, and Midrashic Literature* (New York: Judaica Treasury, 2004).

Kelley, Page H., Daniel S. Mynatt, and Timothy G. Crawford, eds. *The Masorah of Biblia Hebraica Stuttgartensia* (Grand Rapids: Eerdmans, 1998).

Koehler, Ludwig, and Walter Baumgartner, eds. *The Hebrew & Aramaic Lexicon of the Old Testament*, 2 vols. (Leiden, the Netherlands: Brill, 2001).

Seow, C.L. *A Grammar for Biblical Hebrew*, revised edition (Nashville: Abingdon, 1995).

Tov, Emanuel. *Textual Criticism of the Hebrew Bible* (Minneapolis: Fortress Press, 1992).

תורה נביאים כתובים והברית החדשה (Jerusalem: Bible Society in Israel, 1991).

Unger, Merrill F., and William White. *Nelson's Expository Dictionary of the Old Testament* (Nashville: Thomas Nelson, 1980).

Historical Sources and Ancient Literature

Aristotle: *Ethics*, trans. J.A.K. Thomson (Harmondsworth, UK: Penguin Books, 1979).

_____: *Politics*, trans. Ernest Barker (New York: Oxford University Press, 1995).

Bettenson, Henry, and Chris Maunder, eds. *Documents of the Christian Church* (Oxford: Oxford University Press, 1999).

Eusebius of Caesarea: *Ecclesiastical History*, trans. C.F. Cruse (Peabody, MA: Hendrickson, 1998).

González, Justo L. *The Story of Christianity*, Vol. 1 (San Francisco: Harper Collins, 1984).

_____. *The Story of Christianity*, Vol. 2 (San Francisco: HarperCollins, 1985).

Harrington, Joel F., ed. *A Cloud of Witnesses: Readings in the History of Western Christianity* (Boston: Houghton Mifflin, 2001).

Herodotus: *The Histories*, trans. Aubrey de Sélincourt (London: Penguin Books, 1954).

Irvin, Dale T., and Scott W. Sunquist. *History of the World Christian Movement*, Vol. 1 (Maryknoll, NY: Orbis Books, 2001).

Josephus, Flavius: *The Works of Josephus: Complete and Unabridged*, trans. William Whiston (Peabody, MA: Hendrickson, 1987).

Judaeus, Philo: *The Works of Philo: Complete and Unabridged*, trans. C.D. Yonge (Peabody, MA: Hendrickson, 1993).

Murray, Oswyn. *Ancient Greece*, second edition (Cambridge, MA: Harvard University Press, 1993).

Plato: *The Laws*, trans. Trevor J. Saunders (London: Penguin Books, 1970).

_____: *The Republic*, trans. Desmond Lee (London: Penguin Books, 2007).

Pliny the Younger: *Pliny the Younger: Complete Letters*, trans. P.G. Walsh (Oxford: Oxford University Press, 2006).

Seneca: *Letters from a Stoic*, trans. Robin Campbell (London: Penguin Books, 2004).

_____: *On Benefits*, trans. Aubrey Stewart (Hard Press, 2006).

Shanks, Hershel, ed. *Ancient Israel: From Abraham to the Roman Destruction of the Temple* (Washington, D.C.: Biblical Archaeology Society, 1999).

Staniforth, Maxwell, trans. *Early Christian Writings: The Apostolic Fathers* (Harmondsworth, UK: Penguin Books, 1980).

Tacitus, Cornelius: *The Histories*, trans. Kenneth Wellesley (London: Penguin Books, 1992).

Xenophon: *The Persian Expedition*, trans. George Cawkwell (London: Penguin Books, 1949).

_____: *Conversations of Socrates*, trans. Hugh Tredennick and Robin Waterfield (London: Penguin Books, 1990).

Jewish Reference Sources

Cohen, Abraham. *Everyman's Talmud: The Major Teachings of the Rabbinic Sages* (New York: Schoken, 1995).

Eisenberg, Ronald L. *The JPS Guide to Jewish Traditions* (Philadelphia: Jewish Publication Society, 2004).

Encyclopaedia Judaica. MS Windows 9x. Brooklyn: Judaica Multimedia (Israel) Ltd, 1997.

Frank, Daniel H., Oliver Leaman, and Charles H. Manekin, eds. *The Jewish Philosophy Reader* (London and New York: Routledge, 2000).

Harlow, Jules, ed. *Siddur Sim Shalom for Shabbat and Festivals* (New York: Rabbinical Assembly, 2007).

Hertz, J.H., ed. *Pentateuch & Haftorahs* (London: Soncino, 1960).

_____, ed. *The Authorised Daily Prayer Book*, revised (New York: Bloch Publishing Company, 1960).

Kolatch, Alfred J. *The Jewish Book of Why* (Middle Village, NY: Jonathan David Publishers, 1981).

_____. *The Second Jewish Book of Why* (Middle Village, NY: Jonathan David Publishers, 1985).

Kravitz, Leonard, and Kerry M. Olitzky, eds. and trans. *Pirke Avot: A Modern Commentary on Jewish Ethics* (New York: UAHC Press, 1993).

Lieber, David L. *Etz Hayim: Torah and Commentary* (New York: Rabbinical Assembly, 2001).

Neusner, Jacob, trans. *The Mishnah: A New Translation* (New Haven and London: Yale University Press, 1988).

_____, ed. *The Tosefta: Translated from the Hebrew With a New Introduction*, 2 vols. (Peabody, MA: Hendrickson, 2002).

_____, and William Scott Green, eds. *Dictionary of Judaism in the Biblical Period* (Peabody, MA: Hendrickson, 2002).

Scherman, Nosson, ed., et. al. *The ArtScroll Chumash, Stone Edition*, 5th ed. (Brooklyn: Mesorah Publications, 2000).

Miscellaneous Texts and Lexicons

Charlesworth, James H., ed. *The Old Testament Pseudepigrapha*, Vol 1 (New York: Doubleday, 1983).

_____. *The Old Testament Pseudepigrapha*, Vol 2 (New York: Doubleday, 1985).

Robinson, James M., ed. *The Nag Hammadi Library* (San Francisco: HarperCollins, 1990).

Sparks, H.F.D., ed. *The Apocryphal Old Testament* (Oxford: Clarendon Press, 1984).

The Scriptures, second edition (Northriding, South Africa: Institute for Scripture Research, 1998).

The Scriptures, third edition (Northriding, South Africa: Institute for Scripture Research, 2009).

Vermes, Geza, trans. *The Complete Dead Sea Scrolls in English* (London: Penguin Books, 1997).

Wise, Michael, Martin Abegg, Jr., and Edward Cook, trans. *The Dead Sea Scrolls: A New Translation* (San Francisco: HarperCollins, 1996).

Young, Robert. *Young's Analytical Concordance to the Bible* (Grand Rapids: Eerdmans, 1977).

Miscellaneous/Unapprehended

Love and the Messianic Age: Study Guide and Commentary (Marshfield, MO: Vine of David, 2009).

Roth, Andrew Gabriel. *Ruach Qadim: Aramaic Origins of the New Testament* (Malta: Tushiyah Press, 2005).

Online Resources

Christian Classics Ethereal Library. <http://www.ccel.org/>.

The Civil Law, trans. S.P. Scott (Cincinnati: Central Trust Company, 1932). Accessible online at <http://www.constitution.org/sps/sps.htm/>.

Plutarch: *Moralia*, by John Thomson, Prebendary of Hereford (1878). Accessible online at <http://www.bostonleadershipbuilders.com/plutarch/moralia/index.htm>.

Software Programs

BibleWorks 7.0. MS Windows XP. Norfolk: BibleWorks, LLC, 2006. CD-ROM.

E-Sword 8.0.8. MS Windows 9x. Franklin, TN: Equipping Ministries Foundation, 2008.

Libronix Digital Library System 1.0d: Church History Collection. MS Windows XP. Garland, TX: Galaxie Software. 2002.

QuickVerse 6.0. MS Windows 95. Hiawatha, IA: Parsons Technology, 1999. CD-ROM.

The Babylonian Talmud: A Translation and Commentary. MS Windows XP. Peabody, MA: Hendrickson, 2005. CD-ROM.

The Essential Christian Library. MS-Windows 95. Coeur d'Alene, ID: Packard Technologies, 1998. CD-ROM.

Messianic Apologetics is dedicated to producing high quality, doctrinally sound, challenging, and fair-minded publications and resources for Twenty-First Century Messianic people. Our broad faith community faces any number of issues requiring resolution—from newcomers to the Messianic movement and those who have been involved for many years. The books, studies, commentaries, and analyses provided by Messianic Apologetics intend to aid the legitimate needs of today's Messianic people, so they can have the answers they seek in their walk with the Messiah of Israel.

Titles are available for purchase at **www.outreachisrael.net** or at **amazon.com.**

Hebraic Roots: An Introductory Study
is Messianic Apologetics' main, best-selling publication, that offers a good overview of the Messianic movement and Messianic lifestyle that can be used for individual or group study in twelve easy lessons

Introduction to Things Messianic
is an excellent companion to *Hebraic Roots*, which goes into substantially more detail into the emerging theology of the Messianic movement, specific areas of Torah observance, and aspects of faith such as salvation and eschatology

The Messianic Helper series, edited by Margaret McKee Huey, includes a series of books with instructional information on how to have a Messianic home, including holiday celebration guides. **After reading both *Hebraic Roots* and *Introduction to Things Messianic,* these are the publications you need to read!**

Messianic Spring Holiday Helper
is a guide to assist you during the Spring holiday season, analyzing the importance of *Purim*, Passover and Unleavened Bread, *Shavuot*, and the non-Biblical holiday of Easter

Messianic Fall Holiday Helper
is a guide for the Fall holiday season of *Yom Teruah/Rosh HaShanah*, *Yom Kippur*, and *Sukkot*, along with reflective teachings and exhortations

Messianic Winter Holiday Helper
is a guide to help you during the Winter holiday season, addressing the significance of *Chanukah*, the period of the Maccabees, and the non-Biblical holiday of Christmas

Messianic Sabbath Helper
is a guide that will help you make the seventh-day Sabbath a delight, discussing how to keep *Shabbat*, common Jewish traditions associated with *Shabbat*, the history of the transition to Sunday that occurred in early Christianity, respecting those in the past who kept a "Sunday Sabbath," and an extensive analysis of Biblical passages from the Tanach (OT) and Apostolic Scriptures (NT) about the Sabbath, rest, and their relevance to modern-day Messiah followers
    also available is the five-chapter mini-book excerpt ***Shabbat: Sabbath for Messianic Believers***, intended as a congregational handout

Messianic Kosher Helper
is a guide discussing various aspects of the kosher dietary laws, clean and unclean meats, common Jewish traditions associated with kashrut, common claims made that these are no longer important for Believers, and an extensive analysis of Biblical passages from the Tanach (OT) and Apostolic Scriptures (NT) about the Torah's dietary laws and their relevance
    also available is the five-chapter mini-book excerpt ***Kashrut: Kosher for Messianic Believers***, intended as a congregational handout

Additional Materials Available From Messianic Apologetics

Messianic Torah Helper
is a guide that weighs the different perspectives of the Pentateuch present in Jewish and Christian theology, considers the role of the Law for God's people, and how today's Messianics can fairly approach issues of *halachah* and tradition in their Torah observance

Outreach Israel Ministries director **Mark Huey** has written Torah commentaries and reflections that are thought provoking and very enlightening for Messianic Believers today.

TorahScope Volume I
is a compilation workbook of insightful commentaries on the weekly Torah and Haftarah portions

TorahScope Volume II
is a second compilation workbook of expanded commentaries on the weekly Torah and Haftarah portions

TorahScope Volume III
is a third compilation workbook of expanded commentaries on the weekly Torah and Haftarah portions, specifically concentrating on the theme of faith

TorahScope Haftarah Exhortations
is a compilation workbook of insightful commentaries on the specific, weekly Haftarah portions, designed to be used to compliment the weekly Torah reading

TorahScope Apostolic Scripture Reflections
is a compilation workbook of insightful reflections on suggested readings from the Apostolic Scriptures or New Testament, designed to be used to compliment the weekly Torah and Haftarah readings

Counting the Omer: A Daily Devotional Toward Shavuot
is a daily devotional with fifty succinct reflections from Psalms, guiding you during the season between the festivals of Passover and Pentecost

Sayings of the Fathers: A Messianic Perspective on Pirkei Avot
is a daily devotional for two years of reflection on the Mishnah tractate *Pirkei Avot*, introducing you to some of the key views present in the Apostolic period as witnessed by the Jewish Sages (intended to be read during the counting of the *omer*)

Messianic Apologetics editor **J.K. McKee** has written on Messianic theology and practice, including studies on Torah observance, the end-times, and commentaries that are helpful to those who have difficult questions to answer.

The New Testament Validates Torah
Does the New Testament Really Do Away With the Law?
is a resource examining a wide variety of Biblical passages, discussing whether or not the Torah of Moses is really abolished in the New Testament

Torah In the Balance, Volume I
The Validity of the Torah and Its Practical Life Applications
examines the principal areas of a Torah observant walk of faith for the newcomer, including one's spiritual motives

Torah In the Balance, Volume II
The Set-Apart Life in Action—The Outward Expressions of Faith
examines many of the finer areas of Torah observance, which has a diversity of interpretations and applications as witnessed in both mainstream Judaism and the wide Messianic community

Confronting Critical Issues
An Analysis of Subjects that Affects the Growth and Stability
of the Emerging Messianic Movement
compiles a variety of articles and analyses that directly confront negative teachings and trends that have been witnessed in the broad Messianic community in the past decade

Messianic Apologetics has produced a variety of **Messianic commentaries** on various books of the Bible under the "for the Practical Messianic" byline. These can be used in an individual, small group, or congregational study.

general commentaries:
A Survey of the Tanach for the Practical Messianic
A Survey of the Apostolic Scriptures for the Practical Messianic

specific book commentaries:
Acts 15 for the Practical Messianic
Romans for the Practical Messianic
1 Corinthians for the Practical Messianic
2 Corinthians for the Practical Messianic (coming 2016)
Galatians for the Practical Messianic
Ephesians for the Practical Messianic
Philippians for the Practical Messianic
Colossians and Philemon for the Practical Messianic
The Pastoral Epistles for the Practical Messianic
1&2 Thessalonians for the Practical Messianic
James for the Practical Messianic
Hebrews for the Practical Messianic

Additional Materials Available From Messianic Apologetics

One of the goals of Messianic Apologetics is to always be in the mode of producing more cutting edge materials, addressing head on some of the theological and spiritual issues facing our emerging Messianic movement. In addition to our current array of available and soon-to-be available publications, the following are a selection of **Future Projects**, in various stages of planning and pre-production, most of which involve research at the present time (2015-2016). Look for their release sometime over the next two to five years and beyond.

Salvation on the Line: The Nature of Yeshua and His Divinity
by J.K. McKee

will be a lengthy study defending Yeshua the Messiah as God, evaluating the state of Christology in the broad Messianic movement, and intends to examine a wide array of Bible passages, mainly to be compiled into two volumes: (I) Gospels and Acts; (II) The General Epistles, The Pauline Epistles, The Later New Testament

After the Afterlife: Messianic Engagement With Heaven, Hell, and the Resurrection of the Dead

will be a compilation of teaching about the intermediate state, eternal punishment, the philosophy of future resurrection, and will evaluate the Messianic movement's strengths and weaknesses regarding human composition

Made in the USA
Charleston, SC
04 June 2016